THE REAGANS

THE REAGANS:
A POLITICAL
PORTRAIT

PETER HANNAFORD

Coward-McCann, Inc.

NEW YORK

Library of Congress Cataloging in Publication Data

Hannaford, Peter.
  The Reagans, a political portrait.

  1. Reagan, Ronald.   2. Reagan, Nancy, 1923–
3. Presidents—United States—Biography.   4. Presidents
—United States—Wives—Biography.   I. Title.
E877.H36   973.927′092′4 [B]   81-1817
ISBN 0-698-11083-8   AACR2

Acknowledgments

This book was begun in December 1980, in Pasadena, California, and completed in Washington, D.C., in December 1981. In the twelve months between, it went with me wherever my travels took me. Parts of it were written in airplanes, hotel rooms, airport waiting rooms, on a ship, and in the back seat of an automobile. It was written in several states and on three continents. The resulting narrative would not have been possible without the help of many people.

I owe special thanks to my wife, Irene, for her encouragement and support, her skillful proofreader's eye, and a willingness to type manuscript pages on a moment's notice.

My thanks go also to my secretaries, Carol Fields and Esther Lihn, and staff member John Williamson for typing and collating manuscript pages.

Special thanks also go to Molly Sturges Tuthill, chief archivist of the Reagan Collection at the Hoover Institution at Stanford University, and her staff for their unfailingly cheerful and invaluable verification of dates, place names, and other documentation.

Many others helped in a variety of ways: by sharing recollections and perspectives, providing insights, giving advice, and, in some cases, offering weekend hospitality to my typewriter and me. Among them are Richard Allen, Martin Anderson, Douglas Bandow, Paul Boertlein, William Casey, Lou Cannon, Elaine Crispen, Michael Deaver, Dottie Dellinger, James Fuller, Richard and Dorothy Harville, Al Hunt, Kevin Hopkins, Jack Germond, Robert K. Gray, Ken Khachigian, Don Livingston, Ed Meese, Lyn Nofziger, John Paty, Margen Penick, Nancy Clark Reynolds, Roger Stone, Peter Teeley, Jules Witcover, Richard Wirthlin and Helene von Damm.

Finally, my thanks go to my agent, Bill Adler, and his assistant, Julie Rosner, and to my editor, William Thompson, for their patience and guidance.

—PETER D. HANNAFORD
Washington, D.C.
December 8, 1981

Dedicated to
Irene, Dick, and Don

1

November 4, 1980:
End of the Beginning

WE EMBRACED BRIEFLY; then Nancy Reagan looked at me and, with a half-smile, said softly, "Did you think it would ever *really* happen?"

I could not find the right answer. I was numb, but I did manage to say, "What a glorious evening!"

She had summed up perfectly the mood of the three or four dozen old friends, advisers, and staff members who had gathered in the Reagans' suite on the nineteenth floor of the Century Plaza Hotel in Los Angeles on election night, November 4, 1980.

Everyone there had worked so long and hard to help Ronald Reagan become president of the United States that now that he had won the prize it was almost hard to believe.

A few minutes later Ronald and Nancy Reagan went downstairs to the hotel ballroom, where he gave a short speech acknowledging his victory.

It was a victory of such scope that it took virtually everyone but Reagan's and President Jimmy Carter's pollsters and close advisers by surprise. Ronald Reagan was elected the fortieth president of the United States by 51 percent of the vote, with 41 percent going to Carter, 7 percent to John Anderson, and 1 percent to the Libertarians' Ed Clark and other "third party" candidates.

Up to the night before the election, the networks and the major polling organizations had a near consensus that it was "too close to call." John Sears, Reagan's former campaign manager, said on National Public Radio's "All Things Considered" on Monday night, the third, that he could not hazard a prediction. The final *New York Times*–CBS poll gave Reagan a 1 percent margin, and the Gallup Poll showed him 3 points ahead. Both were within the range of statistical error. Only Louis Harris among the major public pollsters predicted a definite Reagan victory, but only barely—by 5 points.

In the Reagan headquarters in Arlington, Virginia, however, it was a different matter. Senior strategist and pollster Dr. Richard Wirthlin and his staff showed a margin of 10 or 11 points by November 3. And that night on Air Force One, as it flew President Carter from Oregon to Georgia, where he would vote in Plains the next morning, Press Secretary Jody Powell was telling the President that, according to Patrick Caddell's polling data, the incumbent was not going to make it.

The pundits had been discounting possible Republican gains in Congress during much of the campaign, so the Republicans' capture of the U.S. Senate came as a surprise to everyone, probably even the party's Senate leaders. The Republicans took twelve seats from the Democrats, displacing such liberals as George McGovern of South Dakota, Frank Church of Idaho, Birch Bayh of Indiana, and John Culver of Iowa. The Republicans' winning control of the Senate—for the first time in twenty-six years—broadened the impact of Ronald Reagan's election. In the House, the Grand Old Party picked up thirty-three seats, narrowing Democratic control and giving the House a decidedly more conservative tilt. Further, Republicans added four governorships to their ranks, took control of two more state legislatures (with redistricting based on the 1980 census coming up), and made a net gain of some two hundred legislative seats.

The people in the Reagan suite on the nineteenth floor alternated affectionate greetings and mutual congratulations with expressions of disbelief as the large television set brought the news of their party's victories piling on one another. "After so many years in the Wilderness," one of them said, "it's a little hard to believe that all this is happening."

It had been sixteen years for some of them, such as Justin Dart and Holmes Tuttle. They were among the small group of California businessmen who concluded after the Goldwater-Johnson campaign of 1964 that Ronald Reagan was just the man to run for governor of California in 1966. During the final days of the Goldwater campaign, Reagan had gone on national television with a thirty-minute speech on behalf of the candidate. Across the nation, it galvanized what was to become a core of supporters that was to grow as the years went on; by 1980, it had become a virtual army of dedicated campaign backers and workers that outorganized the opposition at every turn.

I was to learn just how great an impact that Reagan speech for Barry Goldwater had made when, a decade later, I began accompanying then-Governor Reagan on his campaign swings around the country in the fall of 1974 on behalf of congressional and gubernatorial candidates. In state after state we would run into volunteer drivers and event organizers who said that it was Reagan's 1964 speech that first caused them to get actively involved in politics.

Dart, Tuttle, and the others who made up the small group that later became his "kitchen cabinet," persuaded Reagan, by then host of a television series called "Death Valley Days," to go on the knife-and-fork circuit around California to test out sentiment for a run for governor in 1966. They were enthusiastic about his prospects because they saw him as the most effective spokesman for free enterprise that the United States had had in generations.

A lot of people thought differently. They made up another army, although their ranks thinned from time to time. This army consisted of the people who underestimated Ronald Reagan. California did not manifest the cultural and geographical bias that Reagan was later to face in the East, but many refused to take him seriously because he had been a movie actor or because he had not been in politics. I know—because I was one of them.

At about that time, I had become active in local Republican politics in Alameda County (Oakland and environs) and, along with many of my friends, found Ronald Reagan to be a likable man to meet but "unelectable." I remember when he attended the Republican state convention in San Francisco in February 1965. He strolled around the Hilton Hotel with an aide or two, shaking hands with everyone, beaming that wide, Irish grin of his, and stopping here and there to chat for a moment. You could not help but like him. But his opponent in the upcoming primary would be George Christopher, the seasoned mayor of San Francisco, and according to the conventional wisdom, we would need a seasoned politician, such as Christopher, if we were to stop Edmund G. ("Pat") Brown from winning a third term as governor.

Brown and his people subscribed to the conventional wisdom, too. They were convinced that Reagan would be easy to beat. They hoped he would win the primary and did not hesitate to say so. Jimmy Carter and his strategists made the same mistake fourteen years later, in the spring and summer of 1980.

Reagan went on to win the primary over Christopher, and the party united behind him in the general election. He beat Brown by nearly a million votes, and the Republicans swept all but one of the statewide constitutional offices. During the campaign, Brown had belittled Reagan, not really taking him very seriously. At one point, Brown semifacetiously told a youngster at a campaign stop, "Remember little girl, it was an actor who shot Lincoln." Underneath his joking tone, Brown seemed to be saying that it was preposterous to think that he had to campaign against an *actor*. This unconscious bias was to make Ronald Reagan's climb toward that ultimate victory on November 4, 1980, perhaps the steepest of any modern American politician, for he encountered it time and again in the ensuing years.

Having been an early skeptic about his electability, I was pleased both by his victory in November 1966 and by the quality of his appointments. There were a few early mistakes, but by and large his approach to appointments and to the organization of his administration showed common sense and seemed to reflect a belief on his part that being governor was a matter of good management rather than an extension of the game of politics.

Because of the size of Reagan's victory and the conviction that the voters had approved a mandate for better management of government (what became known as Reagan's "cut, squeeze, and trim" philosophy), the Reagan administration began in high spirits. There was talk of a "prairie fire" of conservatism that might sweep the country. The new administration soon put out brochures extolling the "Creative Society." Underlying all this exuberance was an abiding conviction on Reagan's part that the American people, if given the motivation and incentives, will be willing, individually and collectively, to solve the nation's problems, that we need not automatically look to government to solve our problems. He wanted to bring out the best in people in California, and in those early days, the enthusiastic mood of his appointees had a contagious quality.

Reagan did not take long to put his conviction about volunteerism to the test. He called a group of business and professional leaders to a luncheon in Sacramento. He told them he wanted 250 volunteers for approximately ninety days to conduct a full-scale management audit of all the offices of state government. Soon the volunteer auditors were swarming all over Sacramento and other state facilities. They came up with nearly eighteen hundred recommendations, ranging from improvements in food service in the prison system to standardization of the size of file folders. (In later years, whenever he recounted the work of this task force, Reagan enjoyed telling the story of the file folders. It seemed that most offices used letter-size file folders, but a few departments used legal-size even though it was not necessary, thus requiring costlier special orders and outsized transfer cases for storage.) Nearly 90 percent of the task force's recommendations were adopted, saving an estimated $100 million a year. At that time the figure amounted to the equivalent of a little more than 1 percent of the state budget. It set the tone for Reagan's cut, squeeze, and trim program.

Reagan and his advisers also overhauled the cabinet system. They found that all forty-five departments of the state government reported direct to the governor. It seemed obvious to Reagan and his people that this was far too many people competing for the governor's attention, so they created four "superagencies," grouping the working departments by affinity under them. Each superagency—Health and Welfare; Business and Transportation; Agriculture and Services; and Resources—was headed by a secretary who was a member of Reagan's cabinet. Each secretary had a deputy and a small staff. Department heads would bring their problems to the secretary. If the problems could not be solved at the superagency level, the secretary would bring the problem to the cabinet. As a result, problems began to be dealt with in a more logical manner than before. This system remained basically unchanged throughout Reagan's eight years in Sacramento, and the level of productivity of his cabinet had a good deal to do with his belief that the federal cabinet system could be used more effectively than it had in recent years.

Reagan looked at the size of California's state work force during the eight Pat Brown years and was alarmed. Although the state's population had continued to grow steadily during those years, putting added pressure on state government for services, the state government's labor force under Brown grew at a galloping rate, approximately 75 percent. Reagan immediately froze state hiring.* It was known that retirements, deaths, and resignations accounted for an annual turnover of about 10 percent of the work force, so Reagan reasoned that attrition following a hiring freeze would result in increased productivity. He believed that if managers instituted more-efficient business methods in the departments of the government, fewer people could process more work without serious difficulty. In most cases he was correct. He often cited the case of the Department of Motor Vehicles. Before the hiring freeze took effect, a typical driver's license application took forty-four work days to process. A few months after the freeze had taken effect and with the state's population continuing to grow, the Reagan administration had pared the license-processing time down to an average of ten work days.

Not everything Reagan did in those early days in Sacramento was done with such enthusiasm—or greeted with enthusiasm by the citizens. Take income taxes. During the transition from the Brown to the Reagan administration—a time when Reagan and his people became frustrated and embittered by a general lack of cooperation on the part of outgoing officials—Reagan learned the state was spending about $1.5 million more each day than it was taking in. Brown, during his final year in office, in order to meet the state constitution's mandate for a balanced budget, had switched part of the state's accounting system, income, to the accrual method. Meanwhile, expenditures were kept on the cash

* By the time Reagan left Sacramento, the state government's work force had grown slightly, by 6 percent, to a total of 106,000. This was largely the result of new staffs created by newly legislated programs. The University of California system is not included in these figures, since its hiring is not controlled by the governor.

basis. As Reagan often said, "They were using fifteen months' worth of income to cover twelve month's worth of expenses."

The significance of this problem hit home very quickly for Reagan. It meant he would have to raise income taxes right away in order to balance the books by the end of the fiscal year, June 30, 1967. Reagan's frequently stated belief that "taxes should hurt" (meaning that you are more likely to question the validity of government programs when you are acutely aware of how much you are paying for them in taxes) came back at him with sharp irony.

This conservative governor found himself making taxes more "progressive" than ever before. The highest bracket went up to 11 percent, and the upper brackets were broadened to take in more taxpayers. At the same time, the new tax program eliminated any state income-tax liability for those earning less than $8,000 a year. Had this been done by someone with a reputation as a liberal, it would probably have been hailed in editorials as a model of enlightenment. As it was, in later years Reagan sometimes found this tax increase cited in the press as evidence that his conservatism "did not work."

Wherever he went in the state, explaining the need for the tax increases, Reagan in the same breath promised that as soon as the state's finances were healthy again and surpluses began to develop, he would return the surpluses to the taxpayers. For the most part, that is what he did over the next seven years.

One of his favorite anecdotes involves the first such surplus. News of it came in the spring of 1968. Reagan's state director of finance, Caspar W. Weinberger (now secretary of defense) came into Reagan's office.

Weinberger said, "We've just learned that the state will have a surplus of about a hundred million dollars. In fifteen minutes the folks upstairs [the legislature] are going to know about it, and they'll have a hundred-and-one ways to spend it. I thought you ought to know about it first. What do you want to do with it?"

Reagan replied, "Give it back to the taxpayers."

"Give it back? That's never been done before."

"No, but then you've never had an actor for governor before, either," quipped Reagan.

By the end of his second term, Reagan had turned back $5.7 billion to the taxpayers in the form of tax credits, rebates, and lowered bridge tolls. He had wanted to reduce the actual tax rates, but the surpluses never seemed predictable enough and the possibility of a Democrat-controlled legislature going along with rate reductions seemed slight. By the time he left Sacramento, Reagan left behind a surplus of $500 million for his successor, Pat Brown's son, Jerry.

Brown *fils* saw that surplus grow as inflation forced Californians into higher and higher income-tax brackets. Throughout his first year, his administration and the legislature (still fully controlled by the Democrats) wrangled about how to dispose of a surplus that was heading toward $5 billion! Reagan, when asked by a *Los Angeles Times* reporter what he would do with it if he were still governor, replied, "Give it back."

The fact that Brown and the legislature did not give the surplus back to the taxpayers and also failed to adjust the tax rates downward, led directly to Howard Jarvis and Paul Gann's now-famous Proposition 13, which gave tax relief in the form of sharply reduced property taxes.

Reagan was not long into his first term when he was advised that to insure a steady cash flow for the state, he should shift the collection of the state income tax from an annual to a payroll-withholding basis. That was the occasion of his "taxes should hurt" remark, for he reasoned that if taxes were withheld from paychecks, the taxpayer would be lulled into forgetting just how big a bite they took from his pay and would not question the legislature as closely as he would on writing a check for the taxes once a year.

He adamantly opposed withholding and told the Sacramento press corps that "my feet are in concrete" on the issue.

In 1971 he bowed to the inevitable. The state simply could not pay its bills unless the system was shifted to withholding. He reluctantly agreed to the change. Once having made the painful decision, he exhibited the bounce and humor that are so characteristic of him. He went across the hall from the governor's office to the press-conference room for his regular weekly news conference and said, "The sound you hear is the concrete around my feet cracking." The press corps so enjoyed this remark that they later gave him a disk of concrete in which were embedded a pair of brown leather shoes. He kept that in the governor's office as a memento, and for the five years when his personal office was housed inside the offices of Deaver & Hannaford, Inc.,* in Los Angeles, he kept the shoes-in-concrete in plain view for all his visitors to see.

The shoes-in-concrete episode illustrates well Ronald Reagan's practicality. This aspect of his character, which he and those close to him took for granted, was for years a constant source of surprise to others, especially non-Californians, and more especially the people in the media-academic-financial axis along the Boston-Washington corridor.

There were other Reagan initiatives in Sacramento that drew heated opposition and caused him to be portrayed as insensitive and hardhearted. In later years, he found himself explaining again and again the details of these issues to journalists and audiences in many parts of the country.

* The public relations/public affairs firm Michael Deaver and the author founded in January, 1975.

During the early years of the Reagan administration, for example, relations with the University of California were frequently tense. Reagan believed that the university was letting student disturbances get out of hand and frequently said so. He also trimmed budget requests from the university, infuriating its officials. Over a period of time they managed to make stick the notion that Reagan had somehow "gutted" higher education in California. The facts were otherwise. During his eight years, state funds for the University of California system went up 105.4 percent, from $240.1 million in 1966–67 to $493.2 million in 1974–75; enrollment, meanwhile, was increasing by 43.9 percent during this period. All that he had failed to do was to increase the funds by as much as university officials wanted. Across the board, the Reagan administration in California made heavy commitments to improved funding of education.

He withstood a fire storm of criticism over the state's mental hospitals, too. Under Pat Brown, the state had developed a plan to close down the state's big mental hospitals and move most of the mentally ill and mentally retarded patients into smaller facilities in their own communities. When he learned of the plan, Reagan supported it. It seemed inhumane to him to "warehouse" people in mental hospitals when they might be able to lead partly normal lives closer to home and family. Systematically, he began closing down the hospitals. Unfortunately, not every county was ready with adequate local facilities, and so, problems developed in a number of communities. At the same time, those who had a stake in keeping the big hospitals open, such as the hospital workers, moved to save their jobs by accusing Reagan of attempting to "dump" the mentally ill and retarded on the communities. This conjured visions of dangerously unstable people roaming the streets. The criticism and fear was never fully overcome and kept Reagan's reform program from ever being more than a partial success.

Reagan fared better with his welfare reform program, although it faced the greatest barrage of criticism, especially from liberals who mistrusted his motives. Considering the confrontational atmosphere that pervaded American society in the late 1960's and early 1970's, this hostility was not surprising.

Reagan critics were predictable when it came to this subject. They forecast routinely that "the poor would starve in the streets," as Reagan himself recounted often in later years.

California had virtually become the nation's welfare capital. The number of persons on welfare was climbing much faster than the population. In 1961, the welfare caseload was 620,000. Ten years later, when Governor Reagan presented his reform proposals, it was 2.3 million.

During the early years of his administration, Reagan had let the bureaucrats tinker with the process, listening to their assurances that they could tighten the system and that the increases would level off. Instead, the case load kept climbing.

By 1970 it was clear that if the case load continued to grow, the state would be bankrupt in a few years. Reagan turned again to a task force to look for solutions. In this case, he asked his task force to examine every procedure and rule of the welfare operation. By December 1970, the task force submitted its report and recommendations. A number of the recommendations could be put into effect by executive order of the governor; others would require legislation. Although his task force suspected that a good number of welfare recipients were not actually qualified and that eligibility cross-checks were lax, Reagan knew it would not be easy to persuade a Democrat-controlled legislature to agree with this assessment. He was right.

He asked the legislature for an opportunity to address a joint session in order to unveil his proposals. They refused to hear him. It was a major error on the part of the Democratic leadership, as things turned out. As so many have before and since, they underestimated Ronald Reagan's exceptional abilities as a communicator. In the years since, Reagan has enjoyed recounting the story of his welfare reform campaign. "That speech they wouldn't let me give was like a book banned in Boston. Everyone wanted to know what was in it," he would say. Beginning with an address to Town Hall, a major Los Angeles civic forum, on March 3, 1971 (the same day he transmitted his printed proposals to the legislature), he went up and down the state speaking to civic groups and being interviewed about his reform proposals. Members of his administration and sympathetic civic groups fanned out to rally support for his program.

The administration feared that time was running out for the state's coffers. Its projections indicated that the case load could increase by as much as six hundred thousand persons by the end of the current fiscal year.

For weeks a battle was played out across the state. Reagan and his supporters talked of the need to bring under control a system that had gone haywire. In one instance, a newspaper reporter set out to test the Reagan task force's contention that it was ridiculously easy to get on welfare: he applied for welfare under three different names in the same welfare office on the same day and had been accepted in all cases. The task force had also found an alarmingly high percentage of welfare *workers* on welfare, handling each other's cases.

On the other side, Reagan's opponents seemed to assume that anything the governor said on the subject was motivated by antipathy to the poor and insensitivity to human suffering. They seemed to believe that anyone who applied for welfare deserved and needed it, as if it were not conceivable that in a state of some 20 million persons there might be some who would bend the rules for gain.

Reagan put the executive orders into effect in March and kept up his campaign into the summer. Finally, as he tells it, Assembly Speaker Bob Moretti came into his office one day with his hands held up in mock surrender, saying, "Stop those cards and letters." Then, the two sat down in Reagan's office to forge a compromise that would later be converted into legislation. By his own reckoning, Reagan got "about 70 percent" of what he wanted. Moretti and the Democrats negotiated an increase in the welfare grants that ultimately averaged 43 percent (these were made possible by the savings created by Reagan's tighter eligibility and cross-check procedures). The bill was passed and signed into law. The welfare rolls, which had already peaked in the spring and had begun to turn downward as a result of Reagan's administrative reforms, now took a sharper, faster drop as the effects of the legislation were felt. By the time Ronald Reagan left office in the first week of 1975, the welfare rolls had declined by 364,630 from their peak, 2,459,800, in March 1971, on the eve of the implementation of the administrative reforms.

A durable myth about conservatives is that they are dogmatic, unbending and uncompromising. Yet, in the case of the welfare reforms, Reagan proved once again that he was practical, true to his convictions, confident of what he was doing, and skilled in the art of compromise.

Several years later, using the welfare reforms as an example, Reagan told me that if he could get 70 percent of what he was looking for from a hostile legislature, he would take it because he figured that the 70 percent would work well enough that he could go back later for the other 30 percent and have a fair chance of getting it.

Reagan inadvertently gave his critics ammunition from time to time. He was determined to restore order to those publicly owned universities and colleges where disruptions and demonstrations had seemingly made education a secondary matter. He gave wholehearted support to school officials, such as S. I. Hayakawa at San Francisco State, who stood up to the mobs, but he wanted to awaken alumni and others who could influence those college and university administrators whose resistance to radicalization was weaker and less effective.

At a meeting of the California Council of Growers at Yosemite on April 7, 1970, Reagan said, "Some of you who are alumni of these institutions—you've got to stand up some more. You keep thinking the school's pretty much like it was when you were there. It isn't, and sometimes these administrators need your backing and your insistence that they stand up and 'bite the bullet.' . . . We know it will not work to say, 'Well, it might alienate the moderate students; might radicalize them.'

You've radicalized all you're going to; and now is the time to say, 'If it takes a bloodbath now, let's get it over with. Appeasement is not the answer.' In some instances you've got to be forceful enough to recognize that on some campuses in [the] administration, but particularly in faculty groups, there are groups—a minority to be sure—but groups who are part and parcel of the revolution."

The press seized on the "bloodbath" phrase, largely to the exclusion of the context of the remarks. Reagan's metaphor for "showdown" made his critics furious.

For as long as I have known him (and probably for much longer), Ronald Reagan has consistently believed that the nature of government is such that it will always find a way to spend any available money and that the only way you can curb a government's appetite is to limit the source of its sustenance—taxes. (During a legislative debate on one of his periodic proposals to turn surpluses back to the taxpayers, Reagan's theory about government's appetite was verified. One state senator rose to declare of Reagan's proposal, "I consider this an unnecessary expenditure of public funds!")

Often during the 1980 campaign, Reagan voiced his belief that government had to "go on a diet." True to his word, fiscal restraint has become central to his policies as president.

In California, in early 1973 he began to think seriously about putting his belief into practice. He talked about it at length with his staff and members of his cabinet. He talked with financial experts and economists such as Milton Friedman. He became convinced that the state constitution could be amended so as to put a limit—a fixed percentage—on the amount of the people's total income that state government could take to run its affairs. His economic advisers showed him that California's projected economic growth over the next several years would cause the aggregate income figure of the state's citizens to rise steadily, thus providing the state under a tax-limitation measure with automatic increases to deal with growing demands for services. At the same time, the actual percentage of income taken in taxes could decline over a period of years.

From this, Reagan's Proposition 1 of 1973 was born. It was to have these features: a 20 percent refund on 1973 state income taxes; reduction of state income taxes in 1974 and subsequent years by 7.5 percent; exemption of families with annual incomes of $8,000 or less from any state income-tax liability; prevention of the state budget from rising in the future faster than the cost-of-living index and the state's rate of economic growth; prevention of future state programs from falling below the 1973 level of services; provision of an ample emergency fund for the state; and return of all future surpluses (above emergency-fund needs) to the taxpayers.

His legal experts drew up the measure. They worried that the state legislature, faced with restriction of its funds, would look to the cities to pick up expenses it had been having the state treasury pay. Reagan's people knew they had to make the measure airtight to prevent such a tax "shift." They did. It prohibited the state from shifting costs of services to local governments without also paying for them. It imposed a ceiling on local property-tax rates except as required by normal growth, hardship, or a vote of the people of the community. And, it prevented the legislature from raising any state tax except by a two-thirds vote.

It was a well-crafted measure; however, for it to anticipate attempted tax shifts and the need for emergency contingencies, it was necessarily long—some five thousand words. Its length proved to be a disadvantage once the campaign to pass it began.

Meanwhile, Governor Reagan and his staff turned their attention to getting it on the ballot. The idea of a special one-issue election in the fall began to take hold. Would the people be angry at having a special election? Perhaps, but that had to be weighed against the concentrated attention of angry taxpayers that such an election would provide.

There was also the matter of getting the measure qualified. California has had the initiative process for more than six decades, and it has worked well. One reason for this is that it is not easy to qualify a measure. Thus, faddish or frivolous measures have great difficulty in qualifying. In order to qualify Reagan's tax-limitation measure, it would be necessary to get signatures of between 350,000 and 400,000 registered voters in some seven weeks in order to meet the deadline in June 1973. If it was not done by then, the next earliest time the measure could go to the voters would be in the June 1974 primary, when voter attention would turn to state and congressional races and to the usual dozen or more initiative issues. This unique effort to limit spending and taxes might thus be swamped by other issues and contests.

It was decided to go ahead with a signature drive despite the fact that starting such a signature drive from scratch to gain the needed signatures in only seven weeks was virtually unprecedented. Mike Deaver, then assistant to the governor and director of administration, was handed the job of organizing the signature drive. Public-opinion polls were commissioned from Dick Wirthlin's Decision Making Information (DMI). The polling data was encouraging. Support for the idea outpolled opposition approximately three to one. People were beginning to be upset by the rising levels of spending in the state. The seeds of a taxpayer revolt seemed to have been planted and might be ready to sprout.

A citizen's organization was formed, Californians for Lower Taxes. Money was raised to conduct the petition campaign. Deaver's army of signature-gatherers did it. In seven weeks they had obtained a record 900,000 signatures, many more than necessary and more than their target of 570,000.

The measure was scheduled for a special election on November 6.

Up and down the state Reagan and his staff organized battalions of allies to work on the campaign. Presentations were made to chambers of commerce, taxpayer associations, and many other groups. Enthusiasm ran high. Reagan spoke out for the issue in speeches and in countless television and radio interviews. How could the voters not vote for such a sensible measure, especially when its passage would not result in cuts in state services but only force the legislature to add to those services more prudently?

Indeed, the logic of the measure seemed so unassailable that the DMI polls continued to show the voters in favor of it by as much as 58 percent to 27 percent three weeks before the election. Yet, by election day it went down to defeat by 54 percent to 46 percent.*

What had happened? First, the Reagan forces were lulled by the early poll results into believing that the measure was so appealing to the voters they would not become skeptical about it. By midsummer, this euphoria permitted the opposition to organize and then begin an end run against the tax-limitation forces.

At the time, I was running my own small public-relations firm and Deaver recruited me to take on an organizational assignment in eleven Northern California counties. I attended many meetings at Californians for Lower Taxes in Sacramento and rode the circuit of those eleven counties. At the beginning, I felt the same sense of confidence the others felt. How could the voters turn the measure down? But the midsummer calls began coming in from all over the state. The opposition, made up principally of the powerful California Teachers Association, the California State Employees Association, the League of Women Voters, and most Democrats in the legislature, began sending teams around to city councils, county boards of supervisors, and boards of education, making anti–Proposition 1 presentations and requesting resolutions opposing the measure. Their technique was simple but effective, and it threw the Reagan forces on the defensive: they planted seeds of doubt. The measure was so long and complicated, they would say, that it must be imperfect. They told their audiences it would cause a shift in tax burdens from the state to the communities. Although this was not true, the length and apparent complexity of the measure discouraged many from reading and analyzing it. Furthermore, even the suggestion of a tax shift

---

* No, 2,284,705; Yes, 1,945,123.

made many local officials nervous, for local budgets in many instances were strained and under severe pressure from constituents with competing priorities.

By the time the full force of these "flying squads" of opponents had been assessed, the Proposition 1 field people found themselves defending the issue at every turn. We had to explain and reexplain at virtually every stop that the measure prohibited the state from shifting tax responsibility to the communities without passing along the money to pay for such responsibility.

Whereas the pro–Proposition 1 news-media exposure and advertising had been dominant throughout the early months, the passage of anti–Proposition 1 resolutions by many local bodies began to give the other side a good deal of exposure in the media. A number of newspapers were weighing against the measure editorially.

There is an axiom in politics that if the voters become uncertain about a ballot measure involving taxes they will vote against it.

The turning point seemed tangible to me in Oakland on October 23. There I debated a representative of the League of Women Voters in a church meeting hall in a prosperous apartment-house district that had several high-priced retirement developments in it. The voters in this neighborhood should be for the Reagan tax-limitation measure, I thought. Yet, their questions in the period following the debate told me they were worried and uncertain. They were not convinced that it was airtight and would not cause the tax shift the opponents had been claiming it would. Colleagues in the campaign were reporting that they were experiencing similar skepticism throughout the state.

It was discouraging and at times infuriating that the opposition was using deception to beat us, but it was not too surprising, since many of the opponents relied on access to a full public trough and saw their jobs as being threatened by Proposition 1.

What was to have been a great victory of the forces of tax prudence and common sense over the "big spenders" (as many Reaganites called the opponents) turned out to be an unexpected defeat. Ronald Reagan's carefully crafted tax-limitation measure had turned out to be ahead of its time, although, of course, we did not know that in November 1973. In time, the tax revolt did come about, and it exploded with the force of a political Mount St. Helens with the passage of Proposition 13 in June 1978. Reagan's Proposition 1 probably laid the foundation for the tax revolt that later swept the country and has not really abated yet. It is doubtful there would have been a Proposition 13—let alone a successful one—had not Reagan's Proposition 1 created the climate for tax and spending limitation and had not Governor Jerry Brown and a Democratic legislature failed in 1977 to lower income-tax rates and return to the people the growing state treasury surplus, which was actually a legacy of the Reagan years.

Proposition 1 did not draw the kind of national media attention that 1978's Proposition 13 did. Nevertheless, Ronald Reagan was hardly invisible at a national level. This was partly because of the sheer size of California as the nation's most populous state. It was also partly because of Reagan's skill as a communicator. He gave conservatives throughout the country hope. He campaigned tirelessly in congressional, legislative, and gubernatorial elections in many states and was especially popular in the South during the years when the Republican party was beginning to take root.

To this day, many journalists routinely date Ronald Reagan's quest for the presidency as having begun in 1968, after he had been governor of California for barely a year and a half. Reagan himself never took his last-minute candidacy in Miami Beach at the 1968 Republican convention this seriously. He described it as a "favorite son" effort, although some of his supporters saw it as far more than that. Some of his staff and key supporters were for him challenging Richard Nixon; others did not want him to and thought the effort was wrongly timed and might harm his image in the party.

While Reagan had always intended to lead a favorite-son delegation to Miami Beach and was lukewarm about challenging Nixon, he did not take steps to remove his name from presidential primary ballots in Oregon and Nebraska. He was persuaded to declare his candidacy on the eve of the convention, but it was too late. Nixon had it sewed up well in advance.

Even though the 1968 effort was late, partial, and a failure in the short term, a number of Reagan's strongest adherents and most effective supporters first got behind him at that time. Among them were James Edwards, today secretary of energy (and from 1975 to 1979, the first Republican governor of South Carolina since Reconstruction); Jimmy Lyon, an outgoing, irrepressible Houston banker (who helped keep Reagan's 1976 campaign alive during its darkest hours); and Frank Whetstone, a jovial publisher who proved to be a top field organizer in later campaigns.

Nixon, during his first term, apparently took a shine to Reagan, too. In 1969 and 1971 he asked Reagan to represent him on three different overseas trips, calling on heads of state and other dignitaries. In October 1971, for example, Reagan was in Taipei at Nixon's behest, reassuring Chiang Kai-shek that the United States would stand by him. Meanwhile, Henry Kissinger was in Peking, making arrangements for Nixon's historic trip there.

Governor Reagan also got considerable attention when he went to

Washington in February 1972 to testify before the Senate Finance Committee against the advisability of its adopting the Nixon administration's Family Assistance Plan (known by those who dealt with the issue as FAP). This plan was essentially designed to replace existing welfare programs (except for the aged, blind, and disabled) with an "income floor," or guaranteed annual income. Although the Nixon administration's statistics were attractive at first glance, suggesting an overall reduction in welfare costs through this apparent streamlining, Reagan and his people felt they had learned from the welfare-reform experience in California that the political realities of the issue were such that if the FAP were passed, clamor would soon be heard for various "supplements." Before long, they reasoned, the costs under a totally federal program such as the FAP would be far greater. Reagan argued persuasively before Senator Russell Long's committee that it would be far better to turn more, not less, responsibility for welfare-program management back to the states. Reagan was, and is, a believer in making decisions at the most local level possible. He argued that welfare programs that were not only administered, but also formulated, by the states and communities would be more effective and efficient than a fully "federalized" system.

Ironically, it was Ronald Reagan's good friend "Cap" Weinberger, who, as Nixon's secretary of health, education, and welfare, was assigned to lead the pro-FAP forces.

Reagan, through his testimony and his rallying of support for his position, is widely credited with having been the greatest single factor in the defeat of the FAP. At the hearing, Senator Long passed a handwritten note to the other senators present, Paul Fannin, Len Jordan, and Clifford Hansen. The note read, "Several of us here think that Governor Reagan has made the *best* statement of any witness from those serving in government. Do you agree?" All three agreed. No effort to federalize welfare or replace it with a guaranteed annual income since then has met with success, either.

Reagan's success as governor, his increasing visibility nationally, and his growing popularity with a national conservative constituency all contributed to the belief on the part of many of his close advisers and supporters by 1973 that he would be a logical choice as the Republican party's nominee for president in 1976. There was a growing feeling in the Reagan camp as the year went on that his Proposition 1 tax-limitation measure would pass and that it would give his prospects a major boost. Some may have thought back to the days of "prairie fire" talk. Proposition 1 might rekindle that fire and cause a Reagan-led tax revolt to sweep across the nation.

Considering all that has passed since those days, it is well to remember that in early 1973 Richard Nixon had just been inaugurated to a second term as president and scarcely anyone would have believed that a year and a half later he would be out of office. Spiro Agnew's resignation as vice-president in October that year increased the belief in Reagan circles that the governor would be the logical Republican choice in 1976.

At that time the days of intense scrutiny by the national press were far in Reagan's future. And, although he made a number of trips to the Northeast for Republican fund-raising and campaign endorsement appearances, he was still treated as something of a novelty in the media in the Northeast, where so much of America's opinion-shaping takes place. While those in the media, academic, and financial centers along that Boston-Washington axis saw him as a political celebrity, they also saw him as "a former actor" and not yet a serious possibility for the presidency.

While the prospect of a Reagan candidacy may have seemed unlikely or even fanciful to many in the intelligentsia in 1973, Reagan advisers were comparing notes with a network of Reagan stalwarts in other parts of the country—especially in the West, Southwest, and South—and finding growing enthusiasm. Reagan's success as governor and his vaunted abilities as a communicator of conservative ideas had been weaving for him a network of dedicated followers.

The Reagan circle believed that logic was on their man's side in terms of the 1976 nomination for three reasons: first, the new vice-president, Gerald Ford, had promptly and emphatically disavowed interest in seeking the nomination; next, only Ronald Reagan among nationally known Republicans had a sizable national constituency; and third, the belief that Nelson Rockefeller would never be nominated by a Republican convention, for such conventions were dominated by conservative activists and many harbored an abiding resentment of Rockefeller over his role in the 1964 primary campaign and at the convention where Barry Goldwater became the party's nominee.

Against this background of upbeat thinking, the loss of Proposition 1, while not seriously damaging Reagan, robbed him of the national surge that passage of the measure would have given him. And, as 1973 drew to a close, President Nixon's deepening difficulties over Watergate were the subject of more and more conversation in California among Reagan's leading supporters. No one, at that point, could predict with any accuracy where and when the Watergate matter would end, nor could they predict how its outcome—whatever it was to be—would affect the dynamics of Republican national politics.

2

"Finish Strong"

"LET ME TRY OUT an idea on you," said the voice on the telephone. It was early January 1974, and it was Don Livingston calling from Sacramento. An old friend from Oakland, he was assistant to the governor and director of programs and policy, one of Reagan's four senior assistants.

"How about coming to Sacramento to be Governor Reagan's director of public affairs for his final year in office?" he said. He explained that Dr. Earl Brian, the state's secretary of health and welfare, was resigning to enter the Republican primary for the U.S. Senate, and his place was to be taken by Jim Jenkins, the current assistant to the governor and director of public affairs.

I was surprised and flattered. Of course, I would like to do it, I told Livingston, but I did not see how I could leave my small public-relations business. At that point it consisted of me, an assistant, and a secretary. Livingston argued persuasively; however, I asked for some time to think about it. I promised to call him back the next day.

Weighing the offer, I thought that afternoon about the years of Ronald Reagan's terms in Sacramento. Back in early 1966, like many other California Republicans, I doubted he could be elected. Gradually, I shifted from being a skeptic to a Reagan enthusiast as I saw the way he approached the problems of his sprawling, diverse state. I was impressed, too, by the quality of the people he had taken into his administration. The fact that a number of them were friends whose opinions and judgment I valued reinforced my positive views of the Reagan administration.

That evening over dinner my wife, Irene, and I talked it over. She encouraged me to take the job. Even though it would mean taking leave of absence from my small business, she convinced me I should be able to rebuild it in a fairly short period of time after I left government service the following January.

I thought back over my work for the Reagan administration up to that point. In early 1972 I had been invited to be a member and vice-chairman of a Reagan task force on consumer fraud. The yeasty experience of working with this diverse group—racially and politically mixed and with business, consumerists, and the judicial system all represented—had fired my enthusiasm for the Reagan approach to problem-solving.

We on the task force were not paid for our work, just reimbursed for expenses. Nevertheless, we tackled our job as if our livelihood depended upon it, in two intense all-day meetings every month for fifteen months. We tugged and pulled over many issues, but all of us were proud of the final report we submitted to Governor Reagan in May 1973. Several of our recommendations found their way into legislative and executive action. At no time had the governor or anyone on his staff attempted to dictate the direction of our work or the conclusions to be reached. I learned that this was typical of Ronald Reagan's approach to personnel appointments. He believed in finding the people he thought would be well qualified to do the job at hand and then let them get on with their work without looking over their shoulder.

Not long after the Governor's Consumer Fraud Task Force finished its work, Ned Hutchinson, the governor's appointments secretary, called to say that Allen Bray, the governor's original appointee to the then young bistate (with Nevada) Tahoe Regional Planning Agency, was resigning. He asked me if I would be interested in being appointed to this board, which governed the development of the Lake Tahoe basin in the high Sierra. I was. I had been interested in conservation for many years, and my family and I spent most vacations hiking and climbing in the Sierra Nevada. Also, I owned no property at Lake Tahoe, so I felt I could look disinterestedly at the issues affecting this ecologically fragile area. The appointment came soon after. Again, not a word of instruction was given me by the governor or his staff. I was impressed by the fact he had placed so much confidence in me, and this, of course, made me doubly determined to do the best job possible in representing him.

I soon found myself immersed in the problems of that beautiful and rugged-looking lake that straddles the California-Nevada border in the high mountains. Like the consumer-fraud task force, this was a nonpaying job, but it took many hours of meetings, study, and telephone conversations each month. I had been at the job about six months when Don Livingston called to invite me to join the governor's staff.

The next morning I called Livingston back. Would I have to resign from the Tahoe board if I took the job in the governor's office? I asked. Yes, he replied; Governor Reagan believed that members of his staff should not also sit on policymaking boards and commissions.

Although I knew I would miss the Lake Tahoe work and I was still a little apprehensive about leaving my business, I decided to take the job. A few days later I was in Sacramento to meet with Edwin Meese III, the governor's chief of staff (with the title of executive assistant). Ed, who is also from Oakland, told me that the opportunity I had was unique. Ronald Reagan would be the first California governor in many years to voluntarily retire from office. Early in his first term he had declared that two terms were enough, and he was keeping to his promise. Therefore, since he did not have an election battle to fight in the final year of his second term, he could turn his attention to tying up loose ends, completing unfinished projects and even doing some things he had always intended to do but had not yet found time for. "If we had a motto for this year, it would be Finish Strong," Meese told me. As director of public affairs in the governor's office, my job would be to recommend activities that would help Ronald Reagan fulfill that motto.

Meese also told me that while it was much too early for Governor Reagan to come to any decision regarding the 1976 nomination for the presidency, nothing in his final year in Sacramento should serve to close off his future options.

It was agreed I would start work in about thirty days. Meanwhile, I went home to Piedmont to wrap up my business affairs.

At about this time, Governor Reagan made a trip east to attend several events in New York and New England. At nearly every stop, at either a press conference or an audience question-and-answer session, he was asked about running for president in 1976. He gave virtually the same answer each time. "I don't want to sound coy," he would say, "but it's much too early to be thinking about that." It was a truthful answer, but he was to learn that what sounds plausible to each of several audiences may bore reporters accompanying the party and can even be twisted to give the opposite impression on the evening news. One network crew filmed his remarks at every stop. Once, the evening news ran—in sequence—several instances of only the "I don't want to sound coy" remark, thus making him seem disingenuous. This would not be the last time, as Reagan came more and more into the national spotlight, that his remarks would be made to seem different from their intent when they were reported. In this case, he was careful afterward to vary his answers about the presidential question.

In those early days of 1974, three news events held the attention of Governor Reagan and his staff: the kidnapping of Patricia Hearst, the publishing company heiress; the oil embargo by the Organization of Petroleum Exporting Countries (OPEC); and President Richard Nixon's ongoing and deepening Watergate troubles.

As the Hearst kidnapping dragged on from days into weeks, frustration mounted. It seemed to be an attack on society itself. It was to be many weeks before most of the members of the kidnapping group, the self-styled Symbionese Liberation Army, were to meet their end in a fiery shoot-out in Los Angeles.

The more I talked with members of the governor's staff when I got to Sacramento, the more I realized how seriously concerned they were that he might be subjecting himself to undue criticism for what was considered to be his defense of both Richard Nixon and the oil companies. Reading over his press conference transcripts and other public statements, I could understand their concern.

He did seem to give the embattled president the benefit of the doubt on most occasions, but this stemmed from his deep respect for the office of the presidency, along with the fact that because he has a basic sense of fair play, he was disturbed by what he thought was a tone of hypocrisy in some of the attacks on Nixon.

As for the oil companies, he was not a champion of them. Rather, he was bothered that many people—as frequently became apparent in news conference questions—seemed to be looking for scapegoats for the OPEC embargo and the long gas-station lines in early 1974. The U.S. oil companies were a convenient target.

I was to learn that Ronald Reagan felt that one service he could perform was to help dispel what he called "economic mythology," the sort of mythology embedded in the then-popular belief that almost any problem could be solved if enough government—that is, taxpayer—money were spent on it. He often found himself explaining that businesses, for example, did not pay taxes: "Only people pay taxes and business acts as a very efficient tax collector for government." He was impatient with the notion that there was an economic "free lunch." It irked him, for example, that some state and local politicians would willingly hold out "tin cups" to Washington on the grounds that federal grants were "free" money.

But if he was impatient with the prevailing economic orthodoxy, he had plenty of patience for visitors who were willing to talk economics. He enjoyed the give-and-take of talking economics with academic economists (and he did quite a bit of it that year in Sacramento), but he seemed to enjoy these discussions most when they were with young people. Many small delegations of high school and college students called during the course of every month, and scheduled ten-minute visits to the corner office or the large council room would frequently end up lasting twenty-five or thirty minutes, with the governor's secretary, Helene von Damm, finally coming to the door with a wistful smile, reminding him of his next appointment. The concerns of young people were of special interest to him, for he worried that the cynicism of the late 1960s and early 1970s was in danger of robbing a generation of young people of idealism and the kind of values they would need to succeed in the world. He was always the warm and earnest teacher in these sessions.

The doubt, suspicion, and even hostility of some of these young visitors would almost always be converted to respect—and Reagan treated them with respect, too. Frequently, he would win them over with his anecdotes and good humor.

Ronald Reagan's role as teacher extended in those days to his weekly press conferences, too. He was genuinely interested in being helpful in answering questions. He would, on occasion, launch into a detailed explanation of an issue quite innocently, not realizing that the reporter might be more interested in the possibility of sharpening a controversy than getting an education in the subject. As time went on, he tightened his news conference answers, making them more concise, especially in his presidential campaigns.

Although Reagan treated the press with an openhandedness that they often did not associate with conservative politicians, he still found himself being plagued with the label of apologist for Nixon and the oil companies during many of the months of 1974.

Cynicism, or at least skepticism, is part of the reporter's professional equipment. If he does not come to his craft with it, he soon develops it. Although Reagan was then, as now, very straightforward with people (the phrase "what you see is what you get" is close to the mark), it was hard for California news people (as it was to be even harder for national ones) to believe he did not have a politician's "hidden agenda" or that his statements and policy ideas, which stemmed from an unadorned Midwestern common sense, were anything other than oversimplifications of complex issues.

Some years later, I heard one of Reagan's advisers say with a sigh that he suspected that the news media hold Republicans to a higher standard of conduct than they do Democrats and that they hold Ronald Reagan to a higher standard than other Republicans. While it was a generalization, there was a kernel of truth in it, for many of the men and women of the working press, especially at the national level, had gotten their start in the days of Kennedy idealism, in the early 1960s, and seemed, at times, still to be in search of Camelot. Reagan was a different phenomenon altogether.

In time, as he went through one presidential campaign and on into another, it did seem that what was often called the "Eastern Establishment"—the media-academic-business axis referred to earlier—had an instinctive geographical and cultural bias against a man who was at once a conservative, a Westerner, and a former actor. No one understood this better than Ronald Reagan himself and, in time, he overcame the bias.

The governor's office in Sacramento is a complex centered around a court. It occupies one large corner of the first floor of the state capitol building. The governor's personal office is at the southeast corner of this complex and is commonly referred to in Sacramento as the Corner Office. ("Upstairs" refers to the state legislature, which has its offices on the floors above the governor's office.)

Set squarely in the middle of a large park, the capitol building is surrounded by deep-green lawns and a canopy of large, handsome trees—specimens of both hardwood and conifers found in various parts of the state. The governor's private office and the large cabinet room right next to it look out on this cool, restful scene through high windows. It is hard to imagine a more attractive environment in which to conduct business. In the months to come, I was to wonder if that beautiful California scene outside did not contribute to Ronald Reagan's rarely ruffled calm, confident manner.

I had visited the governor's office complex a number of times in the past and had been impressed by the quiet but industrious atmosphere of the place. I had only been at work there a few days when several other things became apparent. As I became acquainted with the people on the governor's staff, I was struck by their universal cheerfulness and high morale. They got along well together. There were no "turf" disputes that I could detect and the people had mutual respect. There seemed to be a sense of mission. It is as if everyone in the place—all 105 of them—had tacitly agreed to "finish strong."

A few days after I had begun to work there, I remarked about this to Mike Deaver, the governor's assistant and director of administration (in effect, his number-two man, after Ed Meese). Deaver laughed and said, "Remember, we've had seven years' practice." While it is true there had been plenty of time to iron out any bugs in the operation, there was another factor at work. It was loyalty to Ronald Reagan himself. He inspired those around him to do their best. The people who worked for him genuinely liked him. In all the time I have known him and been part of his team, I have never heard him speak crossly to anyone working for him. On the contrary, he would always take time to thank a staff member for extra effort expended or would drop the person a note. He was thoughtful in many small ways which, added together, told his staff he appreciated them. He has often said that it did not matter who got the credit so long as the job got done. This matched well with his belief that if you picked the right person for any given job, the job would be done well. The resulting atmosphere in the governor's office and throughout the departments and agencies of his administration was a positive one in which the individual felt that what he did was worthwhile.

No sooner had I joined the governor's staff than I found myself automatically included in many meetings. There were frequent informal planning meetings over breakfast at the nearby Sutter Club with the rest of the senior staff and the members of the cabinet. Ed Meese usually presided at these.

About every two weeks a smaller group would meet over breakfast. It was called the Nofziger Group, after Lyn Nofziger, then a consultant.* A onetime communications aide to the governor, Nofziger had been associated with him since his first gubernatorial campaign in 1966.

Bob Walker, a special assistant to the governor who went east about once a month and quietly tested the political waters, usually gave his reports at these breakfast meetings. He passed along the views of a handful of longtime Reagan supporters from around the country and talked of potential allies should the governor decide to try for the 1976 presidential nomination. It was at one of these meetings in the spring of 1974 that John Sears's name was first discussed. Sears, a Washington lawyer, had been recruited by Nixon from his New York law firm in 1968 to become chief delegate-hunter at the Republican convention. It was widely agreed in party circles that he had done an excellent job. Certainly, those who engineered the last-minute Reagan nomination effort at Miami Beach that year were well aware of the effectiveness of Sears's delegate work.

While the basic mission of the Nofziger Group was to monitor the national political picture, Mike Deaver presided over scheduling meetings, which occurred frequently. I had an interest in these because the press office reported to me and would be involved in dealing with news people at virtually every future public event on the governor's schedule.

Reagan usually held a press conference every Tuesday morning in the press-conference room across the hall from the governor's office. Briefings were held for about one hour just prior to the press conferences. The afternoon before, the press secretary—Clyde Walthall in 1974—would talk with reporters to determine which issues were on their minds and then develop a set of possible questions for circulation to the governor, his senior staff, and his cabinet officers. At the briefing, Walthall acted as inquisitor, going through the questions one by one. The governor would give his answer and then any of us could add our comments and suggestions about his approach to the answer.

There were frequent cabinet meetings as well. The number in-

---

* In 1981, Nofziger became assistant to the President for political counsel. He returned to private life in early 1982.

creased as we got closer to the June 30 cutoff for gubernatorial action on bills from the spring session. Along with the schedule of cabinet meetings, which often involved presentations by department heads, any department chief who was having a public-relations problem over an issue involving his department was usually dispatched to visit with me, both to get advice and to help us keep the governor briefed in case he got press questions about the problem.

The cabinet meetings provided the best example of Ronald Reagan's management style. Ordinarily, they were scheduled once or twice a week in the large cabinet room in the governor's office. Paneled in birch and decorated with California memorabilia, the room had a rectangular table in the center for the governor and the cabinet and about twenty chairs around the room for senior staff members and department heads. The governor always sat at the end of the table nearest his private office. Ed Meese sat at the other end. The cabinet members—the secretaries of health and welfare, agriculture and services, business and transportation, and resources, and the director of finance—sat along either side. In the middle of the table was an octagonal leather box with brass studs. Inside was a supply of the famous Reagan jelly beans.

I will digress at this point to say that Ronald Reagan's celebrated fondness for jelly beans, while real enough, was not quite so intense as reported. It seems that many years before, when he decided to stop smoking, a friend recommended that every time he had the craving to light up he pop a jelly bean in his mouth for relief. He did, and it worked. For a time he became accustomed to carrying a small supply in his coat pocket. The story got around that he liked jelly beans, so they became something of a trademark. By the time he got to Sacramento, there were jelly beans everywhere: in lobbies and private offices and, of course, on the cabinet table.

All the time I have known Ronald Reagan, he has been a moderate eater of jelly beans. Still, in the cabinet meetings in Sacramento, they often served a useful purpose for him and the others around the table. Sometimes, as the discussion around the table got intense, with alternative proposals being debated and this secretary or that staking out a position, someone would suddenly command, "Pass the jelly beans," and the leather box would make its way around the table with the governor and the others each taking one or two to break the tension.

By June, the cabinet meetings increased to almost a day-long, all-week level. The early and mid-1970s were hyperactive years for the legislature. In 1974, as I recall, nearly a thousand bills had to be considered by the governor, his cabinet, and his staff in the final thirty days prior to the constitutionally required deadline for gubernatorial action.

Governor Reagan used the cabinet somewhat as if it were a board of directors, with himself as chairman. Prior to the meeting, he and interested members of his staff and the agencies and departments involved would receive a memo setting forth the nature of the issue, the options available, the probable costs, and, in most cases, a staff recommendation. The memos were usually one or two pages long, but sometimes longer. There was always detailed technical backup material available, and Reagan often took that home to read.

At the cabinet meeting, the agency secretary would usually bring along the department head involved with the issue to make a presentation. Discussion would follow. Anyone who had regular access to the meetings (about thirty people) was welcome to make a contribution to the discussion. The legislative liaison people would indicate if any organizations or particular constituencies had commented on the issue.

In time, Ed Meese would summarize the arguments. He has a keen ability to synthesize complex material and state its essence clearly and concisely. After long discussions involving several people and points of view, his summaries brought the issues at hand back into sharp focus.

The discussions in the cabinet room would end in one of several ways. Governor Reagan would often say, "I think we've heard enough on this." Then he would say which of the alternatives he had decided on. Or, he might say, "I'd like to sleep on this. Let's take it up at the next meeting." He would take the technical material home to study that evening. (I never saw him leave the office that year without a briefcase filled with reading material. In fact, soon after I joined his staff, one of my colleagues warned me not to send material of marginal value to the governor, for he had a reputation for carefully reading everything in his "In" box.)

Governor Reagan used the cabinet system to give competing points of view a full opportunity to be heard and, frequently, to test new policy approaches on his own people.

There were many one-of-a-kind meetings held that year, often over lunch in the governor's conference room, a modern, low-ceilinged room at the other end of the complex, with a square of tables and a small adjacent kitchen.

One meeting was on the subject of confidence in American institutions, public and private. Dick Wirthlin had shown us polling data indicating that, in light of the Vietnam and Watergate turmoil, the public mood was becoming very sour about such American institutions as Congress, the presidency, business, and the professions. Only a few years before the institutions had enjoyed relatively strong public support. Ed Meese recommended that we put together an all-day conference with several economists and other scholars who might give us insight into ways to improve the situation.

I was given the task of organizing the conference. Although some of the invitees were at first a little suspicious that we were politically motivated, I assured them that this was not the case and that, indeed, one purpose of the meeting would be for the governor to leave a sort of "early warning" issues list for his successor at the end of the year.

On April 10 the scholars arrived to meet with the governor's senior staff. They were Dr. John Bunzel, then president of San Jose State University; Dr. Kenneth Kramer of the Public Policy Research Center at the University of California, Irvine; Dr. Merrill Shenks of the Survey Research Center, University of California, Berkeley; and Dr. Alex Sherriffs, vice-chancellor for academic affairs of the California State College and University System and formerly Governor Reagan's education adviser.

It was a lively session that lasted through lunch. The consensus of the scholars was that "the confidence of the American people in the nation's institutions is rather stable when looked at over long spans of time." This was reassuring, despite the fact that the conferees felt that the short-term alienation toward government would deepen and might have sharply negative consequences for incumbents at election time. The heavy Republican losses at the federal and state levels that November proved them correct.

Other guests for conferences and lunch that year included Dr. Paul McCracken, former chairman of the President's Council of Economic Advisers, and Louis Kelso, originator of the Employee Stock Ownership Plan (ESOP) concept and documenter of the two-factor theory of capitalism. His theories have since been embodied in federal tax laws that give businesses additional tax credits for broadening stock ownership among employees through ESOP. (Senator Russell Long, when he chaired the Senate Finance Committee, became a strong advocate of Kelso's concepts. Reagan, too, was intrigued by them.)

One of our most unusual conferences that year had a man-bites-dog quality about it. It was with Ed and Joyce Koupal, founders of a gadfly group calling itself the People's Lobby. This group was causing quite a stir in California, having gathered enough signatures on petitions under the initiative process to put on the ballot a sweeping reform of the state's election law. This was Proposition 9, which passed in November 1974. It involved detailed disclosure of lobbying expenditures and severely limited the amount of money that lobbyists could spend entertaining legislators. (Reagan's successor, Jerry Brown, was to quip about the Proposition 9 limits that they were enough for a lobbyist to buy a legislator "a hamburger and a Coke.")

The Koupals and Governor Reagan had exchanged verbal blows from a distance and were thought by the capitol press corps to be mortal enemies. Don Livingston pressed for a meeting, saying that it would not only demonstrate the governor's ability to bury the hatchet but would also provide some ground for common cause on future issues. The governor agreed.

The meeting came off with good humor. The Koupals proved to be outspoken, ebullient, and earnest. They had a libertarian streak, and since Ronald Reagan does, too, they did find common ground. At one point, Mrs. Koupal declared that she was in favor of "repealing a law a day." This struck a responsive chord in the governor, who felt that too many legislators measured their success by the number of bills they could sponsor and the notion that the legislature could somehow mandate human perfection. He was the one, after all, who had to cope with the products of their passions, peeves, whims, and causes when the flood of bills came to his desk each year.

The Koupals, only half-jokingly, asked Governor Reagan if he would like to join them in sponsoring a drive for a national voter initiative. They reasoned that the process had worked so well in California for many years that federal legislation should be sought to make it available on a national level. The governor agreed that it worked in California and that he thought the people usually used good judgment on issues, so he saw merit in their idea and promised to take a serious look at the material they had given him. This meeting occurred late in the year, however, and nothing developed directly with the Koupal group, although several times in the years that followed he declared that he liked the principle of a national voter initiative, provided such a measure were carefully written to safeguard the integrity of the federal system.

In mid-April 1974, the Reagans had a meeting of another sort, one they looked forward to with some apprehension. Some time before, the governor had promised the student body of the Davis campus of the University of California that he would appear there before his term was over. This was a time when there was still much residual tension and anti-Reagan sentiment at several UC campuses. Although the Davis campus had always been calm, even at the height of the anti–Vietnam War student unrest, the governor's security people were concerned that someone might use his appearance there to create an incident.

The prospect of facing jeers and catcalls from a gymnasium filled with several thousand people was not a happy one, but Nancy Reagan insisted she would go to Davis with the governor and be at his side. It was characteristic of her to want to be with him, despite the adverse circumstances.

On the evening of April 17, the Reagan motorcade set out for Davis, nineteen miles west of Sacramento. All the previous week, scraps of information had come in to Ed Hickey's security office, suggesting a possible demonstration or picketing. The student newspaper at Davis ran sharply critical articles about the Reagan appearance.

As we arrived at the gymnasium, we saw many anti-Reagan signs about and some pickets. The gymnasium was full. The crowd was orderly, but when the Reagans appeared on stage there was a chorus of boos.

Governor Reagan knew that the crowd would be eager to "get at me," as he put it, so he made his opening remarks brief. The rest of the hour-and-a-half session was devoted to questions and answers. Microphones were placed in several aisle locations. During his opening remarks and the early portion of the question period, Reagan was frequently interrupted by catcalls and shouted slogans, usually radical in nature. Several of us from the senior staff were seated at the side of the gym, slightly above the crowd. It was soon obvious that the interruptions were planned and were being executed, more or less on cue, by about a dozen persons planted at different points in the audience so as to appear to be spontaneous opponents of what Reagan was saying. The tactic did not work. In fact, it backfired. Rather than setting off a shouting match (as the radicals had done often in California, at various events in recent years), the interruptions soon brought forth a strong reaction of disapproval from the crowd. Shouts of "Sit down," "Let him talk," and the like rang through the gym. Although Reagan's answers to many questions were not popular with the crowd, some were, and in all cases he kept his composure and showed flashes of humor, his wife sitting calmly by his side.

When he was asked for his stand on filling the new Melones Dam, a huge project that would end white-water rafting on the Stanislaus river, he replied that he was not fully familiar with the issue but would give it serious study. He listened carefully to the students' objections to the project and, back at the office the next day, ordered a detailed study and presentation of the issue that ultimately came close to halting the project. (Several years earlier he had withheld the traditionally requested gubernatorial approval of a federally built dam because it would have flooded an Indian reservation.)

Legalization of marijuana was still a major topic on California campuses in 1974, and Governor Reagan's answer to a question about it proved to be the climax of the Davis evening. He said, as he often had, that he opposed legislation; he had studied everything he could find on the subject and believed that the medical evidence, which was beginning to come in, indicated that marijuana might have harmful long-range effects. Asked why alcohol should be allowed to be sold but not marijuana, Ronald Reagan brought the house down with his answer. He said, "Why not be the generation that doesn't need to get high on a drug; why not get high on your own accomplishments?" He ended to a standing ovation. Students circled around the stage and engaged him in another ten minutes or so of informal questioning. He had won the respect of the crowd, if not its active support for his positions. It was indicative of things to come, with Reagan's sincerity, calmness, and good humor carrying the day. The Reagans went home happy that the event was over and with the knowledge that it had gone well.

At the Davis event it had not taken long for Ronald Reagan to hit his stride. He was, and is, masterful at give-and-take exchanges. Throughout that last year in Sacramento, he had an opportunity to sharpen his skills even further with a biweekly television program with high school seniors in a format that was rather like a press conference. It was the idea of Joe Holmes, a television producer (and, in the 1980 campaign, associate press secretary). In late 1973 Holmes proposed a series of half-hour programs to be broadcast on the state's public television stations. The target audience would be high school civics classes, and the program would be broadcast during school hours.

It did not take much persuading to get the governor's approval, considering his fondness for discussing issues with young people. It was presented to representatives of the state's department of education and the public television network, and after they were assured that it would be nonpolitical in nature, they agreed to support it; however, they had no money with which to produce it. Ultimately, it was underwritten by the Institute for Contemporary Studies, a San Francisco–based nonprofit public-policy research foundation that had been organized two years earlier by several Reagan allies.

The series was launched early in 1974. High schools would write in, requesting to have their civics classes participate in the videotapings. Joe Holmes had suggested that the program be taped in various cities, depending upon the governor's schedule, so that a wide geographical range of schools could be seen on it.

The format was informal. Governor Reagan sat on a stool facing some twenty students. He greeted them and then asked for their questions. The only restriction on questions was that he was not to be asked about partisan political matters. Anything else was fair game. His warmth and good humor quickly put his young audiences at ease. They were not inhibited; on the contrary, many of the questions were tough, probing ones.

Throughout the year the program was broadcast widely on the public television network. Letters from high school teachers throughout the state told us it was a success and especially appreciated at a time when public confidence in institutions and leadership was registering sharp declines in opinion polls. Ronald Reagan on "YPTV" (for Young People's TV), as his schedule listed it, was showing the state's young people that leaders can and should be accessible, approachable, and accountable.

In December, Don Livingston and I briefed Governor-elect Jerry Brown on the program, recommending that he continue it and conveying the Institute for Contemporary Studies' willingness to continue underwriting it, but he decided against participating in the program. After an effort to use other state officials for a program or two, Holmes folded it.

The same week Ronald Reagan went to the Davis campus he was scheduled to attend his final annual Republican state convention as governor. On Monday of that week, April 16, Ed Meese, Mike Deaver, Don Livingston, Press Secretary Clyde Walthall, and I flew to Los Angeles to brief the governor at his Pacific Palisades residence prior to his weekly news conference, scheduled this time at the Los Angeles Press Club. Willard ("Barney") Barnett, a retired California Highway Patrol officer who served as driver and aide to the governor, met us at the plane and drove us to the governor's home in the hills overlooking Santa Monica Bay on one side and most of the Los Angeles basin on the other.

The governor greeted us with the news that General Alexander Haig had called from the White House to ask him to go to Washington at the end of the week to meet with President Nixon, whose presidency was continuing to unravel. Governor Reagan felt he could not go at that time, since he was committed to address the Republican convention in San Jose that Friday night and would introduce Vice-President Gerald Ford at the same gathering the next morning. (Ultimately, the Washington meeting took the form of telephone conversations.)

My journal for April 16 notes, "We briefed the Governor on a range of state topics of interest to the capitol press corps, but not, as it turned out, to the Los Angeles press. Virtually all the questions centered around Patricia Hearst's involvement in the San Francisco bank robbery and the Zebra murders. There was a question on [Lieutenant Governor Ed] Reinecke's troubles and one on the 55-mile-per-hour speed limit, but little else.

"On the way out, a television reporter and cameraman stopped the Governor as he was about to step into the limousine. They asked him why he was using a limousine during the energy 'crisis.' Ronald Reagan neatly parried by pointing to the staff members accompanying him and noting that we had started out in two cars, but had consolidated on the way to save gasoline. Thereupon, seven of us piled into the limo."

Driving to a luncheon to kick off ticket sales for a June Republican dinner in Los Angeles, we discussed with Reagan the implications of the campaign-reform package he was scheduled to announce Friday at the San Jose Better Business Bureau luncheon and again that night to the Republican convention. (This comprehensive package, along with a sequel to his well-known welfare reforms of 1971, typified the Finish Strong motif of his final year in Sacramento.)

The governor's own favorite reform in the package was a limitation of campaign contributions to those from individuals only. (In California, corporate contributions were, and still are, legal.) Some in the car noted that since a good portion of the tickets for the big June dinner were expected to be sold to corporations, there was a seeming contradiction. "Not really," the governor said. "I think the rules must change, but to unilaterally apply this new rule to our own party before legislation is passed would put it at a serious disadvantage. The Democrats are raising large sums from corporations this year. The new law should apply equally to all from the same starting date." It was logical, and he was not challenged by the press on his proposed reforms. In the face of a strong Democratic majority in the legislature, however, his bills did not make much progress after they were introduced.

Another of Governor Reagan's 1974 legislative initiatives might have fared better if the Nixon administration had not been so preoccupied with its Watergate troubles. This we called Welfare II, a second round of welfare reforms recommended by a task force and based upon the experience of the three years since the first reforms were put into practice. At the center of this second round was reform of eligibility standards for food stamps. Implementation would have required federal cooperation and this was not forthcoming. Increasingly, the decision-making processes in Washington slowed down as Nixon's troubles deepened. Still, Ronald Reagan dramatized the laxity of the existing standards from the speaking platform. The task force had uncovered many outrageous examples such as the one the governor told audiences about the telephone call he had received from a midwestern businessman making $100,000 a year who was furious when he discovered that his son, a college student in California, was getting food stamps. Reagan pointed out that, outrageous as this was, it was legal under federal regulations (which have since been changed).

Not long after Gerald Ford became president, his administration began talking up a new version of the guaranteed-income scheme which Governor Reagan's people dubbed "son of FAP" (after the FAP, which Reagan had helped kill). Reagan privately worried that the new administration was following in the footsteps of the old on this issue.

Although the governor and his people wanted to finish as many things as they could that final year in Sacramento, not every moment was concerned with serious issues. There were plenty of lighthearted, even sentimental moments. Soon after I joined the staff, for example, a letter from a third-grader at the Holbrook School in Concord, east of San Francisco Bay, came to my desk. It was an invitation to the governor to "get out of the rat race and go at a snail's pace. Please come judge our Third Annual Snail Race." I was touched. I thought the governor would be, too, so I proposed it at the next scheduling meeting. He said, "Let's do it; it sounds like fun." So one fine April morning we set out for Concord in a bus, with the press corps along.

A band was playing when we got there, dozens of children were cheering, and a lot of parents were on hand. The school officials were clearly proud of their school and the fact they had been singled out. (When I had called the school officials earlier to tell them the governor would accept their invitation, they were dumbfounded.) The snails, with numbers sticking up from their shells, were creeping about the brightly painted concentric-circle racing board. The race was over in about eight minutes. To this day I do not know if the contestants ended up in retirement on tomato vines or as escargots, but everyone had a grand time. The governor was right in the spirit of the thing and bestowed on the winning classroom the Governor's Snail Race Perpetual Trophy, a jar of jelly beans on which was the gubernatorial seal.

Time and again Ronald Reagan has shown that warm, unaffected human touch in the midst of otherwise serious business. Once, during the Vietnam War he received a letter from a Sacramento soldier who enclosed a money order asking the governor if he would get some anniversary flowers for his wife. On the day of the soldier's anniversary, the governor had his driver, Dale Rowlee, detour to a florist's shop on the way home. He bought the flowers and drove by the soldier's home, astonishing the young man's wife with his personally presented bouquet.

One of my earliest assignments was to develop a list of one-of-a-kind activities the governor might consider doing during his final year. Ronald Reagan is something of a sentimentalist, and there was the likelihood that he might want to take some sentimental journeys. I asked him if there was anything special he wanted to do. He said he would like to go to Round Valley. This valley, in Mendocino, one of the northern coastal counties, was the site of the Indian reservation Reagan had saved some years earlier when he withheld permission for a federal dam on the Eel River that would have flooded the valley. The Indian ranchers were so appreciative that they presented him with a hand-carved plaque commemorating his decision. It was perhaps his favorite memento of the hundreds on the walls in the main rooms of the governor's office. (Later, when he had his office within the Deaver & Hannaford, Inc., suite in Los Angeles, the Round Valley plaque was one of the few from his collection that graced the wall.)

He told me he had also promised Jim Stearns, secretary of agriculture and services (and now an official at the Department of Energy) that he would officiate at the hundredth opening of the Modoc County Fair. This would be held at Cedarville, close by the Nevada border in northeastern California. Perhaps we could visit Round Valley on the same day. We did, as it turned out, on August 22. Both events underscored Ronald Reagan's deep love of the land and his belief in conservation.

The governor's trip to Round Valley, on August 22, 1974, was not only a sentimental journey, but also a personal testament to conservation and to the land that provides California with so much abundance. California summers are hot and dry, but there was a cool breeze when we landed in the Governor's Cessna Citation at the little Round Valley airport. It was the first jet ever to land in the valley. Everyone in the valley, it seemed, had turned out to welcome the governor. Richard Wilson, a young rancher who had organized the morning's visit, escorted the Reagan party to his ranch to inspect a large vegetable plot being tended by college-age "interns" who would soon go out into the Third World to teach the French intensive method of vegetable production, using high-yield, closely spaced beds intensively tended. We examined tables laden with mountains of high-quality produce from the gardens. This was followed by an outdoor luncheon and a reception with Indian leaders, who asked the governor to intercede for them with federal authorities to find funds to rebuild a burned-out clinic. In midafternoon we flew over the mountains to Cedarville for a county fair that, without a parking lot of automobiles and people in modern dress, might have been held a century ago. The town had a comfortable, weathered look; the people were healthy and sturdy. The governor presided at the opening ceremonies, judged a potato-sack race, and enjoyed himself greatly.

On the leg home to Sacramento, Governor Reagan invited a former lieutenant governor, Harold ("Butch") Powers to ride with us. Powers had had a falling out with the Reagan administration some years before, but Ronald Reagan is not a man to hold a grudge. This gesture of reconciliation was met with open gratitude by Powers, then old and long-retired from politics.

In the years since, Ronald Reagan has been photographed in dungarees and cowboy hat at his Santa Barbara County ranch so many times that most people today take for granted his love of the outdoors and his care for the land. In 1974, however, the climate was different. The environmental movement, which was especially strong in California, saw Ronald Reagan and his administration as an adversary. He had a strong record as a conservationist, but it was treated a little like his record in education: if you did not use all the modish rhetoric and support 100 percent of the advocates' programs, you were, ipso facto, the "enemy."

Reagan did not like extremists at either end of the spectrum, and he did not hesitate to say so. In those days he would often make the point to audiences that we had to "strike a balance between those who would bulldoze everything in the name of 'progress' and those who would prevent you from building a house unless it looked like a bird's nest."

Although Ronald Reagan was to prove in time that he would turn upside down many of the assumptions of the nation's political, media, and academic establishments, in those days of left-right politics he was thought of by California campus radicals and, for that matter, by the environmentalists as a pillar of the establishment. In 1974 the environmental movement was still riding high in California, a state with a strong history of interest in conservation. (John Muir founded the Sierra Club there in the late nineteenth century.) Looking back, the environmental movement's heyday in California seems to coincide closely with the rise of the hippies, antiwar demonstrations, and campus disruptions with their strong antieducation flavor. Did all these reflect a deep-seated desire to escape the complexities of modern industrial society, to escape competition, to prolong adolescence? Ultimately, the historians will have to decide upon the answer, but it does seem that the failure of the national leadership to provide young Americans sufficient reason for fighting a war in distant jungles unleashed not only a strong wish on the part of the young not to risk their lives but also the underlying fears that every generation has about entering the adult world.

The yearning for a simpler, more rustic life that seemed so strong among young people in California in the late 1960s and early 1970s seems now to have been closely related to those fears. The back-to-nature aspect of the hippie movement was only one side of the environmental coin; the other was the push by organized environmentalists to restrict the use of private land. As Governor Reagan's second term progressed, legislative attacks on private land use increased, and Reagan, a strong advocate of private property rights, found himself battling what he felt was extremism. Encouraged by a string of victories on the environmental front (especially the 1972 ballot initiative that created coastal commissions to regulate the use of land along the state's thousand-mile coastline), the leadership of groups such as the Sierra Club and the Friends of the Earth became increasingly militant. Reagan was frequently attacked as being an antienvironmentalist. It was not true.

During Reagan's eight years in Sacramento, the state added more land to its park system than under all his predecessors combined. Encouraged by his imaginative state parks director, William Penn Mott,

Reagan campaigned right into his final year to add more land to the system. I remember trips by him that spring to a surfers' beach in Orange County and to Angel Island in San Francisco Bay to dramatize the acquisitions and improvements that would be made as a result of a large 1974 parks-and-recreation bond issue.

In the early 1970s, clamor for a new trans-Sierra highway had reached the point of climax. Several highways cross the huge chain that forms a spine several hundred miles long on California's eastern border. Some are all-year highways, although those in the central part of the Sierra close with the first snows. For years businesses in the San Joaquin Valley had promoted a new all-year highway. The one they proposed would cross through one of the few areas of the Sierra where hikers, campers, fishermen, and climbers can get more than ten miles away from a road—a beautiful near-wilderness area called the Minarets, just south of the border of Yosemite National Park. Reagan examined the facts and decided against the road. To underscore his point, the following summer he and his family took a high-country pack trip into the Minarets.

It was also during Ronald Reagan's years in Sacramento that he signed the nation's toughest air-quality laws. Although it has taken several years, one result is that the Los Angeles basin today has many more clear-sky days a year than it once had.

Northern California is blessed with many cloudless days in the spring and summer, and it was just such a day, May 25, 1974, when a high-level delegation from the Soviet Union arrived, on relatively short notice. Bernice Behrens, wife of the *San Francisco Chronicle*'s Earl ("Squire") Behrens, then longtime dean of the capitol press corps, had called one day in mid-May. She headed the State Department's hospitality center in San Francisco. The center arranged local itineraries for visiting dignitaries, of whom there were many because San Francisco has so many foreign consulates. It seems a delegation of Soviet officials, scholars, journalists, and factory managers headed by Boris N. Ponomarev, secretary of the Central Committee of the Communist party of the Soviet Union and an alternate member of the Politburo, was coming from Washington to San Francisco and had asked to meet Ronald Reagan, whom the delegation apparently thought might become president. The only time they could come was the Saturday of Memorial Day weekend. The legislature would be away, but the governor cleared his schedule.

The Soviet delegation pulled up at 3 P.M. The governor greeted them on the capitol steps. Their limousines and bus were directed to the garage beneath the capitol building because it was expected that demonstrators protesting Soviet policies on Jewish emigration might appear during the visit.

Ponomarev, a dour man in his midsixties wearing a shapeless gray suit, listened soberly as the governor took the group on a tour of the capitol's marble corridors (with portraits of his predecessors looking down) and the senate and assembly chambers. We ended up in the cabinet room for the customary "exchange of views." Governor Reagan, with his ever-present sense of humor, managed to coax a smile out of Ponomarev with one of his anecdotes.

Mrs. Reagan had planned a garden reception at the executive residence, about three miles away. At the appointed time to leave the capitol, the demonstrators had materialized and had blocked the main garage exit, so the entire party slid out by way of a back entrance.

Several of us had wondered, but had not asked, what the Soviet visitors had thought on their ninety-mile drive from San Francisco as they passed miles and miles of prosperous suburbs and farms on a six-lane freeway filled with late-model autos and trucks.

Ponomarev, despite his mild looks, is in charge of coordinating Soviet party activities with those of Communist parties throughout the world. He had with him a KGB security detail worthy of such a senior official. They were young and acted not much different from American security men. They said little and kept their eyes moving about.

At the climax of the reception, Governor Reagan and Ponomarev mounted the arbor steps above the rose garden, where the governor gave a short toast. Just as Ponomarev began a toast in response, two National Guard jets shrieked by right overhead almost as if we had planned it.

Earlier that week Governor Reagan made one of those first-time visits he had talked about; he visited the California Maritime Academy, on Carquinez Strait, where the Sacramento and San Joaquin rivers empty into San Francisco Bay. Reagan frequently noted in his speeches that California's economy was so large that if the state were a separate nation, it would have the world's seventh or eighth largest economy. That economy is heavily involved in international trade, much of which moves by sea, and so, not surprisingly, California is the only state to operate its own maritime academy. On that clear afternoon in May, the governor and his party were piped aboard the *Golden Bear*, the academy's training ship, where he addressed the several hundred young men and women students. Afterward, we drove the short distance to the United States Naval Yard on Mare Island, opposite Vallejo, where he inspected a nuclear submarine.

The first week in June, Ronald Reagan attended his eighth and last National Governors' Conference in Seattle. For several weeks the senior staff had been "round-tabling" the conference format and the level of "visibility" the governor should take. All the national political writers would be there, including the major columnists. The television networks would be looking each day for stories for the evening news.

Deaver and I conferred quietly with friends in the news media to help determine how best to time the governor's news conference at the two-day event. One man said we should consider not one news conference but two. "Provided he has more than one issue he wants to talk about, I'd recommend a morning news conference one day, which is best for network television, and an afternoon one the next day, which favors the newspapers, most of which come out the following morning. That way, everyone should be satisfied."

There were two issues: compulsory national health insurance and federal land-use planning legislation sponsored by Senator Henry Jackson and Congressman Morris Udall.

Senator Edward Kennedy, the leading spokesman for compulsory national health insurance, was scheduled to appear at the opening session of the conference, on a panel on the subject with Secretary of Health, Education, and Welfare Caspar Weinberger and Dr. Russell B. Roth, president of the American Medical Association (AMA). Both the Nixon administration and the AMA had taken a defensive posture on the subject, offering their own national health insurance proposals in an apparent effort to forestall the more extreme Kennedy proposal.

We proposed the idea of two news conferences to Governor Reagan. He liked it because he felt strongly that compulsory national health insurance was the wrong way to solve the health-care problems of a relatively small percentage of the population not already covered. And, he liked the opportunity of campaigning against the Jackson-Udall land-use legislation because he saw it as a fundamental assault on private property rights.

I left for Seattle several days before the conference, to make arrangements for the two news conferences and to call on local news media to alert them to the issues Governor Reagan would be discussing.

The preconference festivities began with a salmon barbecue on an island in Puget Sound on Sunday, June 2. Riding over to the island on the boat, I talked with several national media people and learned that they saw this as a sort of test round in the 1976 presidential sweepstakes. Two oft-mentioned candidates, Reagan and Kennedy, might square off, they thought. A number of other governors were talked about as having presidential ambitions. David Broder, in a *Washington Post* column after the conference, named Democrats Dale Bumpers of Arkansas, Reuben Askew of Florida, Jimmy Carter of Georgia, Dan Walker of Illinois, Wendell Anderson of Minnesota, and John Gilligan of Ohio; and Republicans William Milliken of Michigan and Daniel Evans of Washington. (At this writing, in 1981, only Milliken and Bumpers still hold public office.)

While we originally thought of the device of two news conferences as a way to accommodate best the large, diverse press corps that covered the National Governors' Conference, we began to realize that the act of scheduling two news conferences served as a signal to the media that Ronald Reagan was serious about 1976.

Looking over the clippings from that conference, I find that most reporters concentrated on covering what the other governors thought about Reagan's positions on the issues at hand (he did not have many supporters among them) rather than the fact that he had picked two national issues, beamed his message beyond the conference, and articulated his basic philosophy about the role of the federal government.

At the morning session the panelists tossed the issue of Kennedy's compulsory national health insurance bill back and forth. As soon as they had concluded, Reagan tried to be recognized in order to respond. Others were recognized first, and it was nearly an hour before he got his chance. Robert Shogan, reporting in the *Los Angeles Times*, described Reagan's comments this way: "When his turn finally came, Reagan said that 182 million Americans already had some kind of medical insurance, that 19 million received Medicaid benefits and that 20 million were eligible for Medicare.

" 'Who has asked for this nationalized health insurance?' Reagan wanted to know. 'I find no evidence whatsoever that there is great public demand.' . . .

"Reagan asked, 'Have we ever checked up . . . to see how unsuccessful government medicine has been in the rest of the world?' "

Reagan, in effect, had challenged Kennedy to an impromptu debate. According to Shogan, "Kennedy was given a chance to answer Reagan, by the moderator of the discussion, Gov. Cecil D. Andrus of Idaho. But to the disappointment of the audience that filled the conference room, he chose to pass."

Kennedy, in fact, had not really warmed to his own topic very effectively, according to Broder's account: "Despite the fact that he has made that issue his specialty, specific questions from several governors on the cost and implementation of his plan set Kennedy searching for answers in the memoranda from the Library of Congress he had brought with him."

Reagan, buoyed by his experience in the general session, went directly from there to his first news conference, where he delivered his prepared statement, which elaborated on his extemporaneous remarks. Underscoring his contention that there was no popular support for Kennedy's scheme, he said, "In a recent Louis Harris survey, a cross section of the American people ranked health at number 15 out of 16 national problems. What we definitely do not need is a massive $55-billion-a-year inflationary national health scheme that will deliver very little more than smiles to the faces of the bureaucrats in Washington."

The next day, Reagan took on the land-use legislation. The Jackson version of the bill had cleared the Senate, and the Udall version was scheduled for a House vote a few days after the conference. Back in Sacramento, during the planning for the conference, the governor had said he wanted to go all out against the bill, sending letters to the President and to members of Congress urging its defeat. This was done two weeks prior to the conference.

Much as the White House and the AMA had done on national health insurance, the Republicans in the House had taken a defensive stance, offering a substitute for the Jackson-Udall bill. Reagan's view was that *any* federally supervised land-use planning would lead to federal control and diminution of private property rights.

The Jackson-Udall legislation did not mandate specific land-use plans for the states. Reagan described it this way at his news conference:

> It says, if you will agree to develop land-use planning in your state, we will give you some federal money, but you will have to let us approve and interpret your plan in Washington.
>
> Land-use planning is so intricately bound up with the question of basic property rights that the only proper place to deal with it is at the state level. And, a land-use plan which works well in one state may not in another. Surely, it should be for the individual state to decide, and not rest in the hands of a bureaucrat or social engineer in Washington.
>
> In April, California advised Congressman Udall of its opposition to his bill. Judging from his response, I must assume he misunderstood our concerns. We have two: first, the potential damage to states' rights; second, the pipe dream—nurtured by the bill—that a centrally directed economy is somehow beneficial to the quality of our lives.

He went on to describe how California was developing legislation to deal with its own needs in the area of land-use planning. He concluded by saying, "When all is said and done, we must ask ourselves: has the talk about states' rights at this conference been simply a rhetorical gesture or will it usher in a new era when the states will say to the federal government, 'No thanks. We'd rather do it ourselves.' I am convinced it must be the latter if we are to control our destinies."*

Ronald Reagan's statements at the Seattle Conference did not win him many laurels from his peers (thirty-seven of whom were Democrats),

---

* The Udall bill was ultimately defeated.

but they effectively telegraphed his philosophy on national issues to a nationwide audience. In retrospect, it turns out to have been a dry run for the 1976 campaign. At the time, prevailing orthodoxy among a predominantly Democratic governors' conference and a Democrat-controlled Congress (echoed by many in the news media) was that such things as federal control of land-use planning and imposition of compulsory national health insurance were desirable goals. If Ronald Reagan was swimming upstream at Seattle, he did not act as if he were. He had spoken, as usual, with the courage of his convictions. Those statements of 1974 have a familiar ring to them today because they spring from the same straightforward philosophy of government that animates the Reagan administration in Washington in the 1980s.

Throughout that summer President Nixon's troubles deepened. Finally, on Monday, August 5, came the "smoking gun" revelation: the President had admitted knowing more about the Watergate cover-up than he had previously acknowledged.

Governor Reagan was scheduled to fly to Sacramento from Los Angeles that morning. Meese, Deaver, Livingston, and I met in Ed's office in anticipation of his arrival. We agreed that the governor should issue a statement to the press shortly after he arrived. His plane was delayed, so the scheduled staff luncheon was late. Over lunch all discussion focused on the Nixon admission. There was pressure from the media for a statement from the governor, and as we talked over lunch, he handwrote the following:

> As you know, I have done my best to follow the progress of the Watergate investigation. Until now I was not convinced that evidence of an impeachable offense had been presented to the Congress or the people.
>
> Now, for the first time, it has been revealed that neither the Congress nor the people had been told the entire truth about Watergate.
>
> In view of the President's statement I believe it is absolutely imperative that he go before Congress and make a full disclosure of all the information he has in this matter and that he do so immediately, answering any and all questions they may have. The constitutional procedure should then be followed in order to bring about a speedy resolution of this issue. The American people are entitled to this as well as to the whole truth once and for all.

By evening the networks were talking about a "death watch" on the Nixon presidency. The next morning a friend in the White House called me to say that there was a flurry of activity in Vice-President Ford's office in the old Executive Office Building, with many people coming and going. Also, Nixon's two sons-in-law had appeared. "Things are coming to a head quickly," my friend said.

Thursday, August 8, soon after I arrived in the office, the same friend called to tell me the signature machines that automatically sign the President's name to correspondence had been ordered shut down. Given all the other evidence, this meant that the Nixon resignation was imminent. I rushed into the governor's office with the news. Meese and Deaver were there. The governor looked grim. Although he kept his thoughts to himself, considering all the conversation we had had with him about Nixon's problems, I think he felt a sense of disappointment that Nixon had let his country down, mixed with anger over what he felt was the hypocrisy of many of the Nixon-haters, who had finally run their quarry to ground.

Nixon announced his resignation about two hours later. Governor Reagan agreed to appear later in the afternoon at a Sacramento station for a televised news conference. I was delegated to draft a short statement for him. As usual, he worked it over himself on one of his yellow pads. Here is the final version:

> It is a tragedy for America that we have had to come to this, but it does mean that the agony of many months has come to an end.
>
> It is a personal tragedy for Richard Nixon who, despite these events and his recent revelations, gave so much of himself to his country over the years and who accomplished so much, especially in the area of foreign affairs. Now, though, we must turn our full attention to the other problems that face our nation.
>
> I join with all Americans in pledging my full support to President Ford as he leads the nation into more tranquil times.

While one presidency was dying in Washington that week, another may have been born 3,000 miles away in Sacramento. By coincidence, Ronald Reagan's first meeting with John Sears took place that week.

On Tuesday the sixth, Sears flew from Washington to San Francisco and then to Sacramento to have dinner with what my journal describes as the "National Politicial Group," actually an extension of the Nofziger Group which met every two or three weeks at breakfast. This meant the governor's senior assistants: Meese, Deaver, Livingston and I, Lyn Nofziger, Jim Jenkins (secretary of health and welfare), Dick Wirthlin (head of Decision Making Information), who did the governor's polling, and one or two others.

We had heard so much about Sears' abilities as a delegate-hunter that they had taken on a legendary quality. It was a relaxed, cordial dinner, but Sears' comments, which we had expected to be the high point of the evening, were rather rambling. I recall being disappointed, but in retrospect, I imagine that the fatigue of all-day flying, combined with the uncertainties surrounding the political future as a result of Nixon's probable resignation, caused Sears to be quite cautious.

The next morning Sears met the Reagans at the executive residence.

The only definitive thing that came out of the Sears visit was that the group that met with him over dinner agreed to keep in regular contact and to meet periodically to assess the presidential political situation. But, looking back, this was the embryo of what was to become a presidential campaign some months later.

Gerald Ford had not been in the Oval Office long when he declared that he intended only to serve out the remainder of his appointed term. This seemed to make good sense. The American public clearly wanted a respite from the wrenchings of months of Watergate, and if the new president could turn his full attention to the healing process, it would probably proceed faster and more completely. Also, in the Reagan camp there was the feeling that Ford had no "natural" constituency (other than the Fifth Congressional District of Michigan, which he had served for a quarter-century). On the other hand, there was some fear that what might be called the Republican establishment (the national committee and most incumbent officeholders) would coalesce behind Ford if he ran, in order to prevent Reagan from getting the 1976 nomination. Still, if Ford stuck to his announced intentions, many in the Reagan circle believed, their man's time was coming because his constituency was national in scope, was willing to work hard for him, and believed wholeheartedly in the conservative cause.

As August wore on, planning went ahead for Governor Reagan's customary biennial campaign tour for Republican candidates. All during the year requests had flooded in from congressional, gubernatorial, and other candidates from many states requesting his appearance on their behalf. Mike Deaver and his scheduling people had planned two intensive out-of-state trips, one in September and the other in October, plus a number of appearances in California for Republican candidates.

It was in Chicago, while Governor Reagan was addressing an audience in a downtown hotel for a congressional candidate, that President Ford called to thank him for his public support of Ford's pardon of Nixon.

We went on to South Dakota to campaign for Leo Thorsness, a former Vietnam prisoner of war who was challenging Senator George McGovern. Reagan brought tears to virtually every eye that night with a moving tribute to the men who had fought in Vietnam. For the first time I heard him say, as he was to many times in later years, that "never again must we let Americans fight in a distant land without permitting them to win."

There were appearances for former members of Congress trying to regain their seats, for incumbents trying to hang onto theirs, and for challengers. The trips took us to New Mexico, Colorado, North and South Carolina, Washington, Georgia, and Florida, to name a few states.

It was my first taste of dawn-to-dusk cross-country campaigning. Almost every stop followed a similar pattern: a welcoming party at the airport, a cocktail reception (for larger contributors to the candidate's coffers), a banquet (with cuisine so homogeneous that if you were blindfolded, you would never know you had left the first city), individuals and small delegations coming to the governor's suite afterward, and sometimes a breakfast the next morning. Often there was a news conference sandwiched between the arrival and the reception so that the local candidate could get a picture and headline.

Back in California, Houston Flournoy, the highly regarded state controller, was the party's candidate for governor. (Lieutenant Governor Ed Reinecke had earlier been considered the most likely candidate, but his implication in the scandal over the San Diego site selection for the 1972 Republican convention had sidelined him and, ultimately, led to his resignation from office.) Reagan had offered to campaign anywhere and anytime Flournoy wanted him.

At my level this translated into talking with Flournoy's campaign people about television and radio. They were clearly resistant to using Reagan at all. Several of them saw him as being narrowly "right-wing" (despite his high approval ratings in Wirthlin's polls throughout 1974), and they wanted Flournoy to convey a "moderate" image to voters in the immediate post-Watergate election. Edmund G. ("Jerry") Brown, Jr., then California's secretary of state, was running circles around Flournoy early in the campaign, answering questions with questions and extolling the "small-is-beautiful" fad. Reagan spoke out for the Flournoy-led ticket whenever he could. Late in the campaign Flournoy began pressing Brown very hard, so that the latter's victory on election day, November 5, was razor-thin. In fact, considering the onrush of Flournoy in the last days of the campaign, had it lasted another week Jerry Brown might never have been governor. But, elected he was, as was most of his ticket.

From holding all but one of the six state constitutional offices in Reagan's second term, the Republicans sank to holding only one, the attorney generalship, which Evelle Younger won. Republican delegations in both houses of the legislature slipped. Nationally, a number of candidates Reagan supported held on to their seats or were elected, but most of these failed to support him when he ran for president in 1976. (They came around in 1980).

Ed Meese had organized several meetings in October to lay plans for the transition to a new administration, so that we were well prepared for the meeting Governor Reagan called in the cabinet room on Thursday, two days after the election. He had invited Brown to meet with him and to bring whomever he wished. Several of us from the senior staff attended with the governor. Brown brought Warren Christopher, a Los Angeles attorney who became deputy secretary of state in the Carter administration, and several other close political associates. All enjoyed the joke when we served each for lunch "a hamburger and a Coke" which Brown had extolled during his campaign support of Proposition 9.

Because Brown's father's transition had gone so poorly and there had been so little cooperation with the Reagan people, Ronald Reagan was determined that this transition would go smoothly. It did. The first meeting was cordial, as were all the others that were held. We worked out a schedule of work sessions with various persons in the Brown entourage who would be in charge of particular areas. Brown himself had at least one extensive meeting with each of the senior staff members to get a personal feeling for what each office within the governor's purview did. Everyone got on well. The meetings skirted philosophy and specific policies and kept to functional matters.

At the conclusion of that first meeting in the cabinet room, Brown asked Reagan for an opportunity to speak privately. They retired to the governor's office, where Brown told him that he admired much of what Reagan had done and worked for and that, in any case, he did not intend to "bad-mouth" him after he left office. Reagan expressed similar intentions. Both stuck to their word.

Throughout 1974 the governor received a variety of offers for his future. He knew he wanted to go on the lecture circuit when he left office to fight, as he put it, that "economic mythology" which was crippling the American enterprise system. There were plenty of requests for his presence on platforms, according to Mike Deaver's scheduling people. In addition, there were offers from newspaper syndicates, television producers, book publishers, and others. One day in late spring, as we finished going over some papers in his office, the governor said to me, "Efrem Zimbalist says he's doing a syndicated radio program with a chap in Hollywood who has an idea of doing one with me next year. He thinks there's a market for conservative commentary. Will you look into it?" I said I would.

The next time I was in Los Angeles on business, I called on Harry O'Connor, the radio syndicator. We recognized each other at once. Comparing notes, we realized we had done business together a number of years before. He was convinced, he told me, that the country was ready for commonsense commentary of the sort Ronald Reagan dispensed so well. He saw it as approximately three minutes of commentary in a five-minute program segment, five days a week.

Later, in response to some inquiries, I explored the idea of a Reagan newspaper column with several syndicates and decided to recommend the San Diego–based Copley News Service.

By late summer, as several of the governor's senior people had begun to decide on their future careers, Mike Deaver and I began to talk about going into business together. Perhaps better than anyone else in the Reagan circle, he could sense the Reagans' interests and needs. I was reporting to him about my findings on newspaper and radio syndication one day when he said, "You know, come next January the Reagans are going to need some kind of organization or they'll find themselves at home one morning, fresh from Sacramento, with the phone ringing off the hook and bags of mail pouring through the door."

Before long we had decided to join forces. We developed a proposed staffing plan that would include several people from the governor's office. We would form a new company and would put the remainder of my small public relations business into it. One Saturday in October, we flew to Los Angeles to present our plan to the Reagans at their home in Pacific Palisades. We showed them how a combination of lecturing, radio commentary, and newspaper columns would provide income; we outlined the costs involved and how it would be managed. They liked the plan. Not long after, they told us they wanted to engage our new company to implement it.

One day early in December, Ronald Reagan had lunch with his kitchen cabinet (then consisting of Justin Dart, Holmes Tuttle, Ed Mills, William French Smith, and David Packard), Meese, Deaver, and me at the Los Angeles Country Club. The governor's friends had met periodically with him during the year, and his future was a frequent topic. They agreed that he was probably the best spokesman in the nation for the free-enterprise system, and they talked over possible activities. Even though he had invested wisely in his years in film and television, Ronald Reagan still needed to work for a living. (A hostile legislature had recently crafted a bill that would have the effect of keeping his gubernatorial pension at a very low level.) Although I am sure he appreciated his friends' interest and concern for his well-being, Ronald Reagan had a special sense of satisfaction at that luncheon when he thanked them and told about his program plan, which rested solely on his own abilities, with just managerial and administrative help.

The December days became fewer. There were many receptions and "final" visits in offices in Sacramento and with various constituencies. December has an especially wistful quality in Sacramento when the winter ground fog settles in. Often, the sky seems as if it will never clear, with the light soft and diffused. These are cold days, too.

On December 10, Mike and Carolyn Deaver had a small dinner at their home for the Reagans and just a few members of the senior staffs and their spouses. It was a warm, happy evening, filled with laughter and reminiscences.

There were many other warm moments in the final weeks of the administration. Nancy Reagan invited representatives from all of the state's Foster Grandparent Program units to a garden luncheon at the executive residence. She had first become interested several years earlier in this program, which brought together lonely elderly people with mentally retarded or disturbed children. She had visited many state hospitals and other facilities that participated in the Foster Grandparent Program, often presiding at their awards ceremonies. A visit to the final gathering was testimony to how well the program worked. The love that flowed from the old people to the children and vice versa was tangible. Nancy Reagan had seen it many times before and so had Nancy Reynolds, the assistant to the governor who worked most closely with her, but it was new to me and a revelation. One of the caseworkers at the luncheon told me that in case after case, the children had advanced far beyond what was thought to be their potential, as a result of the love and attention given them by their foster grandparents. Nancy Reagan took quiet pride in this project, for she had had a good deal to do with its expansion, not only in California but in other states as well.

In mid-December there was the lighting of the state's huge Christmas tree near the capitol entrance. And, there was a "raffle" in the council room at which all members of the governor's office staff received memorabilia from the Reagan years as gifts.

There was even a two-hour session set aside for photos in the large council room. This was an opportunity for staff members, their families, and Reagan appointees to have their pictures taken with the governor if they did not already have them. A few days before the photo session I received a call from Herman Rowlands, of the Herman Goelitz Candy Company in Oakland. Rowlands, it turned out, had been supplying the Reagan administration its jelly beans gratis for nearly eight years. He asked if he might have a picture with the governor. So, on "picture day," along with the staff, Rowlands and his family stood there, beaming, with the governor. Little did Rowlands know how many arguments his smaller-than-standard-size delicacies had cooled in the cabinet room during those eight years.

The day after New Year's Day, the Reagans were back in Sacramento, where the governor had a final interview scheduled with one of the local television stations. I was to accompany him. As we headed away from the capitol in the soft, half-light of the late afternoon, he said, "Ford called me at home yesterday. He wants me to join his cabinet." "Really," I said. "Which department?" "Well," he replied, "he didn't say specifically, but he said there might be several things coming up, maybe Transportation. I thanked him but declined." We laughed.

The next day, January 3, was the final day in the Corner Office. There seemed to me to be a huge amount of work to process—reports to approve, letters to sign, memos to leave to transition successors. Just before 6 P.M., Betty Nakashoji, secretary to both Don Livingston and me, said, "Pete, it's time to go to the reception." I had almost forgotten it was the final day. I went through the halls hung with historical drawings and photos of California that Nancy Reagan had rescued from the capitol basement. I poked my head in several offices. A few of my colleagues were still there. It was only a few days earlier, sitting in Governor Reagan's office that he had said, with that characteristically mischievous look in his eye, "Let's not leave. I like it here."

But, at 6 P.M. that Friday night we left, much as if it had been any other Friday, expecting to be back on Monday. Several of us drove out to the Northlake Inn in the near suburbs for the farewell reception for the entire staff of the governor's office. There the Reagans were presented with the staff's gift, a California landscape by painter Bob Rishell, who had already been commissioned to paint the governor's official portrait for the capitol halls. The gift painting was a scene to warm any Californian's heart: the savannah topography of the coast range, and summer-gold grassy hills spotted with oaks at sunset.

I had turned in my state car that day and rented a sedan, filling it with the contents from my rented studio apartment near the capitol. After the reception, I headed toward Piedmont, eighty miles away, for the last time.

Sunday, the Reagan era would end in Sacramento, but a new one would begin Monday in Los Angeles.

3

Thanks for Listening

DEAVER & HANNAFORD, INC., opened for business Monday, January 6, 1975, and, along with it, private citizen Ronald Reagan's new office.

Mike Deaver and I had assembled a small staff, most of whom were assigned to the Reagans' account. Those who joined us from the governor's office were Helene von Damm, the governor's secretary; Nancy Reynolds, who had assisted Mrs. Reagan and would now also do advance work for Governor Reagan's lecture tours; Dennis LeBlanc, on leave from the state police, where he had been on the governor's security detail; and Barney Barnett, for eight years one of the governor's drivers and aides.

Our new public-relations firm's suite, including the Reagan private office, was on the eighth floor of the Tishman Building in the Westwood area of Los Angeles. It had been readied while we were still working in Sacramento. In December, Mrs. Reagan had visited it to plan the governor's private office. When it was finished, it looked much like his corner office in the state capitol, with the same antique desk and drum table; the mother-of-pearl-inlay coffee table that had been a gift of the president of South Vietnam; the nineteenth-century American prints on the wall; and some of the governor's memorabilia (such as the shoes-in-concrete, the pillow embroidered with the word *Jellybeans,* and the octagonal leather jelly-bean box).

Deaver & Hannaford had other public relations clients, including several based in Northern California, but Mike and I decided that the principal office should be based close to the Reagans, since we expected their account to generate the most activity in our new firm. In fact, we joked about our "branch" offices: the basement of my home in Piedmont, in the hills above Oakland on the east side of San Francisco Bay; and the Deavers' rumpus room in their Sacramento home. Both of us had decided not to move, so we began commuting regularly to Los Angeles.

From Governor Reagan's office you could watch the planes landing and taking off at Los Angeles International Airport, and frequently you could see Catalina Island, about twenty-five miles out to sea. Mike's office was next to the governor's, and mine next to Mike's. There were two more private offices and what we thought was an ample general office. We soon outgrew it, for we had not anticipated that several Republican women activists would volunteer to handle the Reagan mail, which was coming in a heavy flow. Everyone bore the crowded conditions with good cheer. Birthdays and anniversaries of each staff member—and the governor—were faithfully observed with homemade cakes and cookies, and sometimes strawberries. During those first few months, the volunteers—Dottie Dellinger, Gwen Pruter, Leslie Ohland, Leslie Dutton, and Joyce von Schock—pitched in one or two at a time to help Helene and the other secretaries.

The Reagans had just bought a mountaintop ranch in Santa Barbara County, Rancho del Cielo ("Ranch of the Sky"), and the governor (we all continued to call him by that title even though he was now a private citizen) was anxious to spend time out of doors remodeling and expanding the small adobe ranch house. Still, the demands of his new schedule that month did not allow as much ranch time as he had hoped.

There was the newspaper column to get started, a trip back to Sacramento on the twenty-first for the unveiling of the official Reagan portrait in the capitol building, the first radio taping on the twenty-third, and, on the thirtieth, the start of his first lecture tour.

The Sacramento trip went well. It was a clear, crisp day. The new governor, Jerry Brown, welcomed the Reagans back to the capitol and made a short but gracious speech about Ronald Reagan's tenure in Sacramento. Reagan gave an equally gracious response. All seemed to enjoy it. The Reagans liked the portrait by Robert Rishell. It shows a smiling, confident Ronald Reagan standing in front of the capitol, looking as if he had enjoyed every minute of those eight years.

On the afternoon of the twenty-third, Barney Barnett drove us to Harry O'Connor's Hollywood recording studios. It is doubtful if the intersection of Hollywood and Vine ever lived up to its legendary fame as a place where one could see the mighty of the motion-picture business. By the mid-1970s its fame rested on that durable legend and the fact that it is a gathering place for a fascinating variety of eccentrics. When Ronald Reagan alighted from the car in front of the Taft Building, it took only a minute or two for a crowd of them to gather, greeting him with quips and cheers.

Up on the eighth floor, Harry O'Connor had prepared a surprise party. His production crew was there, as were Art Linkletter; Jack Webb; Doug Willis of the Associated Press Sacramento bureau; and Sally Cobb, widow of Bob Cobb, founder of the Brown Derby down the street. We all crowded into the small studio suite. Reagan worked through his scripts smoothly and comfortably. We had decided to record three weeks' worth at each taping—fifteen programs in all. Among the topics of that first round were a federal bill to create a consumer-protection agency, one to tie congressional paychecks to budget balancing, and a new guaranteed-income plan like the FAP, which he had helped defeat several years earlier. Every program ended with, "This is Ronald Reagan. Thanks for listening."

No sooner had he finished the last script than Sally Cobb's Brown Derby staff appeared with champagne and hors d'oeuvres. The Reagan daily radio commentary was thus launched. Initially, O'Connor had signed up nearly 100 stations; it was to grow to more than 350 by the early fall that year.

Copley News Service kicked off the once-a-week Reagan newspaper column the same week.

From that time until the radio programs and columns ended when Reagan declared for the presidency in November, he never used them in a partisan political sense. They were always issue-oriented and provided Reagan with an opportunity to comment on current issues from the perspective of his free-enterprise, limited-government philosophy. Some journalists began to note that Reagan on the lecture circuit and in the media commentaries was becoming more philosophical—or, as they often decribed it, "ideological." It was true to a degree; since he no longer had to make policy decisions on individual issues, he could and did speak out in more philosophical tones. He was deeply concerned that the federal government was growing larger and, consequently, more elitist and unresponsive to the citizens, despite the fact that the Republicans held the White House. He worried about America's declining defense posture in relation to the Soviet Union, and he believed that the process of détente basically served the Russian intention of conducting a one-way arms race. He did not hesitate to talk about these issues.

For his lecture tours, Governor Reagan developed what he called his "business" speech and another he called his "political" speech. Some items were the same in each, but the political speech, readied for use at the several Lincoln Day dinners he had agreed to address, put the blame for most of the nation's ills squarely on the Democrat-controlled Congress. The business speech concentrated on examples of hilarious and superfluous overregulation of the economy.

Over the years I would hear reporters who accompanied us on some of these trips (which usually mixed schedules of trade conventions and

Republican gatherings) complain that "all Reagan's speeches are the same." Since he was not campaigning for any office, we did not draft inserts of daily news items for him (standard practice in campaigns), so the newsmen along for the ride were frustrated because there was not new material each day. In most cases they had to write articles that fell into the a-week-on-the-road-with-Ronald-Reagan genre. But, as to the Reagan speeches being all the same, the journalists were wrong. There were no two literally the same, although the themes that swept through them were constant—such themes as the stifling of American ingenuity by too much government; the attempt by government to solve problems with schemes that cause new ones ("Government invents cures for which there are no known diseases" is the way he put it); the fragility of freedom; and the danger of forgetting that vigilance is the eternal price of liberty.

I marveled at the subtleties of the changes in the Reagan stump speeches. He was constantly working them over on airplanes (either Mike Deaver or I, as part of our agreement with the governor, accompanied him on all these trips). He kept stacks of four-by-six-inch file cards bound with rubber bands in his briefcase. He had a stack of quotations he had gathered over many years, and another of anecdotes and one-liners, of which he seemed to have an endless and timely supply; we rarely supplied any to him. His current speeches—business and political—were also "carded" by him in a personal shorthand he had devised. These, too, were bound with rubber bands and in the briefcase. He read a good deal on the air legs of the tours—daily newspapers; monographs friends and advisers had sent him; such periodicals as *Human Events, National Review, American Spectator;* the news magazines; and books, always nonfiction. He was forever delving into that briefcase to pull out a blank card on which to copy a passage or some statistics from something he had read. Thus, the speeches were constantly changing, with new examples of bureaucratic excess and government folly.

January 1975 was still young when talk of a third party began to set the conservative movement abuzz. William Rusher, publisher of *National Review,* was probably the chief theoretician behind the idea, but many were talking it up. Rusher even wrote a book about it. He was concerned that what he called the "yes-but" Republicans were dominating the party, so anxious to protect what little power they had as a minority that they were willing to make that minority status permanent. The name came from the view that the congressional Republican party for years had, in effect, been saying to the Democrats, about Democratic legislative initiatives, "Yes, but a little less" and "Yes, but a little more slowly."

"Movement" conservatives were restless with the Ford administra-

tion. Many telephoned us to vent their frustrations about an administration they felt was too pliant in dealing with liberal orthodoxy, which
seemed to guide the Democrat-controlled Congress. In truth, President
Ford was to use the veto many times during his tenure to check the Congress. In early 1975, however, this was not yet apparent. Furthermore,
the veto is a negative device, and conservatives, depressed from the
losses in the 1974 congressional election, were yearning for outspoken
leadership based upon a clear philosophy—namely, their conservative
principles of limited government and a strong foreign policy. They were
suspicious of détente with the Soviet Union, and Ford's retention of
Henry Kissinger as secretary of state brought out their worst fears that
the new administration might adopt a posture of defeatism and an acceptance of the decline of America that so many ultraliberals and radicals were not only proclaiming but apparently working for.

Then there was Base-Broadening. Under Mary Louise Smith, Ford's
choice as chairman of the Republican National Committee, party leaders (echoed by many congressional Republicans) began to say that the
party had done so poorly in the election because it had too narrow a
base; it needed to broaden that base of membership in order to win in
the future. While ways and means were never defined, it was widely assumed by conservatives that what the leaders had in mind was to make
the party more liberal, more like the Democrats. The leaders spoke of
appealing to young voters and minorities. Ronald Reagan wanted to do
that, too, but he was convinced that the best way to do it was to reduce
the influence of government on the economy. He was concerned, as
were many around him, that the base-broadeners were thinking in terms
of yet more government programs to appeal to this group or that. This
would be yes-but Republicanism at its worst, he felt. It would rob the
party of its reason for being, on the one hand, and would not succeed in
attracting new adherents, on the other. After all, if one believed in cen-
tralized government, one needed only to turn to the Democrats to find
the most active practitioners.

Reagan, in his speeches to Republican groups, spoke of the need for
the party to have a banner of "bold colors—no pale pastels." Establishment and liberal Republicans (who invariably called themselves "moderates") as well as many commentators in the media, interpreted this
oft-repeated phrase of Reagan's as a call to "purify" the party, to drive
out all but the most ardent conservatives. This is not, of course, what he
meant. What he did mean was that a political party should stand for
something, as opposed to being a collection of people who came together out of expediency to bend to the whims of the moment in trying
to win an election every two years.

Those conservatives who were talking energetically about a third party in early 1975 saw it forming around the conservatives from the Republican party (a majority of Republicans, in public opinion polls, continued to identify themselves as "conservative"), conservative Democrats (mostly from the South and Southwest), and blue-collar workers in the industrial cities (particularly white ethnics, who were very conservative by heritage). In retrospect, this fledgling formulation in 1975 laid the foundation for the Reagan coalition that swept to victory in November 1980.

Would Ronald Reagan lead the coalition and form the third party? No. Although it had been the subject of many conversations early that year, he never changed his belief that the Republican party could, and should, be salvaged. It was far more in his nature to be a party-rebuilder than a party-wrecker. The climax came on Saturday, February 15, when he was to address the annual midwinter Conservative Political Action Conference in Washington. This event brought together the leadership of the various elements of the conservative movement. The number of calls from news people and conservative supporters mounted steadily for two weeks before he was to speak. Would he use this dinner to announce the formation of a new party? "No" was the reply. And, at the dinner, while he called again for a party with a banner of bold colors and no pastels, he said that it should be the Republican party.

Thereafter, talk of a third party was less noticed by the press, although elements of the grouping that called itself the New Right continued to say that the Republican party was dead and useless. Indeed, some of these people were only lukewarm about Ronald Reagan, believing that he was willing to settle for a less-than-perfect party in this less-than-perfect world. They were the true purists. Had they examined Ronald Reagan's gubernatorial record closely, they would have known that while he was always true to his principles, he was willing to reach an objective by stages and, along the way, might settle temporarily for partial success.

In February, President Ford, in an effort to blunt the growing demands of Democratic liberals in Congress to curtail sharply the nation's intelligence system in general and the Central Intelligence Agency (CIA) in particular, named a presidential commission to study alleged excesses of the CIA. Vice-President Nelson Rockefeller was to be chairman, and Ford asked Reagan to become a member. This Reagan felt he could do, since the meetings would be intermittent and he could still keep up his heavy traveling and speaking schedule. He had been told not to worry if he occasionally had to miss a meeting; the commission staff would brief him to keep him up to date. Yet, when he did find that a previous engagement kept him from one meeting in Washington, he took a salvo of criticism from the press. After that, he instructed us to adjust his schedule to make sure he was at every meeting.

On one of Reagan's trips to Washington for a commission meeting,

Ford's chief of staff, Donald Rumsfeld, met with him to sound him out again on a cabinet position. Ford and his people, had they studied Reagan more carefully, would have known that these offers were not the way to keep him from running against Ford in 1976. While it would be months before he was actually to decide to run, this effort to co-opt him—and those that followed—in fact served to inch him a little closer to entertaining the idea of running. He told Rumsfeld that he felt he could be of greater service by being a communicator, using his various forums to fight the liberals' economic mythology and to build support for the free-enterprise system.

The Ford administration's next round of co-option had a much stronger—and more negative—effect on Reagan. Paul Haerle, once Reagan's appointments secretary in Sacramento and now the California Republican chairman, met with him during one of our early spring trips to Washington. At that meeting he urged Reagan to back away from any idea of running. He expressed a view we were to hear many times in the months to come: the party's only chance to keep the White House in 1976 was to rally behind Ford as the incumbent. A challenge would be "divisive" he said. That was a word that we were to hear over and over again before we got to Kansas City in the summer of 1976.

Back in California, Bill Banowsky, president of Pepperdine University and Reagan's handpicked Republican national committeeman, began talking in a similar vein. As the spring wore on, several other California Reagan supporters declared their support for a Ford candidacy in 1976. That spring Meese, Deaver, Nofziger, Wirthlin, and I met frequently (together or in various combinations), usually over breakfast, and the growing number of "name" Californians who had supported Reagan in his state races but were now coming out for Ford was the central topic. We agreed that the tactic was transparent and would not work. There were no grass-roots leaders among those named, and Reagan's kitchen cabinet was effectively untouched by the Ford blandishments. Indeed, several members of the kitchen cabinet were enthusiastic about a possible Reagan candidacy. In short, the effort to discourage Reagan by creating the idea that his friends were deserting him had the opposite effect on him.

Meanwhile, some in Washington still sought Ronald Reagan's views on policy. Senator Russell Long invited Reagan to meet with the members of the Senate Finance Committee over breakfast on March 10 at the Capitol, to brief them on his food stamp reform proposals, which had been announced toward the end of his term in California.

In early April, the Reagans took their first overseas trip since 1973. Governor Reagan had accepted an invitation from the Pilgrim Society in London to give an address at its annual dinner. (The society's American counterpart group always invites a speaker from the United Kingdom.) The Reagans and I left Los Angeles for New York on Friday, April 4, and for London the next day. The Reagans stayed at Justin Dart's London house, and we had arranged some briefings for the governor there, one from William Schneider, then a defense adviser to Senator James Buckley (and now a member of the Reagan administration) and another from Robert Conquest, a noted British conservative scholar. Schneider had just arrived in London from Saigon and painted a dark picture of the situation there. Conquest spoke principally about the Soviet Union. Although the Reagans were scheduled to be in London only four days, several interviews were arranged with the news media.

The Pilgrim Society black-tie dinner was held at the Savoy Hotel on Monday, April 7. Reagan had decided to make the North Atlantic Treaty Organization (NATO) alliance the theme of his speech, suggesting ways of strengthening it without appearing to dictate them. Reagan also wanted to show that he was aware of the various sensitivities of our European allies. Jeff Bell and Schneider assisted him in developing the speech theme. The speech was measured in tone and was well received by the audience. More important, I thought, was that it was reported straightforwardly in the next morning's *London Times*. Having that account of the speech echo back across the Atlantic to the American press had longer-range implications than the audience's immediate reaction.

On Tuesday we called on Roy Hattersley, minister of state for foreign and commercial affairs, at the Foreign Office at Whitehall. We were met in the courtyard by an official and escorted into the building through high-ceilinged, dark stone corridors with the portraits of British diplomats gazing down on us. As we rounded a corner, we startled a group of middle-aged women employees who, on seeing Ronald Reagan, began giggling like schoolgirls. We stopped to say hello and learned that all of them had seen several of his motion pictures. (We were to learn, too, that when much of the British press referred to him, it wrote of him as a former actor rather than a former governor.)

The following day we went to the Houses of Parliament to meet Margaret Thatcher. She had recently replaced Edward Heath as leader of the Conservative party. Her offices were small, but the wood paneling made them warm, and Mrs. Thatcher's ready smile, poise, and earnestness made them seem all the warmer. The two seemed, moments after meeting, like lifelong friends. Each having heard and read much about the other, they found that their basic philosophies of government were very much alike.

After the Thatcher meeting, we met with Sir Keith Joseph, Sir Geoffrey Howe, and Reginald Maudling, all members of Mrs. Thatcher's "shadow" cabinet, for a stimulating hour's exchange. Sir Keith in particular was interested in many of the Reagan California programs, such as welfare reform and increased productivity of the bureaucracy.

After his arrival back home, Governor Reagan's spring speaking tours drew enthusiastic crowds and much questioning about a possible run for the presidency. In late April we went to Des Moines and Marshalltown, Iowa; the Detroit suburbs; New Jersey, where we had four events in one day, two in the north and two in the south, with an armada of small planes flying the guest speaker and party leaders from one end of the state to the other; Jackson, Mississippi; and Boca Raton, Florida.

The event in Jackson was a dinner in support of a Republican candidate for governor, so it attracted some national press attention. Robert Novak of the Evans and Novak column and Remer Tyson of the *Detroit Free Press* joined us for the trip to Boca Raton in a small, slow, propeller-driven plane. While the trip lasted about an hour longer than our printed schedule had indicated, the time went by swiftly as Reagan swapped anecdotes with his guests, drawing from his seemingly endless memory.

On May 1, back in Los Angeles, we had a meeting of what we now called the Madison (or M) Group that lasted nearly all day. This had taken the place of the Nofziger Group of Sacramento days and ultimately became the cadre of senior advisers and staff for the 1976 campaign. We met first at Deaver & Hannaford and then went up to the governor's home in Pacific Palisades to review the political situation with the Reagans.

Sears was beginning to emerge as the chairman of this group, and we listened attentively to his reflections on presidential politics. The M Group at the time consisted basically of Sears, Nevada Senator Paul Laxalt, Meese, Nofziger, Deaver, and me. Others attended certain meetings and the group itself enlarged with time.

Laxalt, who had become friends with Reagan when the two governed neighboring states, was to agree by early summer to become chairman of the Citizens for Reagan Committee. He was to be one of only a handful of members of Congress who endorsed the Reagan candidacy. Some congressmen whom Reagan was instrumental in helping get elected in 1974 were to turn the other way when their endorsements were solicited for 1976.

The day after our M Group meeting, Sears met over lunch at the California Club downtown with Governor Reagan and his kitchen cabinet.

At these meetings, Ronald Reagan gave no inkling of what his decision would be about running, but he was clearly listening closely to the various reports from his friends and advisers. I think by then that all of us around him assumed that, in time, his answer would be yes.

Pressure had been growing from some of the most ardent conservative activists around the country. They wanted him to declare early. This was in part because of the natural restlessness of activists as election season draws closer and in part because of the nervousness over the Ford efforts to co-opt Reagan. The M Group was not of a single mind on the matter. Deaver and I both felt that an announcement should come as late as possible so that Reagan would have his valuable media forums for a maximum period of time. Others thought he should declare by summer, before Ford could pick off any more potential supporters.

After the Conservative Political Action Committee met in midwinter, the Committee on Conservative Alternatives (COCA), an ad hoc group headed by North Carolina's Senator Jesse Helms, was formed to "review and assess the current political situation and to develop future political opportunities." It became the rallying point for New Rightists who still wanted to replace the Republican party with a third party consisting of Republican conservatives, blue-collar Democrats, and George Wallace's supporters. In fact, some associated with the COCA movement saw a Reagan-Wallace independent candidacy as a "dream ticket." This idea made Governor Reagan uneasy, as it did most of his advisers.

On Sunday, June 1, an expanded version of the M Group (but not including Governor Reagan) met at Sears's law offices in a building across the street from the Old Executive Office Building (which is next to the White House) in Washington to discuss this and other aspects of the current political climate. Governor Reagan had continued to say to groups he addressed that he felt Ford deserved more time to try to solve the nation's problems. He did criticize the growing national deficit, however, and told his audiences that he was very worried that the SALT II negotiations might produce an agreement disadvantageous to the United States. The group also discussed whether or not it should urge Governor Reagan to declare for the presidency by midsummer. We left without a resolution of this question.

Everybody who attended the meeting (about fifteen in all) was asked to keep the fact we were meeting confidential. Despite this, the fact that we had met was reported in the Los Angeles Times the following day, fueling speculation that Reagan would soon make an announcement. We realized after we had met that the paper's Washington bureau was in the same building as Sears's offices and that a Times reporter had probably seen our names on the security register in the lobby.

Earlier, I had accompanied Governor Reagan on a speaking tour that included a two-night stop in Washington, where on May 5 he and I had dinner in his suite with Senator Barry Goldwater and on the sixth with

Bryce Harlow, who had advised several Republican presidents but not yet met Reagan.

The Reagans and Goldwaters were longtime friends, and Reagan's emergence as a national political figure really began with his eleventh-hour televised fund-raising speech for the Goldwater campaign in 1964. That night in Washington he hoped to find out what Goldwater's feelings were about the presidential campaign for 1976. Goldwater told us that Dean Burch had told him that President Ford wanted to meet with him (Burch) that week to discuss plans for his campaign committee. The senator said to Governor Reagan that he told Burch that "we [the Republicans] have a viable alternative: Reagan." He added that he hoped that Ford would "get the message" about needing conservative support when Burch met with him. On balance, it was difficult to know where Goldwater would come down in the event of a Ford-Reagan contest, although at one point he did say, "Just keep on doing what you're doing [meaning the speeches, radio, and newspaper commentaries]. We know what you're up to."

The COCA was not idle while Ford and his advisers went ahead with their plans. It began to research the feasibility of getting an independent ticket on the ballot in every state.

Pennsylvania's Senator Hugh Scott, the minority leader, countered this with a petition supporting President Ford that he asked every Republican senator to sign. This became known among conservatives as the "loyalty oath." Senator James Buckley of New York headed a group that responded by calling for an "open" Republican convention in 1976.

All this was prelude to a dinner meeting called by some of Reagan's most staunch conservative supporters in a Madison Hotel suite the evening of June 16. The group also included a number of New Right leaders (most of whom were not thought of as primarily Reagan supporters) and representatives of George Wallace. A concerted effort was made to keep any of Reagan's close advisers—including Deaver, who had accompanied him on the trip—from the dinner.

At the dinner, exponents of a new party, largely New Rightists such as direct-mail executive Richard Viguerie, Howard Phillips, Paul Weyrich, and columnist Kevin Phillips gave the strongest pitches they could for Reagan to abandon the Republican party and make common cause with an independent movement, basically along the third-party lines discussed so much over the winter. Those who spoke worried that if Reagan got the Republican nomination, he would be co-opted by Republican-establishment types and thus be rendered ineffective. Although they were at the opposite end of the spectrum from the liberals who so routinely underestimated Reagan in those days as little more than a "retired movie actor," the New Right leaders, in their anxiety that Reagan would succumb to the hated establishment, also underestimated him. Their anxiety seemed to disguise a belief that Reagan lacked the courage of his convictions.

The group pressed him to make his decision and declare soon. From them he learned that Senator Carl Curtis of Nebraska had signed the Ford-Rockefeller loyalty oath. (It had been assumed that in the event of a Reagan candidacy Curtis would support him.)

Reagan told the group that he had not yet made up his mind about running, but that if he did, he would run in the Republican party and would make the strongest appeal he could to blue-collar northern Democrats and conservative southern and southwestern Democrats, who, he believed, shared his views about limited government and the need for a strong defense.

Not long before the June 16 dinner, Reagan had learned that Goldwater had told a group of Republican senators that he was sure Reagan would not run. As a result of this apparent misreading of Reagan's mood at the dinner in May, Reagan called each of the senators who had met with Goldwater to assure them that he had not yet made up his mind.

While Reagan had once and for all shut the door on an independent candidacy, he did tell the group it was his hope that if he ran, he could appeal to a conservative coalition cutting across party lines and if he won, his hope would be to reorganize the Republican party to include conservative Democratic officeholders. He said accommodations would probably have to be made for seniority in Congress and the party might have to adopt a new name.

A month later, on July 15, the Citizens for Reagan Committee opened its doors on L Street in downtown Washington. Senator Laxalt had agreed to be its national chairman. John Sears was executive vice-chairman (campaign director). Lyn Nofziger was soon to join it, and its first permanent employee was Jeff Bell as research director. Bell had first joined the Reagan operation in the late summer of 1974 to do political research for that year's speaking tours on behalf of Republican candidates. For a time in the spring of 1975 he did research work in Los Angeles at the Deaver & Hannaford offices.

The committee was formed with Governor Reagan's acquiescence, of course. Under federal election law, when such a committee is formed, the person it is designed to benefit must declare within thirty days whether he recognizes it as officially representing him. Since Reagan had not yet decided whether to run, he informed the Federal Election Commission that *if* he did become a candidate, he would use Citizens for Reagan as his campaign committee. Meanwhile, he would have no direct contact with it.

The committee began fund-raising efforts with direct mail and built a staff in Washington with the expectation (shared by all of us around Reagan by now) that the governor would ultimately decide to run. To this day, I do not know when he finally decided to run, for he never told us and we never asked, although I believe it must have been sometime in the early fall. By then, preparations at the committee's headquarters had become extensive and intense, and he did not talk about bringing them to a halt.

The pressures for Reagan to announce in summer continued. Most of these came from grass-roots leaders around the country, for they were feeling the pressure from their workers, who were anxious to get a formal campaign going. Some in the news media tried to create the impression that the Reagan inner circle was divided into two camps, those who wanted him to run and those who did not; Deaver and I, being based in California, were presumed to be in the latter category. This was incorrect. By midsummer, the only disagreement the Washington- and Los Angeles–based Reagan advisers had was over timing.

President Ford meanwhile embarked on what amounted to a campaign swing through California in a last major effort to demonstrate to Reagan that Ford was so strong in Reagan's own state that a challenge would be futile. While he was in the state Ford escaped assassination attempts by two deranged women. Other than that scare, the Ford visit was uneventful and did not serve to frighten Reagan from the race.

Reagan's visibility as a potential candidate increased sharply in September. On the eleventh he participated in a panel sponsored by the American Enterprise Institute and the Hoover Institution on "Government Regulation: What Kind of Reform?" at the Washington Hilton. His fellow panelists were Minnesota's Senator Hubert Humphrey, consumerist Ralph Nader, and Harvard University economics professor Hendrik Houthakker. Eileen Shanahan, then of the *New York Times*, was the moderator.

Reagan was at his best in the kind of rhetorical hand-to-hand combat that ensued. It was clear from the beginning that the evening would be a Nader-Reagan duel. Nader's technique is to overwhelm and intimidate his opposition with a staccato delivery of statistics mixed with scorn for anyone not sharing his views. Listening to his philippic about the need for compulsory national health insurance (a subject about which I had read quite a bit because of Reagan's interest in it), I thought Nader defied logic. Reagan thought so, too. From the look on Nader's face, I gather he assumed that Reagan would trip over his shoelaces in his rebuttal. Instead, Reagan delivered a clear, concise recitation—with detailed statistical references—of the failures of socialized medicine as practiced in the United Kingdom and elsewhere.

The irrepressible Humphrey arrived late and was given an opportunity to make his own opening statement. After the Reagan-Nader duel (which, the audience seemed to agree, went to Reagan) Humphrey provided light relief. He did a nonstop fifteen-minute monologue about deregulation (especially of aviation), ending with a smile and the line "And that's just for starters!"

On September 26, Ronald Reagan was to give a speech to the Chicago Executive Club that later would nearly wreck his campaign and, still later, form the philosophical foundation for the new president's efforts to redefine federalism and redirect the energies of the federal government.

The speech carried the title "Let the People Rule." The title was not an afterthought. In four words it synthesized Reagan's belief that the people should dominate their own lives rather than have a government elite dictate to them. That Reagan was a conservative populist was not fully realized by the press and the electorate until 1980, but the basis for it was clearly spelled out in the 1976 campaign and that September 26 speech at McCormick Place on the shore of Lake Michigan.

As is often the case with a major political figure, an important speech may result from a scheduling decision. The Chicago Executive Club is an important civic forum, one of the best in the country. About three months beforehand, an invitation had been accepted for Reagan to be its guest speaker. In conversations with Sears, Deaver, and Nofziger, we agreed that the speech to this group should be different from Reagan's regular "mashed potato circuit" speech about free enterprise. This would be an opportunity for Reagan to discuss his vision for America. My own schedule was full, assisting Reagan with his radio and newspaper commentaries, so we agreed that Jeff Bell would be asked to find someone who would help research it. He ended up doing it himself. He talked to several of us about it: Sears; David Keene, Sears's deputy; Nofziger; and me. Jeff made the point that a recurring theme of Reagan's was that when the states sent money to Washington and Washington sent it back, it did so after "extracting a healthy carrying charge and putting plenty of strings on how you could spend it." Citing the California welfare reforms, Reagan often told his audiences that he believed the states and communities could do a better job of setting priorities and managing programs than could the federal bureaucrats. Jeff wanted to develop this into a larger theme, a vision of systematic reduction of federal dictation of programs, replaced by increased state and local autonomy and responsibility.

At a luncheon with the Reagans at their home on August 28, I reported to them and to Laxalt, Sears, Deaver, Meese, and Nofziger that we would have a draft in the governor's hands shortly after Labor Day.

Bell's draft arrived ten days later. I was excited about it and thought the governor would be, too. It captured the essence of much that he had been saying and then went forward with a bold proposal consistent with his view of government's role. I called Sears and told him I thought Bell had sent us "one helluva speech." I took it to the governor. As was his custom when he had one of us work on a draft for a special-occasion speech, he tucked the draft into his briefcase to work on during the drive up to the Santa Barbara ranch on his next speaking tour. He brought it back, marked with his notations, about the fifteenth of the month. He liked it, but as was usually the case, he changed many phrases, improving on them. Experienced as a writer for the ear, he had a better understanding than most of those who drafted things for him of how the sound patterns would fall on the ears of the audience.

We telecopied the annotated draft to Bell in Washington, and I asked him to prepare enough copies for distribution to the press on the morning of September 26 in Chicago. The Chicago stop was but one on a speaking tour. I was not scheduled to accompany the governor, but I flew into Chicago the night before because I did not want to miss the speech. Bell came in from Washington the morning of the twenty-sixth, but the copies of the speech were late. So, while Reagan and the several hundred members of the Chicago Executive Club dined upstairs, the press (Dick Bergholz of the *Los Angeles Times* and Martin Schram, then of *Newsday*, along with some local reporters) were in a downstairs room restlessly awaiting the text of the speech so that they could follow it when Reagan spoke. The package of speeches arrived at the last minute.

I had only a moment to glance at the first page but did note that there was an addendum attached to the text. That was the first I had heard of an addendum, but since Reagan was about to begin the address to his audience and time had run out, I did not closely examine the addendum, let alone assess its political ramifications. I suppose that at the time I assumed that someone in Washington had approved it, so I merely asked Bell about it. He said it contained supporting references for Reagan's assertion in the speech that the transfer program he proposed could save $90 billion in the federal budget. The addendum was to come back to haunt us in New Hampshire that winter. Despite that, "Let the People Rule," reread today, is a remarkably accurate preview of much of President Reagan's agenda.

Reagan set the stage for his audience with an opening reference to Jefferson: "In his first inaugural, nearly a century and three-quarters ago, President Thomas Jefferson defined the aims of his administration: 'A wise and frugal government,' he said, 'which shall restrain men from injuring one another, shall leave them otherwise free to regulate their own pursuits of industry and improvement, and shall not take from the mouth of labor the bread it has earned—this is the sum of good government.' " This was a favorite quotation of Reagan's and one that perfectly matched his own philosophy.

"If Jefferson could return today," he said, "I doubt that he would be surprised either at what has happened in America, or at the result. When a nation loses its desire or ability to restrain the growth and concentration of power, the floodgates are open and the results are predictable." He went on to note that government at all levels was absorbing 37 percent of the gross national product (GNP) and 44 percent of the nation's total personal income. He added:

> That is taking from the mouth of labor the bread it has earned. If government continues to take that bread for the next twenty-five years at the same rate of increase it has in the last forty, the percent of GNP government consumes will be 66 percent. . . . This absorption of revenue by all levels of government, the alarming rate of inflation and the rising toll of unemployment all stem from a single source: the belief that government, particularly the federal government, has the answer to our ills, and that the proper method of dealing with social problems is to transfer power from the private to the public sector, and within the public sector from state and local governments to the ultimate power center in Washington.
>
> This collectivist, centralizing approach, whatever name or party label it wears, has created our economic problems. By taxing and consuming an ever-greater share of the national wealth, it has imposed an intolerable burden of taxation on American citizens. By spending above and beyond even this level of taxation, it has created the horrendous inflation of the past decade. And by saddling our economy with an ever-greater burden of controls and regulations, it has generated countless economic problems, from the raising of consumer prices to the destruction of jobs, to choking off vital supplies of food and energy.
>
> As if that were not enough, the crushing weight of central government has distorted our federal system and altered the relationship between the levels of government, threatening the freedom of individuals and families.

Having set forth the problem, he moved on to his proposal:

> It isn't good enough to approach this tangle of confusion by saying we will try to make it more efficient or 'responsive,' or modify an aspect here or there, or do a little less of all these objectionable things than will the Washington bureaucrats and those who support them. This may have worked in the past, but not any longer. The problem must be attacked at its source. . . . We can and must *reverse* the flow of power to Washington; not simply slow it or paper over the problem with attractive phrases or cosmetic tinkering. . . .
>
> What I propose is nothing less than a systematic transfer of authority and resources to the states—a program of creative federalism for America's third century.

Federal authority has clearly failed to do the job. Indeed, it has created more problems in welfare, education, housing, food stamps, Medicaid, community and regional development and revenue sharing, to name a few. The sums involved and the potential savings to the taxpayer are large. Transfer of authority in whole or part in all these areas would reduce the outlay of the federal government by more than $90 billion, using the spending levels of fiscal 1976.

While the programs he cited were intended as illustrations of the principle, the addendum had the effect of turning them into specific recommendations—at least that is how the Ford campaign was later to treat them in New Hampshire.

Reagan did spell out several federal functions that he said would *not* be candidates for a transfer program: national defense, space, Social Security, Medicare, federal law enforcement, veterans affairs, the TVA and similar projects, and various agriculture, energy, transportation, and environmental-protection functions.

Having described one vision, he swept on to others, several of which have since become part of his presidential program:

> In our regulatory agencies dealing with nonmonopoly industries, we must set a date certain for an end to federal price fixing and an end to all federal restrictions on entry.... We must take steps to keep the spending and borrowing of off-budget agencies under control.... We must reform our major trust funds to ensure solvency and accountability. Particularly important is the need to save Social Security from the colossal debt that threatens the future well-being of millions of Americans, even while it overtaxes our workers at a growing and exorbitant rate.... We must put a statutory limit on the growth of our money supply, so that growth does not exceed the gain in productivity. Only in this way can we be sure of returning to a strong dollar.... And we must radically simplify our method of tax collection, so that every American can fill out his return in a matter of minutes without legal help. Genuine tax reform would also make it more rewarding to save than to borrow, and encourage a wider diffusion of ownership to America's workers.

Of the transfer program he added, "The decision as to whether programs are or are not worthwhile—and whether to continue or cancel them—will be placed where it rightfully belongs: with the people of our states." Nearly six years later, in 1981, the same view underlay President Reagan's proposal for replacing categorical federal grants with block grants to the states for many programs.

Of the status quo, Reagan said:

> The present system is geared for maximum expenditure and minimum responsibility. There is no better way to promote the lavish outlay of tax money than to transfer program and funding authority away from state

and local governments to the federal level. This ensures that recipients of aid will have every reason to spend and none to conserve. They can get political credit for spending freely, but don't have to take the heat for imposing taxes. The French economist Bastiat, one hundred years ago, said, "Public funds seemingly belong to no one and the temptation to bestow them on someone is irresistible."

So long as the system continues to function on this basis, we are going to see expenditures at every level of government soar out of sight. The object is to reverse this: to tie spending and taxing functions together wherever feasible, so that those who have the pleasure of giving away tax dollars will also have the pain of raising them. At the same time we can sort out which functions of government are best performed at each level. And that process, I hope, would be going on between each state and *its* local government at the same time.

In a speech of barely twenty minutes length, Ronald Reagan had set forth a plan to alter radically a relationship between Washington and the states and communities that had been going on for four decades and had been accelerating rapidly since the mid-1960s. The speech was well received, but looking about at the faces of the audience, I was not sure they understood just how significant his proposals could be. Evidently, the news media at the time did not understand either. Marty Schram of *Newsday* was scheduled to ride with us to the airport to interview the governor. Schram concentrated on Reagan's intentions about running and ignored the substance of the speech, although he mentioned it in passing in his story. A Chicago reporter for the *Washington Post* wrote a story about the "$90 billion transfer plan." It ran inside the paper and was not picked up by others in the national political press, indicating they thought it had little significance.

An axiom in politics is that a candidate should be a small target and not a stationary one. The more detailed and explicit his recommendations, the more easily his opponents, media critics, and affected constituencies can seize on them and force the candidate to the defensive. Ultimately, this is what happened in New Hampshire. Stuart Spencer, back in 1966 co-director of Reagan's first gubernatorial campaign but then a consultant to the Ford campaign committee, recognized the potential political significance of the plan. The addendum to the speech had listed twenty-four programs for transfer, adding up to $81.9 billion, with then-expected budget growth bringing the total to $90 billion. (As it turned out, many of the programs on that list were among those to undergo cuts in fiscal 1982 as a result of President Reagan's initiatives to reduce the rate of increase of the federal budget in his first year in the White House.) Spencer put some associates on a research project to see just how they could make the best use of Reagan's words and figures in New Hampshire. Since Reagan had talked of transferring both the authority and the resources (that is, taxing ability) of federal programs to the states, Spencer and his associates saw the possibility that voters in New Hampshire might think of the transfer only in terms of the possibility that it might require a statewide income tax. If there is anything that will throw a candidate on the defensive in New Hampshire, it is the merest suggestion that he favors a broad-based statewide tax in a state that has never had one.

On October 2, the M Group met at the Marriott Hotel near the Los Angeles airport. We discussed the Chicago speech and agreed that it would have been better had we not had an addendum, but that politically speaking, the speech text itself was defensible. Furthermore, there had been no "second looks" by the press at the vulnerable data, so we went on to other matters.

Interest was increasing in a possible Reagan run. On the sixth, I accompanied the governor on a short speaking tour to central Pennsylvania, Cleveland, Houston, and San Francisco. At one of the Pennsylvania stops, at an impromptu news conference at a small airport, a local Republican congressman was seated near Reagan when a reporter asked the governor if the rumors were true that he might select this congressman as his running mate. The question came as a surprise, but Reagan handled it diplomatically, and we left for Cleveland. Minutes after we sat down to lunch with his host group there, I was called away to the telephone to take a call from a national reporter half a continent away, asking me if it were true that Reagan was considering this particular congressman.

In mid-October, Reagan gave his permission for plans to go forward for a late-November presidential announcement, probably during the week of the seventeenth. Several of us M Group members met October 17 in Washington to review assignments and plans. Meanwhile, Reagan's schedule of radio tapings for his program, his newspaper column, and his speeches continued unchanged.

The Panama Canal, which was to figure so prominently as an issue in the 1976 primaries, received an increasing amount of Ronald Reagan's attention as 1975 wore on. My first recollection of a conversation with him about it took place in Charlotte, North Carolina, in late October 1974. We were there for an appearance by the governor on behalf of Senator Helms. We had about twenty minutes to wait in his suite before leaving for the auditorium where the dinner was to be held. Helms and Reagan were talking over various issues when the senator mentioned that he was disturbed that the Ford administration was permitting near-secret negotiations to go forward between the United States and Panama for the purpose of eventually turning the canal over to Panama. The governor expressed surprise at this and said he wanted to look into it.

By early spring 1975, we were beginning to get some letters about the subject. In April, as I recall, *Human Events* ran an article critical of the negotiations. Reagan consulted with an attorney friend, Lawrence Beilenson, who had written a scholarly history of treaties titled *The Treaty Trap*. Reagan was impressed with Beilenson's argument that nations observed treaties that served their purposes and that no nation that had relied primarily on treaties for its security had ever succeeded at the exercise over the long run. He worried that a new treaty with Panama which called for an eventual turnover of the canal might be breached, considering the volatility of Panama's strongman government.

We got copies of the Hay–Bunau-Varilla Treaty, which had established the basis for the Canal Zone and U.S. operations of the Canal. And, we read a number of legal cases that tended to reinforce the language of the treaty that stipulated that the United States would govern the Canal Zone "as if it were sovereign" and "in perpetuity." We read treaty amendments and delved into the history of the canal. Reagan did his first radio scripts and columns on the subject in the late spring and early summer.

Most correspondence dealing with issues came to my desk before it went on to the governor. By monitoring the issues mail, we could determine if a particular issue was growing in interest. This one was. We received several letters from people who claimed special knowledge about Panama and the Canal Zone, and I met with several of these. Almost before I realized it, we had a network of correspondents who cared deeply about the issue and kept us supplied with news clippings.

Considering that Panama's strongman, Omar Torrijos, and national guard had overthrown an elected government in 1968 and had not permitted elections since, Reagan was skeptical about Panamanian intentions. And, considering Torrijos's much-publicized adulation of Fidel Castro and his flirtation with the Russians, Reagan believed that little good could come out of turning over the canal to Panama.

He recognized, however, that Panamanian national pride was involved, and he came to believe that negotiations aimed at updating the existing treaty relationship might have value in this regard. A straight giveaway of the canal, however, was another matter.

As the year went on, I noticed that he would often bring the subject up in small conversational groups. Some of his speeches to conservative and Republican groups began to mention it in passing. It was not until a warm early November evening in Coral Springs, Florida, however, that I heard him say to an audience (and he said it with fervor), "We bought it, we paid for it, it's ours, and we aren't going to give it away to some tinhorn dictator!" Strong medicine, but he had come to feel strongly about the issue. Nearly everyone he had spoken to about the issue expressed surprise and shock about the canal negotiations. His declamation to the Republican group in Coral Springs was a logical culmination of a process that had been going on for nearly a year. It had also come at the end of a momentous day.

That morning, Monday, November 3, at Boca Raton, where Reagan had given a breakfast speech to a trade association, he met briefly with Dr. Arnulfo Arias, the last elected president of Panama. Although Arias was now old and living in Florida, probably never to return to Panama (he ultimately did), Reagan was impressed by his dignity and his declared love for his country and for democracy.

Leaving Boca Raton, we went to a nearby junior college for an assembly with students and local citizens. As we got out of the car, a reporter rushed up and asked Reagan what he thought about Nelson Rockefeller's announcement that he would not be on the ticket with Gerald Ford in 1976. Reagan was surprised. Would this alter his plans, the reporter asked? No. In retrospect, Rockefeller's move seems to have been designed to appease conservatives in the Republican party so that they could get behind Ford. If so, it was a miscalculation. While Rockefeller was unpopular with many grass-roots conservatives in the party, they were motivated to support Reagan not so much as a result of Ford's unacceptability, but because in Reagan they had the genuine article, a conservative leader.

Reagan and Rockefeller had always gotten on well personally as governors, and Reagan never failed to say so when a supporter spoke critically of Rockefeller. True to form, his remarks to reporters about Rockefeller's decision to get off the 1976 ticket were diplomatic.

There was another surprise yet that day. By early afternoon, when we arrived at Coral Springs, the news was out that President Ford had reshuffled his cabinet, firing Defense Secretary James Schlesinger and replacing him with his chief of staff, Donald Rumsfeld. This move was unrelated to Ford's efforts to co-opt or deflect the Reagan challenge; rather, Schlesinger's frequent disagreements with Secretary of State Henry Kissinger seemed to be the main reason for it.

A big moon hung over Coral Springs that evening when Ronald Reagan addressed a lively Republican crowd. He gave his "political" speech, but there was a new sense of urgency to it. He seemed like a man ready to wade into a campaign. The audience interrupted him with applause many times and cheered when he made his declaration about the Panama Canal.

By now, the announcement of his candidacy was only seventeen days away. On Sunday, November 16, I took the overnight "red-eye" flight to Washington, where I would work on the draft of the governor's candidacy announcement. On that flight were four members of the House of Representatives from the San Francisco area, including one, Ronald Dellums of Berkeley, whose election opponent I had been in 1972. It occurred to me that these men probably raced home from Washington every Friday, only to return on this flight every Sunday night. I turned over in my mind the irony of the situation. I would make this particular trip only once, to help a man who might become president. Had I been elected to Congress, I would have been doing this in much the same manner as these men, week after week. Things have a way of turning out for the best, I thought.

The Reagans had a few days of rest at home before leaving on Friday the fourteenth for what was to be the governor's final speaking tour as a noncandidate.

The Reagans arrived in Washington on Wednesday afternoon, the nineteenth, and went directly to the Madison Hotel. Sears and Deaver had accompanied them on the flight from Dallas. I met them at the Reagans' suite. The Laxalts had planned a small dinner party for the Reagans, the members of the National Citizens for Reagan Committee and senior members of the Reagan staff. First, however, Governor Reagan had several important telephone calls to make from the suite at the Madison.

Before he did, Mike and I had arranged a small surprise for the Reagans. Once, at a reception during a speaking tour (I do not recall where) when only champagne was being served, Governor Reagan said to me, "I'm not too partial to champagne, but one time Nancy and I had a wonderful trip to Paris and there we had a bottle of Taittinger that we really enjoyed."

That conversation had stuck in my mind, so Mike and I decided to have a bottle of Taittinger delivered to the Reagans' suite just before he began the telephone calls. I recounted his Paris story, and we drank a toast to success in his forthcoming campaign. It was a warm moment.

After that, Governor Reagan telephoned President Ford to tell him, officially, that he would be announcing his candidacy the next morning. Ford was not pleased, according to Reagan. He had told Reagan he thought it would be "divisive."

Reagan called several other party leaders, and then we all left for the Laxalts'.

The next morning at 9:30, Ronald Reagan, his wife by his side, opened a press conference at the National Press Club with the announcement of his candidacy. It was short. "I am running," he said, "because I have grown increasingly concerned about the course of events in the United States and in the world. In just a few years, three vital measures of economic decay—inflation, unemployment, and interest rates—have more than doubled, at times reaching 10 percent and even more. Government at all levels now absorbs more than 44 percent of our personal income. It has become more intrusive, more coercive, more meddlesome, and less effective."

The themes were the ones he had been sounding across the land for a long time, but this time he had the nation's full attention for these few minutes.

> Our access to cheap and abundant energy has been interrupted, and our dependence on foreign sources is growing. A decade ago, we had military superiority. Today, we are in danger of being surpassed by a nation that has never made any effort to hide its hostility to everything we stand for.
>
> Through détente we have sought peace with our adversaries. We should continue to do so, but must make it plain we expect a stronger indication that they also seek a lasting peace with us.

He turned the focus on Washington with a statement that surprised many in the press:

> In my opinion, the root of these problems lies right here—in Washington, D.C. Our nation's capital has become the seat of a "buddy" system that functions for its own benefit—increasingly insensitive to the needs of the American worker who supports it with his taxes.
>
> Today it is difficult to find leaders who are independent of the forces that have brought us our problems—the Congress, the bureaucracy, the lobbyists, big business, and big labor.
>
> If America is to survive and go forward, this must change. It will only change when the American people vote for a leadership that listens to them, relies on them, and seeks to return government to them. We need a government that is confident not of what *it* can do, but of what the people can do.

Reagan criticizing big business? It seemed odd to many observers, but should not have. Reagan held no particular brief for big business, but because in his speeches he often sought to dispel economic myths arising from oversimplified coverage of business news, it was assumed that he was a champion of big business. In truth, for those who followed Reagan's travels with any regularity, the core of his constituency was made up to a great degree of small businesss entrepreneurs.

His conclusion summarized his view of the American people: "I don't believe for one moment that four more years of business-as-usual in Washington is the answer to our problems, and I don't think the American people believe it either.

"We, as a people, aren't happy if we are not moving forward. A nation that is growing and thriving is one which will solve its problems. We must offer progress instead of stagnation; the truth instead of promises; hope and faith instead of defeatism and despair. Then, I am sure, the people will make those decisions which will restore confidence in our way of life and release that energy that is the American spirit."

The restlessness of the American spirit, the desire to solve problems, was a theme to which he was to return time and again in the 1976 campaign, in the years between elections, and again in 1980. It reflected his own upbeat, optimistic nature.

The Reagan party, with a large press contingent in tow, left for Washington National Airport and a chartered airliner, to begin a two-day barnstorming announcement tour. The traveling party, in addition to the Reagans and the press, included Senator Laxalt, chairman of Citizens for Reagan; Sears, vice-chairman and campaign director; Deaver, staff director; Nofziger, press secretary; Nancy Reynolds, Mrs. Reagan's assistant; Matt Lawson and Rose Marie Monk, press assistants; Dennis LeBlanc and Barney Barnett, staff assistants; Tom Malatesta, logistics coordinator; Jack Courtemanche, finance chairman of Citizens for Reagan; and me, research director.

Our first stop was a Miami airport rally. No sooner had Governor Reagan made his announcement remarks than a young man in the audience brandished a toy pistol at him. Before we knew what had happened, the Secret Service detail had wrestled the man to the ground and swiftly moved Governor and Mrs. Reagan into the airport hotel in front of which the rally was taking place. It was a shaking experience, but the Reagans never lost their composure.

We flew on to Manchester, New Hampshire, for a "town meeting" at a hotel ballroom that evening. The place was packed. Hugh Gregg, former New Hampshire governor and Reagan's chairman for the Granite State, introduced the candidate. After a brief opening statement, Reagan opened the meeting to his favorite form of campaigning, a question-and-answer dialogue. He fielded the questions easily. It was a friendly crowd.

From a cool Manchester, we flew Friday morning to Charlotte, North Carolina, for an airport hanger rally. It was clear, windy, and chilly. The crowd of about three hundred cheered enthusiastically. Then, it was on to Chicago, which was bitterly cold, with some snow on the ground. There we had a hangar news conference. After that we flew to Burbank, California, where we landed to a wildly cheering crowd of Southern California Reaganites and a band. It was good to be home in the soft, warm sunshine of a late November California afternoon. The Reagans were buoyant, and so were the rest of us.

The remainder of the year for Ronald Reagan was devoted to studying issues materials and receiving briefings from experts on various subjects. One day in December, Martin Anderson arranged for a daylong session with a group of economists. Anderson, a senior fellow at the Hoover Institution at Stanford, had once been on the Nixon domestic council staff and had agreed to go on leave from his academic work to join the campaign full time. Together, he and I headed the small issues and research group for the balance of the campaign.

At the economists' session, Ronald Reagan for the first time met Arthur Laffer, whose now-famous "Laffer curve" was to become a trademark of supply-side economics.

Another meeting was with Dr. Petr Beckmann, an outspoken energy expert from Colorado. Another arranged by Sears was with James Schlesinger, the deposed secretary of defense. We met him in a Los Angeles hotel for a long briefing on the global situation. Reagan and the rest of us were impressed by his knowledge and analytical ability. He was to become an informal resource on foreign policy and defense issues with whom I had many conversations—mostly on the telephone—in the coming months.

There was one final trip to be made in 1975, three days to Florence, South Carolina, and to Alexandria and Lafayette, Louisiana. It was an easy trip, and the crowds were enthusiastic. There was, looking back on it, a euphoric feeling that everything was going to be fine. On the political horizon, however, there was a small black cloud. It was a $90 billion cloud. In early December, Bob Novak called me to ask if we were worried about what the Ford people might do with the $90 billion matter. Since the matter had attracted so little press attention in the months following the September speech, I told Novak I did not expect it to cause us trouble on the campaign trail in New Hampshire. Yet, after the conversation I felt a sense of nervousness. Sears did not say much, but I think he was concerned. Anderson and I talked about it, but put it out of our minds until after the holidays.

The year ended with the Reagan camp in high spirits, unaware that in a few weeks the campaign would be on the ropes.

4

The First Primaries, 1976:
The Gordian Knot Retied

RONALD REAGAN had concluded his "$90 billion" speech in September 1975 with a reference to the Gordian knot of Greek mythology: "The Gordian knot of antiquity was in Phrygia, and it was Alexander the Great who cut it, thereby, according to legend, assuring the conquest of Persia. Today, the Gordian knot is in Washington, and the stakes are even higher."

His intention was to offer the voters an opportunity to cut the Gordian knot represented by overly complex, unresponsive government. But, while he set out for New Hampshire to strike rhetorically through that Gordian knot, President Ford's campaign managers were working hard to tie him up in another one, a political one.

New Hampshire in January 1976 looked much as it had when last I had seen it in midwinter twenty years before. Then, in 1956, when I was in the army at Fort Devens, Massachusetts, a few miles south of the New Hampshire state line, we lived on a farm near Pepperell and often went north on weekends for winter country drives and cross-country skiing in southern New Hampshire. The winter days are often cloudless, the sky is a white blue, and there is a stillness over the round, wooded mountains and the valleys. In early January snow lies over the state like a white down comforter.

On Monday the fifth, the Reagan campaign's chartered United Airlines 727 left Los Angeles at 6:30 in the morning, bound for Manchester. The 1976 presidential primary campaign was officially under way.

We landed in early afternoon. The tarmac at Manchester was covered with snow and ice as Ronald Reagan alighted from the plane (Mrs. Reagan would join him later in the week). Jim Lake was there to greet the governor, along with Hugh Gregg, John Sears, and a team of advance men.

Lake, who had headed the state of California's office in Washington during the last year or so of Governor Reagan's second team, had signed on to coordinate campaign activities in New Hampshire. He had done a thorough job—and a diplomatic one—in organizing Reagan committees throughout the state. New Hampshire has a high proportion of political activists, and Republican politics has a long history of feuds and factionalism. Sears and Lake had succeeded in persuading Gregg, seen in New Hampshire as a "moderate," to take the state chairmanship. Gregg was a good organizer and a tireless one. Governor Meldrim Thomson, an outspoken conservative, and William Loeb, publisher of the *Manchester Union Leader* (the only statewide daily), represented another part of the Republican spectrum, and Lake had to keep all these elements focused on the basic objective: winning the primary for Reagan. It was not an easy job. Each of these men, and many other Granite State activists, had strongly held beliefs and strong egos. Sears's reasoning was that Reagan was generally perceived as a conservative and, in New Hampshire terms, that meant identification with only one faction of the party, a faction not large enough to carry a primary.

Sears believed that if Reagan's record in California could be effectively presented to New Hampshire voters, they would like it. Furthermore, Reagan's affability and platform style would help dispel stereotypes of him. With Gregg as state chairman, Sears hoped to show that Reagan could appeal to all elements of the party. This was important, for Sears was banking on a near knock-out blow in New Hampshire.

The first day was typical of the many we spent in New Hampshire. People there like give-and-take campaigning between the candidate and the townspeople at each stop. This probably has its roots in the town-meeting form of government, still common in rural New England. In any case, New Hampshire people liked it, and so did Ronald Reagan. It matched his long-held preference for the question-and-answer format in campaign appearances. For him, this method dated back to his first campaign for governor in 1966. Its roots were deeper, however, going back to the 1950s and his days with General Electric, when he visited factory after factory to meet and talk with the workers.

Our motorcade—with a staff bus, press bus, the governor's sedan (with Sears and Gregg riding with him), and the Secret Service cars—left Manchester for Meredith and a shopping-center walking tour, followed by a gathering in the Municipal Building in Center Harbor. Then, it was on to the Lion's Club in Moultonborough. After that, it was West Ossipee and North Conway. After dinner, we went to Kennett High School auditorium for the evening's main event, a "citizens' press conference" that lasted for an hour and a half, followed by autograph signing and handshaking by Governor Reagan for another fifty minutes.

Also present at the first town meeting was a film crew sent by the campaign's advertising agency. It had been decided by Sears, Harry Treleaven (once Nixon's television adviser), and the agency to build commercials from footage taken at these town meetings. "Cinema verité" the agency men were calling it. They were worried that commercials featuring Reagan talking directly into the camera would conjure up the image of the actor, even though Wirthlin's polls found that Reagan's "star quality" was a positive factor. They went so far as to make sure that the quality of their town-meeting footage was slightly below average in terms of color and light so that it would look more "natural" and not contrived. They felt, too, that television spots based on the give-and-take sessions would counter any worries about "stridency," a word that had been applied to Reagan by some New Hampshire Ford supporters.

One memory of the first evening in New Hampshire is the question about the Panama Canal. I was surprised when it came from a member of the audience. This was the first I recall hearing the issue mentioned north of the Mason-Dixon line. Governor Reagan noted it, too, for he later remarked to audiences elsewhere that the issue of the canal negotiations had been raised in New Hampshire by his audiences, not by him. And, it is true that his "stump speech"—the three or four minutes of opening remarks he gave at each stop and at the evening town meetings—made no mention of the Panama Canal. Instead, he usually declared that the people were fed up with the Washington "system" (the Gordian knot). He would say, "Unless we elect to the highest offices men with no ties to the system, men at the top who are not afraid to tangle with it and take it on head first, we will never change it."

The second and third days of the trip we spent in the northern part of the state in the White Mountains. We visited Dixville Notch, a resort that traditionally is the first community in the state to report its votes, soon after 12:01 A.M. each election day; looked up at Mount Washington, the highest point in New England; visited Berlin, a paper-mill town; and traveled down through Franconia Notch and on back to Manchester, from where late Wednesday afternoon we left for North Carolina.

The New Hampshire air had been bracing, and spirits were high—with Reagan obligingly pitching snowballs for the cameras in Conway, a popular ski resort. But, as the national political reporters began to interview informally those of us on the senior staff riding the bus, we found that the $90 billion transfer plan was the focus of their attention. And at stop after stop, townspeople asked the candidate if his plan would not force new taxes on New Hampshire.

Late that week, Howard ("Bo") Callaway, Ford's campaign manager, told a group of reporters in Washington that Reagan's proposal was a "ninety-billion-dollar boondoggle." He added that the American people "do not want elderly people thrown out in the snow." Since this comment was similar to the ones made by California legislators in response to the Reagan welfare-reform proposals, we laughed at its preposterousness when we heard about it. Who, we thought, would believe it?

Despite the flurry of questions about the $90 billion plan, we remained confident. The polls showed Ronald Reagan ahead. A Gallup poll in late November had Reagan ahead of Ford among Republicans and independents by 40 percent to 32 percent. This was a complete reversal of the polls taken prior to Reagan's announcement of candidacy. It was too early to draw firm conclusions from Wirthlin's New Hampshire polls for the Reagan campaign; but they showed us ahead, so we went through that first trip with our sense of optimism intact.

The full force of Stu Spencer's strategy for the Ford campaign in New Hampshire was yet to be felt. We had an inkling of it at some of the later stops on that first trip when we began to notice a laconic, flatfooted young man bundled up in a shapeless parka, holding a tape recorder. It took us a while to realize he was not from the New Hampshire Reagan committee. In fact, he was a Ford operative assigned to record everything Reagan said publicly, in the hope that our candidate would say something that could be used against him by Ford "truth squads" later.

It should be noted that we, too, recorded everything Governor Reagan said, to minimize surprise questions. Dana Rohrabacher, a young radio reporter from Los Angeles and now a White House speechwriter, had been recruited for this little-noticed but important job.

In North Carolina, where we arrived on Wednesday evening, the nucleus of the Reagan campaign was made up of supporters of Senator Jesse Helms, a former television commentator who had been elected to the Senate in 1972. Governor James Holshauser was the leader of the Ford forces in the state. Both sides seemed well organized, and each was determined to best the other, for control of the state party was at stake.

The $90 billion questions would not go away, but Ronald Reagan began to find ways of defending the issue well enough to make it fade. In a large rally in High Point, he answered the now-common question about a tax shift from the federal to state governments by emphasizing that the transfer of the programs would be accompanied by "a transfer of federal tax sources along with them." (This point later became crucial in New Hampshire, where Martin Anderson's research gave Reagan a concrete example: federal inheritance tax revenues shared with the states by formula.) The Ford people, of course, had no intention of letting go an issue they believed would trap Reagan in a skein of Gordian knots, so they busily flooded the early primary states with flyers showing that important programs would have to be sharply cut or eliminated unless state taxes were raised to make up for the Reagan-proposed federal cuts.

Thursday ended with a large civic dinner in Wilmington, the seaport. Helms's people had arranged for the Reagan dinner speech to be televised live locally. Anderson and I had been worrying about the best way to handle the $90 billion questions, so we stayed upstairs to watch the governor on television. He handled it well, we thought, but the audience was basically one of supporters, unlike those at street rallies and shopping centers, where the Ford campaign could plant questions. The Panama Canal issue came up again. Reagan dug into it eagerly. This audience clapped vigorously at his positions on this and other defense and security issues.

Friday we went to Tallahassee for a call on Florida's Democratic governor, Reuben Askew (Reagan and he sipped tea and orange juice) and visits to the state senate and a large shopping center.

Politically, Florida is more like three states than one. The northern tier of counties is southern-state Florida, conservative and mostly Democratic. (Unfortunately, we remarked to one another, crossover voting in primaries is not permitted in Florida). The west coast is midwestern-state Florida, with the largest concentration of Republicans, mostly retired. The southern portion of the Atlantic coast is eastern-state Florida but with an important Cuban émigré community.

Tommy Thomas, Reagan's ebullient Florida chairman, a Panama City auto dealer, was already predicting to newsmen that Reagan would carry the state by two to one. In his enthusiasm he later said it would be by even more.

The first week of campaigning ended in Miami, where the Reagans, together now, spent the rest of the weekend quietly as houseguests of friends. The staff and the press spent the time at a hotel complex near the Miami airport, arranging for clean clothes, resting, and preparing for another week on the road.

One thing you quickly learn on the presidential campaign trail is that the average day begins early. Baggage call that next Monday morning in Miami was at six. This meant arising at five or earlier in order to get dressed and packed. Our plane left for Springfield, Illinois, at eight.

The weather in central Illinois was clear, dry, and not bitterly cold. Congressman Philip Crane, long a Reagan supporter, and Don Totten, a state legislator serving as Reagan's state chairman, took the candidate on a tour of the campaign headquarters in downtown Springfield. There was a visit to the state capitol for a press conference and meetings. Then it was on to Bloomington, in the center of the rich, black-soil farm country, for a rally at the big James Bell farm. In his speech there, delivered in a large, metal farm-equipment shed, Reagan emphasized the need to let farmers compete by selling wheat to anyone on the world market, including the Soviet Union. If anyone was surprised in 1981 when President Reagan lifted the grain embargo that Jimmy Carter had placed on the Soviet Union, they should not have been. In 1976, Reagan was telling the wheat farmers that they should not be singled out to bear the burden of a national policy designed to penalize the Soviets; rather, "if we are going to invoke such a policy," he told his farm audience, "we should spread the burden." He also made the point that the Soviets were having to deplete their gold reserves to make the purchases.

This was Reagan's first farm speech, and the traveling press had been anxious to hear it, even though he made similar statements on farm issues in the course of question-and-answer periods at campaign appearances.

When I learned that we would be stopping in Bloomington, I remembered that the late Adlai Stevenson, the Democratic standard bearer in 1952 and 1956, was a native son. I dug out a book of Stevenson's 1952 campaign speeches and was surprised to find how much like a 1976 Republican this liberal Democrat had sounded on foreign policy and defense matters. I thought Governor Reagan would enjoy the irony, so I suggested a Stevenson quote to underscore a Reagan point, and he worked it into the speech, which was received well by the farm audience. After a hearty lunch in the Bell home, we were off to Rockford, where Crane, a handsome man with a strong voice and dynamic oratorical style, gave a rousing introduction of Reagan to a packed rally in a theater.

The next day took us into Wisconsin and snow in Janesville, Oshkosh, and Milwaukee. At the Pfister Hotel in Milwaukee, the national right-to-life group was having a convention, and a hastily arranged meeting with its leaders took place that evening. Dr. Mildred Jefferson, a soft-spoken black physician who was president of the group, greatly impressed Governor Reagan, who several years before had come to believe that abortion was the taking of a human life and therefore not permissible unless the mother's life was endangered. Following their meeting, Lyn Nofziger and I continued with Dr. Jefferson and some of her board members. One of them was pressing very hard for what seemed to us a strident position they wanted Reagan to take. This woman reminded me of zealots for other causes, right and left, I had run into over the years: rigid in her views, constantly pressing them, not listening to others, and tolerating little interference with her agenda. We told the women we would discuss with Governor Reagan the development of a position paper on the issue.

While Reagan opposed abortion, he did not offer it gratuitously at campaign appearances as an issue. He answered audience questions about his views on the subject willingly, but some of the right-to-lifers wanted him to go much further. The issue was a deeply divisive one. Polls showed, if anything, more people favoring abortion than opposing it. Furthermore, it crosscut other issues and political loyalties.

Thursday, Friday, and Saturday were devoted to hours-long bus rides in New Hampshire, a numbing process. By now, Governor Reagan was riding one of the busses. Jim Lake had arranged for a different weekly newspaper editor or publisher to interview him on each leg of our bus trip. As for the New Hampshire dailies, they had a tendency to oppose whatever the fiery William Loeb of the *Manchester Union Leader* supported, and vice versa, so Gregg and Lake had not been making much headway with them.

Reagan never appeared to tire of this routine. Although it was repetitious, he was always friendly and supplied his interviewers with flashes of his anecdotal humor. He also explained carefully to each that his transfer plan would not result in new taxes for New Hampshire. Still, the questioning at the evening town meetings was getting sharper. Furthermore, the traveling press was beginning to write that the questions, because they were persistent (we believed them to be planted), were "hurting" the Reagan campaign. It is not uncommon in a campaign for reporters to draw such conclusions (even in the absence of polling data to support them) and for the campaign in question to react as if the conclusions were true. In fact, the longer we campaigned, the more acutely we learned how important it is for neither the candidate nor his staff to overreact to news reportage. We were beginning to learn just how hermetically sealed a traveling presidential campaign can be. Most of the reporters must file a story every day from the campaign trail. The campaign must attempt to make some "news" every day, for if it does not, the reporters, acting out of frustration, may draw the wrong conclusions from chance observations or tangential events; the campaign may then find itself unexpectedly on the defensive as a result of the new questions generated by these conclusions.

Sears—who, when he traveled with us, would often look out the bus window for long periods of time, deep in thought—was obviously bothered by the endless questions about the $90 billion transfer plan. He was thinking out a plan to get the issue behind us, once and for all. Toward the end of the trip, he asked Martin Anderson to drop off the campaign trail a few days and develop a comprehensive "white paper" on the program that would serve as the definitive Reagan document. (News people were forever asking us for "position papers" on this or that issue, but we learned that few read them with any intensity when we did provide them.)

On Saturday the seventeenth we headed for Los Angeles and a week at home. Reagan spent some of that time at his ranch, splitting fence rails and riding horseback. ("There is nothing so good for the inside of a man as the outside of a horse," he often said.) Meanwhile, Anderson went to work on the white paper.

The next trip, on the twenty-fifth, took us again to Florida, this time Pensacola, Panama City, and Fort Walton. Then it was on to Asheville, North Carolina, in the heart of the Republican mountain counties of the state, an area where Ford's popularity exceeded Reagan's. Asheville was the birthplace of the novelist Thomas Wolfe, and I thought recognition of the fact by Governor Reagan would be appreciated locally (although Asheville still has mixed views of its most famous son, author of *Look Homeward, Angel*). I suggested a Wolfe quote that Reagan liked, and he used it. Even when he was using his stump speech for day-in, day-out use on the campaign trail, Reagan liked to make a local reference whenever possible, provided it did not seem "that we dragged it in by its ears," as he put it.

We headed again for Manchester on the twenty-eighth, going directly to the New Hampshire Highway Hotel, not far from the state capitol in Concord. Over the years, the Highway Hotel, a sprawling imitation of a colonial manor house, has been headquarters to many itinerant primary presidential campaigns, especially Republican ones. (Sears and Richard Whalen once regaled several of us with recollections of Richard Nixon's "I've got a plan to end the Vietnam War," which the then-candidate blurted out at a Highway Hotel press conference.) In "real life," it thrives on the business of state legislators and the lobbyists and delegations that call on them.

While the food is simple but good and the average room is simple but clean, the Presidential Suite in 1976 had come through a recent remodeling and boasted a parlor, two bedrooms, and a sunken bathtub large enough to float a motorboat (we encountered another just like it, in a campaign stop in Kankakee, Illinois).

We set up a permanent staff room down the hall from the Reagans' suite. There we had a profusion of telephones, a photocopier, typewriters, and a telecopier, from which we received facsimile clippings of leading stories from the next day's first editions of the New York and Washington papers at about eleven each night. From these, we prepared a news summary each day for Governor Reagan to read over breakfast the next morning.

At the end of each day's tour, the staff room had platters heaped with sandwiches and large plastic wastebaskets filled with iced soft drinks and beer. It is easy to gain weight on the campaign trail.

Early in the campaign, Marty Anderson gave me the three cardinal rules for a presidential-campaign staff member on the trail: "(1) When you see food, eat it. You may not get another chance that day; (2) when you see a bathroom, use it—for the same reason—and (3) at a campaign event always position yourself between the candidate and the door (when it's time to go, the Secret Service worries only about the candidate; his staff is on its own)." Marty's advice proved true many times that winter and spring, but it also resulted in a nearly all-carbohydrate diet. This, combined with little sleep and little real exercise, meant that most of us on the trail were putting on weight.

Reagan held a press conference just before lunch that first day at the Highway Hotel and then spent the afternoon in a bus motorcade, touring several small communities. The midwinter thaw had set in, and along the roadsides the snow had turned to gray slush.

During this tour and on a similar one the next day, Reagan still got the questions about his transfer plan, but we began to notice something new. After some of the stops and the question-and-answer periods, reporters traveling with us began to come up to Deaver, Nofziger, Anderson, and me to ask us where Reagan got this or that fact he had cited. Within a few hours it had taken on the proportions of a game of Twenty Questions. The questions all ultimately ended up in Anderson's and my hands, since we were the issues men. We compared notes. Despite a press conference on this leg of the trip, we detected restlessness among the reporters traveling with us. There was not much going on. The $90 billion story was, for the moment, not generating new initiatives by the Ford people nor verbal missteps by Reagan. So, someone had apparently decided to try something new and challenge Reagan on his facts. Soon, others in the press group picked up the idea, and we had a flood of inquiries.

Probably the most noted of these diversions was the case of the so-called Welfare Queen of Chicago. For months prior to his candidacy, Reagan had been telling audiences about a news story reporting the case of a woman who had received some $150,000 in welfare and widow's grants by using false identities to make fraudulent claims. She was under indictment for having misrepresented herself as the widow of several deceased navy men. She was also reported to own expensive autos, furs, and other luxuries.

I do not recall who first raised the question, but soon many reporters traveling with us were challenging Reagan. I remembered having seen the original account Reagan was quoting from (in fact, I was sure he had used it in a radio commentary or newspaper column), but it was not to be found in our traveling research file. I telephoned our office in Los Angeles, where we had kept extensive research files for Reagan's use. Still it was not to be found. The story had been widely reported in the press when it first surfaced several months earlier, but most of the news people traveling with us acted as if they had never heard of it before.

Finally, Anderson contacted Chicago-area authorities and learned that Reagan's recitation of the charges had been, for the most part, correct, but that the charges had been reduced in a plea bargain and the woman had been found guilty of defrauding welfare of about $8,000 instead of $150,000.

While the saga of the Welfare Queen generated plenty of light banter between the staff and the press, it was bothersome that this degree of hair-splitting was taking so much time. The few days we were immersed in the Twenty-Questions phase of the campaign showed us that there were still some in the traveling press who did not take Ronald Reagan seriously.

For a few days the questions had come at us so thick and fast that we decided to answer only a few, but to answer those in careful detail. We realized that much of the questioning was designed to test our reaction, so every evening during that time, we called our research office in Washington and got a report on the day's fact-digging from Jeff Bell or Larry Uzzell (we never had more than two researchers during the primaries).

The trip ended with a day in Sarasota and Melbourne, Florida. It was a long day, ending at one o'clock the next morning back in Los Angeles. While we had been feeling confident about Florida (and early polls showed us ahead), the Ford campaign was beginning to pull itself together. They had hired Bill Roberts, Spencer's former California partner, who knew Reagan well from the 1966 campaign. Roberts was assigned to organize Florida, where Ford's chairman, Congressman Lou Frey, was torn between his friendship for Ford and his desire not to alienate the Reagan forces, because he was considering running for governor. It was to take a while, but the Reagan campaign would eventually feel the full effect of Roberts's organizational rebuilding.

Our California sojourn was short—barely three days. Early Tuesday morning, February 3, the Reagan jet was off again, this time for a thirteen-day trip that would take us to Florida three times, New Hampshire twice, and once each to North Carolina, Illinois, and New York City.

Tuesday evening and Wednesday morning in West Palm Beach and Fort Lauderdale went well, but there were new worries about New Hampshire. Ford's people had been soliciting, and getting, statements from some California officials criticizing Ronald Reagan's record as gov-

ernor. The number was not large (four or five), but any sign of lack of
solidarity in Reagan's home state was disquieting and made news. San
Diego's Mayor Pete Wilson was the most prominent California Republican to issue a statement (after 1976 he and the Reaganites made up),
and it was followed by several legislators who, like Wilson, had served in
Sacramento when Reagan was governor. The statements were similar in
that they drew attention to the fact that income taxes had increased
under Reagan. They left out the fact—mentioned by Reagan before
many audiences—that, as a new governor in 1966, he had inherited a
nearly bankrupt state government and had reluctantly turned to tax increases as the only short-term means of balancing the budget.

At each stop in New Hampshire, Reagan was questioned by someone
in the audience about the allegations of these Californians. A similar
barrage of statements was being issued by New Hampshire legislators
(always Ford supporters, as it turned out), quoting this reading of the
California record and suggesting that millions of dollars of new taxes
would have to be raised in New Hampshire in order to cope with Reagan's transfer plan. This, on the eve of a Ford visit to New Hampshire
the coming weekend, was intended to throw the challenger on the defensive while preparing the way for a triumphal tour by the incumbent.
We learned that the Ford campaign people intended to use as much
pomp and circumstance as possible to make the visit highly "presidential." In fact, their ads in the local papers that week urged people to
come to the Manchester airport to "see Air Force One, see the President's limousine, see the President," and so forth.

By the next time Reagan held a press conference we had obtained a
copy of a fill-in-the-blanks press release that had been used by the Ford
people to generate their blitz of criticisms from the California and New
Hampshire legislators. Reagan opened his press conference with a grin
and read the sample press release, including every " 'Blank' said today."
That ended the canned-criticism blitz.

Other than the $90 billion transfer plan and its implications, what
were the issues on the minds of the voters? Audiences at the citizens'
press conferences at the evening stops brought out similar concerns
across the state. (The real press people could not join the audience in
asking questions at these sessions, and they did not like that.) My notes
from campaign stops at Colby-Sawyer College and Kearsarge list questions about unemployment, deregulation of natural gas, the $90 billion
plan (several questions), foreign policy, the Seabrook nuclear plant,
abortion, Angola, Social Security, euthanasia, aid to New York City,
welfare, compulsory national health insurance, federal matching funds,
the equal-rights amendment (ERA), nuclear waste, Kissinger as secre-

tary of state, the Panama Canal negotiations, and problems of independent gasoline retailers.

We were once again in rural New Hampshire with its mountains, forests, and fresh snow. We spent two nights at the handsome Hanover Inn in Hanover, the site of Dartmouth College. The students were preparing for their winter carnival. The holiday spirit would have been contagious, had it not been for the fact that each day in Hanover we had to be out early and back late.

Friday morning we left for North Carolina, spending the night in Raleigh. Saturday morning we flew to Daytona. Reagan was in a relaxed mood and so were the rest of us. The main event of the day would be the Florida Jaycees' convention luncheon at Daytona Beach. From there we would go to Miami to spend the remainder of the weekend in rest and relaxation. We did not think much ahead about the press conference scheduled at Embry-Riddle Aeronautical University just prior to the rally there, on the way to the Daytona luncheon. As it turned out, one question and one answer at the news conference were to cause serious damage to Ronald Reagan's Florida campaign.

Most of the questions came from the national press traveling with us. They were not unlike the verbal shadowboxing that usually takes place at such events. At its best, a traveling press corps tests the mettle of a candidate. Part of this process is to ask repeatedly for "specifics." The candidate, of course, wants to stick with principles and concepts as much as possible. The more detailed his answers, the more likely he will make himself an inviting target for his opponent.

The press conference had wound its way through eleven questions without any headlines developing when Dick Bergholz of the *Los Angeles Times*, who had been covering Reagan for several years, began a series of inquiries about Social Security. Other reporters added questions. One asked, "How do you invest a fund [the Social Security trust fund] that is heading toward a two-trillion-dollar imbalance?" Reagan replied by saying that the trust fund had never been put to work earning income. When pressed for an example of how it might, he said some economists had suggested using "the industrial might of America." He went no further. While he had not made an actual proposal to invest in, say, the stock market, the Ford campaign quickly translated it into that. Ford operatives wasted little time in spreading the word around Florida that Reagan was willing to speculate with the Social Security trust fund. Even the President took up the refrain, saying that government investment in the stock market would amount to "back-door socialism."

The story itself was not a big one in the media, at least not at first, but the slant the Ford people put on it in Florida temporarily undermined Governor Reagan's credibility on the issue and threatened to waste valuable time by putting him on the defensive. From then on, when reporters traveling with us came around for their frequent "backgrounder" visits with Nofziger, Anderson, and me, they pressed very hard on Reagan's views on every aspect of Social Security.

By the time he got to Florida again a few days later, Ronald Reagan opened every remark about Social Security with the flat assurance that the nation had an obligation to provide with benefits those who rely on the program or expect to rely on it. Anderson recommended that the governor propose that, if elected, he would appoint a blue-ribbon commission of experts to make long-term recommendations to strengthen the system. Reagan liked this idea and used it without exception from then on. It ultimately ended the issue, although not before Ford campaign forces had caused us damage in Florida.

We left the news conference with a feeling of nervousness, but this went away at the Jaycees' luncheon, in a huge hotel ballroom on the beach. The Jaycees whooped and hollered in support of almost everything Reagan said.

The press often asked Reagan and the rest of us when he was going to announce his foreign policy. Although he had answered many foreign-policy questions, they wanted it in a package. Sears had been resisting this because Reagan's image, as shown in our polls, was already strong in terms of national defense and security matters. To underscore his concerns for Soviet advances would tend to put too much emphasis on the subject. Wirthlin's tracking polls, however, were beginning to show that the American public was concerned about the United States actually falling behind the Soviet Union. Sears told me that weekend that he thought it was time we put a foreign-policy section in a speech. Governor Reagan was scheduled to address the students at Phillips Exeter Academy in Exeter, New Hampshire, the following Tuesday, February 10. Because it was a nonpartisan audience, he could not use his stump speech, but could use some education proposals we had been talking about. The remarks he had been working on were brief, however, so that he would have time for a question period with the students. We decided that we could graft on about ten minutes on foreign and defense policy to the remarks about education. Sears asked me to call James Schlesinger to get his ideas. I did and then worked up a draft, which I took to Governor Reagan. As usual, he improved on it.

Tuesday morning, when he addressed the Exeter student body, Reagan made a smooth transition from his remarks about education to a discussion of détente, which had become increasingly controversial, even to the point where Gerald Ford declared that the very term would no longer be used. Reagan said:

We are told that détente is our best hope for a lasting peace. Hope it may offer, but only so long as we have no illusions about it. When we sit down at the bargaining table, we must always remember that the Soviet Union's representatives across the table will give up as little as they have to and take as much as they can get. They have a history of being tough negotiators, and we should be, too. Détente, if it is a one-way street, will fail. As a two-way street it may succeed.

When the stakes are war and peace, we can bargain successfully only if we are strong militarily and only if we are willing to defend outselves if necessary. We must also have a sense of unity and a national purpose in our foreign policy.

In a free society, these things can be accomplished if the government will confide in the people. They must know why a particular policy is in our best interests as a nation. They must know what dangers are involved if the policy isn't adopted. Given the facts, they will make the right decisions and their elected representatives will know of it soon enough.

He traced the history of the growth of the Soviet arsenal, of the worries of our European allies, of opportunities lost in various parts of the globe.

Secretary of State Henry Kissinger had been scolding the Russians about meddling in Angola, but the U.S. government had said nothing about postponing Kissinger's trip to Moscow to prepare for SALT II talks. Reagan turned his aim thus: "If you were a Russian official and you heard the American secretary of state deliver stern warnings to you for trying to dominate the situation in Angola, but all the time you knew he was packing his bags to come to Moscow to negotiate a new arms-limitation agreement, would you really take his words seriously?"

Reagan spoke of the importance of the cruise missile to the rebuilding of U.S. strength. He questioned the need to telegraph our intention to give up the Panama Canal. (In early 1974, a time when Nixon was distracted by Watergate, Kissinger had gone to Panama and signed a memorandum with the Panamanian foreign minister which, in effect, set forth the points that would later provide the framework for Carter's Panama Canal treaties.)

About SALT II he said, "The best way to have an equitable SALT II agreement is to negotiate from a firmly established position. We should not be so eager for an agreement that we make unnecessary concessions, for to grant such concessions is to whet the Soviets' appetite for more."

Reagan was proposing peace through strength, a position that went against what seemed the tide of opinion at the time. That tide contained views that ranged from a feeling that Americans would no longer tolerate an assertion of strength, to contention from the Left that the United States should actually cast off any remaining vestiges of world leadership—the New Isolationism. The Ford administration was in an awkward position, trying to follow its instincts to keep up U.S. defense strength while bucking the antistrength tide, which was exemplified by outspoken liberal elements in Congress. Kissinger's statements and writings tended to convey a pessimistic view about the willpower of the American people, and this made many conservatives uneasy. Thus, there was an opening for Reagan that he used to advantage in this, his first foreign- and defense-policy speech.

The students clapped politely, but the speech was really intended for the news media, Washington, and a national audience. When we climbed aboard the bus I knew it had been a success, for several members of the national press were complimentary about it. Later that week the *Wall Street Journal* reprinted it—a surprise to us.

By giving the speech at that point in his campaign, Ronald Reagan had done two things: he achieved new momentum (briefly, at least, he would again be the main focus of press attention), and he had defused the stereotype nurtured by Ford partisans of a man who would be a trigger-happy president.

The rest of the week included a quick side trip to New York City to address a Republican dinner (Sears was working hard behind the scenes to line up some New York delegates) and ended with a visit to Disney World, outside Orlando, Florida. Election night in New Hampshire was a little over a week away when we landed in Los Angeles, late Sunday afternoon, the fifteenth.

Despite the fact that Ford's strategists had thrown Ronald Reagan on the defensive at the beginning of the New Hampshire campaign and had kept up their attack, Reagan and his staff still believed he would win.

Martin Anderson's suggestions for dealing with the negative aspects of the transfer plan had provided Reagan with a defense of the issue that permitted him to rebound; our polls showed that voters in New Hampshire and elsewhere liked the basic concept. By offering such specifics as the possibility of diverting federal alcohol and tobacco tax revenues to the states, Reagan gave the concept new believability.

The Social Security issue, although it worried us, seemed to have been weathered by Reagan's frequent repetition of his assurance that no one counting on the program would be denied benefits.

Yet, throughout the New Hampshire campaign, all of us around Reagan were concerned about the perception by the press that our candidate "had" to win in New Hampshire. Hugh Gregg, Reagan's state chairman, insisted repeatedly that if Reagan got 40 percent to 45 percent of the vote he would be doing very well. This seemed a sensible position. Although the Reagan camp had been confident from the outset (buoyed by polls showing him ahead), New Hampshire politics could be mercurial, and the ground was shifting in Ford's favor in the final days of the campaign. Sears often kept Wirthlin's poll results to himself. The result was that the traveling staff (and sometimes the candidate himself) did not have early warning of growing dangers. I suspect that Sears's reason was that he wanted time to think out the implications of the polls before exposing them to the superheated atmosphere that is sometimes felt out on the campaign trail.

Reagan and the rest of us kept trying to shake the "must win" perception by reminding the press that if history were a guide, Reagan did not need to win New Hampshire literally. After all, in 1968 Eugene McCarthy had lost to the incumbent, Lyndon Johnson, by 6 points and was still declared the "winner" by the news media. A month later, Johnson withdrew his candidacy, so potent was the perception that he and his policies had "lost." In 1972, George McGovern lost to Edmund Muskie by more than 9 points, but because the press considered McGovern the winner, it proved to be the beginning of the end for Muskie.

Thus, Gregg kept making the point that if Reagan received between 40 percent and 45 percent of the vote, he should be declared the "winner" against an incumbent president. In this case, however, history was not a guide. The reporters listened to Gregg, but they did not really believe him. They thought Reagan was going to win; therefore, he "had" to. Conversely, Ford, the unelected President, without the usual incumbent's "right" to party loyalty, also "had" to win in New Hampshire in order to remain a credible candidate.

Ford's strategists knew this, and at one point Ford himself declared that he would enter every primary, apparently apprehensive about a possible loss in New Hampshire and trying to minimize it in advance.

Sears's strategy had been built on a victory in New Hampshire with a quick follow-up in Florida (we were not actively contesting Massachusetts or Vermont), with the finale in Illinois, thus avoiding a costly war of attrition through some thirty primaries.

Although there was no detailed contingency plan to fall back on if that one failed, most of us assumed that the only thing that would dry up campaign contributions would be a series of defeats and the consequent demoralizing of Reagan's army of supporters. There was, however, a "wild card" we had not counted on that later almost put the Reagan campaign out of business.

On January 30, the Supreme Court had ruled that some provisions of the Federal Election Campaign Act amendments of 1974 were flawed and would have to be corrected by Congress. Meanwhile, the Federal Election Commission suspended federal matching funds to the candidates, pending the outcome in Congress. Serious cash-flow problems were to arise later, but at first they were not felt by the Reagan campaign. In fact, in some respects, Reagan's fund-raising had been more successful than Ford's.

From the beginning, the Reagan campaign went for the small contributor. A creative young direct-mail specialist, Bruce Eberle, tested list after list of donors to conservative causes, tapping large numbers of pro-Reagan people in every corner of the country. The resulting "house" list was turned to again and again, and a steady stream of small checks flowed into the Reagan headquarters in Washington. Ford's campaign, on the other hand, had gotten off to a bumpy start in its 1975 fund-raising. Industrialist David Packard, Ford's first finance chairman, had concentrated on one-to-one contacts with major Republican donors, ignoring the potentialities of direct mail. Federal Election law, with its $1,000-per-person contribution limit, had rendered this traditional large-donor approach much less effective than before. Direct mail was to become the campaign-financing tool of the future, and the Reagan campaign was already on to it.

Yet, after the January 30 court decision the advantage began to turn to Ford in terms of the effect of cash flow on campaign mobility. As president, Ford could have the government bill his committee for the use of Air Force One, whereas Reagan's campaign had to pay cash in advance for his travels.

As the final week of the New Hampshire campaign began, the Reagans and their traveling staff were taking a four-day respite in California, planning for the final swing through the Granite State.

Ford in his appearances (echoed by stand-in speakers in New Hampshire) had throughout most of the campaign emphasized that there was very little philosophical difference between him and Reagan and that therefore, it was safest for voters to trust his experience and keep him in office. Lately, however, Ford had begun saying that Reagan was to his right philosophically, implying that the governor was out of the mainstream of Republican politics. We gathered this was designed to conjure up the notion that Reagan was an "extremist," something that presumably would not set well with New Hampshire voters.

In one conversation with his staff that week, Reagan noted wryly that Ford had not thought him too extreme to ask him twice to join his cabinet. Sears immediately saw this as the perfect rejoinder and urged Reagan to open his press conference in Manchester that Friday evening with it. He did. Although Reagan had spoken of these Ford offers to individual reporters before, his opening statement in the crowded hotel ballroom that Friday seemed to come as a revelation to the assembled reporters. He reviewed Ford's telephone call in late 1974 and the

Rumsfeld conversation in the spring of 1975, as well as the fact he had been appointed by Ford to the Rockefeller CIA Commission in 1975. A reporter asked him why he thought Ford had asked him to take those jobs. Was it to co-opt him as a possible opponent? Reagan let a few seconds pass as the question sunk in. His face took on a mischievous expression I had seen many times when he was savoring an irony. "No," he said slowly, "I just thought he recognized my administrative ability."

John Sears's theory that "politics is motion" seemed to have been fully verified at the press conference. The momentum had suddenly passed to Ronald Reagan. Still, our earlier lead in the polls had been whittled away until, in recent days, the race was statistically a toss-up.

A last-minute problem of another sort had developed for the Ford campaign that had the President's strategists very nervous. Richard Nixon had accepted an invitation from the Chinese Communists to visit Peking just three days before election day in New Hampshire. Watergate was still fresh enough in voters' minds that Nixon's travels monopolizing the news media would bring back reminders of Ford's pardon of him.

Ford, when asked about it, told reporters that Nixon, as a private citizen, could go wherever he wished. Reagan, true to character, did nothing to capitalize on this political hand grenade and said much the same thing when asked.

In order to dispel any press perception that Reagan was either "too old" or "not up to" a full campaign, Sears had arranged a particularly intense, exhausting schedule throughout the New Hampshire campaign. Thirteen- and fourteen-hour days were common, and the candidate, if anything, bore up under it better than his staff and the press. Indeed, a week or so after the first day's swing in New Hampshire, all the "too old" and "not up to" questions had ceased altogether. Now, by the final week, Reagan had so thoroughly covered the state and drawn such large and generally enthusiastic crowds that Gregg and Sears told him there was nothing more that he could do and that he should leave the state the last day or two. Gregg and his people would get to work on the effort to get out the vote. So, on the final Sunday, we flew in midafternoon to Illinois, not returning until Tuesday evening.

On election day the Concord Highway Hotel was headquarters once again. It was swarming with aides and reporters. Early returns showed Reagan leading by a few thousand votes. The lead held throughout the evening. No one, however, was claiming victory, including Governor Reagan, who, when he went downstairs to speak to assembled campaign workers, stopped short of declaring the battle won.

It was nearly one in the morning when we learned that Ford had inched ahead. Ronald Reagan, resilient and optimistic by nature, cheered those around him and talked of comparisons with the McCarthy and McGovern "victories."

By breakfast time we learned that Ford had won. The final margin was 49.4 percent for Ford, 48 percent for Reagan, and 2.6 percent for others.

When he met with reporters, Reagan smiled and said he was happy with the results. If he was disappointed, he did not show it. Following his example of cheerfulness, those of us with him bantered with the reporters as if we were pleased with the outcome. The fact is that most of us were worried about what this meant to the future of the campaign. It would certainly have some negative carry-over effect in Florida, where we already had problems. Still, there was a sense of relief that the first primary was over and, buoyed by our candidate's seeming good spirits, we headed for the airport, where we took off at midmorning for a day of campaigning that would end in Tampa, Florida.

This was the second visit to Illinois in three days. Memories of the first had been crowded out by the onrush of the New Hampshire primary night. I suddenly realized that it had only been yesterday morning, clear and cold, when our motorcade had made its way from Peoria through the rich farm country of Ronald Reagan's youth to Tampico, the small town where he was born and on to Dixon, the city where he spent his teenage years and which he considered his real hometown. Both communities turned out in force for his return. In Tampico, his classmates from elementary school were assembled on the school auditorium stage to greet their old friend "Dutch." Later, we visited his first home, a flat above a store on the main street. (A few years later, when driving by the White House and being asked what he thought of living there, Reagan quipped, "Not so bad, I guess. When I was a kid we lived above the store.") In Dixon, the gymnasium of Reagan's old high school was jammed with students and townspeople. The band and the cheers made a deafening roar. That, followed by the long, quiet drive up the course of the Rock River—the same river where Reagan had worked as a lifeguard in his teens—made me wonder if this peaceful part of the world and the people with their plain, solid values did not have a lot to do with Ronald Reagan's consistency of purpose and sense of self-confidence. He often spoke lovingly of this land. It was easy to see why.

The morning after the New Hampshire primary, Sears spoke to Governor Reagan about changing the content of his stump speech. Sears and Wirthlin had been poring over the polling data. Sears felt the time had come for Reagan to shift emphasis to foreign- and defense-policy issues. He wanted to get away from the pitfalls associated with Social Security and to lay aside the transfer plan, too.

Wirthlin's polls showed that Florida voters, to a greater degree than the nation as a whole, were worried about the decline of U.S. defense capability in relation to the Soviet Union. Since Reagan's first foreign-policy speech (at Exeter) had been well received, Sears recommended that the governor begin working elements of it into his basic speech. He did so on the Florida leg of the trip that week, but the press did not really pick up on the changes—at least, the local press did not and, in terms of Florida votes, that is what counted. Still, the crowds were enthusiastic and cheered when Reagan said we should be "second to none" in our defense capability.

An intricate game of code words had begun to develop. While there was evidence that our defense strength had declined in a number of categories, the administration insisted that, on balance, there was "rough equivalence" between the United States and the Soviet Union. This was hard to refute, although Reagan and his advisers believed a rebuilding of eroded strength was necessary. So, judging from the response of his audiences, did many voters. Yet, for Reagan to call for clear superiority in all categories would bring charges that he wanted to engage in an arms race, which he did not. His image was already quite strong on the defense issue, and to sharpen his rhetorical points even more would make him appear too strong, so he settled on the "second to none" phrase to describe his objective.

Wednesday was a long day, and we arrived at the Riverside Hilton Hotel in downtown Tampa ready to welcome the three-night stay we would have there. The hotel, however, was not prepared for the combined onslaught of the Reagan entourage and a convention, and for many on the staff and in the press corps, fatigue quickly turned to irritability when hotel services buckled under the load. Food and laundry service were next to impossible to obtain, and room assignments were scrambled. Still, there was work to do. Governor Reagan was scheduled to leave the hotel each morning for motorcade tours through neighboring cities.

Thursday morning, the senior staff met with him in his suite before setting out for the day. The advertising account executive had flown in, to review the television commercials. Most of us on the Reagan staff had felt from the beginning that the commercials were bland. Nofziger returned to a favorite theme of his: Reagan is his own best advertisement. He got plenty of agreement from the rest of us. We needed new television spots to feature Reagan's positions on the defense issue, to let our candidate speak for himself directly to the voters in the most personal of all media, television. The advertising agency man gave us the bad news: between the tightness of the campaign traveling schedule and the production and delivery time for new television materials, there was no time left in the Florida campaign to produce anything new. All we could do, he said, was to cut and edit new spots from the old footage. Reagan looked intensely frustrated, although he said little. Some of the rest of us were seething because so little contingency planning had been made by the advertising people. As it turned out, they had done their last work for the campaign. Not long afterward it was decided to let their contract lapse at the end of March.

That day there was a noontime Bicentennial rally in a park in the center of St. Petersburg. If Ronald Reagan was upset about the television commercials, the crowd never knew it. He addressed them with good humor and verve, hitting all the new issues he had woven into his speech. Mike Deaver and I had often commented how Ronald Reagan and an audience reacted on one another. As he warmed to his topic, they would respond with laughter, surprise, or applause, and it would give him an extra lift. He in turn would lift them until, by the time he reached his final peroration, he and the audience were locked in a sort of partnership. His well-developed sense of timing had a great deal to do with this successful relationship he developed with so many audiences.

This time the crowd was in a festive mood. Before and after the governor's speech, they cheered and laughed when a man in an Uncle Sam suit went by the front of the stage on roller skates followed by a small terrier. With such a lighthearted mood prevailing, it was hard to remember that Ronald Reagan's lead in Florida—never more than a few points, despite the intensity of feeling of his supporters and Tommy Thomas's cheery predictions—had ebbed away, and President Ford was now ahead in the polls.

From the beginning of his candidacy, Governor Reagan had said he would stick by the Republican "Eleventh Commandment" ("Thou shalt not speak ill of a fellow Republican"), an idea created by Gaylord Parkinson, the California Republican chairman after the bitter Goldwater-Rockefeller fight of 1964. Thus far, Reagan had managed to criticize policies and to offer alternatives without overtly criticizing his opponent or those around him. The time was coming closer, however, when this would be impossible to do any longer.

On Friday, we would be campaigning at a big retirement community in Sun City and at the baseball park in Winter Haven where major-league teams did spring training. We talked over the issues. Reagan decided to focus on the Panama Canal for the day. An insert was drafted, based on reports we had been getting from Latin America that the U.S. and Panamanian negotiators might already have reached agreement on the elements of a new treaty. The semisecrecy of the negotiations and the apparently foregone conclusion that the U.S. would divest itself of the canal became a sort of lightning rod for voter frustration over

American impotence in the world generally, especially among conservatives.

Ronald Reagan poured it on in Sun City, and the crowd roared its approval. He got a similar reaction in Winter Haven. The traveling press picked up the story (and his other foreign- and defense-policy themes), but the local press focused less on it than we had hoped. It was crucial that the new themes sink in with the Florida media, for Ford was pulling way ahead. Under Bill Roberts's direction the once ineffectual Ford campaign had been shaped into a powerful one. The President had visited the very area we were now in, campaigning from an open car in a rainstorm with obvious gusto. The administration had been bestowing presents on Florida as if it were Christmas: completion of an interstate highway, a new veterans' hospital, a Miami transit grant, a defense contract. Roberts had also hit on the idea of having Florida editors and broadcasters invited to the Oval Office for interviews with the President. They went and promptly reported back to their readers, listeners, and viewers. There was no way we could top that. Ronald Reagan, despite his star quality in attracting and winning crowds, was not, after all, the incumbent. If politics is motion, as John Sears often reminded us, most of the motion was with the Ford campaign.

We flew home to Los Angeles on Saturday, February 28, after a day of campaigning in Jacksonville. We were scheduled to return to Florida late the next Thursday afternoon, March 5, for the final push in the Sunshine State.

What Sears, Wirthlin, and David Keene (who was coordinating the Florida effort) knew, but the candidate and the rest of us did not, was just how far in front Ford had moved. He was now ahead by 17 to 20 points in our own polls. We had expected, and dreaded, a negative carry-over effect from New Hampshire, but nothing this bad. We got this news after we returned to California. Sears wanted the Reagans to have a chance to relax at their ranch before he broke the news to them.

On Monday, March 1, Sears called me from Washington. He said he was going to recommend to the governor that on arrival in Orlando on Thursday, he open a live-on-television press conference with a blast at the Ford-Kissinger foreign policy. "It means we'll have to put aside the Eleventh Commandment," he said, "but we have no choice and it's time to take the gloves off." He cited Wirthlin's polls. He told me he would send a draft opening statement to me on the telecopier. He asked me to edit it and then take it to the governor for approval. The next morning I received it. It was stronger than anything Ronald Reagan had used before. For example, "Henry Kissinger's recent stewardship of U.S. foreign policy has coincided precisely with the loss of military supremacy." Ford had of course inherited his secretary of state from Richard Nixon, but since conservatives tended to be critical and mistrustful of Kissinger and were also concerned about the decline of U.S. defenses, this linkage with Kissinger's stewardship seemed logical.

Sears had also told me in that telephone conversation that from then on, we should draft at least one insert each day for Governor Reagan to include in his stump speech, building on the basic theme of growing U.S. weakness vis-à-vis the Soviet Union. "And don't stop," he chuckled. Marty Anderson and I talked over the idea and then set the research staff to work looking for every available quotation from experts to back up the assertions in the Reagan statement. Next, I went over the statement and reiterated Sears's comments with Governor Reagan. He toned down the statement, but it was still plenty vigorous.

When we arrived in Orlando, the party went straight to the studios of WFTV, the local ABC affiliate. Ronald Reagan gave his short opening statement and then fielded questions in the on-the-air press conference. He seemed both determined and sure of his ground. Politics was motion once again, and the motion this time was in Reagan's favor. The media people caught the new mood in an instant. It remained to give them the sustained follow-through.

On Friday, Saturday, Sunday, and Monday we crossed and recrossed the state. Each day Anderson and I gave Governor Reagan two inserts quoting defense experts and citing facts and figures with as much news value as we could muster. Reagan addressed crowds at shopping centers, retirement communities, parks, recreation centers, colleges, and luncheon and dinner rallies. He meant to finish strong, and the enthusiastic crowds were helping him do it.

Late Monday afternoon we left Jacksonville for Illinois once again. After a full day of campaigning and long motorcade rides between towns, we ended Tuesday, March 9, in Rock Island. We received the Florida results in the hotel there. Ford's 17–20-point lead of a week ago had been reduced to a win by fewer than 6 points. Ronald Reagan had made up a great deal of lost ground in the final days, losing with 47.2 percent to Ford's 52.8 percent.

While the news media were focused on the two-primary losing streak Reagan had suffered (Massachusetts and Vermont were often added, although we had not contested them), the candidate and his staff were more cheerful than the news reports indicated they should be. Reagan had opened a new front in the campaign with his Orlando statement and its follow-throughs, and he intended to press on. That he had made up so much ground in so short a time told him and those around him that he had found a winning formula.

One event in the final Florida trip, which had been added to the schedule only in the final days, proved to have a positive effect on the future of the Reagan campaign, although at the time we did not know it.

A Miami television station had offered both Ford and Reagan a half-hour of live time that final weekend. We decided to accept. The Ford people did not. Governor Reagan talked over the speech. We would take the main points he was hitting on the stump and expand upon them to fit the twenty-seven-minute segment. Reluctantly, Thursday night he parted with his stump-speech cards long enough for me to make photocopies so that I could develop the longer version. The final speech hit his familiar themes, with emphasis on centralization of authority in Washington, on overregulation, and on foreign policy and defense, with a good dose of the Panama Canal issue.

The television studio was short on what is called in the business "production values." They consisted of a huge desk and a blue backdrop. Off to one side, out of camera range, was the TelePrompTer. Because I did not want to take any chances, I monitored the feeding of the TelePrompTer myself so that it would work at Governor Reagan's normal speaking pace. Reagan, not surprisingly, delivered the address flawlessly.

This speech came to be called the "talking-head speech," because his head and shoulders were about all the camera and the audience saw. Unbeknownst to us, some days later Tom Ellis, the North Carolina campaign chairman, arranged to buy a videotape of the speech. He arranged with Nofziger to have the Florida references edited out, and then he began to run it in every television market in North Carolina. It would go down well with the voters in his state, he reasoned, but he budgeted it and ran it over the objections of Sears and the Washington headquarters.

Back in Illinois, the campaign wound its way through the state in search of votes. Ford had locked up the entire Republican establishment, but as elsewhere, the Reagan volunteers were dedicated and undaunted. Reagan pressed his attack on the foreign-policy issues. Kissinger counterattacked in a speech in Boston, and Ford rushed to Kissinger's defense. This meant to us that the issue was beginning to take hold. Reagan announced that if elected, he would appoint a new secretary of state.

Originally, Sears had intended the Illinois primary to be the end of the campaign, after presumed victories in New Hampshire and Florida. Now, the Reagan campaign was fighting to come from behind. We did not expect to win in Illinois. In fact, Reagan himself had been saying for some time that he would be satisfied with 40 percent of the vote. On election day, March 16, he got 40.1 percent; Ford, 58.9 percent; and Lar Daly, a perennial candidate in the state, 1 percent.

The North Carolina primary was a week away, and we would head there the day after next for the final swing. Reagan and the traveling staff were in California for a short breather on the day of the Illinois primary. While the results were not unexpected and the Illinois loss in itself was not enough to depress the candidate or his staff, the next morning's news brought a new, more ominous piece of information. Rogers Morton, in Ford's Washington campaign headquarters, began to put together announcements from prominent Republican members of Congress, mayors, and other leaders suggesting that it was time for Reagan to withdraw.

Wednesday we were scheduled to fly to North Carolina in the afternoon. There was some doubt that morning that we would even be able to go. The cash flow, in the absence of matching funds, had become so tight that the money from the morning's mail in Washington had to be counted before it was known whether there would be enough to pay for the chartered jet.

No one said anything as we departed, but the worry written on Nancy Reagan's face was matched by the feelings of all of us on her husband's staff. We were staring another defeat in the face, and if it came true, the perception of the news media would probably be that the campaign had lost its credibility and to continue would be futile. In presidential politics, such abstractions can be as important as vote tallies. To make matters worse, we were running out of money.

We landed at Greensboro at about ten that night. As was often the case, there were local reporters crowding the fence at the edge of the tarmac. The Reagans went over to greet them. "When are you going to get out of the race?" shouted one. Another said, "A group of Republican congressmen are saying that you've made your point, so now it's time to quit. Are you going to?" Ronald Reagan was taken aback, but he mustered a reply: "The ball game is still in the first inning, and that's not the time to take your bat and go home."

It did not stop there. The next morning it was worse. At every stop, local reporters hammered away with similar questions and reports of new groups of Republican luminaries calling for Reagan's withdrawal. Reagan kept answering the questions, but he was beginning to sound testy. "I won't quit; tell *him* [Ford] to quit," he said at one of these impromptu press conferences.

At lunch that day, while the governor was addressing the audience, Mike Deaver took me aside. We had both noticed the grim set of Ronald Reagan's jaw. This was a sure sign he was digging in against the heavy odds that were building against him. That could be a plus in terms of determination but a minus if he was goaded too much. Mike had an idea. Senator Paul Laxalt had joined us. Mike said, "Paul should ride with the governor after lunch and before the next stop get him to put away his speech cards and just speak straight from the heart." That is what happened. Laxalt, a trusted friend with good instincts and a calm, deliberate manner, told him to do just that. At the next stop, a shopping center, the "stage" was a flatbed truck trailer. Reagan leaped aboard it eagerly. He threw himself into his off-the-cuff remarks. He was intense and earnest. He pulled from his memory some of his strongest issue points. He hammered away at the foreign policy and defense issues. He used barbs to jab at the Ford administration's cornucopia policy of bestowing give-aways on primary states. "I don't know whether they're the Easter Bunny or Santa Claus," he said. He was back on the offensive. He meant to go all the way to Kansas City, he said, and the crowd cheered, letting him know that was fine with them.

So it went in town after town. At one point we passed an airfield with a huge C5-A on the runway about to disgorge its cargo: the President's limousine! There was to be a repeat that weekend of the New Hampshire and Florida presidential visits. Somehow, it did not matter. All that mattered at the moment was Ronald Reagan's newfound zest for campaigning.

It was a tiring few days that ended Saturday night in Asheville, in the green hills of western North Carolina. Sunday was quiet. The Reagans went to church that morning, and the staff relaxed. That evening, the Reagans hosted the senior staff at a quiet dinner at a country club housed in a building on what had once been Biltmore, the Vanderbilt estate. It was a pleasant evening—the quiet before the storm, I thought, for it still seemed likely we would lose on Tuesday.

Little did we know that late that week Sears had met with Rogers Morton (now Ford's campaign chairman, following the resignation of Callaway) to probe the possibility of a Reagan withdrawal. Sears was worried about the money problem. The campaign was about $2 million in debt. If we lost North Carolina and were forced out, it would be helpful if the Ford campaign would agree to cover that debt. Despite the meeting with Morton, a couple of days later Sears told us that if Reagan could hold on until the Texas primary in May, the tide would turn in his favor.

Sears's strategy in talking with Morton was one with high risks—Reagan and those of us close to him would have been furious, had we known about it at the time—but, in retrospect, his motives seem to have been to protect his candidate's flanks in case of a loss in North Carolina.

Monday, after a series of airport news conferences across the state, we left North Carolina for Green Bay, Wisconsin. The day ended in Racine, on the shores of a bleak, icy Lake Michigan. As we arrived at the hotel, a cheering group of right-to-lifers greeted Governor Reagan and his party.

Sears had flown in to join us. That night, he advanced a startling idea: Ronald Reagan should end his Wisconsin campaign the next day, draw a "bottom line" under the first round of primaries, use the money saved to deliver a nationwide television speech to raise money, and then go on to win the May primaries, which favored him. We were not going to win Wisconsin anyway, Sears reasoned. Indeed, according to Dick Wirthlin's polls, 40 percent was about the most we could hope for.

The more we talked about Sears's audacious idea, the more appealing it became. Governor Reagan mulled it over but seemed favorably disposed, so the next morning, Sears, Anderson, and I stayed behind while Reagan and the motorcade went out to campaign in the chilly late winter air. We sat in the hotel room, looking out at that frozen day in Racine and talked over themes to be used in the television address. By midday, the outline of the speech had taken form. It was time for us to rejoin the governor and his party. We met them at the Milwaukee airport, Mitchell Field. A little after three in the afternoon, we left for La Crosse. After a staff conference, greetings to well wishers at the hotel, and a quiet supper, Ronald Reagan left to address some twelve hundred members of Ducks Unlimited at the Civic Auditorium. This was an annual dinner of the hunters' club, and the members were in high spirits when we arrived. In a room behind the stage we asked Governor Reagan what themes he wanted to emphasize in his speech. "Nothing serious," he said. "I've been saving up some one-liners in my briefcase. I don't think this crowd wants to hear weighty arguments about the issues." He was right. He kept his remarks light and full of humor and his audience happy.

The rest of us were standing off to the side, next to the stage. Frank Reynolds of ABC came up to Deaver, Anderson, and me. "I thought you fellows would like to know that you're winning in North Carolina." We did not believe him at first, but he filled in the details. As soon as Reagan finished his remarks and left the stage, we headed for an office in the building and called North Carolina. It was true. He seemed to be on the way to a clear victory.

When the wheels of our chartered airliner lifted off the Wisconsin ground for the last time, it took a jubilant Reagan campaign party back to California. We were back in the race—for good. It was Reagan, with 52.4 percent to Ford's 45.9 percent and others 1.7 percent.

Two weeks later, on April 6, although we had scrubbed further campaigning in Wisconsin, Reagan got a respectable 44.3 percent of the vote. Important, but little noticed at the time, was the fact he had done very well with Democratic crossover voters in the blue-collar industrial cities south of Milwaukee. (In a crossover state, Democrats can vote for Republicans and vice versa.) It was a sign of the Reagan coalition to come four years later.

Back in California, we set to work on the draft of the nationwide television speech, March 31. The time had been cleared with NBC. Matt Lawson, who had been doing television and radio interview advances during the primaries (and who met his future wife, Mary, when she was a Reagan volunteer in Tampa), recommended a Los Angeles production team for the taping of the speech on the morning of the thirty-first. Ron Phillips, Bruce McGee, and their crew and a studio were engaged. After Governor Reagan worked over the draft I had taken him, we set about to have it put on the TelePrompTer. The producers wanted to produce the speech in short tapings, about one or two minutes each. On the day of the taping, it was clear this was not going to work for Ronald Reagan. He was used to working straight through, breaking only for technical problems. He was right, as it turned out.

The speech embodied virtually all the themes Ronald Reagan had been stressing that winter and spring: inflation, overregulation, détente, the Panama Canal, Soviet arms growth. About inflation and unemployment, he said, "Ending inflation is the only long-range and lasting answer to the problem of unemployment. The Washington establishment is *not* the answer. It's the problem. Its tax policies, its harassing regulation, its confiscation of investment capital to pay for its deficits keeps business and industry from expanding to meet your needs and to provide the jobs we all need."

He reviewed again his record as governor in California, saying, "In those eight years, most of us never lost the feeling that we were there representing the people against what Cicero called 'the arrogance of officialdom.' We had a kind of watchword we used on each other: 'When we begin thinking of government as *we* instead of *they*, we've been here too long.' "

Another theme, along with these, presaged his 1980 campaign and, indeed, the themes of his presidency: "I believe that what we did in California *can* be done in Washington if government will have faith in the people and let them bring their common sense to bear on the problems bureaucracy hasn't solved. I believe in the people."

The transfer plan was no longer an issue that put Ronald Reagan on the defensive, but it was one that was philosophically dear to him and that he did not want to leave out: "The truth is, Washington has taken over functions that don't truly belong to it. In almost every case it has been a failure. Understand, I am speaking of those programs which logically should be administered at state and local levels."

Henry Kissinger's pessimism about American willpower—the real key to voter discontent with Ford's secretary of state—was the subject of this Reagan statement: "Dr. Kissinger is quoted as saying he thinks of the United States as Athens and the Soviet Union as Sparta. 'The day of the United States is past and today is the day of the Soviet Union.' And, he added, 'My job as secretary of state is to negotiate the most acceptable second-best position available.' "

Reagan then observed, "Ask the people of Latvia, Estonia, Lithuania, Czechoslovakia, Poland, Hungary, and all the others—East Germany, Bulgaria, Rumania—ask them, what is it like to live in a world where the Soviet Union is Number One? I don't want to live in that kind of world, and I don't think you do, either."

It was Reagan at his oratorical best. He had risen above the skirmishes of the primaries and spoken right to his own national constituency. Although Ford and his campaign strategists had many party leaders in their corner and Ford had seemingly come from behind to win the two toughest early primaries, he still did not have Reagan's devoted national following. Reagan's constituency responded to his address. Lyn Nofziger, ever mindful of the importance of what followed a televised political address, insisted on a strongly worded appeal for funds following Reagan's remarks. It paid off. Within a few days the return from the speech had climbed to $1.25 million. It was enough to carry us through to the late primaries and to the caucus states, when the demographics strongly favored Reagan.

Round One was over.

5

"A Shining City on the Hill"

WHEN JOHN SEARS recommended that Ronald Reagan abandon his Wisconsin campaign to save enough money to do a nationwide television speech, he knew there were risks involved. Reagan's Wisconsin volunteers would be upset. They were. They pleaded with the national headquarters to keep their campaign going. Wisconsin was a crossover state. George Wallace's campaign had been fading rapidly since his Florida defeat at the hands of Jimmy Carter, and the conservative Wallace had been a strong second in the Wisconsin Democratic primary in 1972.

In the Republican primary in Wisconsin, delegates are apportioned by congressional district to the presidential candidate who wins the district. Dave Keene, the Reagan coordinator for the state, was convinced we could take three or four congressional districts. The trouble was that we did not have enough money to conduct a poll in Wisconsin to determine which districts to target. Left to guesswork, we thought it better to pull out than to take chances with the trickle of cash then available to the campaign. The Federal Election Commission, as a result of the Supreme Court's ruling, had to stop issuing matching funds on March 22. Approximately $1.5 million was due the Reagan campaign at that time; we had debts of about $2 million.

The other risk involved in the decision to pull out of Wisconsin had potentially greater consequences. The decision had been made on the assumption that we would be able to clear a half-hour of time on one of the three television networks.

It had been decided not to renew the contracts of Treleaven and the advertising agency, which expired at the end of March. Because I had several years of advertising agency experience, I was asked to take on the job of coordinating with television directors and producers who would be engaged to tape Governor Reagan's nationwide speech and with Ruth Jones, the seasoned professional in New York who had been doing our media buying from the beginning.

The morning after we returned to Los Angeles from the North Carolina–Wisconsin trip, I talked with Ruth Jones and with Loren Smith, the Citizens for Reagan legal counsel. Ruth called the networks. All three balked. Their reluctance had nothing to do with political bias. It was a matter of revenue. A network can sell a half-hour's commercial time as "spots" for a good deal more, in the aggregate, than they can as a "bulk" unit.

Jones and Smith worked furiously for several days, Ruth rushing across Manhattan several times on short notice to plead with network executives. Governor Reagan himself was enlisted to send telegrams to the heads of each of the networks, asking them to grant him the time "in the interest of fairness." Finally, NBC, which had a low-rated show on the 10:30 P.M. slot on Tuesdays, agreed.

The success of the March 30 speech, with its strong appeal for funds tagged on at the end (a "beggar," in political parlance), led us to talk immediately about a follow-up broadcast or even a series of them. At the same time, we decided to edit short excerpts from the speech to use as television commercials. Within days, Ruth Jones was able to offer them to the various Reagan state committees.

The question of a follow-up speech was not easily answered. Throughout the winter, Governor Reagan, remembering his pulling-power on television from the 1964 Goldwater speech, had wanted to go on the air himself. The campaign high command had resisted. When Sears had finally proposed the speech strategy in that Racine hotel room, it took little time to convince Reagan. On the other hand, he did not want to wear out his welcome with his constituency. Another full-length television speech too soon might not be productive. Instead, we decided on a five-minute speech, exclusively about national defense, emphasizing the growing disparity between Soviet and U.S. strategic capabilities.

Martin Anderson and I met with two defense experts, Sam Cohen, then with a subsidiary of the Rand Corporation (and the man generally credited with the concept of the neutron weapon), and William Van Cleave, who was with the advanced international studies school at the University of Southern California. Van Cleave had been a member of Nixon's "B" team, which had critically analyzed the SALT I agreement.

Their thorough briefing gave us the necessary foundation for developing a draft for Governor Reagan to work from. They even suggested some props: scale models of U.S. and Soviet missiles. Although Reagan felt that props tended to be distracting in a television speech, when he saw these models, which effectively conveyed the potency of the Soviet arsenal and the relative modesty of ours, he decided to use them. This address aired on CBS on April 28. It raised another $250,000.

For both television speeches we took care to make the sets similar to Governor Reagan's own office. We brought in many items from his office: books, bookends, the leather jelly-bean container, an antique perpetual calendar. One item became something of a trademark in all his subsequent television addresses that I can recall (in fact, it was there in its customary place in late July 1981 when *President* Reagan gave the address that clinched the vote for his tax-cut program). That item was a photo of his wife. It was placed on a table behind his desk so that the viewer would see it as the camera panned across the room and moved to its first close-up of him. This photo of Nancy Reagan was taken at their ranch. In it she is wearing a blue leather jacket, her arms folded. She looks out with a soft, warm, but confident smile. Her picture close at hand symbolized the closeness of their relationship.

If the events of late March 1976—the North Carolina primary and the thirty-minute television speech—had put the brakes on Ronald Reagan's decline, April and the first half of May were to see him move into the lead for the presidential nomination.

At first glance it might not have looked as if it would turn out that way. On April 6, the same day Ford was winning Wisconsin's forty-five delegates (Reagan had, indeed, received many blue-collar Democratic votes but not enough in any one congressional district to win it), the Reagan campaign was bypassing the New York primary. Sears had reasoned that to contest New York, with Nelson Rockefeller still in command of the party there, would take a large amount of money that was not available and that the risks would be too great even if it were. Instead, Sears intended to go back later to negotiate for some delegates. The same reasoning was applied to Pennsylvania, which had its primary on April 27—the watershed primary for the Democrats, the showdown between Carter and Senator Henry ("Scoop") Jackson.

Initially, it had been decided to treat Ohio and New Jersey the same as New York and Pennsylvania, but the feeling was not unanimous among Sears and his regional field coordinators. The Reagans, Deaver, and others on the traveling staff believed we had a chance in these two states. This view prevailed, and there was a last-minute scramble to qualify delegates in both states. On the campaign plane heading back from Wisconsin the night of the North Carolina primary, Ronald Reagan was interrupted in his victory celebration by the need to sign a stack of Ohio petitions that Sears managed to file in the nick of time so that we could field delegates in fifteen of the twenty-five Ohio districts, as well as a statewide slate. In New Jersey we were too late.

Right along, Sears had been pointing out to Reagan and the rest of us that April would be a comparatively light month. No one expected us to win in the states that were up, and the May primaries favored Reagan. Texas was the big one, on Saturday, May 1. It would be Texas's first presidential primary. Like Wisconsin, it would permit voters to cross party lines. More important, it was being held at a different time from state and legislative primaries. This was of major importance to the Reagan campaign.

In state elections, Texans still vote overwhelmingly Democratic, but being for the most part conservatives, they could go for a conservative Republican for president. With the presidential primary on a different day from the state and legislative primary, Reagan's followers were not presented with the unenviable task of asking Democrats to set aside party loyalty. This way, they would appeal to Democrats to vote on presidential primary day for the candidate most likely to be closest to their own thinking—Ronald Reagan.

Reagan's Texas campaign leaders—Ray Barnhart, Ernie Angelo, Jimmy Lyon, and others—were enthusiastic about our chances. Victory seemed to be in the air. Local advertising agencies were engaged to create television and radio spots beamed directly to conservative Texas Democrats, inviting them to cross over.

Texas had always given Ronald Reagan a rousing reception, both as governor of California and as a private citizen. His themes of individualism, self-reliance, and patriotism brought whoops of approval from Texas audiences whenever he spoke. If anything, the reception was louder and more enthusiastic now than ever before.

The Panama Canal became a key issue in Texas, helped along by unexpected events. At one point, testimony from a congressional committee hearing made the news when Ambassador Ellsworth Bunker, head of the U.S. negotiating team in Panama, told the committee that he had direct orders from Ford to negotiate a turnover of the Canal Zone and ultimately the canal itself over a period of time. This was just what Reagan had been warning about for months. Unfortunately for Ford, Bunker's testimony seemed to contradict a Ford press conference statement in Dallas a few days earlier. Ford had said rather emphatically that the United States would not relinquish its defense or operating rights of the canal. White House efforts at clarification seemed to make matters worse, and Reagan kept pressing on this and the other issues that he had been emphasizing.

On election day, the Reagan strategy worked. Large numbers of Democrats crossed over, adding to Reagan's argument that he could appeal across party lines and thus broaden the Republican base.

While the Texas campaign was looking good, we had to squeeze our budget wherever possible. Back in late March, when a visit to Virginia was deemed essential because we expected to get most or all of the state's delegates, it had been decided to fly Governor Reagan from Los Angeles to Richmond, visit three receptions, have him address a large dinner, and then fly home again the same night, thus saving the cost of hotel rooms for the traveling party.

Because of the money shortage, we dropped the chartered 727, flew into Texas on commercial flights, and then boarded a propeller-driven airliner pulled out of retirement by Texas International Airlines. Altogether, the Reagan party puddle-jumped this way all over the Lone Star State for a total of seven days in April.

One advantage of going to and from California was that it was easy to drop in on other western and southwestern states on the way. Visits were made to several with upcoming primaries or delegate-selecting state conventions, including Colorado, New Mexico, Wyoming, Idaho, and Washington. In addition, during April, Reagan campaigned two days in Indiana and one each in Alabama and Georgia. All three would have their primaries on the same day, May 4, just three days after Texas.

We had expected to win in Texas, but I think none of us in the Reagan camp expected the enormousness of the victory: Ronald Reagan had won in every one of Texas's twenty-four congressional districts and had taken all ninety-six delegates.

The campaign party was in Indianapolis when the news came in. Paul Laxalt had flown out from Washington. Sears was there. So was Jimmy Stewart, who, along with other Hollywood notables such as Lloyd Nolan, Efrem Zimbalist, and Ken Curtis, had given unstintingly of his time to campaign for his old friend.

Next morning, Senator Barry Goldwater was the guest on one of the Sunday network television panel shows. He was very critical of Reagan's stand on the Panama Canal. This was not the first, nor would it be the last, time he would voice this criticism. We all watched it in the Reagans' suite. The Reagans were puzzled and, I think, hurt because they had always considered Goldwater a good personal friend. Although the friendship was strained for a time, the problem resolved itself before long, and they again resumed their close ties.

The following Tuesday, despite that criticism from a fellow conservative, Ronald Reagan made a near-clean sweep of the day's three primaries, Indiana, Georgia, and Alabama. Of 139 delegates to be chosen that day, Reagan got 130 to Ford's 9. Now, for the first time, the Californian was in the lead in the race for national convention delegates, 313–241.

To add to the euphoria of the Reagan campaign (and the long faces in the Ford campaign), Rogers Morton, at Ford campaign headquarters in Washington, told reporters he was not "going to rearrange the deck furniture on the *Titanic*."

With West Virginia and Nebraska primaries coming up a week later and both of them closed to crossover voters, Ford strategists were beginning to say that Reagan could only win with the help of crossover Democrats, that he needed to win a "closed" primary to prove his popularity within his own party. They expected to win both states, although the Reagan forces in Nebraska had organized early and well under a volunteer cadre led by Milan Bish, and we knew from the response that Reagan got to his criticism of the government's embargo on grain sales to the Soviet Union the previous year that he would probably do well in Nebraska. Primary day, May 11, produced a split. Ford won West Virginia with 57 percent; Reagan took Nebraska convincingly, with 55 percent, putting to rest the argument that he could not win a closed primary.

A week later would come a big one—Michigan. By now, Ford was seen as having to win his home state or he would be finished. For Reagan, on the other hand, there was the tantalizing possibility of pulling in crossover Democrats. (Wallace had carried the Democratic primary in 1972, although partly with the help of Republicans crossing over.)

If we threw all our resources into Michigan and did not do well, Sears reasoned, the perception would be that Reagan was slipping and that Ford had rallied his constituency and had the momentum with him. A strategic tug-of-war between Sears and the national headquarters on the one hand, and some of the conservative Reagan Michigan cadres on the other, ensued. Meanwhile, the Ford forces took no chances. The Republican establishment in the state, from Governor William Milliken on down, turned out in force to support the Ford effort. Ford himself did an old-fashioned whistle-stop train trip through the state to campaign on a frank native-son basis.

The money situation made a full-scale Reagan effort in Ford's home state virtually an impossibility. It was decided that the governor would go into the state for little more than a day. Meanwhile, we threw as much television and radio money as we could muster into increased schedules there. Reagan's cutting issues worked for conservative Republicans and pulled many Democrats over on primary day, but Ford had effectively turned it into a native-son popularity contest on his own turf and pulled back into the fold large numbers of Republicans who had apparently voted for Wallace in 1972 not on the issues but to play hob with the Democratic primary. The final results gave Ford 65 percent to Reagan's 34 percent (Ford got fifty-five delegates; Reagan, twenty-nine).

On the same day, Ford took all forty-three Maryland delegates in a primary not contested by the Reagan campaign. Ford's slide had been arrested and the delegate count was getting now nearly even.

From mid-April on, the Reagan traveling squad had changed its composition. With the added duties involved in coordinating the campaign's advertising, I began spending more days in Los Angeles than on the road with the Reagans and their party. Marty Anderson continued with the issues work on the traveling team, and we talked two or three times a day. In fact, I was still drafting daily inserts for Governor Reagan's stump speeches, after conferring with Marty and having our research people in Washington provide the necessary background material. Thanks to telecopiers, I was able to send Marty the one-page inserts each day when the team made its final stop for the night. He would present this to the governor for his use—or modification—the next day.

Lyn Nofziger dropped off the traveling squad at about the same time to take on the major job of organizing the state of California for the big winner-take-all primary in June. Jim Lake took his place as traveling press secretary.

A week after the Michigan primary there would be a record number of primaries—six in one day, May 25. A total of 176 delegates would be contested in Arkansas, Idaho, Kentucky, Nevada, Oregon, and Tennessee.

Just prior to the big day, Nelson Rockefeller played a card in Ford's favor: the New York delegation, heretofore formally "uncommitted," decided to give Ford 119 of its 154 delegates. In Pennsylvania (through no coincidence) 88 members of the 103-member delegation voted for a resolution in support of Ford. Despite this, Sears still expected there would be quite a lot of negotiating room with these delegations. Still, this support for Ford came at a critical moment.

On the twenty-fifth, Reagan carried Arkansas, Idaho, and Nevada by more than 60 percent of the vote in each. He came close to upsetting Ford in Oregon, losing with 48 percent and getting fourteen of the thirty delegates. Kentucky and Tennessee did not go as well as we had expected. Former Kentucky Governor Louie B. Nunn had already successfully led a Reagan state convention effort that had garnered twenty-seven of the state's thirty-seven delegates. The primary was being held (a closed one, with no crossovers), in effect, to instruct those delegates on whom to vote for on the first ballot. We went into Louisville and surrounding areas, and Reagan campaigned hard, but Ford carried the state with 51 percent. In Tennessee, while Reagan won a majority of the delegates (twenty-two of forty-three), Ford clung to a tiny popular vote lead to win that aspect of the contest. Not surprisingly, but maddeningly, the headline out of Tennessee was that Ford was the winner. A chance comment by Reagan that the TVA had grown well beyond its original purpose and was competing with private enterprise had been seized upon by the Ford forces. As much as they could, they made it seem as if Reagan had repeated Goldwater's 1964 idea of selling off TVA to private enterprise. This last-minute flap no doubt cost Reagan votes at a time when he badly needed them.

The primary season had only two weeks to go. All but two of those days, scheduled for Ohio, would keep the Reagan campaign in California. Reagan "had" to win his home state, just as Ford had "had" to win Michigan. California was a big prize: 167 delegates and it was winner take all. Ford's strategists persuaded him to campaign in California in order to force Reagan to concentrate much of his energy there. Meanwhile, Spencer and the other Ford strategists were banking on New Jersey, where Reagan was not on the ballot and there were 67 delegates to be won. (A number of key Reagan supporters continued to criticize Sears's failure to contest New Jersey and his decision to field only a partial campaign in Ohio.)

Meanwhile, three smaller primaries were held on Tuesday, June 1. Reagan took Montana, while Ford won in Rhode Island and South Dakota.

All the polls showed Reagan in a strong lead in California, but Nofziger was not taking any chances. He had organized the state thoroughly, with battalions of volunteers and phone banks. There was as much broadcast advertising as the budget and the federal spending limits would allow. Going into the final week, Mervin Field's California poll showed Reagan ahead by 24 points (56 percent to 32 percent).

Then, on Wednesday, the second, something happened that at first looked to the press and the Ford campaign as if it might throw Reagan into a tailspin. Rhodesia at the time was in the grips of intensive guerrilla warfare, with no end in sight. Appearing before the Sacramento Press Club, Reagan was asked how the United States could help guarantee peace there. Would he send in troops or observers?

The question had not come up recently. Back in late April, when the Reagan party was in Georgia campaigning, Marty Anderson had telephoned me from Atlanta. He told me the governor had been questioned about Rhodesia that day, that he said we should use our good offices to try to help achieve peace there, but that he did not offer anything specific to back it up. Ed Noble, a strong Reagan supporter in Atlanta, had suggested they call Richard Allen for some ideas on this. This was to be Allen's first involvement with the Reagan operation. Marty had called him and was now calling me to ask me to talk with Allen the next morning to work up a position paper. I did, and found Allen's ideas sensible. He suggested that since the British were the residual constitutional authority in Rhodesia, it should be up to them to make any peace initiatives. If they did and then asked us to assist them in some way, we should give serious study to such a request. We talked over the language and edited it. (He had sent me a copy over the telecopier; he was in Washington, and I was in Los Angeles.) Then I telephoned Marty and sent him the final version. He told me later that the governor liked it and would develop his platform statement from it.

Rhodesia had not come up often in the weeks since, so that when it was raised in Sacramento, it was something of a surprise. Governor Reagan covered the idea of U.S. helpfulness but did not discuss the role of the British. It became what we called a "traveling question," wherein his answer leads the journalist to another question, then another, and so on. Reagan had indicated that we might go in as part of a UN peacekeeping mission, as in the Middle East. He had been talking about a token force. When pressed on the token force, he said he did not think it would be needed. "Would you, if you had to?" the newsman asked. Reagan replied that if we had pledged to help, he assumed we would, but he emphasized that in the Middle East such help had not involved us in a war and that he did not think it would in this instance either.

We did not think much of the matter at first, since it did not differ greatly from Reagan's earlier statements on the subject. In any case, he stated it all hypothetically, not as a proposal. Nevertheless, we underestimated the parochial factor. We used to say of the Washington press, "If it didn't happen in Washington, it didn't happen," and the Sacramento news people treated this one the same way, like a brand new issue.

It made big headlines in California, and the Ford people did not lose a minute capitalizing on it. Rogers Morton sent off a salvo questioning Reagan's "qualifications" for the job. Elliott Richardson, in California at the time, said, "This kind of thinking is frightening." The next day, as the campaign made its way back down the coast, Governor Reagan figured it would be brought up at each stop, so he included remarks about the issue. Anything he did would have kept the story alive. The Ford people loved it. They quickly scrapped the relatively bland television spots they had been running, produced a new one that said that Reagan *would* send troops to Rhodesia and ended with the line "When you vote Tuesday, remember: *Governor* Ronald Reagan couldn't start a war. *President* Ronald Reagan could."

Nofziger thought the Ford campaign had gone too far. He asked Wirthlin, who was doing nightly tracking polls of California voters to monitor last-minute changes in opinion, to call him the minute any slippage or backlash turned up. The backlash did, within twenty-four hours of the airing of the Ford commercials. Nofziger, who has both a good

sense of humor and an occasional flare for the dramatic, hit upon an audacious tactic. He set up a videotape camera and taped one of the new
Ford spots right off the television set. He put that line about starting a
war in to a new Reagan spot, urging voters to watch for the Ford spots.
He was on target. The backlash grew. In addition, a last-minute maneu-
ver by Ford supporters in the legislature to abandon the winner-take-all
aspect of the primary and apportion the delegates by popular vote failed
in a vote in the Republican caucus in the state senate.

The Reagans went to Ohio for most of the weekend, campaigning in
five major cities. He ended up with 45 percent of the popular vote there
the following Tuesday, compared with Ford's 55 percent. Reagan got
nine Ohio delegates from the brief, lightly funded campaign. For
months afterward, Reagan partisans debated among themselves what
would have happened had a full commitment been made in Ohio.

On Tuesday, Reagan swamped Ford in California, 66 percent to 34
percent. However, in New Jersey, where Ford went unchallenged, he
picked up all of the delegates. The day's total delegate count was 176 for
Reagan and 155 for Ford. The overall count toward the convention in
Kansas City was neck-and-neck by most tallies. More than two months
remained before the Republican National Convention in Kansas City,
where it would take 1,130 delegates to secure the nomination.

The evening of the California primary, the Reagans met with many
of their closest, oldest friends and some members of the senior staff and
their wives for cocktails and dinner at the home of friends and then went
on to a huge victory celebration at Los Angeles's Ambassador Hotel.

The next day the Reagans began a three-day vacation at home that
would end that Friday evening with a flight to Springfield, Missouri. The
Missouri state convention would pick its delegates on Saturday, the
twelfth, and we had a chance of getting them.

Meanwhile, the Reagan senior staff went on a two-day retreat to
Lake Tahoe to plan strategy for the ten state conventions still to come
and to discuss the hunts for individual delegates that Sears predicted
would be necessary. There were still four hundred delegates, at the
minimum, to be chosen or to state a candidate preference.

So far, Reagan had done better than Ford in the so-called caucus
states. This was owing partly to the intensity of dedication of Reagan
volunteers in most states and partly to the widespread belief by party organizations (most of which favored Ford) that Ford would eliminate
Reagan fairly early. Thus, they had not done as much grass-roots organizing as had the Reagan campaign.

This was nowhere better demonstrated than in Missouri. Ford was
persuaded to fly in to address the state convention. Nineteen at-large
delegates were to be chosen. Reagan was there, meeting with delegates

singly and in small groups. The Reagan grass-roots volunteers were there, too, in strength. Reagan got eighteen of the nineteen delegates that day.

The two campaigns began settling into a sort of political equivalent of hand-to-hand combat, with one or the other of the candidates present at a state caucus nearly every weekend for the next several weeks, personally leading his "troops." On June 19, Reagan flew to Des Moines for the Iowa convention. The Ford forces had expected to do well, but deft maneuvering by the Reagan field people kept them to a near-even split of the delegation (nineteen to seventeen). The same day, Reagan took the Washington state delegation (thirty-one to seven) and Ford won thirteen of Delaware's seventeen (four were uncommitted).

A sampling of headlines from the second half of June reflects the intensity and closeness of the contest:

FORD IN TROUBLE AS STATES PICK 240 MORE DELEGATES
REAGAN, FORD SCRAMBLE FOR 36 IOWA DELEGATES
GOP DELEGATE SWEEPSTAKES SEEN ENDING IN DEAD HEAT
REAGAN RAIDING FORD'S DELEGATES
FORD DELEGATE LEAD SLIPS, IS EXPECTED TO DROP TO 27
REAGAN CLOSING GAP STILL FURTHER

On Tuesday evening, July 6, Ronald Reagan gave another half-hour television speech, broadcast on the ABC network. This time the purpose was not to raise money to keep the campaign alive, although we did ask for money at the end of the speech and the broadcast paid for itself as a result. Instead, the main purpose was to address millions in order to persuade a few hundred uncommitted or yet-to-be-selected Republican delegates that Ronald Reagan could win in November. The themes were designed for the electorate in general, not just Republicans. He talked of his vision of a more responsible, less intrusive government; restored American self-respect; and the hopes of minorities. He reviewed some of his California record, highlighting aspects of it that he thought would best relate to how he would approach the presidency.

Rogers Morton had recently recruited James A. Baker, then an undersecretary of commerce and today President Reagan's White House chief of staff, to shape up the Ford delegate-hunting operation. As Jim Baker's work began to take effect, the weekly caucuses began to be more and more exercises in making trade-offs. The caucus process finally came to an end on July 17, with Reagan taking all of the Utah delegates and Ford getting all of Connecticut's. The overall delegate count stood at Ford 1,102, Reagan 1,063, with 94 uncommitted, according to the *New York Times*. (None of the published tallies could be considered "hard" at that point.)

In the Reagan camp we were beginning to worry that many of the national political reporters would soon conclude that Ford had it wrapped up, despite the fluidity of the uncommitted-delegate count. Sears kept alluding to "softness" among several Ford delegate groups and hoped to make some breaks in the New York, Pennsylvania, and New Jersey delegations. At the beginning of the week following the final caucuses he even told reporters that Reagan would go into the national convention with 1,140 delegates, 10 more than needed for the nomination. Sears knew he could sustain this claim for only a short time without providing concrete evidence.

Meanwhile, we had slippage problems in the South. Harry Dent, once Nixon's political adviser in the White House and now a Columbia, South Carolina, lawyer who had signed on with the Ford campaign as southern coordinator, had been working furiously to have the Mississippi delegation go for Ford.

Mississippi, generally believed to be solid for Reagan, had declared that it would go to the convention uncommitted and would vote by the unit rule. That is, whoever got a majority of the delegation in caucus would get all the votes. There were thirty delegates but also thirty alternates, and each of the sixty persons had half a vote in the caucus. Leading the delegation was Clarke Reed, for some years a leading Republican in the South and party chairman in Mississippi.

The tall, soft-spoken, silver-haired Reed had been one of Bob Walker's regular contacts during his forays from Sacramento in 1974, and Reed had been brought into the early, tentative candidacy-planning discussions by the Reagan group in early 1975. Further, Reed had promised David Keene, the Reagan coordinator for the region, that he would go for Reagan.

This commitment masked two problems. The previous fall, Gil Carmichael had run an unexpectedly strong race for governor and was now seen as an emerging power in the Republican party in Mississippi. Carmichael was also solidly for Ford. (Ironically, Reagan had gone to Jackson in the fall of 1975 to campaign for Carmichael at Reed's request.) The other problem was that Reed thought the nomination would be sewed up by one candidate or the other well before the convention. Thus, he did not pay as close attention to the composition of the state delegation as he might have.

Carmichael's candidacy for governor had attracted some new party workers, whose enthusiasm Reed wanted to maintain, so Reed scheduled the state convention for early April to choose the delegation. The regulars were all there, but many of the newcomers were added to the delegation, especially as alternates. Many of these, as it turned out later, favored Ford.

Keene and Billy Mounger, the Reagan chairman in Mississippi, on the one side, and Dent and Carmichael, on the other, began to tug and pull at the delegation. White House invitations to Mississippi delegates flew thick and fast. Reagan went to the state to meet with the delegation. We knew that if Mississippi went over to Ford before the convention, it would be a serious blow to Reagan's candidacy, for virtually all the news media were counting Mississippi in the Reagan column in their tallies. Without it, there would be no plausible way for Sears to claim enough votes for a first-ballot victory.

Meanwhile, very quietly, Sears and Senator Laxalt were looking for a vice-presidential candidate for Reagan. Not long after the California primary, Governor Reagan had asked them to bring him recommendations. He liked the idea of having his choice made (at least privately) before he got to the convention.

At one point, Sears met with William Ruckelshaus, the former deputy attorney general who had resigned back in 1973 on the night of Nixon's famous "Saturday Night Massacre." Ruckelshaus, from Indiana, was a Catholic, and there was reason to believe that Carter's support among Catholic voters was soft. But Ruckelshaus was also thought by conservatives to represent the most liberal wing of the party. There was no follow-up meeting, however, and Reagan was unaware at the time that Sears had met with Ruckelshaus to discuss the vice-presidency.

As it became clear to Sears that the process of prying delegates loose one by one would not in itself produce a large enough vote count for us going into the convention, he began to evolve a northeastern strategy. With Reagan's strength lying in the West, Southwest, and South, a running mate from the Northeast would offer him a chance in November to challenge Carter seriously in what would otherwise be Democratic territory. Furthermore, it had the chance of pulling over some northeastern delegates for the upcoming convention.

Sears had asked Reagan to begin making telephone calls to individual delegates from northeastern states. In fact, a daily checklist was prepared, and Governor Reagan would sit in his study at home or at the ranch for hours at a time making the delegate calls. A short visit was also scheduled to Delaware, New Jersey, and Pennsylvania. While it did not produce a rush of delegates to Reagan, it probably helped keep the uncommitted ones in that column.

Sears talked with Laxalt about the running-mate selection. If the northeastern strategy made sense, when you got to actual names, the list kept narrowing to one: Senator Richard Schweiker of Pennsylvania. Sears also went over his strategy (for some time not getting into the matter of names) with some of his political strategists at the national headquarters (Keene, Charlie Black, Andy Carter). Finally, Laxalt and

Sears decided to contact Schweiker. A meeting was arranged for Tuesday, July 20. They presented the case to him. He called back the next day to say he would be willing to go to Los Angeles to talk with Reagan about it. (They had told him that Reagan himself did not know they were meeting with him.)

Sears flew ahead to present the case to Reagan. Although Schweiker had a reputation in the party as liberal, it was only partly deserved. Sears pointed out that on many issues—abortion, gun control, school prayer, among others—Schweiker and Reagan would see eye to eye. Laxalt, who had been Schweiker's seat mate in the Senate, personally liked him and that counted heavily with Reagan.

The next day, July 24, Schweiker was at Reagan's home for lunch and what turned out to be a six-hour meeting. Their personal "chemistry" was right almost from the moment they met. After they had talked for some time, Reagan asked Schweiker to be his running mate. Schweiker agreed, and the remainder of the meeting was spent discussing ways and means of announcing their decision.

Sears said it had to be done quickly. Late that week rumors had surfaced that one of the networks was going to declare flatly that Ford had the votes for a first-ballot victory. Sears knew his 1,140-vote claim could not be left dangling much longer. Furthermore, with no more caucuses between then and the convention in mid-August, the press would be restless and looking for movement of any kind. It was time for "politics is motion." The Schweiker selection process up to then was known only to the two men, their wives, Sears, Laxalt, and a few of us on the senior staff. The secret could not hold for long.

If the announcement were made the following Monday, it would completely stop the drift of the press toward declaring a Ford victory. All the action would move to Reagan. Yet, some risks—all of which had been weighed—would be incurred by making the announcement.

It was agreed Reagan would make a statement to the press in Los Angeles at nine o'clock Monday morning. Schweiker would hold a press conference in the caucus room of the Russell Senate Office Building in Washington on Monday afternoon. Beginning Sunday evening, a few key conservatives, especially in the South, would be called by Reagan, Laxalt, and Keene.

At one point, Keene had said, "If we can keep our southern delegates from breaking ranks for the first forty-eight hours, I think we'll be all right."

The worst trouble came in Mississippi. Reed saw the choice of Schweiker as ticket-splitting, something he had long opposed. The next forty-eight hours saw heavy pressure placed by the Ford forces to get Reed to cross over (thus, presumably breaking the delegation that way, too). Keene argued intensely, trying to buy time to allow things to cool off.

A corresponding pickup of delegates in the Northeast was not materializing. Drew Lewis, leader of the Pennsylvania delegation and today secretary of transportation, was a close personal friend of Schweiker's, but on being told the news by Schweiker, he said he would have to stick by his commitment to support Ford. Lewis was the key to any major break in the Pennsylvania delegation, so if he stuck, there would not be a break. Schweiker talked with him several times, but Lewis did not waver.

The shock of the announcement was beginning to wear off. Key southerners such as Governor James Edwards of South Carolina, now secretary of energy, and Senator Jesse Helms were still aboard.

Ford flew to Jackson that Friday, accepting an invitation to address the Mississippi delegation. The Ford strategists were undecided whether to press for a caucus vote at that time, still not sure they had the votes to prevail. Despite the fact that Reed had said often throughout June and July that Reagan's support in the South was softening (which some Reagan operatives saw as a wish being father to the deed), the hearts of a majority of the delegates still seemed to be with Reagan.

One benefit of the Schweiker selection, Sears said, would be that pressure would mount on Ford to choose his running mate. The Ford people had gone through an elaborate process of soliciting the top choices of several thousand Republican party leaders. The resulting list of a dozen or so names covered every point on the Republican spectrum. One name that Ford operatives (starting with Dent in the South) had been dangling for several weeks was that of Ronald Reagan. This apparently started as a ploy to soften Reagan support, the idea being that no one who supported such a ticket could be accused of "divisiveness" (that oft-heard 1976 word). Everyone would be off the hook. It also caused Reagan to have to deny the story. "I'm not interested," he would say. "Only the lead dog gets a change of scene."

Other things were happening in July. While all the delegate hunting was going on, Martin Anderson and I had been in touch with the platform drafters assigned by the Republican National Committee, especially John Meagher, a House committee minority counsel, who was organizing domestic and economic issues, and Richard Allen, who was doing the foreign-policy portion.

We had agreed within the Reagan campaign that the platform should probably be broad enough so that either candidate could run on it without the Democrats embarrassing him with it in the fall. Historically, candidates ran as close to their platforms as was comfortable, in any case. Still, we knew that Reagan delegates would want more than rhetorical pabulum. What we did not anticipate was that by late July some of the most ardent Reagan supporters would want to turn the platform into the political equivalent of a holy war.

In the late spring we had begun talking about the desirability of strengthening Governor Reagan's credentials internationally, should he become the nominee. We talked over the idea of sending Reagan emissaries to various capitals around the world to outline his views and to correct any misimpressions foreign leaders might have. "A fine idea," Sears said one day in late June, "but I don't see how we can afford it." So, Project Emissary, as it was called, turned out to be me riding around Washington in a taxicab calling on a number of ambassadors and other diplomats the week of the Schweiker announcement. France, Germany, Saudi Arabia, Argentina, Nicaragua (whose ambassador at the time was dean of the Washington diplomatic corps), Egypt, Brazil, Israel, the Republic of China, and the United Kingdom were among those visited.

That same week, although he did not know it at the time (and I am not sure I did), supply-side economics was entering Ronald Reagan's life. Jude Wanniski, then an editorial writer for the *Wall Street Journal*, called me and asked me to have dinner with him when I got to New York. Earlier that month, at Wanniski's urging, I had arranged for him to bring Bob Bartley, editorial-page editor of the *Journal*, to California, to have lunch with the Reagans; but it was largely a get-acquainted meeting, and Wanniski did not make supply-side economics a part of the discussion.

We met for dinner at the Palm on Thursday night, the twenty-ninth. Wanniski wanted Reagan to embrace the idea of across-the-board tax cuts in his campaign as an incentive for increased production. He talked about the Laffer curve (economist Arthur Laffer's now-famous illustration which demonstrates that taxes spur or depress human incentive and production, depending upon whether they are low or high).

Wanniski was writing a book, *The Way the World Works*. He said he had uncovered some elemental truths. One of them was that most people operate most of the time in what they believe to be their self-interest. I thought this was stating the obvious and told him so. What I did not see at the time was the link between this and the likely effect of major across-the-board tax cuts. I also could not envision Ronald Reagan opening up a broad new front of economic argumentation at this late date in the campaign. The issue now was delegates, I said. Any uncommitteds left to be wooed and any Ford delegates to be pried loose would be gotten on the basis of a conclusion that Reagan had the better chance of winning in November, not on the basis of some arcane new tax scheme. I sensed that Jude was disappointed in my failure to leap at his ideas with enthusiasm. As it turned out, however, I underestimated his tenacity.

Shortly after Gerald Ford's visit to Mississippi, Reagan and Schweiker began a tour through several southern states (South Carolina, Virginia, Alabama, Mississippi) and West Virginia so that delegates could meet Schweiker and question him in person. The tour ended in Jackson, August 4. By now, the Schweiker announcement was ten days old, and much of the initial shock had worn off. Reagan told the delegates that in picking Schweiker he was being true to his belief that running mates should be philosophically compatible. Schweiker had satisfied Reagan that first day they met that he would be a team player so long as he could speak his mind in the internal councils of the Reagan organization—a condition in accord with the way Reagan had worked with his cabinet in Sacramento.

The Mississippi delegation decided to remain uncommitted, although behind-the-scenes maneuvering by both sides did not let up.

Reagan and Schweiker went on to Pennsylvania, New Jersey, and New York and managed to get nine or ten delegates, mostly from Pennsylvania.

Meanwhile, on the last weekend in July, a group of southern conservatives met in Atlanta to discuss the platform, with some Reagan staff members in attendance. The southerners wanted a very strong platform so as to force a major ideological battle on the convention floor. They believed that the majority of the delegates would be conservative (which was true) and that only the party hierarchy, controlled by the Ford campaign, stood in the way of the convention expressing its true feelings.

During late July Sears had been carefully studying procedural challenges that might force the hand of the Ford organization. He worried that an ideological battle could lead to fratricidal warfare in the party and sure defeat in November, with Reagan and his supporters getting the blame. Our people did not consider the Atlanta session as much more than a venting of frustrations. We should have taken it more seriously.

On the weekend of August 7–8, Martin Anderson was scheduled to fly to Kansas City and Ed Meese was taking leave from his law practice and university teaching to join him. They would represent the Reagan campaign at Platform Committee hearings beginning Monday, and I was to join them later in the week.

Sunday evening Anderson telephoned to say that Senator Helms had just called a meeting of several dozen delegates (a sequel, as it turned out, to the Atlanta meeting) and that all hell was breaking loose over the platform. "It's wild here," he said. "You've got to get here. Two of us can't cover all this by ourselves." I flew to Kansas City the next day. He was right. The group Helms had called together was clearly not going to settle for the mild platform the drafters had brought to Kansas City. They wanted "red meat," as one of them put it.

Tom Ellis, who headed Helms's North Carolina delegation, and John East, then the North Carolina national committeeman and now a U.S. senator, became the principal spokesmen for what came to be called the Helms Group. Others who attended the many meetings we had with this group included Rich Williamson, Congressman Phil Crane's administrative assistant; our Texas leaders, Ernie Angelo, Ray Barnhart, and Jimmy Lyon; and Tom Curtis, former congressman from Missouri, a constitutional-law expert and, as it turned out, a Reagan stalwart on the Platform Committee.

By day, Meese, Anderson, and I took turns covering the various platform hearings and sitting on the stage of the Municipal Auditorium where the full Platform Committee was debating the various segments as hearings were finished and the drafts sent over.

By night, we found ourselves in the midst of meetings with the Helms Group, which kept pressing for a major platform showdown with the Ford forces.

Early in the week Senator James Buckley of New York announced that if his name were placed in nomination, he would not withdraw it. We were baffled by this move, although we soon learned that Crane had inspired it. Some of our strategists suspected that it had been done in order to force platform concessions from us, since any serious effort by Buckley would only drain delegates from Reagan. The other side saw it the other way, however, and Richard Rosenbaum, the New York party chairman, told Buckley that if he did not withdraw, he could expect no party support for reelection that fall. Buckley withdrew.

Sears, meanwhile, was unfolding the Reagan campaign strategy before the Rules Committee of the Republican National Committee. While it is standard practice in a presidential campaign for the "issues" people to belittle the role of the "political" people, and vice versa, both know they are indispensable, that there is a time to stress issues and a time to concentrate on political strategy and often a need to do both simultaneously. While those of us on the issues side of the campaign had thought that Sears's plan to fight the climactic battle with the Ford campaign over a procedural matter would hardly ignite the passions of our own delegates, we had to admit that a heated platform fight had high risks for the party's fortunes in November, whoever won.

During "platform week," the week before the actual convention,

Sears had been keeping up a steady barrage of criticism at Ford for not naming his running mate. He proposed to the Ford-dominated Rules Committee of the party that there be a change in the rules (Rule 16-C), to require announcement of vice-presidential candidates by all presidential candidates in advance of presidential nominations.

The Ford people thought that Sears just wanted the Ford campaign to share the presumed misery he was experiencing as a result of having persuaded Reagan to accept Schweiker. Not so. What Sears had in mind was to begin a stampede away from Ford. Since Ford had solicited recommendations from so many party leaders about his running mate, the rumor mill had been grinding at full speed for weeks. The list of names kept growing. It was somewhere around twenty. It included Ruckelshaus, John Connally, and Senators Buckley, Mark Hatfield, Howard Baker, and Charles Percy, among others. Sears had made the point to several of us that if Ford were forced to name his choice prior to the convention, he was going to make a lot of would-be vice-presidential candidates angry, and their followers along with them. Furthermore, the appearance of various names on the list began to draw fiery challenges from some of the delegations. Some delegates began to say that if so-and-so was going to be Ford's choice, Ford would have to do without their support. For example, at one point, a group of Ford delegates from Maine said they would abstain from voting on the first nominating ballot if Ford picked Connally, but Ford's Mississippi people favored Connally. Such was the potential misery for Ford.

Obviously, if Sears could force this issue, the Ford campaign just might unravel. The party Rules Committee predictably turned down the proposal. Sears would then take it to the *convention* Rules Committee (which also turned it down) and then to the floor the following week.

Although the move was a political one, there was an issue side to it, although not one that would stir the passions of many delegates. At its 1972 convention, the party had voted to create a special committee to propose reforms in the method by which vice-presidential candidates were to be chosen. This committee was not expected to bring any recommendations to the Kansas City convention, however, and Sears would fill the vacuum with his Rule 16-C.

The plan of the Helms people, to contest Ford on several issues fronts, was still very much alive. They felt they could begin forcing some of the issues at the full Platform Committee deliberations later in the week. They reasoned that the Platform Committee, which, like the convention, was split virtually fifty-fifty in terms of apparent candidate preference, was actually more conservative when it came to issues. They believed that if they could force a series of overtly conservative votes out of the committee, the process of cracking open the Ford campaign would have begun. Their plan was then to complete the process with a platform battle on the floor of the convention.

The discussions went on, including two "negotiating" luncheons in the mahogany-paneled grill room of the Radisson Muehlebach Hotel over champagne with Helms's deft, good-humored, and determined aides, Jim Lucier and John Carbaugh.

Even while we had been debating behind the scenes with the Helms Group, all of us on the Reagan side were working in the Platform Committee meetings to strengthen the platform in our candidate's favor. The Helms Group usually wanted more fiery language than we did, of course.

As the committee deliberated, off to the side of the stage Martin Anderson, Ed Meese, and I took turns manning the Reagan table, while Stan Ebner and Mike Duvall sat at the Ford table. Their operation was more sophisticated: they had a walkie-talkie link with Bill Timmons, the Ford convention director, who was directing things from his hotel room. In our case, whoever was at the table made decisions on the spot on behalf of the Reagan campaign and then passed them by way of memo to our key delegates on the committee.

Several senators and congressmen attended these plenary sessions of the Platform Committee, some to make comments on a single matter. Others stayed and pitched into the deliberations time and again. Congressman John Anderson was one of these. I recall that his manner when addressing committee members who asked questions or made comments from the Reagan perspective was quite condescending.

By the week's end Sears had agreed to develop a foreign-policy initiative. There were two reasons: to end the time-consuming deliberations with the Helms Group and to back up the 16-C strategy with one that, if we were successful on 16-C, would force a floor contest with a weakened Ford campaign and would probably go our way.

Saturday the backup initiative took form. Sears, Meese, Anderson, and I talked it over. We decided that it should omit a detailed recitation of foreign-policy issues, since that portion of the platform had already been improved during the course of the week. Instead, we hit on the idea of a thematic statement, "Morality in Foreign Policy," that would become a preamble to the foreign-policy section of the platform. It would mention no names, but it would be written in such a way as to be unacceptable by the other side, thus ensuring a second floor fight after our presumed victory on 16-C.

While most delegates, if asked, would almost certainly have said they liked Gerald Ford, whether or not they supported him, Secretary of State Henry Kissinger, the master of realpolitik, was widely unpopular at the grass-roots level in the party. "Morality in Foreign Policy" was aimed squarely at him.

Sunday was hot and clear. The Reagans arrived to a cheering reception and thousands of balloons at the Alameda Plaza Hotel in early afternoon. The Fords had arrived in town and gone to their headquarters hotel, the Crown Center. Governor Reagan visited several delegations. In the evening, the Reagans; the Schweikers; Dave Newhall, Schweiker's administrative assistant; Sears; Meese; Deaver; Nofziger; Martin Anderson; Lake; and I met in the Reagans' suite for dinner and a briefing. Sears covered the 16-C strategy, and Anderson, the foreign policy. Governor Reagan approved both. Late that evening, Meese, Anderson, and I left for a downtown hotel to meet for the last time with the Helms Group. We presented the new strategy, and they agreed with it in principle. We got back to the Alameda Plaza, exhausted, at two in the morning.

Monday, Anderson and I did the final editing on the "Morality in Foreign Policy" draft. I typed it on my portable in my room at the hotel. As agreed, I called Senator Helms and read it to him. He said it was fine but asked that we consider adding specific references to the Panama Canal issue and U.S. support for Taiwan. I told him we would take it up with the others. Marty and I took it down the hall to Sears's room, where most of the senior staff had gathered. We discussed the Helms additions, but the consensus was that we should keep it on as high a rhetorical level as possible and should leave detailed issues to the actual platform planks that had already been voted on.

The final statement squared with Ronald Reagan's positions. Part of it read, "Ours will be a foreign policy which recognizes that in international negotiations we must make no undue concessions; that in pursuing détente we must not grant unilateral favors with only the hope of getting future favors in return." Reagan had said as much before and would make similar statements many times in the future.

There was a favorable reference to Alexander Solzhenitsyn, whom Kissinger had counseled Ford not to receive when the Russian first came to the United States; there was a warning about the Helsinki agreement in relation to captive nations; and a veiled reference to the Panama Canal negotiations.

By now, lobbying by both sides over 16-C was feverish. The Ford forces were swarming over the Mississippi delegation, alternately trying to get all its votes or a compromise that would break the unit rule and give half the state's thirty votes to Reagan on 16-C and half to Ford. Clarke Reed, like the proverbial reed, bent in the wind, back and forth, wishing to displease neither side and thus frustrating both.

Harry Dent, playing the role of weaving spider, told the Mississippians that if 16-C passed, Ford could not consider Reagan as his running mate or even seek his advice on a choice. Thus, he revived the rumor that Reagan would take the second place on the ticket, causing Reagan, in his many visits to delegations, to deny repeatedly that he would consider the matter.

Finally, late Tuesday afternoon, the Mississippians caucused and voted. They went for the Ford position (that is, against 16-C) by thirty-one to twenty-eight. Having not voted to abandon the unit rule, this meant that all thirty votes that night would go into the Ford column on the issue.

Down in the bowels of the Alameda Plaza, Nofziger, the Reagan convention director, had assigned our issues-and-research unit two rooms. Annelise Anderson, Marty's wife and a scholar in her own right, organized the unit for us, using our two research assistants from Washington and several volunteer aides, including my teenage son Donald.

Marty and I were never in our office suite for long, because our duties usually took us to the upper floors, where the Reagans and the senior staff were housed. This left Annelise and the others to listen to the many special-issues groups that came seeking an audience and a sympathetic ear.

Rushing out of the office about noon that day, I bumped into Jude Wanniski, who pressed me to give him a few minutes. "Okay," I said, "but I'm late for a meeting." He proceeded to urge me again to get Reagan to make a statement in favor of major across-the-board tax cuts. He said that if Reagan would do so, he thought he could persuade Congressman Jack Kemp, who had espoused the tax-cut philosophy, to endorse Reagan. I had no idea whether he had talked to Kemp or not, and under the circumstances the idea again struck me as irrelevant. "I'm sorry, Jude," I said. "I'm sympathetic, but no sale," and rushed away. This did not daunt Wanniski, who, long after Kansas City, kept sending me materials and calling me periodically.

The 16-C lobbying kept up in Kemper Arena that night. Several of us were dispatched around the floor to buttonhole particular delegates. Some were Reagan delegates who did not seem to understand the importance of their vote to their candidate's chances. Others were suspicious about "reforms." Most did not see the rule change as a make-or-break issue. This was the flaw in the strategy. It had been incompletely sold, and as an intraparty issue, its very bloodlessness was working against us.

That afternoon there had begun to appear, in photocopy form, an article from the *Birmingham* (Alabama) *News* with the headline FORD WOULD WRITE OFF COTTON SOUTH. It was based on an interview with Rogers Morton in which he implied that in a general election most of

Ford's time would have to be spent outside the South because there was not much chance against Carter there.

Southern delegates were furious, especially Billy Mounger and some of the other Reagan partisans in the Mississippi delegation. As the delegates began to assemble on the floor (with the alternates in the galleries) for the evening's business, Mounger and Charles Pickering, who would soon replace Reed as state chairman, called for another caucus and another vote on 16-C.

At about that time, Sears, who was in the Reagan command-post trailer outside the arena, called Reed, who was with the delegation on the floor. Sears told him that every vote counted, that 16-C would decide the nomination, and that he wanted Reed to get the delegation to open the unit rule so that Reagan could get at least fourteen of the thirty votes when the roll call was taken on 16-C.

This puzzled Reed. Mounger had repeatedly told him that the Reagan campaign did not want to bypass the unit rule. Indeed, Dave Keene did not think they should and called Sears. He asked Sears if a handful of votes, at the expense of Mississippi's unit rule, would make the difference on the overall vote count on 16-C. (The roll call had begun and Mississippi had already passed while these discussions were taking place.) Sears said he could not guarantee that these votes would make the difference. Keene went back to the delegation and told it to stay with the unit rule. At about the time he did, the convention clerk began to go through the alphabet a second time, to pick up the states that had passed. When she got to Florida, its votes went against 16-C, insuring its defeat. Mississippi, for all the attention that had been paid it, did not, in the end, decide the nomination as both sides thought it would.

While many delegates understood the significance of the vote and knew that Ford would now be nominated, many did not or, if they did, still wanted to mount the make-or-break challenge.

The convention rules having been adopted, the convention's officers moved to the platform. When they got to the "Morality in Foreign Policy" amendment, it was clear the Ford forces had been told not to fight it. They had just won a crucial vote and had decided to swallow the pill, even if it tasted bitter. Congressman John Rhodes, chairman of the convention, called for a voice vote and quickly ruled that it had passed. Pandemonium broke out on the floor. Reagan's most intense partisans had realized that Rhodes was going to deny them the moment they had been waiting for.

I was standing near the North Carolina delegation at the time. Tom Ellis motioned me over excitedly. He was so hoarse I could barely hear him. "We've got petitions from seven delegations—enough under the rules to force a roll-call vote. We can win it big enough to stay in the ballgame. We want an okay to go for it." I stepped to the nearest phone, called Sears, and relayed the message. "Let's try it," I urged him. "What do we have to lose?" "Okay," he replied, but his answer sounded perfunctory. To him, the war had already been lost.

I raced back to Ellis to tell him to go ahead. He jumped up on his chair, waving at the podium and croaking as loudly as his hoarse voice would let him. The man next to him said that their microphone had gone dead. Ellis was waving at Rhodes like a signalman on a battleship—but got no response. In a few moments Rhodes announced that the platform had been adopted and the business of the convention that evening was concluded.

Afterward, recounting with a colleague the events of the last tumultuous hour or so (running up from the floor to the trailer at one point, not looking, I nearly bowled over nonagenarian Alf Landon, the party's 1936 standard-bearer), my friend, who had been in the trailer throughout the 16-C vote and after, said, "You know that one of our telephone lines is hooked into the podium. It couldn't have been long after you called in with the Ellis message that I heard one of our people answer a question on that podium telephone." "What did he say?" I asked. "Shut him off," was the reply.

We were never sure if this fragmentary conversation had actually alluded to Ellis's microphone. In any case, the battles, and indeed the war, had been lost.

The next morning, Governor Reagan's senior staff assembled in his suite as he was finishing breakfast. He said he would go, as planned, to talk to several delegations that day. He had already gotten several calls from key supporters, urging him to take the vice-presidential nomination if offered. Dick Schweiker, with all of us sitting there, offered to step down if it would help, but Reagan had not changed his mind. Unlike those who had been calling, Reagan said that since he had been critical of some of Ford's policies during the campaign, he could not get enthusiastic about the idea because both he and Ford would be constantly asked about their differences if they were campaigning as a team. He said he thought he could be more helpful campaigning for the ticket as an individual not on it.

After the meeting a couple of us hung back. "I guess we've never talked about an acceptance speech," I said. "Any idea of what you'd like to talk about in case the need arises?" Reagan then told us that recently he had been asked to write a statement to go into a Los Angeles time capsule that would be opened a century later, at the time of the city's tercentenary. The story he told—of riding home from the ranch one day, looking out the car window alternately at the Pacific Ocean and the Santa Ynez Mountains—became the basis for what he was to say in an extemporaneous speech the following night.

That evening, both candidates' names were placed in nomination, Reagan's by Laxalt. The Reagan delegates, frustrated and disappointed, but with all their energy still pent up, unleashed a long, loud demonstration on the floor. When all was done, however, the vote went predictably—1,187 for Ford, 1,070 for Reagan.

It had been prearranged by the candidates' staffs, with Ford's and Reagan's approval, that the winner would go to the loser's hotel to confer after the evening's nominating session. At about 1:30 in the morning, President Ford arrived with Dick Cheney, his chief of staff, two or three others, and his Secret Service detail. By prearrangement also, he and Reagan went alone into the living room of the Reagan suite.

Reagan congratulated him and pledged his support; then Ford asked for his thoughts about the vice-presidency. Sears had an understanding with the Ford staff that Ford would not ask Reagan to take the vice-presidential nomination, so that question did not come up. Ford mentioned several names to Reagan, most of which had been on his preconvention list and one that had not received much previous notice, that of Senator Bob Dole of Kansas.

Thursday morning after breakfast, the senior staff again assembled with the Reagans in the suite. Most of the faithful kitchen cabinet was there, too—Justin Dart, Holmes Tuttle, William French Smith, and Joseph Coors.

The phone rang. It was President Ford. When Reagan came back into the room, he said, "It's Bob Dole." He told us that when Ford had presented his list of names to Reagan and asked for his comments, he had tried to avoid negatives, instead complimenting several of them, perhaps Dole a little more than some of the others.

That apparently had been a factor in Ford's thinking and his deliberations with his own staff that night. His choice presented him with no trouble on the convention floor, either. Dole was quickly added to the ticket as the first order of business that night. Then Gerald Ford gave his acceptance speech. For a man whose speaking style had often been described as "wooden," he gave a spirited, animated speech that lifted the mood of the crowd.

Some of us on the staff learned that Ford was going to invite the Reagans down to the podium; however, Governor Reagan himself did not know about it until Ford, over the podium microphone, invited him. It was a warm, gracious gesture, and Reagan responded with a short, stirring speech that had most eyes in the house moist. He told the story of the time capsule. "Suddenly it dawned on me," he said. "Those who would read this letter a hundred years from now will know whether those missiles were fired [he had posed the question of whether our defenses would be used in a future war]. They will know whether we met our challenge. Whether we will have the freedom that we have known up till now will depend on what we do here. Will they look back with appreciation and say, 'Thank God for those people in 1976 who headed off the loss of freedom; who kept us now, a hundred years later, free; who kept our world from nuclear destruction'?

"And, if we fail, they probably won't get to read the letter at all because it spoke of individual freedom and they won't be allowed to talk of that or read of it. This is our challenge, and this is why we're here in this hall tonight. Better than we've ever done before, we've got to quit talking about each other, start talking to each other, and go out and communicate to the world that we may be fewer in number than we've ever been, but we carry the message they've been waiting for. We must go forth from here united, determined. What a great general said a few years ago is true: 'There is no substitute for victory.'"

You could almost hear a collective sigh. Reagan, on the heels of Ford's uplifting speech, had given the several thousand people packed in that arena a great emotional release. After all the fury had been spent, the party was unified.

It was not quite the end of the Reagan cause in Kansas City. During those convention nights the Texas delegation had flooded into the lobby of the Alameda Plaza chanting, "Viva! Ole!" for Reagan, their emotions running high. Now, the emotions would run more deeply and quietly as Reagan said his farewells. First, it was to the media people, among whom he now counted quite a few friends. After the late-night press conference he called on the California delegation.

Finally, after breakfast Friday morning, we met with the army of young volunteers who had descended on Kansas City to work for his candidacy. He urged them to keep working for what they believed and to make the system work. He ended, his voice very soft, with these words: "We who are privileged to be Americans have had a rendezvous with destiny since the moment, back in 1630, when John Winthrop, standing on the deck of the tiny *Arabella* off the Massachusetts coast, told his little band of Pilgrims, 'We shall be as a city upon a hill. The eyes of all people are upon us so that if we shall deal falsely with our God in this work we have undertaken and so cause Him to withdraw His present help from us, we shall be made a story and a byword throughout the world.'

"A troubled mankind looks to us, pleading for us to keep our rendezvous with destiny; that we will uphold the principles of self-reliance, self-discipline, morality, and—above all—responsible liberty for every individual; that we will become that shining city on a hill."

Tears streamed down most of the faces. The Reagans themselves were not immune to the emotional intensity of the moment, although they did not lose their composure.

At last, the Reagan traveling party moved toward the motorcade that waited to take them to the airport and home.

On the chartered 727, heading for Los Angeles, Mike Deaver and I talked briefly with Governor Reagan about the future. Governor Reagan was in a cheerful mood. "Well, it's back to work now fellows," he said, as we made a date to meet the next Monday at his old office in the Deaver & Hannaford suite in Los Angeles.

Ronald Reagan left Kansas City not as a defeated candidate but as the leader of a large segment of his party and with the respect of those who had not supported him. He almost certainly believed that his political career, in terms of any future candidacy, was at an end. From our conversations with him in the days ahead we got the impression that he would be happy to stay on the lecture circuit, do his radio commentaries and his newspaper column, and enjoy his ranch. He would be a senior statesman in the party (he would be sixty-six on his next birthday). Neither he nor his wife seemed to have any regrets.

He did want some ranch time, he told us when we met that next Monday to talk over the fall schedule. I had begun discussions with Harry O'Connor, the producer and syndicator of the Reagan radio program, before Kansas City on a "what if" basis. O'Connor said the program could be on the air by late September. We set the first taping for September 1. And, that night I would fly to New York to keep an appointment with executives of King Features, the largest of the newspaper syndicates, who had expressed an interest in taking on the Reagan column. This came about, and the column, running twice a week instead of once, was resumed in early October.

Deaver had told me that he had asked the Ford people to have their fall schedule requests to him within three weeks. He said our office had been deluged with campaign-appearance requests from Republican candidates for Congress and state offices. He added, "I'm worried that the Ford people won't get their requests in on time, that we'll have to go ahead with our scheduling, and that they'll come to us at the last minute with a handful of emergencies." He was right, as it turned out.

Reagan campaigned in twenty-five states for the Republican ticket, but the Ford campaign had made few specific requests until near the end of the campaign when they wanted him in a place he could not get to one day without scrubbing several other long-promised appearances.

At the request of the Republican National Committee, Reagan taped a number of television presentations for the Ford-Dole ticket: a half-hour speech, a five-minute speech, and several commercials. We did all of this in one marathon session in a Hollywood studio. This time the director was Phil Dusenberry, a friend of Jim Lake's, who had been recruited to supervise the lighting of the Reagan suite in Kansas City so that it had a natural quality during the many television interviews Reagan was to have there. Dusenberry, a creative director at BBDO, the advertising agency, flew from New York for this Reagan taping.

Several dozen Republican candidates had sent us copy they wanted the governor to tape for them so that they could have their own Reagan commercials. Several even showed up at the studio to appear on camera with him. It was a little like a day of campaigning. And, like those days, he never lost his good humor, no matter how repetitive the activity may have seemed. Phil understood that Reagan liked to go from start to finish through his material, stopping and redoing a segment only if there were technical hitches. They worked well together.

Deaver and I divided up the fall trips, one of us accompanying Governor Reagan on each trip. Toward the end of the campaign a story appeared in one of the Washington papers in which a Ford campaign aide said he did not think Reagan had worked hard enough for the ticket, implying that if Ford lost it would be partly Reagan's fault.

This did not sit well with the Reagans, Deaver, and me. Mike asked Stu Spencer, an old friend, to tell the aide to stop spreading such stories. But the damage had been done. After Ford lost to Carter in November, it was a long time before he and Reagan were fully reconciled as friends. Mutual friends started the building process the next year. It would be 1980 before it was really completed.

From September on, we were back into familiar routines. Mike and Helene von Damm held scheduling meetings with the governor; I met with him frequently to talk over subjects for radio broadcasts and newspaper columns. In one of our first meetings in September we talked over some of the tax-cut information Wanniski had given me. Reagan had also been hearing about Kemp's "jobs-creation bill," the first bill to carry with it the incentives-through-tax-cuts philosophy that is at the heart of supply-side economics. "Let's do both a script and a column about it," he said. And we did. This is from his script, aired in October 1976 by the 150 or so radio stations that were by then carrying his revived daily broadcasts:

> We've been spending our way to prosperity for more than four decades and it hasn't worked. . . . Twice in this century, in the 1920s and in the early '60s, we cut taxes substantially and the benefit to the economy was substantial and nearly immediate.
>
> Unfortunately, the Washington climate is one in which it is believed that any tax cut must be for the greater number of people beginning at

the lower end of the earning scale and only if it is matched by increases for the lesser number at the other end. . . .

Jack Kemp, a young Congressman from New York, who used to quarterback the Buffalo Bills, has introduced a jobs-creation bill five times and each time he got more support—the last time 195 votes, across party lines. We should help him. . . .

It would substantially cut the income tax across the board in every bracket. People would have more of their money to spend as they wish, and there would be more incentive to invest to expand our economy. And, history shows that the government would increase its revenue, thus reducing the deficit which causes inflation, because the tax base would be broadened by increased prosperity.

An October 8 newspaper column, one of his first for King, started: "Warren Harding did it. John Kennedy did it. . . . The 'it' that Harding and Kennedy had in common was to cut the income tax. In both cases, federal revenues went up instead of down." He goes on to describe Kemp's bill and concludes: "The Presidential candidates would do us all a service if they would discuss the pros and cons of the concept. Since the idea worked under both Democrat and Republican administrations before, who's to say it wouldn't work again?"

I wish I could say that this early commentary on supply-side economics was planned as a harbinger of what was to come, but I cannot. It was done more innocently than that, for although Ronald Reagan and those around him felt he had a bright future as an influential commentator on public policy, we did not, in the fall of 1976, think he would be his party's standard-bearer four years later, let alone one with tax cuts as the economic centerpiece of his campaign.

6

1977: "Back to Work"

BY THE TIME Ronald Reagan completed his fall 1976 campaigning for Republican candidates, the scheduling desk back at the office in Los Angeles was laden with speaking invitations for 1977.

The United States is probably the world's greatest convention-going nation, and this creates a constant demand for "name" speakers. Everyone, it seems, has a trade association that has an annual convention. We had invitations from such diverse groups as the Indiana Highway Contractors Association, the National Polled Hereford Association, the Mid-Western Gas Association, and the National Asphalt Pavement Association, to name a few.

Governor Reagan had decided to devote seven to ten days to speaking tours each month. They would be interspersed by visits with political friends and acquaintances from different times of his life. There were interviews, radio tapings, and time for the ranch, where the Reagans themselves (with the frequent help of Barney Barnett) reroofed their adobe ranch house and added a glassed-in veranda.

Both Ronald and Nancy Reagan seemed to slide comfortably into their new routine. Their travels began soon after New Year's Day. On January 5, for example, Governor Reagan called on President Ford for lunch at the White House. Jimmy Carter would soon be its occupant.

On the eleventh, back in California, Reagan renewed his old acquaintance with Ed Reinecke, his former lieutenant governor and by then a rancher in Northern California.

There was one piece of unfinished business from the 1976 campaign that Governor Reagan had to talk about in earnest with his former campaign staff and advisers. That was the disposition of his 1976 campaign surplus. It seemed hard to believe that a campaign which, on more than one occasion, had nearly stopped cold for lack of funds, could have a surplus of approximately $1.5 million, but it was true. This had come about as a result of the U.S. Supreme Court's decision to halt Federal Election Commission matching funds until Congress corrected certain deficiencies in the Federal Election Campaign Act amendments. With matching funds suspended, the Reagan campaign had recalculated all its budgets, trimmed its sails even further, and made do with direct contributions, first stimulated by Reagan's national television speeches and then by the momentum of his primary and caucus-state victories. Later, when Congress corrected the act, the frozen matching funds were restored and passed on to the campaign.

Under the law a candidate with a surplus may legally keep it personally if he wishes. Ronald Reagan would never have considered doing that. What did intrigue him, however, was the possibility of helping future candidates who believed, as he did, that the American free-enterprise system was being hobbled by excessive government regulation; that government needed to be streamlined and more responsive; and that we needed to restore our defense capabilities. He conferred with his advisers. The best vehicle for doing this would be a political-action committee (PAC), registered with the Federal Election Commission. Such a committee could contribute up to $5,000 to an individual candidate (the federal limit) and could solicit contributions from individual donors of up to $5,000 per person.

Would cynics say that such a PAC was little more than a repository for Reagan campaign workers to wait out the years until 1980? Or that it was designed to put many people in Reagan's debt? Probably, but since neither was the intent, the best evidence that it was what Ronald Reagan stated it would be was to build on the initial $1.5 million by raising funds continuously, seeking many small contributions.

When Reagan announced his intention to create the PAC, in mid-January, some skeptics did raise these questions. Several media people who called Deaver and me at our office seemed to believe that such a PAC would survive only until 1980, although at the time it would have been hard to find anyone in the Reagan circle who believed he would be a candidate again. All of us expected him to continue to be a force in the Republican party and among conservatives in general, but not a candidate.

In early February the Reagans flew east for a trip that took them to Toronto, where Governor Reagan addressed the annual Mississauga North dinner of the Progressive Conservative party, and to Peoria and Eureka, Illinois, where they made several appearances on behalf of the Eureka College endowment fund (Reagan's alma mater had also been periodically receiving from him souvenirs of his travels, which it would house in a Reagan Room on campus). On the fifth, they went on to Washington, where he spoke at the annual Conservative Political Action Conference dinner. The enthusiasm was, if anything, even greater than in previous years.

It was like old times, and there was no lack of interest in what Ronald Reagan had to say. The next day, Sunday, he was the guest on ABC's "Issues and Answers." On Monday, he had lunch with Katherine Graham, publisher; Ben Bradlee, executive editor; and the editorial board of the *Washington Post.* And during these early days of February, both the Reagans were guests on Merv Griffin's and Phil Donahue's television shows.

On the tenth, Reagan's PAC, Citizens for the Republic (CFTR) officially opened its doors in Santa Monica with a headquarters reception. The Reagans were there, of course, smiling and laughing with old friends and volunteer workers, mostly from the Los Angeles area.

Lyn Nofziger, who had worked with Ronald Reagan in many roles since the 1966 gubernatorial campaign in California, was to be executive director of CFTR. A steering committee had also been formed. It consisted of men and women in every corner of the country who shared the Reagan philosophy. All were united in a desire to elect candidates to Congress and state legislatures who would halt the course of government growth. Among them were Martin Anderson, Ernie Angelo, Constance Armitage, Ray Barnhart, Milan Bish, William Boeing, Monroe Browne, John Cade, Anderson Carter, Jack Courtemanche, Mike Curb, Tom Curtis, Michael Deaver, Charles (Arleigh) Foster, Robert K. Gray, Ray Hagie, Douglas Hofe, David Keene, Jim Lake, Senator Paul Laxalt, William Love, Dr. Henry Lucas, James Lyon, Ed Meese, Ed Mills, John Powell, Virginia Rice, Dick Richards (today, chairman of the Republican National Committee), Eleanor Ring Storrs, Senator Richard Schweiker, John Sears, Loren Smith, Reese Taylor, L. E. "Tommy" Thomas, Dr. Gloria Toote, Clarence Warner, David West, Frank Whetstone, and the author. The chairman was Ronald Reagan.

It was decided to launch a direct-mail campaign to solicit contributions for the few off-year elections in 1977 and to begin building CFTR for the 1978 congressional races. There would also be a monthly newsletter for contributors, and Nofziger planned to have grass-roots workshops in major cities, featuring veterans of various aspects of campaigning—polling, getting out the vote, relations with the news media, organizing, fund-raising, and so forth. The audience would be made up of persons from the regions in which the workshops were to be held who were interested in local grass-roots campaigning. These were to be workshops in practical politics. As chairman of CFTR, Reagan agreed to appear as the featured speaker (usually at a luncheon).

Meanwhile, CFTR held its first steering-committee meeting at the

Hyatt Hotel near the Los Angeles airport on March 10 with nearly 100 percent attendance.

Reagan's interest in the issues was livelier than ever. He tackled his radio commentaries and newspaper columns with zest and sought out specialists in various fields to give him new perspectives. On March 14, for example, he met in Chicago over dinner with a group of University of Chicago economists and Martin Anderson.

The schedule was varied. In late April, King Features, now carrying his twice-a-week newspaper column in more than one hundred newspapers, invited him to be guest of honor, along with columnist Nicholas von Hoffman and cartoonist Milton Caniff ("Terry and the Pirates") at a large reception that its parent company, the Hearst Corporation, was holding at the annual American Newspaper Publishers Association convention in San Francisco. He was in a lighthearted mood and regaled the group with anecdotes and good-humored accounts of his trips on what he called "the mashed potato circuit." A few days later he was in Washington, meeting the editorial board of the *Washington Star* over lunch. Within a week, on the first Sunday in May, he was the guest on NBC's "Meet the Press."

Not one of those events had been stimulated by our firm, Deaver & Hannaford, Inc., which again was under contract to Governor Reagan to provide administrative, research, and scheduling services for him. All were unsolicited.

I believe that much of that 1977 interest on the part of the news media and other opinion-shaping circles in the man who nearly took the Republican nomination from an incumbent president stemmed from pure curiosity. What was he thinking about the issues of the day? It may have reflected the first stirrings of concern about the Carter style (if not yet the substance) and a desire to keep in touch with anyone who might conceivably play a role in 1980 presidential politics. In any case, the interest was real and constant.

Nancy Reagan accompanied her husband on a number of these trips and, when in Washington, took the opportunity to meet over lunch with people from a variety of spheres of activity in the capital, making a number of new acquaintances. Nancy Reynolds, who had accepted a corporate-government relations position in Washington, continued as a good friend of Mrs. Reagan's and often participated in these gatherings.

As it turned out, 1977 was to be the year of the Panama Canal treaty. Under the new administration, negotiations with the Panamanians had gone forward, with President Carter naming Sol Linowitz (with the rank of ambassador) to join Ambassador Ellsworth Bunker as coleader of the American negotiating team.

In late April, Linowitz called me to ask if he could meet with Governor Reagan and brief him on the treaty situation. It came as a surprise because Linowitz obviously knew of Reagan's skeptical views on the subject. I was impressed by his directness. Governor Reagan was intrigued, too, and said he would be interested in hearing what Ambassador Linowitz had to say. A luncheon was arranged for Saturday, April 30, in the Reagans' suite at the Madison Hotel in Washington. That morning, Roger Fontaine, a young scholar at the Georgetown Center for Strategic and International Studies, came to the hotel to brief Governor Reagan on his latest visits to the Panama region. Roger (today the President's Latin American specialist on the National Security Council staff) had proved to be a very helpful adviser on Caribbean and Latin American issues from midsummer of 1976 on, when I first met him. He had often supplied Governor Reagan with memos on current issues in the region. His observations found their way into a number of Reagan radio broadcasts and newspaper columns. Fontaine had been studying Panama closely and had visited the country as well. In addition, he was a close student of Castro's Cuba and was concerned about the friendship of Panamanian strongman Omar Torrijos and Fidel Castro.

Sol Linowitz arrived at noon. He, Governor and Mrs. Reagan, and I were the only ones in attendance. Linowitz, who had retired wealthy at a relatively early age to devote himself to philanthropy and foreign affairs (especially in the Caribbean and Latin America) but stayed involved with certain business interests, proved to be earnest, direct, soft-spoken. It was a cordial meeting on all counts. We were pleasantly surprised that despite his espousal of policy views for the region that Reagan and his supporters would consider somewhat to the left, Linowitz was not at all tendentious. He argued his point of view quietly and with conviction, building his case piece by piece. He said that he believed that we would end up with a treaty which protected U.S. interests and that a treaty which recognized the nationalistic aspirations of the Panamanians would also improve our relations with all Latin America.*

At the conclusion of the luncheon, Linowitz asked only for the opportunity to contact Governor Reagan again. This was readily granted. We talked it over afterward, agreeing that it was something of a com-

---

* This did not square with the intelligence we were getting from a number of sources in Latin America. Aside from Venezuela, Mexico, Costa Rica, and a few neighboring states, there was little noticeable enthusiasm for Panama's position. The "Southern Cone" nations in the lower half of South America were indifferent; those on the west coast, who depended most on canal traffic for their commerce, were privately saying they worried about Panama operating the canal.

pliment for the Carter administration to assume that Ronald Reagan might have it in his power to mount so strong a campaign against a new treaty as a private citizen that he could derail its course.

On May 3, Governor Reagan had a day devoted to scholars and their work and reveled in it. He spent the entire day at the Hoover Institution on War, Revolution, and Peace at Stanford University in Palo Alto, forty-five miles south of San Francisco. He was the first of the institution's honorary senior fellows (Nobel laureates Alexander Solzhenitsyn and Friedrich Hayek have since joined his company with that title). Director Glen Campbell, his associate Richard Staar, and the resident senior fellows prepared for him.

In late May there began a series of fund-raising events for Republican organizations, usually county central committees. Republican groups traditionally hold Lincoln Day dinners, just as Democrats hold Jackson-Jefferson Day dinners. In both cases, the dates of the historical birthdays can stretch quite a bit. We used to joke that Lincoln's birthday was any time between February 12 (the actual date) and the Fourth of July.

Visits were scheduled in Texas, Rhode Island, Buffalo, New York, and Bergen County, New Jersey. Mike Deaver accompanied Governor Reagan on this first round of appearances before political groups.

"It's different than before," Mike said when he returned. "There's something going on out there." It was hard to put one's finger on it, he said, but dinner chairmen were reporting record ticket sales. The lines of people coming up to shake Reagan's hand or get his autograph after the dinners were greater than ever. And, most of the people were saying such things as "You've got to run next time." By now, the reality of Carter had sunk in. There was more. Deaver reported that people came from everywhere at the airports (most of the trips were on commercial airliners) to offer their support; motorists and taxi drivers would holler, "Give 'em hell." The maids at the hotels would line up the morning of his departure to shake hands and wish him well.

The common assertion that Ronald Reagan was "too old" might prove premature. In any case, Mike said, "See for yourself, next trip out. Then, let's compare notes." I soon had a chance to do so. On June 8 we flew to Pittsburgh for an event in Westmoreland County, Pennsylvania, outside the city. The receptions for donors of larger amounts were jammed, and the big dinner hall did not have a seat to spare. One committee member told me this was the biggest turnout they had had in at least thirty years. The head table included every part of the party's spectrum in terms of elected officials and party leaders. Richard Thornburgh, formerly U.S. deputy attorney general, soon to be a gubernatorial candidate, and generally considered to be a part of the more liberal wing of the party, was much in evidence and gave the introduction of Reagan.

The handshake-and-autograph line after the dinner seemed to have no end. And no matter how much time this consumed, Ronald Reagan would not leave until the last person was greeted. It was an ironclad rule of his that his staff not disturb this process unless some pressing airplane connection required breaking it off. His view was that when people paid good money to attend such a banquet, they were entitled to shake the speaker's hand and ask for his autograph.

The next day, we met Mrs. Reagan in New York, where the governor addressed the Foreign Policy Association and then went on to Washington to a joint CFTR–American Conservative Union "Salute to Ronald Reagan" dinner. The following day, the Governor and I helicoptered to central New Jersey, to Fiddler's Elbow Country Club, set in beautiful farm country, for its annual economics seminar. The club usually invited two major speakers on opposite sides of an issue for a gentlemanly debate, followed by questions and answers and a luncheon. Reagan's debate opponent was to be former Senator Eugene McCarthy in a "Dialogue on the Economy." It might as well have been titled "Duet on the Economy." Although McCarthy's reputation was as a liberal, on basic economic issues he and Ronald Reagan were chorusing one another. The quips and anecdotes flew.

That evening, Governor Reagan addressed the annual dinner of the Camden County (New Jersey) Republican Committee in Cherry Hill. It was another appreciative audience.

That same evening we flew to Memphis, where Governor Reagan addressed the Young Republicans' annual convention at breakfast the next morning.

This pace continued on into the summer. In late June there was a CFTR all-day workshop in Salt Lake City; a county Republican dinner the following night in Eugene, Oregon; and another in Seattle the following night. A few days after the Fourth of July there was a trip consisting of Republican fund-raising events in Toledo; Westchester County, New York; and Middlesex County, New Jersey.

By midsummer it was decided that a small group would meet at the governor's home from time to time to compare notes on major issues and the political climate in the country. Attendance varied, but most often included, in addition to the Reagans, Sears, Meese, Deaver, Wirthlin, Nofziger, Anderson, Allen, Whalen, and myself. Senator Laxalt often attended and kept in close touch with Governor Reagan when he could not. Bill Gavin, once a Nixon speechwriter (now with Congressman Bob Michel, the House Republican leader), participated from time to time.

We agreed that we would stay in touch by telephone as new issues developed so that we could compare notes and make appropriate recommendations to Governor Reagan about his stance on them, inasmuch as there was growing press interest in him. (We frequently got calls at the office asking for off-the-cuff comments from him about breaking issues.)

Except for some time out for an August vacation at the ranch, the Reagans' schedule did not slacken during the summer. On August 23, George Bush and James Baker called on the governor in the office in Los Angeles. Our greatest attention, however, was focused on the Panama Canal treaty (actually two treaties as it turned out).

Carter's team and the Panamanians had announced the completion of their negotiations late the previous week. They had a treaty, but they were not releasing its terms. Ambassador Linowitz called to ask if he and Ambassador Bunker could brief the governor. As it happened, we were headed for an Atlantic City Republican dinner on the twenty-fourth and would be in New York on the twenty-fifth. The Reagans would be staying at the New York apartment of their friends the Justin Darts, and we could have the ambassadors join us there.

Meanwhile, Landon Butler, Hamilton Jordan's assistant, had called me to ask if I would like a prebriefing at the White House. This was arranged for Tuesday morning the twenty-third. It took about forty-five minutes. It was my impression that the Carter people were nervous about what Ronald Reagan might do.

The next day I drove to Atlantic City to meet the governor. I briefed him on what they had told me. After his speech that night we went on to New York.

The next morning dawned clear and comfortable for that time of year. The Reagans received Linowitz and Bunker at 10:30. The East River spread out below us as the tall, elderly Bunker and the younger, wirier Linowitz told us about the general outlines of the treaties. They told Reagan that Carter and Torrijos would sign the treaties at a gala dinner at the Organization of American States (OAS) hall in Washington on September 7.

When they left, Governor Reagan said to me, "Suppose they're right; suppose these treaties fully protect our interests?" He quickly answered his own question. First, we did not have the actual treaties in hand to review (nor would we have had time to analyze them in detail if the ambassadors had brought them), but judging from their outline, there were enough serious questions to be raised to forestall a change in his mind. He was, on balance, skeptical. Earlier, when we had first heard the news that the treaties had been agreed upon, the small advisory group had a telephone conference with the governor. It was agreed that should the governor decide to oppose the treaties after getting the briefing, his opposition should be developed with deliberation. Many newsmen had been calling the office to ask us if Reagan was going to "lead the charge" against the treaties. Clearly, some of them would have been happy to see him in confrontation with the treaty advocates. It would have been good copy.

Dick Whalen, in our telephone conference, made the point that the coming Senate debate over the treaties would provide an opportunity to review our overall relations with Latin America and the Caribbean nations. He proposed that Governor Reagan lift the argument above the canal issue itself to U.S.–Latin American relations. The governor and the rest agreed.

By a coincidence of scheduling, the governor's first speaking engagement after the Linowitz-Bunker briefing was the same night, to the Young Americans for Freedom (YAF), the conservative youth group, at the New York Statler-Hilton. The YAF membership had supported him strongly. And they take their conservative politics seriously. Reagan had intended to use the current version of his on-the-road political speech, which was certain to bring a good response from YAF. "But," he said, "everyone there will know that I've had this briefing this morning and I can't fail to mention it." Indeed, the front of the building had been swarming with reporters, and I had told them there would be no statement until later. He therefore added a short statement at the very end of his speech (we also released it as a separate press statement). There was nothing inflammatory about the statement, but in the running-adrenalin context of a YAF annual dinner, it brought the house down. And, the news media, not surprisingly, assumed we had carefully stitched this scheduling sequence together as evidence that Governor Reagan would lead the charge.

The other things he did in opposition to the treaty lowered the potential temperature of the national debate. The late Senator James Allen, Democrat of Alabama and then chairman of the Separation of Powers Subcommittee of the Senate Judiciary Committee, invited Reagan to testify on September 8, three days after Labor Day. The National Press Club invited him to address its members at a lunch the same day. "Issues and Answers" wanted him to discuss the issue; he agreed to do this back in Los Angeles the following Sunday.

Wednesday night, September 7, the Carter-Torrijos dinner, carried live on television, came off as scheduled. Across town, in the Reagans' suite at the Madison Hotel, the Reagans were having a quiet dinner with Senator Laxalt, Deaver, Nofziger, Whalen, and me to review the entire strategy for dealing with the Panama Canal issue over the coming months.

Laxalt wanted to get the Republican National Committee to mount a campaign against the treaties. (He almost succeeded, but the committee's ultimate failure to support such a campaign became a source of contention between Laxalt and party chairman Bill Brock for some time to come.) Laxalt would also be the floor leader of the antitreaty forces in the Senate.

We had been working intensively on Reagan's Senate testimony, because there was not much time. When the day arrived, the Senate hearing room was packed. Governor Reagan's sober and serious testimony set the stage for congressional antitreaty forces to seek a role for the House of Representatives in the treaty-ratification process in this instance (ordinarily, only the Senate is involved). His testimony ran to nearly fifty minutes. In modified form, the arguments he presented were later published in an article in the foreign-affairs quarterly *Orbis*. There would also be ample opportunity over the next few months to comment on the treaties on his radio program and in his newspaper column. Governor Reagan had decided that he would not make the treaties the focal point of his on-the-road speeches. Rather, he would deal with them in question-and-answer sessions.

The National Press Club speech broadened the discussion. Reagan began it, "This morning on Capitol Hill, I had an opportunity to voice many of my doubts about the wisdom of the canal treaties. This afternoon, rather than covering those same specifics, I would like to broaden the focus to a more general discussion of American foreign policy and the constructive steps that we should consider with regard to Latin America. First and foremost I believe our concern should be our national security and that, in turn, is dependent on hemisphere security."

He traced the then-current state of U.S. foreign affairs and added, "One fundamental reality—indeed, the overriding reality—of our time is the expansion of Soviet power in the world." He cited the decline of American power in contrast to Soviet expansionism. He said, "All the realities that I have mentioned here—the relentless expansion of Marxist power, the relative decline of American power, the rising tide of expectations among less-developed nations—are now converging in Latin America, and it is within that context that I believe the United States should shape its policies toward the region."

He went on to trace parallels in the development of independence in North and South America and of shared values and concerns. He criticized the emerging Carter policy of punishing friends and warming toward foes (at that time, Castro in particular). As to recognizing Castro, which some American liberals and the Left had been arguing for, Reagan said, "Aren't we entitled to ask, 'What's in it for us?' Without his Russian subsidy, how will he [Castro] buy the American goods he admits he needs?" He answered his own question with sarcasm: "I think of one answer to that: We'll provide him with low-interest, soft loans." He added, "It seems to me, normalized relations with Fidel Castro would be more normal if he pulled his troops out of Africa, his revolutionaries out of Latin America, released the thousands upon thousands of political prisoners and compensated us for stolen property. Having done all this it would seem to me we could sit down together and light up a couple of good Havana cigars."

He concluded with several elements he said were essential to improved intrahemisphere relations: continuation of the trend of declining foreign aid and increasing investment capital; free flow of private capital; free trade; encouragement of energy independence throughout the hemisphere; assistance—when asked for—to Latin American nations to curb population explosions; and sound economic policies in the United States. "It is imperative we recognize that the economic progress of Latin America and the United States are tied together; we can fall together or we can rise together. And, we will rise only if the United States government is sound and wise in its economic policies."*

That evening, Robert K. Gray, the well-known Washington public-relations man and a Reagan supporter, welcomed the Reagans to Washington with a cocktail reception that put a relaxing finish to nearly three weeks of intensive work on the Panama Canal issue.

Except for his appearance on "Issues and Answers" that Sunday, Ronald Reagan, as he had planned, moved off center stage in the Panama Canal treaty debate, for the Senate would now be the focus of attention.

The Reagan schedule, including both business speaking engagements and various political appearances, did not slacken. Republican dinners in Jackson County (Kansas City), Missouri, and Fayette County, Iowa; the National Federation of Republican Women (two thousand strong at their biennial convention) in Oklahoma City; the Western States Republican Conference in Salt Lake City; a four-thousand-person "Reagan Day Rally" picnic by Republicans in New Orleans; a CFTR steering committee meeting in Chicago; and countless dinners filled the days and evenings.

The Panama Canal issue was the subject of a meeting in the office in Los Angeles in late September with Norman Lear, the television producer. Lear, who was for the treaties, had requested the meeting. He thought that a nationwide televised debate between Reagan and a major figure on the other side would be an excellent way to inform the public of all aspects of the issue. Reagan listened with interest. The idea did not

---

* David Gergen, now assistant to the President, joined us for the first time on this speech, assisting with the draft.

develop much further. Instead, in early 1978, Reagan ultimately debated his good friend William Buckley, publisher of *National Review*, on Buckley's television program "Firing Line."

During all this time, between trips involving many speeches to business groups and trade associations and the fund-raising events for GOP committees, Reagan also spent another day with the scholars at the Hoover Institution. And he met in December with the Baltimore *Sun's* editorial board.

Another part of his business, his five-day-a-week radio commentary and his newspaper columns, provided plenty of opportunity to give millions of Americans his observations on current affairs. A sampling of his radio scripts during the year shows them covering such topics as Cuba (about the push for normalization of relations and the imprisonment for nearly two decades of Cuban patriot Hubert Matos, he said, "Major Matos is just one of thousands imprisoned in Castro's Cuba. Let normalization of relations with us begin with justice for all of them"); energy (in favor of continued development of the Clinch River breeder reactor); air bags (skepticism—and libertarianism—about government-mandated devices such as the air bag: "Isn't this whole idea another thing that should be left to us and the free market? If any of us would like to install such a device in the family car shouldn't that be our decision to make?"); Cambodia (about the book *Murder of a Gentle Land,* documenting the genocide of the Pol Pot regime when many news media steadfastly refused to believe it was happening); human rights (criticism of the National Council of Churches' lopsided approach to the subject); and the Olympics (noting the irony of the heavy politicizing of the Olympic Games, in light of the protestations of the International Olympic Committee that they are "nonpolitical").

Any subject was fair game. Reagan would stuff his latest reading into his briefcase as he kissed Mrs. Reagan goodby and left the house in Pacific Palisades for the latest round of days on the road. On the air legs of his journeys, he would go through the briefcase, read, and then pull out his lined yellow legal pads and begin to draft commentaries. When next he came to the office, it was always with a grin when he had that stack of yellow sheets under his arm.

In the fall of 1977 an unusual television request came to Ronald Reagan. It seems that Gerald Musgrave, a research fellow at the Hoover Institution, had learned that the public television station in Los Angeles, with a grant of nearly $750,000, was going to coproduce (with the British and Canadian Broadcasting companies) a twelve-part series featuring Professor John Kenneth Galbraith and called "The Age of Uncertainty." The series would be broadcast for college credit in conjunction with the publication of a new Galbraith book. His curiosity was aroused by a statement contained in one of the program proposals: "A short discussion piece will be produced for each program presenting information while providing opportunity for extended and alternative viewpoints on the crucial issues of the series."

Musgrave sought to find out who would provide the alternative viewpoints, only to get a bureaucratic runaround. "Much later I was told Galbraith was so good that no alternative viewpoints would be necessary!" Musgrave related. Undaunted, Musgrave contacted everyone he could think of to bring enough pressure to bear to get the Corporation for Public Broadcasting and the Public Broadcasting System, from whom the tax dollars had come, to make good on supplying the alternative viewpoints to the well-known self-declared socialist Galbraith.

In January 1977, Musgrave found himself named a consultant on the series to select most of the twelve alternative speakers. Among them were scholars Sidney Hook, Peter Duignan, and Robert Conquest and economists J. Clayburn LaForce and Herbert Stein. Then, he asked Ronald Reagan to do the summation on "Democracy, Leadership, and Commitment," which would be taped for inclusion in the final Galbraith broadcast. Reagan's statement sums up his philosophy of the subject:

> I've been watching "The Age of Uncertainty" with great interest. No one could accuse Dr. Galbraith of lacking either an interest in the broad sweeps of history or a sense of humor. Just the same, the program leaves me uneasy. Uneasy, partly because it uses skillful editing to glorify Dr. Galbraith's heroes and make those he disagrees with seem ignorant, unfeeling, or downright villainous. But more important, I am uneasy about his view of just what constitutes democracy, leadership, and commitment.
>
> Early in the program, he give us a glimpse at Switzerland's federal democracy at work. He makes the point that it works because it is close to the people and the emphasis is on problem solving. "The money is spent by the people who pay," he says.
>
> So far, so good. That's an idea that worked pretty well in the United States until some people began getting the idea that they could make government solve every problem that came along, if only they were put in charge of its machinery.
>
> Having allowed government to grow to monster size, we have produced a cadre of professional, lifetime politicians, most of whom ply their trade by periodically raising their constituents' hopes of solving the latest problem. Once reconfirmed by the voters, they always follow the same method, dispensing huge amounts of tax money, passing laws that lead to restrictive regulations, then blaming those they regulated when things break down. And *then,* passing more laws and regulations because things obviously don't work. The ruling class of politicians and bureaucrats we

have been breeding for several decades benefits from bigger and bigger government. And the opposite side of that coin is, inevitably, less liberty for individual citizens.

Dr. Galbraith says that the essence of leadership is "to confront, without doubt or equivocation, the major aspiration, the greatest need, the gravest anxiety of the people you presume to lead." He cites Nehru, Franklin Roosevelt, and John Kennedy as models. But, there is something lacking in his definition. Essential also to leadership, it seems to me, is a clear belief in the limitations of government, coupled with a strong faith in the ability of individual men and women to think for themselves and to make decisions for themselves.

As an academician, Dr. Galbraith understandably places emphasis on education's role in democracy. He says, "The greatest source of democratic power . . . derives from education." He adds that it helps bestow self-confidence, the sense of purpose, the ability to identify with a people's anxieties. He then takes us to the University of California, where much of the anti–Vietnam War movement began. He is impressed by the ability of that movement to change events as it did. He does not also show us its anti-intellectual, antidemocratic side when mobs rampaged through the streets of Berkeley and demonstrators wanted anything *but* free speech for those who opposed them.

The impression comes through in this program that leadership is best left to development by a group of wise mandarins on college campuses. We can forgive Dr. Galbraith his bias in favor of his own profession, but the mandarins did not stop the violence. In fact, some even encouraged it in those days. And today, many of their products enter public service with the view that man was meant to be just an ant in society's anthill.

In the last analysis, Dr. Galbraith and I have different views of man and his relationship to society and government. He extols the submersion of personality and self-interest in what he says is being "part of the team." I am suspicious of people who profess to have no self-interest, only that of the group or community.

Dr. Galbraith seems to believe that it is a simple matter to identify what the community interest is. I am afraid he forgets that the community interest is constantly subject to the reality of pressure from special-interest groups of all kinds. Leaders will act in terms of what they *believe* is the main anxiety of their constituents, but they are far from being always right. As often as not, it is the squeakiest wheel that gets the grease.

Rather than government-by-squeaky-wheel, history has shown us that it is better to leave the individual alone to develop to the fullest extent possible whatever talents God gave him. As for leaders, give us those who know the difference between what society as a whole—and government—can and *should* do, and what it should leave alone.

The last official meeting on Governor Reagan's schedule for 1977 was a meeting on December 20 at his home with his advisory committee. We reviewed the current political climate, Carter's seeming inability to master his job as president, and the Panama Canal debates in the Senate. Looking into the future, 1978 appeared to be a year perhaps more full of activity than even 1977 had been. It would also be a year of foreign travel. Trips to Latin America, Europe, and Asia were under consideration.

7

1978: Moving Closer

As 1977 CAME TO A CLOSE, Ronald Reagan had an important decision to make about his 1978 activities. If, as his small group of advisers recommended, he conducted himself in a way that would enhance his chances for a 1980 nomination, should he seek it, there was the risk (as there had been in 1975) that the news media would conclude that he already *was* a candidate. If that were to happen it could erode his speaking schedule and his nationally distributed radio commentaries and newspaper column.

On the other hand, if his activities were so low key that it appeared he had no interest in the 1980 presidential nomination, his supporters could become disheartened and begin to drift away. Furthermore, he would lose the opportunity to broaden his appeal to a larger audience.

Reagan's personal income was based on media-related activities and erosion of that base was undesirable. At the same time, interest in him as a speaker and a commentator was high precisely because he was a public figure. As speculation grew about the 1980 presidential election, it was clear that he would have to strike a balance between his political profile and his business. As in 1975, it was to become a case of keeping his options open.

Foreign travel was one activity about which decisions had to be made early in 1978. The Reagans had expressed an interest in traveling abroad, both for pleasure and because Governor Reagan wanted to have an updated firsthand understanding of areas of the world constantly in the news.

In the early 1970s the Reagans had made a series of overseas trips on missions for then-President Nixon. Except for a visit to London in 1975, however, they had not made any more.

Dick Allen and I had been especially persistent in recommending an overall travel plan for 1978 and 1979 that would provide Governor Reagan with up-to-date contacts with foreign leaders. We believed that he would impress them with his understanding of international issues and would thus counter stereotypes of him fashioned largely by the foreign press ("cowboy actor" was a recurring sobriquet).

We recommended against media-oriented travel. Doing and saying things designed to get on the evening television news in the United States would require oversimplification of current issues and would also have made foreign officials reticent about meeting with him. Instead, we proposed that the trips be relatively low profile in nature ("look-and-listen" visits we dubbed them), including a limited number of interviews by host-country journalists. Thus, we reasoned, if Reagan became a candidate in 1980, U.S. journalists would seek out foreign leaders and journalists for opinions about him at campaign time. Because we were confident he would make a good impression, we believed the positive opinions would reverberate back to the United States. On the other hand, if he never became a candidate the trips would be informative and useful for him as a popular commentator on current events. (One trip was ultimately for background preparation for a seminar back in the United States.)

The idea of a low-profile set of visits appealed to Governor Reagan. Allen and I were detailed to draft a plan. When it was presented, it included more trips than we believed his schedule would permit, but it was a starting point for discussion. It included Canada, Mexico, South America, Asia, the Middle East, Europe and the Soviet Union.

Under the heading of Asia, we had included a visit to the China mainland, which at the time still did not have diplomatic relations with the United States. Governor Reagan had, for many years, supported the Republic of China—the Nationalist Chinese—on Taiwan, as did most U.S. conservatives (and, according to most public opinion polls at the time, most Americans). On the other hand, we believed that Reagan would be able to speak more authoritatively about Asian—and especially Chinese—issues if he had visited that part of China long-controlled by the Communists.*

Lyn Nofziger, as executive director of CFTR, was also asking for a major chunk of Reagan's time because 1978 would be a congressional election year and CFTR's first major opportunity to support candidates. At the same time, Reagan's popularity as a speaker at business, civic,

---

* He had called on Chiang Kai-shek in Taipei in 1972 on a particularly sensitive mission for Nixon and had been chosen because of his strong support of the Republic of China. In late 1977, when the firm which Deaver and I headed was invited to do work for the R.O.C., we asked Reagan if he had any objection. He not only had none, he also said we should accept.

and professional gatherings had never been greater, and the demand for his time far exceeded the available supply.

Early in the year there were many discussions about priorities, resulting in compromises between the various influences on Governor Reagan's schedule. He, too, found himself compromising, in terms of the time he had hoped to spend at the ranch. (Often, about the second or third day of a trip he would begin to get a certain look in his eye which told us he was counting the days till he could get back to his latest outdoor project at the ranch.)

Eventually, there were two overseas trips during the year. The first, in April and early May, included Japan, Taiwan, Hong Kong, and Iran. The second, in late November and early December, included Britain, France, and Germany.

Meanwhile, early in the year Ronald Reagan's participation in the Panama Canal treaty issue was reaching a climax. He had accepted William Buckley's invitation to debate the issue on "Firing Line," to be taped on Friday, January 13.

Each debater was allowed two advisers as "seconds." Reagan chose the late Admiral John McCain (who had been commander of the U.S. Seventh Fleet) and Roger Fontaine, Latin America specialist at the Georgetown Center for Strategic and International Studies. The taping was to take place in the amphitheater of an historic building on the campus of the University of South Carolina in Columbia.

We arrived from different directions. The night before the debate, Bill Buckley and I found ourselves on the same flight from New York. Ed Meese arrived from California. The next afternoon I met Governor Reagan at the Columbia airport. He had been on a speaking tour all week.

South Carolina Governor and Mrs. James Edwards had invited Reagan, Meese, and me to stay in the stately old governor's mansion the night of the debate. Fires blazed in all the fireplaces, a warm contrast to the chilly January night. The Edwardses were also hosts at a dinner for about one hundred guests just prior to the event. This was held in a building called The Lace House (because of its ornamental iron grillwork), across the street from the governor's mansion. The principals, their seconds and advisers, university leaders, and officials of the state's public television network were on hand and so were former U.S. Senator and Mrs. Sam Ervin, who sat at our table. (Senator Ervin served as moderator of the debate.)

The debate was conducted with good humor, for the two principals are friends of long standing, but each was clearly doing his best to drive his arguments home. Buckley argued that signing the treaties would be a magnanimous gesture on the part of the United States and it would bring continuous long-range benefits in good will to the United States. Reagan emphasized the uncertainty of the canal's security if we were to relinquish control over it.

The evening ended with a cheerful reception at the campus residence of the president of the university. Guests differed as to who had "won." On balance, it seemed to have been a draw, although media commentators afterward based their decision of who won on their own predilections about the issue. Most favored the treaties.

A week later, I accompanied Governor Reagan while he made a stop in Denver, en route to a business convention speaking date in New Orleans. There in the Rockies he fulfilled a promise he had made to Senator Laxalt who was the leader on the Senate floor of the anti-treaty forces. Reagan met with the members of the Panama Canal Truth Squad—Laxalt, Senator Jake Garn and Congressmen Phil Crane, Mickey Edwards, George Hansen, and Larry McDonald—to appear at a joint press conference and later a rally at a suburban high school.

The Truth Squad was sponsored by the American Conservative Union and other conservative activist organizations as it made its way around the country; however, the original plan had been for the Republican National Committee to underwrite its travels. Back in the fall of 1977, Reagan had agreed to a request by RNC Chairman Bill Brock to sign a fund-raising letter, asking for contributions to help oppose the Carter–Torrijos treaties. A companion letter over Brock's signature supported Reagan's. The Reagan letter raised between $500,000 and $1 million and Laxalt asked Brock to direct $50,000 from the proceeds to underwrite the costs of the Truth Squad. Brock declined. Laxalt was furious. During a December visit to Washington, Reagan met with Laxalt and found himself in an often-heated three-way telephone conversation with Brock over his apparent unwillingness to use any of the funds Reagan had raised for the purpose intended.* Reagan felt his honor was at stake, for many contributors had sent in small checks on the strength of his word. There was some residual bitterness from this encounter for many months to come. It finally dissipated, as did most intra-party disagreements from the past, in the wake of Reagan's winning of the Republican nomination in 1980.

Following the Truth Squad appearance and his New Orleans speaking date, Reagan went on to Atlanta for a CFTR steering committee meeting and an all-day grassroots political workshop on Saturday at the Hyatt Regency. Luncheon speakers, along with Reagan, were Senator

---

* Brock's refusal fueled suspicions in the Reagan camp that the RNC staff was strongly anti-Reagan and actively working to help a potential 1980 candidacy of Ford or some other candidate. After 1976, the Ford forces had managed to maintain tight control of the organization and only Charlie Black, of the Reagan staff, held a senior position on the RNC staff.

Jesse Helms, Governor Edwards, and South Carolina women's leader Connie Armitage. Several hundred Republican and conservative activists were in attendance.

Reagan's final major appearance dealing with the Panama Canal treaty issue took place in early February on national television (CBS). The network had invited him to rebut President Carter's televised "fireside chat" in support of the two treaties. There was very little time to work on drafts, but Reagan's arguments were all fresh in his mind and they had been thoroughly researched. We taped the half-hour talk in Los Angeles on the sixth and it was broadcast the night of the eighth. He summarized his arguments this way:

"We're talking about our national security, and where that is concerned we must always be skeptical and on guard against the worst that might happen. In his book, *The Treaty Trap*, Lawrence Beilenson documents that treaties down through history have been broken more often than not."

He went on to offer several specific suggestions for improving relations with Panama and concluded by saying, "Greatness may be measured in many ways. Carrying out our responsibilities as a nation is one of them. Being the middle point—the vital center—of the free world is not an easy responsibility. We have shown in recent years that we can get very weary of shouldering our burdens. But, if not us, then who? The Panama Canal is vital to the free world and that world depends on us . . ."

While relations with Panama have gone smoothly since, and neither the most glowing hopes of treaty proponents nor worst fears of opponents have been realized, Reagan's concluding statement reflects his most fundamental beliefs: that to shrink from responsibilities wherever we find them endangers our own freedom.

February saw much activity on behalf of Citizens for the Republic by Reagan, who was its chairman. Between the twenty-second and twenty-fourth he made appearances in six Texas cities for congressional candidates CFTR was supporting. On the twenty-fifth he was back in Los Angeles for an all-day workshop meeting with the Western States Caucus of CFTR. This event brought grassroots activists from eleven states, many of whom had been Reagan delegates and workers in 1976. Most were actively urging Reagan to run in 1980, as were many other friends, fans, and former campaign supporters in other parts of the country.

On March 17 he renewed what had become an annual tradition. He flew to Washington to address the Conservative Political Action Conference banquet. The ballroom of the Hyatt Regency hotel was filled to capacity. He chose this occasion to speak about U.S. foreign policy. His address was both a detailed critique of the Carter administration's policy and a guide to his own views of how foreign affairs should be conducted.

Since President Reagan took office I have often had friends and acquaintances express surprise at his actions. Some are surprised to find a president who does what he has said he would do; others have had no preparation for his actions. When people ask me what to expect from him as president, I suggest they read what he has said over the last several years. The following passages from his Washington speech that March evening provide a sampling.

On human rights policy—"In practice, they [the Carter administration] have ceaselessly scolded authoritarian governments of countries that are friendly and ignored authoritarian and totalitarian countries that are not. . . . By using a combination of heavy-handed moves against allied countries on the one hand, and making preemptive concessions [the reference is to SALT II negotiations] toward unfriendly and potentially unfriendly countries on the other, the Carter administration has managed to convey the view that it desperately wants the whole world to have democratic institutions that would be the envy of the most ardent ACLU lawyer, and that wishing will make it so."

On Vietnam—"Too often, the president is advised by men and women who are forever trapped in the tragic, but still fresh memory of a lost war. And from Vietnam they have drawn all the wrong lessons.

"When they say 'never again,' they mean the United States should never again resist communist aggression. In saying 'never again,' they imply that the war *should* have been lost; that it is all right for the victors to conduct a brutal campaign against their own people, violating even minimal human rights. . . .

"The lesson we should have learned from Vietnam is that never again will Americans be asked to fight and die unless they are permitted to win."

On basic foreign policy—". . . our fundamental aim in foreign policy must be to insure our own survival and to protect those others who share our values."

On detente—"The Soviet Union has no intention of maintaining the status quo. It does not accept our soft definition of détente. To the Soviet Union, détente is an opportunity to expand its sphere of influence around the world."

On negotiating arms control—"Today, the USSR continues its drive to dominate the world in military capability: on the land, on water and in the air. Meanwhile, the Carter administration seems confused and torn, partly believing the realities and partly listening to those who believe that preemptive concessions by us will result in matching concessions by the Soviets. But the Soviets don't bargain that way. They

Salt II briefings, Summer 1979. An intensive two-day series of briefings was arranged for Governor Reagan, including one from the Carter White House. All took place in his Los Angeles office. Here he is conferring with advisers (clockwise from left) Martin Anderson, William Van Cleave, Fred Ikle, Richard Allen, Charles Kupperman. *Photograph by Roger Sandler.*

Preparing to announce his candidacy for the 1980 Presidential election, Ronald Reagan goes over details of his announcement speech with the author on the New York television studio set, where he pre-taped the speech one day before addressing a large dinner at the New York Hilton, November 13, 1979. *Photograph by Roger Sandler.*

Berlin, December, 1978. The West Berliners were delighted that the Reagans decided to visit their city. They were snapped in mid-tour of the city, in front of the Brandenburg Gate, with the author and his wife, Irene.

Kansas City, 1976. A planning session of the Reagan team at the Alameda Plaza hotel during the Republican Convention. Mike Deaver (center left) illustrates a point. Others (clockwise): Jim Lake (back to camera), Senator Paul Laxalt, Ed Meese, Lyn Nofziger, Andy Carter, the author.

Researching an issue. The author (right) and Martin Anderson traveled as a team on the 1976 Reagan campaign plane. Briefing materials were prepared for the candidate between stops. We carried a facsimile printer (telecopier) aboard. Such equipment was new to campaigning in those days. At airport stops our assistants would carry the telecopier to a pay phone and receive the latest clippings from New York, Washington and Los Angeles. *Photograph by Dennis Brack/Black Star*.

The first victory, 1976. Tuesday, March 23, night of the North Carolina primary. This photo was taken on the campaign plane, homebound for California after leaving LaCrosse, Wisconsin, where we had just heard the news that Ronald Reagan was winning in North Carolina. Seated with Reagan are Lyn Nofziger (l.) and John Sears (center). Standing (l. to r.) Richard Wirthlin, the author, Martin Anderson, Michael Deaver. *Photograph by Dennis Brack/Black Star.*

Taipei, Taiwan, April, 1978. The Reagans inspect a jade carving in the National Palace Museum during their Asia trip. Patricia Allen looks on.

"I paid for this microphone." Ronald Reagan responds to a Nashua newspaper executive who tried to cut him off at the famous Nashua, New Hampshire, debate, February 23. George Bush is seated at right. Standing are the other candidates who were refused participation by the newspaper: John Anderson, Howard Baker, Bob Dole, Phil Crane. *Photograph by Roger Sandler.*

Commuting on the New Haven line, March, 1980. The Reagan campaign was rolling and so was the campaign party, taking an early morning train from New Haven to New York City. Large and mostly friendly crowds greeted Governor Reagan at a series of New York City events that day, which ended with a packaged tour of the floor of the New York Stock Exchange. *Photograph by Roger Sandler.*

First family. Just after Ronald Reagan announced his candidacy, his family joined him on the dais of the New York Hilton, November 13, 1979. Between Ronald and Nancy is Maureen; then Patti, Michael, his wife Colleen, and Ron. *Photograph by Roger Sandler.*

Campaign Chief of Staff Ed Meese and Campaign Director William Casey at the Dallas–Fort Worth airport, 1980. *Photograph by Roger Sandler.*

Nancy Reagan's campaign day begins. Often, during both the 1976 and 1980 campaigns, she would depart for a separate day of campaigning, rejoining her husband each evening. *Photograph by Roger Sandler.*

A campaign day in the California primary, May, 1980. This scene was repeated hundreds of times throughout both campaigns. *Photograph by Roger Sandler.*

Jaffrey, New Hampshire, February, 1980. *Photograph by Roger Sandler.*

"Dutch" returns to Davenport, January, 1980. The candidate looks on admiringly as his wife accepts flowers. Reagan began his career as a radio announcer on the Iowa city's station WOC in the '30s. *Photograph by Roger Sandler.*

understand strength; they exploit weakness and take advantage of inexperience. And, possibly, it was inexperience that led the president to placate the most dovish members of his party by scuttling the B-1 bomber—one of his bargaining chips—even before the SALT II negotiations began."

He reviewed Soviet and Cuban adventuring in Africa and had this to say about Southern Africa—"Whatever we may think of South Africa's internal policies, control of its mineral riches and its strategic position are the Soviet Union's ultimate goal in Africa."

On American leadership—"America will remain great and act responsibly so long as it exercises power—wisely, and not in the bullying sense—but exercises it nonetheless.

"Leadership is a great burden. We grow weary of it at times. And the Carter administration, despite its own cheerful propaganda about accomplishments, reflects that weariness. But, if *we* are not to shoulder the burdens of leadership in the free world, then who will? The alternatives are neither pleasant nor acceptable. Great nations which fail to meet their responsibilities are consigned to the dustbin of history. We grew from that small, weak republic which had as its assets spirit, optimism, faith in God, and an unshakable belief that free men and women could govern themselves wisely. We became the leader of the free world, an example for all those who cherish freedom."

For those of us closely associated with Governor Reagan, the rest of March and early April were filled with preparations for the Reagans' April trip which would take them around the world. Dick Allen coordinated the arrangements for the visit to Japan, the first leg of the trip. Governor Reagan was interested in returning to Taiwan and accepted a standing invitation to address the Chinese National Association of Industry and Commerce. I coordinated the arrangements for this visit and for the Hong Kong visit that would follow it. The Reagans had also been invited several times by the Shah of Iran to visit his country and were now finally able to schedule their time so that they could accept. Mike Deaver coordinated the arrangements for this portion of the trip.

For most of us who were long familiar with the Reagans' scheduling, working out the details came almost as second nature. Mike asked Chuck Tyson (who had been an advance man for Reagan in Sacramento) to advance the Asian portion of the trip. I was to advance the first stop, in Honolulu, where Governor Reagan had two speaking engagements, one to an annual investment and economic conference and the other to a trade association. Richard Allen and his wife, Pat, would meet the Reagans and my wife, Irene, and me in Tokyo. Meanwhile, Mike and Carolyn Deaver would head in the other direction, through Europe to Iran, to meet the Reagans when they arrived in Tehran.

Chuck Tyson met us at the airport in Tokyo late in the afternoon, Saturday, April 15. We had left Honolulu at one o'clock the afternoon of the fourteenth, but had advanced a day on the calendar by crossing the International Date Line. We went straight to the Hotel Okura. The next day, Dick Allen briefed Governor Reagan on details of the Tokyo schedule. On the flight across the Pacific, Reagan had read Allen's briefing books about issues of concern to the Japanese. In Tokyo, Allen had arranged rounds of meetings with leading political and business figures.

Late Sunday afternoon Ambassador (and former U.S. Senate Majority Leader) Mike Mansfield was scheduled to call on the Reagans in their hotel suite. The Allens and we were with the Reagans when he arrived. We had not asked the State Department for any assistance in planning this trip. Rather, once all the arrangements had been made, we notified them of the broad outlines of our itinerary. The Mansfield meeting came about as a result.

A serious, reserved man, Mansfield seemed uncomfortable meeting Reagan, as if, perhaps, he expected the next hour to be an ordeal of listening to oversimplifications and extremist rhetoric about world events. The Reagans, with their warm sense of hospitality, quickly sought to put him at ease. Governor Reagan seemed to sense that Mansfield might be expecting him to match old stereotyped descriptions and began discussing—in well-informed detail—the current issues worrying the Japanese. He ably demonstrated sensitivity to the subtleties of the U.S.–Japanese relationship and, despite the presumed political gulf between host and visitor, Mansfield's reserve began to melt as he realized that he and Reagan saw eye-to-eye on these issues. Indeed, the atmosphere was so cordial after an hour that both seemed to genuinely regret having to end the visit. The ambassador left, inviting us all to a reception, across the street at the embassy, late the next day.

In 1980, Ronald Reagan, as president-elect, decided to ask Mansfield to stay on as our ambassador to Japan. I believe this decision was rooted in that first meeting at the Hotel Okura in April, 1978.

Monday morning began with a breakfast with some two dozen Japanese businessmen, led by Mr. S. Nagano, former chairman of the Japan Chamber of Commerce and of Nippon Steel. The guest list read like a Who's Who of the executive cadres of Japan's major businesses and industries. An even more senior group, including the chairmen of many of the same companies, met with us for breakfast the next day.

Reagan had developed his remarks to these groups with special care. Dick Allen, with his extensive experience in dealing with Japanese businessmen and officials, assisted him. Reagan's remarks were intended to assure these Japanese leaders that he understood their concerns, to recognize the legitimacy of Japanese competition in world trade but at the same time to make it clear that he believed the United States should restore its own ability to compete effectively.

He frequently referred to the U.S.–Japanese relationship as being "special" and a "partnership." He said:

> The basic ingredients of U.S.–Japanese relations are many, but none can be more important than maintaining mutual trust and respect. This requires great patience and an understanding by each partner of how the other partner thinks, how he sees the world and how he is likely to react to changes and alterations in the basic patterns of the relationship.
>
> Beyond that, I believe that the sincerity of each partner must remain above question at all times, and that each side must always demonstrate a willingness to discuss, to negotiate, to compromise and to adjust to momentary or passing differences in the interest of maintaining a smooth working relationship.
>
> At the same time, and in view of the fact that Japan and the United States will not always approach each issue or each problem in an identical way, I firmly believe that there must be a strong element of predictability in our relations. Sudden, unannounced sharp departures from the existing pattern of relations would be harmful, even counterproductive. Neither side must perceive the other as attempting to gain a unilateral or selfish advantage, and we should be patient with each other.

This last point brought vigorous nods from Reagan's Japanese audiences. The Japanese had been upset by various sudden changes in U.S. policy which affected their country, but about which they had not been consulted. Both Presidents Nixon and Carter had sprung such "shokkus" (shocks) on the Japanese, and Reagan wanted them to know that he understood their concern. Implicit in his comments, of course, was the thought that if he were one day president the views he was expressing in Tokyo during this visit would provide the basis for U.S. relations with Japan (and, to a great extent, they have).

After breakfast, we made an official call on Prime Minister Fukuda with whom Reagan had struck up a friendship on his previous visit, when Fukuda was a cabinet member. After that, we called on former Prime Minister Kishi, a wise and venerated man in his eighties whose opinion is frequently sought by leaders of Japan's long-ruling Liberal Democratic party.

In the afternoon we called at LDP headquarters for a meeting with then-party secretary, Masayoshi Ohira who, a few months later, became prime minister (and who died in office in 1980), and afterward with Mr. Nakasone, the party's defense expert and leader of a rival party faction.

At Ambassador Mansfield's reception late that day, Mansfield greeted the Reagans warmly and said to the governor, "We've had some very good reports about your day." We had felt it was a good day, too. Reagan had been warmly received by those he met and they were reassured by his message in support of cooperation, consultation and sincere competition without trade protectionism. He saw the latter as a two-way street and subtly made sure those he spoke with did, too, since it was no secret that the Japanese marketing and distribution system's complexity and "non-tariff barriers" made entry into the Japanese market by outsiders difficult.

Tuesday morning, Mr. S. Ishihara, a young Japanese legislator who was also a successful writer and yachtsman, arranged for a national television interview of Reagan to be taped at a downtown Tokyo studio. That evening, the entire party had dinner with a group of Japanese Diet members, most of whom were allied with Ishihara. As in the other group meetings, there were interpreters' booths for simultaneous translation. At the dinner meeting, both sides used the earphones extensively, but I noticed at the two breakfasts with the business leaders very few of the Japanese were listening to the Japanese translations of Reagan's remarks. They understood him in English, then replied in Japanese. Among our party only Allen had some knowledge of Japanese, so we kept to our earphones.

On Wednesday morning, a breakfast with Japan's special trade representative, Ambassador N. Ushiba, was interrupted by a telephone call from Dan Kingsley, manager of the Deaver & Hannaford office in Washington. "The Senate just voted in favor of the second Panama Canal treaty," he said. I took the news to the others. Reagan's disappointment showed, but an hour later, when he was interviewed at a television station for satellite transmission back to the ABC network in the United States, he said, "As you know, I felt these treaties were flawed and should not have been passed in this form; however, the Senate has completed its action and now we must hope that it proves to have been a wise action." Thus, an issue that had heated so much of the 1976 political campaign and been the subject of so much debate and newsprint, effectively came to an end. Only time would tell if the treaties had been crafted wisely and well.

Our Tokyo schedule came to a conclusion with a lively press conference-style luncheon in the rooftop clubroom of the Foreign Correspondents' Association. In midafternoon we left for Taipei.

We arrived in late afternoon and a wet cloud cover hung over the city. It was rush hour in Taipei and that meant thousands of motorbikes and small motorcycles mingled with automobiles on all the main streets. The main airport has since moved to a site about twenty-five miles from downtown Taipei, but then it was virtually adjacent to the business district. Airliners screamed in below the roof level of the Grand Hotel, seeming to skim just above the busy vehicle traffic on the Keelung-Kaohsiung expressway which passed a short distance in front of it.

The Republic of China greeted Ronald Reagan as a good friend, virtually a hero. Our motorcade, with R.O.C. and U.S. flags flying from the fenders of the autos, made its way through downtown Taipei. People stopped and waved and cheered despite the threatening weather. Reagan was the most important American public figure to visit Taiwan since Vice-President Nelson Rockefeller attended Chiang Kai-shek's funeral in 1975.

That evening, the Reagans and their party were hosted at dinner by Foreign Minister C.H. Shen at the National Guest House. This building, vaguely Victorian in style, is near the presidential palace in the center of the city, and was built around the turn of the century by the Japanese, during the beginning of their fifty-year occupation of Taiwan.

The next morning we flew to Kaohsiung, the large industrial city at the south end of the island, to visit the big new shipyard and the American-designed steel mill. After lunch back in Taipei, hosted by Dr. and Mrs. C. F. Koo (he is a business leader, Taiwan-born, and president of the Chinese National Association of Commerce and Industry), we called on the foreign minister and the minister of economics, Y. S. Sun (now premier). That evening, then-President C. K. Yen was host at a formal and many-coursed Chinese banquet.

The following morning, Reagan met over breakfast privately with Chiang Ching-kuo (son of Chiang Kai-shek), then president-elect and prime minister. Reagan told us afterward that he had said that he trusted Chiang would understand if he traveled to the mainland of China. He reported that "C.C.K." (his popular nickname) replied that he understood, indeed (by then, Allen and I had already made tentative, preliminary soundings about a possible Reagan visit to the People's Republic of China).

After an informal question-and-answer session at the clubrooms of the American Chamber of Commerce and a call on U.S. Ambassador and Mrs. Leonard Unger, we went on to Governor Reagan's featured speaking engagement to several hundred members of the Chinese National Association of Commerce and Industry at a downtown hotel ballroom.

Reagan knew his audience was most worried about possible "normalization" of relations by the United States with the mainland. After detailing the economic accomplishments of the Republic of China on Taiwan, he moved to the subject of normalization.

First, on U.S.–R.O.C. friendship, he said:

Vivid evidence that our friendship is a two-way street was given early this year when you sent a special trade mission to the U.S. for the express purpose of buying more than one-quarter of a million dollars of American goods in order to reduce your trade surplus with us. . . . Here we have evidence of each nation helping the other. First, American aid at a time when you were embarking on modernization and industrialization of Taiwan in order to improve the lot of your people. Now, you are making a special effort to "buy American" at a time when we have a serious trade deficit.

This friendship and mutual trust goes back a long way. Our ties are strong. They bind us, but could they be broken? I am afraid that the answer is "Yes," they could—under certain circumstances. But should they be broken and must they be broken? The answer in both cases is "No!," of course not.

The American view of China today might be likened to a gemstone that is held to the light. If you turn it one way, it reflects the light in a certain way. But turn it, and the light is reflected elsewhere.

Referring to U.S. public opinion polls, he said, "When the average American is asked his opinion of our relations with China, he responds by saying, yes, he would like to have so-called 'normal' relations with the mainland. But, turn the question and you get a much different reflection of opinion. When the question becomes, would you be willing to 'normalize' relations with Peking at the expense of the Republic of China on Taiwan?—then, the average American answers with an emphatic 'no.' "

He added, "Still, we must not underestimate the influence of that relatively small number of American scholars and commentators which is pressing the normalization issue essentially on Peking's terms. They are widely published and quoted in our newspapers and magazines and they have adherents in our federal government. . . . There is an odd quality to their discussion in the arguments they put forth. They talk of Taiwan as if it were something abstract and not a real place populated by seventeen million real people who want nothing more nor less than to be free to determine their own destiny."

He then presaged what would, in the years ahead, become fact so far as Peking's position was concerned: "Those in my country who argue for immediate normalization also contend that if Peking would only give quiet assurances that it would not attempt a military conquest of Taiwan in exchange for 'normalization,' then your security here would be assured. Peking's answer to this, as you know, has been echoed time and again by its leaders. They insist that once 'normalization' is achieved, what they do about Taiwan is nobody else's business."

Based both on his own deductions and the views of several specialists with whom he discussed the issue, Reagan believed that Peking needed the United States far more than we needed them. He did not subscribe to the view, pushed heavily in the Carter administration by national security adviser Zbigniew Brzezinski, that the United States should "play the China card" against the USSR. Involving ourselves in a millennium-old hostility between the Chinese and Russians might have unhappy ultimate consequences for us, he believed. In other words, he did not subscribe to the theory that "the enemy of my enemy is my friend."

The Chinese communists had been pressing determinedly—with as full a propaganda campaign as they could muster—for normalization on their terms. They insisted that these include the breaking of diplomatic relations with the Republic of China, breaking our mutual defense treaty of 1954 and withdrawing our remaining military advisers from Taiwan. Their purpose was to de-legitimize the Republic of China as a government in international eyes so they could eventually incorporate it into the rest of China which they controlled. In the 1972 Shanghai Communique our government acknowledged that all Chinese consider there to be only one China, so, if the People's Republic could get us to switch diplomatic recognition on its terms, the stage would be set for concluding the thirty-year-old Chinese civil war on its terms. Reagan made this point in his address.

He also sought to reassure his audience. "The days ahead will not be easy ones, but you know that," he said. "In my opinion the realities of American politics are such that our government would not be persuaded to move any closer to so-called normalization this year. After all, we have national congressional elections this November, and elected representatives do not like to have to answer for unpopular policies. Depending upon the outcome of that election, though, I think you can expect the advocates of normalization to begin raising the same arguments again next year, perhaps with an even greater sense of urgency and restlessness than before."[*]

The audience gave the Reagans a long standing ovation. After a brief airport press conference we left for Hong Kong. The next day, British officials had arranged for the Reagans and me to go on a helicopter overflight of the entire colony—Hong Kong and the New Territories. The intense shipping and business activity was spread out below us along the harbor. Inland, we passed over great clusters of new high-rise buildings the government was putting up to relieve the congestion of population growth. Despite the population pressures on Hong Kong, it

---

[*] His prediction was only slightly off. Carter announced "normalization"—on Peking's terms—on December 15, 1978.

was amazing to find small villages in the hills along the northern parts of the bay deserted, their inhabitants having moved to the cities.

Sir Denys Roberts, the chief secretary of the Hong Kong government, was host to the Reagan party and to the U.S. consul and his wife at lunch at Victoria house, high on Victoria peak on the Hong Kong side of the harbor, looking over the twin cities of Hong Kong and Kowloon.

That evening, the Reagans asked the rest of us—the Allens, Chuck and Missy Tyson, and Irene and me—to be their guests for dinner at the Peninsula Hotel, before their 11 P.M. departure for Tehran. It was a relaxed and happy evening, with much laughter and reminiscences of the events of the trip. As was his custom, Governor Reagan, with his decaffeinated coffee after dinner, pulled what looked like a ballpoint pen from his pocket, pressed the button and dropped white powder into the coffee. I had seen him do this many times, but it always brought curious questions from those who had never seen it. The gadget was something he had come across some years before. It held a sugar substitute which could be easily dispensed in just the right quantity into one's coffee. Over the years he has bought and given away dozens of the gadgets (I still carry one he gave me which I use for dispensing a salt substitute).

After a long flight, with an intermediate stop in Delhi, India, the Reagans arrived in Tehran on Sunday morning, April 23. The Deavers met them and they proceeded to the Tehran residence of Iran's ambassador to the United States, Ardeshir Zahedi. The next six days were busy ones, viewing historic sites and meeting with officials of the Shah's government. On Thursday that week, the Shah and his empress were hosts at a luncheon for the Reagans, and Ambassador and Mrs. William Sullivan were their dinner hosts that evening.

Governor Reagan met privately with the Shah for more than an hour, during which the Shah told him of his hopes for his people, for the continued modernization of his country, for expanded prosperity and education. At the same time, Reagan told friends later, the Shah seemed like a very worried man when he talked of the future.

On Saturday, April 29, the Reagans and Deavers left Tehran for London and the next day on to Los Angeles. At home, the political temperature was rising.

California's Proposition 13, the Jarvis–Gann initiative, was on the June ballot and was being hotly debated. Reagan had spoken warmly of the measure months before, even though he realized its imperfections. Back in January, he made it the topic of one of his nationally syndicated newspaper columns, noting that:

> Talk of property-tax revolt continues to simmer just about anywhere that inflation-swollen assessments are the rule—and that's just about

everywhere in the United States. But California is the place where the revolt is coming to a boil. It should reach that temperature by June 6, the date of the Golden State's primary election. . . .

Worried that the Jarvis amendment will pass, Governor Brown and the legislature are batting back and forth various tax relief measures. There is one obvious solution they aren't saying much about: give the money back to the people who paid it. When I was governor I proposed that and found that making such a recommendation to a legislative body is a little like getting between the hog and the bucket. You get buffeted about a bit. In fact, one state senator said he considered my proposal "an unnecessary expenditure of public funds."

If the Jarvis amendment has done nothing else it has gotten the Big Spenders' attention in California. They talk of little else. No wonder; if it passes, they will have to set spending priorities. Predictably, the Spenders have gone into a Chicken Little routine. Working from the assumption that public expenditures can never go down and that no economies are possible, they say that cities and counties would have to cut essential services if the amendment passes. It would require a two-thirds vote of the people for local agencies to increase other taxes to replace the property tax revenue, so opponents of the measure have warned solemnly that the state would have to assume the cost of the lost local revenue by jacking up sales and income taxes.

The net result, according to the Spenders, would be a tax "shift," not a tax savings. They used that argument in 1973 when we proposed a limitation on the percentage of the people's income government could take to run its affairs. They scared enough voters to defeat our proposal (though it was so carefully constructed it could not have resulted in a tax "shift"). This time, the taxpayers haven't been buying the tax "shift" argument. In my travels around the state, I am finding just the opposite: most people can't wait to go to the polls to sock it to the Spenders. . . .

Though the Jarvis amendment is not perfect, it will serve to focus attention on a very basic topic: Should government (and taxes) expand indefinitely, or should its role be limited? If the Jarvis proposal passes in California, watch the prairie fire sweep to all points of the compass.

He made it the subject of other radio and newspaper commentaries, believing that the growing support for it was a logical outgrowth of a movement he had helped start with his tax-and-spending limitation, Proposition 1, back in 1973.

Meanwhile, other potential 1980 candidates were keeping the news media busy reporting their comings and goings. George Bush had been in Asia at the time the Reagans had in late April. John Connally was forming a political action committee. Senators Howard Baker and Bob Dole talked about possible candidacies.

The Reagan schedule had plenty of variety. On May 14, Governor Reagan was the guest on CBS's "Face the Nation." On the twentieth, at his Pacific Palisades home, he met with William Clements, then the Republican candidate for governor of Texas, Lyn Nofziger, and Tom Reed (former Republican National committeeman from California). That afternoon, Senator Dole and his daughter called for a visit. The next Wednesday, George Cook, a long-time Reagan supporter and one of the original members of Reagan's 1976 campaign committee, visited from Nebraska. That same day, the Reverend Jesse Jackson had been invited for lunch, but lunchtime came and went and there was no Reverend Jackson. His colleagues later attributed it to a scheduling error.

On Saturday the twenty-eighth, the Reagans and several of those of us associated with them attended the fifth anniversary reunion dinner of the Vietnam War POWs. It was a warm and stirring event at the Los Angeles Marriott Hotel. Commander John McCain, who had spent eight years as a POW, was the master of ceremonies. Mike Curb, soon to become lieutenant governor of California, arranged for stars such as Sammy Davis, Jr., to pay an entertainment tribute to the POWs. It was a special event for the Reagans, for in their Sacramento home they had entertained many of these same men and their wives very soon after their return from captivity.

On election day, June 6, Governor Reagan and I flew to Denver. He had promised Joe Coors that he would be guest speaker at a fund-raising dinner for a group of freshman Republican state legislators. The Republican party was making a comeback in Colorado, and Coors felt that Reagan's appearance would strengthen the reelection chances of these men. We heard the California election results on television later that night in our Denver hotel. Proposition 13 had passed by a wide margin.

Reagan was to return to Los Angeles the next morning to attend a press conference and a unity luncheon at the Century Plaza hotel with the Republican candidates for governor (Attorney General Evelle Younger had won the nomination). Since I was going on to Washington instead, I suggested to Governor Reagan that we go over possible press conference questions. There were only two which I thought might be new ones, and I had discussed them with Deaver, Nofziger, and Meese at what was becoming a weekly meeting. These two issues involved ballot initiatives Propositions 5 and 6, which would be on the November ballot. The first was an anti-smoking measure which would have required businesses to create smoking and nonsmoking work areas for employees and would have imposed a crazy quilt of regulations on smoking in public buildings. The second was designed to ferret out and dismiss schoolteachers who might be homosexuals. I briefed the governor on the measures and said that while our consensus was that both seemed badly flawed, we recommended for the present that he not declare a firm position on either, instead indicating initial concern and his intention to research them thoroughly. As it turned out, this matched his own views closely. He agreed this wasn't the time to take stands and that there should be research of the measures, but he didn't like the sound of either one. His reaction was that Proposition 5 sounded like regulation run amok and that reasonable people working in the same place should be able to work out their own smoking arrangements. As for Proposition 6, he reminded me that in his film days there were people who were widely thought to be homosexuals, but whose private lives never touched upon their professional behavior. He said he thought the same could be assumed of other professions, too.

As it turned out, the press concentrated on Proposition 13 and the candidates at the Los Angeles press conference, so neither of the new issues came up, though in time both were to become the subject of hot debate throughout the state.

Meanwhile, plans were going forward for an event that would ultimately prove to have significance in building the Reagan conservative coalition in 1980. R. Emmett (Bob) Tyrrell, editor of *The American Spectator*, who has been described as a latter-day H. L. Mencken because of his iconoclastic pen, had been arranging a small dinner in New York for the Reagans with some leaders of what was coming to be called the Neo-conservative Movement. The dinner was scheduled for Monday, June 12, at the Union League Club and included Norman Podhoretz, editor of the influential magazine *Commentary*, his wife, Midge Decter, an editor at Basic Books and an author, and Nathan Glazer, coeditor with Irving Kristol of *The Public Interest*, an opinion quarterly. The Neo-conservatives were, for the most part, from New York social democratic, liberal backgrounds who had found the Democratic party—particularly after its capture by the McGovernites—to have moved far away from their own ideals. They had become increasingly alarmed by the military strength of the Soviet Union and its sorry record in the area of human rights.

Also at the dinner were broadcasting executive Frank Shakespeare, former head of the United States Information Agency and a leading conservative intellectual in New York, Tyrrell, Steve Munsen of the *Spectator*, and myself.

About two weeks before we left for New York, I had given Nancy Reagan a copy of Midge Decter's book, *Liberal Parents, Radical Children*. She was absorbed by it, and as soon as the two women met, they fell into animated conversation about it. The dinner went well, generally, although on both "sides" there were old stereotypes to be broken down. Perhaps the highlight was a lively conversation that Glazer and Reagan had over the causes of graffiti on New York subways (this led to an exchange of letters between them over the next several months).

The next day, Reagan addressed a group of corporate public affairs executives at the Plaza Hotel. His friend Justin Dart, working with the Chamber of Commerce of the United States, the National Association of Manufacturers, and the National Federation of Independent Businesses, had organized the event, an all-day seminar. It was to be one of several in major cities around the country. Its subject was the free enterprise system in particular and economics in general. A number of companies, including Dart's, had developed employee information programs about the elements of economics. Such programs set out to identify the causes and effects of inflation, explain the role of profits, define productivity and its importance, and show the role of capital in economic growth. The basic purpose was to make the private enterprise system work more effectively by reducing government deficits and undue regulation. This seminar and the others like it were designed to show more companies how such programs were working. The nuts-and-bolts atmosphere of this economic seminar for business people seemed far removed from the intellectual atmosphere of the previous night's dinner, but in a way it, too, became part of the process of coalition-building, though we did not know it at the time.

At about that time, Reagan assembled his small advisory group at his Pacific Palisades home for one of its periodic meetings. We reviewed the performance of the Carter administration, the state of the Republican party, and the outlook for various issues in the months ahead. This time, though, there turned out to be another subject. We were drawing to a close when one member of the group said with a grin, "Well, Governor, are you going to run?" Governor Reagan said something along the lines of, "Well, I don't know, but let's find out what all of you think." He then asked each of us in the room, one by one, to give our opinion. No one said no and the yes answers had varying degrees of elaboration. When he got to me I said, "If that's where you want to go, I want to help you get there." Like the others, I wanted Ronald Reagan to be president, but at that point it still seemed like a very steep mountain to climb.

The meeting ended over one of Nancy Reagan's beautifully planned and executed lunches and the kind of easy joking and anecdotes that Ronald Reagan enjoyed sharing with his group. He did not declare any personal conclusion from our statements to him about running. He kept his own counsel, but in my mind I always looked back on that meeting as a landmark in Ronald Reagan's road to the White House.

Thinking back, I shouldn't have let my thoughts run to much doubt at the time for, like Deaver and Nofziger, I had been on the road a good deal with Reagan in recent months and had felt the noticeable, but hard-to-measure change in the body politic.* The people—as contrasted to media commentators and political pundits—were moving Reagan's way on the issues. We watched polls as closely as gypsies watch tea leaves, and everything we saw confirmed what we were feeling.

Late in June, on the twenty-fourth, CFTR had another steering committee meeting and all-day workshop seminar, this time in Philadelphia. Governor Reagan was the keynote speaker at lunch. Several hundred persons attended. Late in the day, Robert Strausz-Hupé, whom Reagan had often quoted from the former's farewell speech as our ambassador to NATO, called on Reagan in his hotel suite. Strausz-Hupé, who had been warning about the Soviet military buildup for several years, was now a scholar at the Foreign Policy Research Institute at the University of Pennsylvania.†

Right after July Fourth, Reagan toured several states, appearing at fund-raising events for candidates CFTR was supporting. This included stops in Utah, Nevada (broken by a weekend sidetrip to Senator Paul Laxalt's ranch in the mountains above Lake Tahoe), and Indiana.

On Monday, July 17, he fulfilled a commitment he had made prior to his Asia trip. He addressed a joint luncheon meeting of the Chinese Consolidated Benevolent Association and the Committee to Conserve Chinese Culture at a large restaurant in Los Angeles's Chinatown. Most in the audience had family or business ties with Taiwan, so he used the occasion to report on what he had said in his speech in Taipei and to describe his current impressions of Taiwan.

About relations with the rival Chinese government, he noted, "America's friendship with the people of the Chinese mainland [can] be developed with care, but this can be done only if it does not jeopardize our close friendship with the Chinese on Taiwan. The tradition of friendship of the American people with the Chinese people is a long one, and many individual Americans are desirous of visiting the mainland, while others want to develop more trade. Such things need not be inconsistent with the present strong ties we have with the Republic of China."

This particular passage was designed to ease the way for Governor Reagan to visit the mainland later in the year, should he decide to do so. Conversations about this had gone on, more or less continuously, within his advisory group since late the previous year. We recognized that should he make such a trip, since he was known as a strong supporter of

---

* One instance occurred in June when I was in New York with the Reagans. We had one evening free and Deaver suggested that although both of us would not be there, we jointly have the Reagans as our guests for dinner and the theater. At the show, *Ain't Misbehavin'*, the audience was clearly an out-of-town, vacation-time one. People spontaneously stood and clapped when they discovered the Reagans in their midst. Many came over to shake hands, ask for autographs, and wish them well.

† In 1981, President Reagan named him U.S. Ambassador to Turkey.

the nationalist Chinese, he had to let them know (which he did in Taipei in April) and to let various American conservative leaders know quietly in advance of any publicity, so they would not misunderstand. Something unexpected happened the morning after this Los Angeles speech, however, which put the subject on ice.

Tuesday morning, unbeknownst to any of us in California, John Sears was the featured guest at one of the frequent Godfrey Sperling breakfasts (named after their host, the capital bureau chief of the *Christian Science Monitor*) in Washington. These are attended by members of the national press corps and the guests are usually government or political leaders. Guests often use the Sperling breakfasts to float trial balloons on various subjects. At this breakfast, Sears told the reporters that Reagan might soon go to the mainland of China!

Although Sears was a member of Reagan's advisory group, he had no title, for the group was informal. Nor was he authorized to speak for Reagan. In fact, no one was. Even Deaver and I, as his professional representatives, checked with Governor Reagan first when reporters asked for his opinion on an issue unless we had at hand something current he had already said about it.

Reagan himself and Deaver, Nofziger, and I frequently had to listen to criticism of Sears's handling of the 1976 campaign. We explained, over and over, the reasoning behind the moves that were made and why they took us as far as we could go, but the criticism continued. This announcement by Sears brought on a fresh barrage of calls from friends and supporters around the country.

The reporters, knowing that Sears was still involved with Reagan, assumed that if he were accepting a breakfast invitation to meet with them, he must be speaking for Reagan. Under the circumstances, such an assumption seemed justified. Much of the reportage of the breakfast gave the impression that a trip to China would be part of a remaking of Reagan's image into something more "moderate" (whatever that term meant to the reporters, I cannot say, but to the Reagan supporters who began flooding our switchboard, it meant only one thing: Sears was going to be a sort of Svengali, making Reagan over into something he wasn't).

As soon as the news of the Sears breakfast reached all of us, Deaver, Nofziger, Meese, and I conferred with one another and with Governor Reagan. We all knew there would be many calls from the news media seeking a Reagan reaction to Sears's statement. Governor Reagan felt he should have a statement ready, making it clear that Sears was not speaking for him but only for himself. We could also use it to answer supporters' inquiries.

Sears, when we talked with him, seemed genuinely sorry that he had caused such a commotion. It was not to go away, however. The Reagans were in Washington on the twenty-fifth to serve as hosts to the Republican Eagles at a dinner cruise on the Potomac.* The next day, Reagan had lunch in a private dining room in the Capitol with the Kingston Group. This organization of about two dozen members, is composed of conservative activists who are either on congressional staffs or who are the professional managers of various conservative organizations. They had asked Senator Laxalt to arrange the meeting, and he had urged Reagan to do it. They wanted to talk about Sears. They were upset and worried. If Reagan ran, their support would be important, for they were among the hardest workers in the conservative movement and would be able to attract many energetic volunteers. At the same time, we knew that Reagan would have to appeal to a variety of constituencies, not just the "movement" conservatives. Reagan's continuing themes—of bringing government spending and regulation under control and of creating a coherent foreign and defense policy—had appeal across party lines and even to many people who did not think of themselves as being "political." Reagan and his close associates had no intention of being captured by any constituency; however, it was important that the views of this particular potential campaign cadre be heard. And Reagan heard them that day.

Sears was the main topic. Would he be Reagan's campaign manager if Reagan ran? The governor gave a strong reply. He would use Sears's talents, yes, but he would have a different kind of campaign organization from that of 1976. Did Sears speak for him? No, Reagan said, referring to his statement released after Sears's China-visit comments. In fact, said Reagan, he was not planning to go to the Chinese mainland. That was correct. Sears's comments at the Sperling breakfast had effectively killed the idea.

After the luncheon, Senator Laxalt had planned a series of short visits for Reagan with Senators Carl Curtis, Barry Goldwater, and William Roth (co-author of the Kemp–Roth tax-cut legislation). After that, he stopped to meet Senator Laxalt's summer interns and have his photo taken with them. Then, Congressman Phil Crane came to call. We knew the topic in advance. Crane was going to announce his own candidacy for the presidency.

Crane had been one of Reagan's earliest supporters. He had cam-

* Party Chairman Bill Brock asked leading party figures to be hosts at several such functions throughout the year. The Eagles (and their spouses) are the party's largest contributors. The invitation to Reagan was the beginning of a peacemaking effort after the Panama Canal treaty problem of the previous winter.

paigned long and hard for Reagan. He was an articulate spokesman for the philosophy he and Reagan shared. The two had always had a warm rapport. Today, though, the atmosphere seemed strained. I sensed it was not easy for Crane to say that, assuming Reagan was going to run, he was going to challenge him. But he had made up his mind that he would run and telling Reagan about it privately was a necessary step. Crane emphasized that he would never say anything critical of Reagan, nor any other Republican.

Reagan told him of his concern about two possible conservative candidacies; that it might split support within the most important segment of the party. He also told Crane that although he had not made a final decision about running himself and would not for many months, "On a scale of one to ten, I'm at ten-and-a-half."

Crane nevertheless made his announcement on August 2, the first official candidate of either party to enter the 1980 race for the White House.

There were two nonpolitical events of note during that summer. On July 18, Reagan went to Palo Alto for the dedication the next day of the new federally built Hoover Building, constructed to house the expanded collection of the Hoover Institution on War, Revolution and Peace, next to the Hoover Tower on the Stanford University campus.

On the evening of the eighteenth, George Schultz and his wife entertained many of the dedication participants at their campus home. Schultz, who had been secretary of the treasury under Nixon and Ford, was now on the Stanford faculty part-time and also served as president of Bechtel Corporation, the large San Francisco-based engineering firm. Over coffee after dinner, he invited his guests to have a freewheeling conversation about economics.

There were about two dozen of us in the Schultz's living room to hear a lively, hour-long discussion between Reagan, Schultz, Caspar Weinberger, William Simon, economist Michael Boskin, and others.

The next morning, Reagan, Ed Meese, and I had breakfast with Martin and Annaliese Anderson and Alan Greenspan, former chairman of the Council of Economic Advisors. Anderson and Greenspan were good friends, and Anderson felt that he and Reagan should become better acquainted. Reagan talked about supply-side tax cuts. Greenspan did not take an opposite view, but he stressed the importance of budget cuts in conjunction with any tax cuts.

The Hoover dedication address, under a blue sky in front of the tower, was given by former President Gerald Ford. Senator Mark Hatfield, a leading student of Herbert Hoover's career, gave an historical sketch of the man who had created this institution.

In early August, the Reagans flew to Dixon, Illinois, for Governor Reagan's high school class reunion. The people of Dixon had something special in store for their most famous son: they dedicated a bridge over the Rock River in his honor. Later he told us, "I said 'thanks, I'm greatly honored, but you've called it the Ronald Reagan *Memorial* Bridge and I'm still alive.' "

After a brief vacation at the ranch, Ronald Reagan's fall schedule began. As chairman of Citizens for the Republic, he had committed himself to making a large number of appearances for candidates CFTR would be supporting in its first major election effort. These events were coordinated with his regular business speaking schedule.

Governor Reagan had developed a new speech for the fall political appearances. He had talked over ideas for the speech with his advisory group during the summer. Bill Gavin, who had been a White House speech writer, was a member of this group and was asked to develop some draft material. During his vacation, Reagan molded this into a speech which proved to be a harbinger of his 1980 campaign. A re-reading of it today shows that it contains all the elements of coalition-building that he used to achieve success in 1980.

Because he gave this speech to Republican audiences, appearing on behalf of candidates for Congress or state offices, it took the form of a challenge to Republicans to reshape their party and its message. He said:

> We have to make our successes by our own effort. We cannot count on the ineptitude of the administration or the record of the Democrats in Congress to speak for themselves. The voters will only be aware of the profound difference between our two parties if we point out that difference to them.
>
> This isn't a case of the two parties seeking similar goals with different approaches. The other party has been proud to claim that it seeks bigger government programs in more and more areas of American life. The Democratic leaders have gloried in this philosophy. The Democratic intellectuals have written entire libraries of books telling how good big, centralized government is for you. For the Democratic leaders to turn their backs on what they have always been most proud of is proof that we Republicans have broken their ranks and that we are in the process of driving them off the field of political battle.
>
> But we have to be aware that the Democrats are regrouping. After the shock of California's Proposition 13, many of them have begun to do that well-known political dance, the Waffler's Waltz, over to our rhetoric if not our principles. They are engaged in one of the greatest rewritings of history ever attempted in American politics by telling the American people that high taxes, inflation, budget-busting and other forms of economic lunacy just *happened* and weren't caused by Democratic policies.

He then called for a new Republican message:

> . . . at the heart of that message should be five simple, familiar every-
> day words. No big economic theories. No sermons on political philosophy.
> Just five short words:
>   Family
>   Work
>   Neighborhood
>   Freedom
>   Peace

Republican candidates for every office should make these words the
heart of their message. Anything we have to tell the voters should eventually come back to these five words.

Americans are concerned over inflation, not because they have master's degrees in economics, but because inflation is hurting their families.

Americans are concerned over the future of the job market, not because they are interested in investment theory, but because each of us has
to work in order to eat and clothe ourselves and our families and to edu-
cate our kids.

Let the professors and Washington bureaucrats talk in their jargon
about costly urban "Marshall Plans." We should talk about how our programs and policies affect neighborhoods and their problems, because
that's where the people we have to reach live and raise their families.

Americans want peace and freedom in the world not because they are
interested in the deliberations of the Council on Foreign Relations. To
them peace and freedom mean their kids are going to get the chance to
enjoy the blessings they have and their fathers had before them. And, their
sons won't bleed their lives into the mud of a battlefield.

Family. Work. Neighborhood. Peace. Freedom.

We should repeat those words until they become second nature. We
should meditate on their meaning and how our policies can be applied to
them. They should be on our lips. But, they must also be in our hearts, just
as they are in the hearts of Americans all across this country.

When we talk about inflation, let's drop the textbook language and get
down to facts as Americans experience them. Let's say something like this
to the people we talk to: "Inflation is dangerous to your family's health.
And, inflation-spreaders in Congress and their high-tax colleagues should
be quarantined, just as we quarantine the carriers and spreaders of any
contagion. The way to deal with these economic Typhoid Marys is to take
them out of Congress and the legislature so they won't be harming your
family any more."

When we talk about such ideas as lower capital gains tax, let's throw
out all that economic mumbo jumbo and repeat over and over: "Jobs help
people. Investments make jobs."

And then let's ask: "Where are the jobs coming from if there is no
money to invest?" Let the Democrat candidate answer that one.

Let's stop using charts and graphs when we talk about employment, and say instead: "Work is at the center of our lives. Governmental policies that harm the economy destroy jobs. We want to keep the American economy sound and strong for people, for families, for your kids."

This isn't a change in what we believe. We are simply putting our belief into understandable language.

He then set the stage for his Republican listeners to begin to think in new ways of broadening their party's appeal.

I remember once reading about the great western journey made by the pioneers. It seems that a myth developed among the settlers that Indians had some inherent sense of direction, that they couldn't get lost in the wilderness because of some mystical power.

What actually happened was quite simple. The wagon trains approached each landmark from the same direction time after time. So a settler losing the regular trail might not recognize an otherwise familiar landmark when he saw it from a different angle. The Indians, of course, lived in the area and got used to seeing familiar objects from different vantage points.

For too long we Republicans, like most Americans, have approached the political landscape from one direction and have seen things in the same way.

We got used to and felt comfortable with the old divisions: Labor and Industry. Liberal and Conservative. Rich and Poor. Urban and Rural. These are the landmarks of the American political landscape as we learned them. Unconsciously, we have shaped our policies and our programs, our vision and our hopes by this way of looking at things.

But, the realities of 1978 demand that we get off of the beaten path and start learning new ways of looking at things. Let's decide for ourselves just how the political map should be viewed.

The union member living in a city neighborhood, the executive with a home in the suburbs, the farmer fifty miles away, the pre-med college student at the state university, the bus driver with kids to raise, his mom and dad who still live in the old neighborhood on a small pension, the teenage girl looking for her first job—if you look at such a group as we have been taught to, there is no community of interest.

But suppose we don't look at what the political experts say are the only things that matter, *group interests.* Suppose, instead, we look for a set of principles that link these men and women into a *community of values.* Family, work, neighborhood, peace, and freedom are values shared by each of them.

Instead of seeing them as we always have—stereotyped members of special interest groups—let's look at them as they see themselves. They are unique individuals with family responsibilities, with a love of country and a set of traditional values they share with millions of others. Let's treat them that way.

He then gave several illustrations of his concept of the "community of shared values," such as this one:

> We are told there can be no similarity of interest between the commuter who lives in the suburbs and the union member who lives in the city. They are supposed to be historic economic enemies. What one wants he must get at the expense of the other. Therefore, you have to direct your message to either one or the other.
>
> Don't you believe it.
>
> The suburban commuter wants relief from brutal taxation. He wants his money to mean something. He wants his schools to teach and his neighborhood to be safe. He wants the ordinary common-sense rules of experience to be observed by public officials when they are conducting public business.
>
> Tell me, how does the union member in the city differ from the suburbanite on these points? The answer, of course, is that he does *not* differ because, despite the fact that they make different salaries, may have different interests and styles and tastes—despite the fact they live apart from each other and may not know each other—they share the same basic values. We tend to forget that the suburbanite probably grew up in a union-member family in the city. He hasn't lost the beliefs he grew up with.
>
> The suburbanite's next-door neighbor may be like him in every way except the most important: He may not share the same love of family, of responsibility to traditional values. But the union member does. So, it isn't geographic proximity or even economic class that we look for. It's the way people look at themselves and the world. That is our key to political victory.
>
> Once you begin to look at things this way, the outlines of this community of values become clear. They live on farms, in city neighborhoods, in suburbs. They attend different houses of worship. They have different ancestors with different cultural attitudes and a different heritage. But, on certain basic things, they agree. They are peaceful people, but when they see somebody out to hurt their family or their neighborhood or their traditional values, they get angry. They are angry now, and for good reason. They are the victims of an undeclared war against the things they hold most sacred. And we are their allies in that war.

He moved on to the themes of "peace" and "freedom":

> As Republicans, we must simply and forthrightly bring before the American people the essence of our defense policy: America cannot afford to be Number Two. No matter what the specific defense issue may be, it is in the interest of peace and freedom that we be second to none. It is essential that we keep the technological advantages that have saved us and other nations from the fate of millions in Europe and Asia. Even more essential is that we have the will to use them if necessary.

Next, whether he knew it or not at the time, Reagan drew the battle lines for the 1980 challenge of Jimmy Carter:

Whether we are talking about domestiç or foreign policy, these are the facts that are clear about this election year: It is in the interest of the intellectual and political leaders of the other party to keep the status quo. They want Americans to keep on thinking about politics in the same way.

It is the job of Republicans to shake things up, to get things moving, to throw over the false idols the Democratic leaders have set for all to worship.

It is the job of Republicans to refuse to accept the old way of looking at things and to take a new look, to see opportunities Democrat leaders and their friends have told us no longer exist. It is our job to first stop government from hurting the American family and then to make certain future government policies do not harm it.

His conclusion was an example of "looking at things in a new way."

As my personal contribution to this new way of looking at things, let me close by quoting from a great American the Democratic party has claimed as its own. I challenge that claim, and every Republican should challenge it because Thomas Jefferson belongs to all Americans and not to one party. Indeed, if he were to come back today, it would not be the big-government, regulatory, paternal, meddling philosophy of the present Democratic party he would call his own.

If you've ever visited his home, Monticello, near Charlottesville in the beautiful Virginia countryside, you are suddenly aware of a fact that the history books rarely dwell on.

The country around Monticello is still beautiful today, much as it must have been when Jefferson built his superb home there. You stand on the hill on which Monticello is built, look around and wonder to yourself: *What would ever make a man risk all this?*

Think of it. Although the building was not completed when Jefferson wrote the Declaration of Independence, the dream must have been there. And he was willing to risk that dream, the dream we all share, a dream for his family, for his work, for the surrounding Virginia countryside which was his neighborhood. He was willing to say "farewell" to peace, to risk his freedom for what he *believed* in.

Tell that to the historians who say there was an economic cause of our revolution. Tell that to the cynics who say men and women are always motivated by their base instincts.

If you are at Monticello at twilight, the air is hushed and still. For a moment you are in a kind of timeless state. It could be 1978. Or 1878. Or even March 4, 1801. It was on that day that Jefferson delivered his first inaugural address. He spoke of the need for "a wise and frugal government, which shall restrain men from injuring one another, which shall leave them otherwise free to regulate their own pursuits of industry and improvement, and shall not take from the mouth of labor the bread it has earned. This is the sum of good government, and this is necessary to close the circle of our felicities."

That was the kind of government for which Jefferson and his friends were willing to risk their lives, their fortunes, and their sacred honor. Not for what they could get out of it, but for what they believed. They formed the first community of values in this country.

My friends, tell me: Can we do any less than to try to restore "the sum of good government" for ourselves and our children?

Let us do all we can for family, work, neighborhood, peace, and freedom. Let history record that almost two hundred years after Jefferson's words, there was still a majority of Americans who tried their best "to close the circle of our felicities."

Ronald Reagan gave that speech several dozen times in September and October, 1978. Invariably, the hush of his ending caused his audiences to sit in silence for a moment. Then, many with moist eyes, his listeners would get to their feet and begin clapping, louder and louder in what would become a sustained ovation. Reagan was touching the right chords with his audiences, but reporters who covered these events for the most part did not notice anything different. It was reported as just another political speech given by a man who was already considered one of America's best public speakers.

On September 22 in Chicago, Reagan took part in an event which reflected his challenge to his party to "look at things in a new way." For months the Kemp–Roth bill, designed to cut income tax rates by one-third over a three-year period, was gaining support among Republican members of Congress. Representative Jack Kemp evangelized for supply-side economics in speeches throughout the country. He was talking a new brand of economics and it added up to the politics of hope. Traditionally, most Republican public figures subscribed to the traditional view that if you cut taxes, you had to cut spending; that if you wanted to bring inflation down you had to tolerate more unemployment. Reagan himself used to talk of an "economic bellyache" to describe this phenomenon. Yet, the federal government's policies had begun to lead us into a period of both high inflation and high unemployment and there was no relief in sight. Kemp and the other supply-siders said it was time to look at tax cuts in a different light: If you cut taxes significantly and across the board (not "fine tuning" cuts or income redistribution cuts of the sort usually favored by the Democrats), you give human incentive a great boost. Incentive and production flourish and the economy grows. The federal treasury, after awhile, gets more revenue, not less.

Republicans on Capitol Hill began to see the Kemp–Roth bill as both a way to offer a positive program to the voters and to embarrass the Democrats. Republican National Chairman Bill Brock, a man with a strong desire to dress up the party's image and make it more broadly appealing, saw the value in this. He organized a Tax Blitz, in which Senator Roth, Representative Kemp, and several other Republican members of Congress would barnstorm major cities by airplane, holding press conferences in each to challenge the Democrats to match their tax-cut program.

This was a natural for Reagan who had gradually been moving into the supply-side camp since 1976 when he had done his first radio scripts and newspaper columns on the subject of major tax cuts.

Reagan began to study the subject in detail in 1977. Late that year, a speech of Kemp's was reprinted in *Human Events* and Reagan sent Kemp a handwritten note, praising both the speech and its underlying reasoning. More and more, Reagan began to call for major across-the-board tax cuts in his own speeches, usually referring to the Kemp–Roth bill as the vehicle for doing it.

Reagan met the Tax Blitz group in Chicago and spoke out strongly for the Kemp–Roth bill that day.

The next day another issue came up. Governor Reagan returned to California after the Chicago event for a private dinner near Monterey. My wife and I had flown up with Mrs. Reagan that afternoon to join him. I called the office for messages soon after we arrived. Elaine Crispen, our executive secretary, told me that CFTR had been receiving several calls, including at least one press call, about Governor Reagan's stand on Proposition 6 on the November ballot (the one aimed at school teachers who might be homosexual).

Reagan's practice with so-called social issues (e.g., abortion and the Equal Rights Amendment) was to be prepared to answer questions about them forthrightly, but not to bring them up gratuitously in his speeches or remarks.

He had decided to do this in the case of Proposition 6 and 5 (the anti-smoking measure) in California. He had decided, after studying both issues, to vote against them and he authorized us to draft short statements about each in order to answer letters that might come in requesting his position. This, too, was his usual practice. CFTR had asked our office for these statements (as well as those on other current issues) because they often received mail addressed to Reagan as chairman, requesting his positions. They had been answering inquiries on these two issues, quoting from his statement. Reagan's intention on these, as on other social issues, was to reply to inquiries, but not to promote a position by issuing press releases or making speeches. I knew, however, when Elaine told me that one of the wire services had called CFTR and gotten Reagan's statement on Proposition 6, there would be a story.

The next morning's *San Francisco Chronicle* confirmed my suspicions. Reagan's statement was quoted at length, making his opposition to the measure unequivocal. We discussed it on the plane going back to Los Angeles that day. He decided to stand on the written statement and not amplify it if there were further press calls on Monday.

While Reagan's basic attitude on the subject could be described as live and let live, he did not like ballot measures—such as those cropping up in many city elections—that advanced certain "gay rights." He felt that these tended to promote and advocate such an alternative lifestyle. This bothered him from both the standpoint of his belief in traditional family values and because he felt it was a misapplication of government's role. Just as he was opposed to such things as racial hiring quotas, so too he was opposed to measures which seemed to confer special "rights" on particular groups.

Proposition 6, however, was different. It seemed to have the potentiality of infringing on basic Constitutional rights. The declared purpose of the measure was to make it possible for school districts to fire teachers who "advocate" homosexuality, but according to legal opinions Reagan obtained, its definition of advocacy was so vague that an exemplary teacher who never said a word in public about the subject but was suspected of being homosexual in private could be hauled through a dismissal hearing on the basis of accusations alone.

On Monday we were preparing to fly to Greenville, South Carolina, and the beginning of a week's campaigning for Republican candidates and for some business speeches by Governor Reagan. We left in mid-afternoon and there was still a stack of telephone message slips on my desk. I stuffed them in my briefcase. In the air, I looked through them and found two from State Senator John Briggs, the sponsor of Proposition 6. We landed in Amarillo, Texas, to refuel the chartered plane and I put in a call to Briggs in Sacramento. He lost no time making it clear he thought Reagan's opposition to his measure amounted to proposing that the schools should seek out homosexuals to hire as teachers. I was surprised by this distortion of Reagan's position. I knew Briggs's people had a copy of his statement, so I said, "That's not true and you know it." I went on to describe Governor Reagan's concerns about infringement of Constitutional rights; concern that the measure might be misused in a sort of "witchhunt." (My impression from Briggs's response was that he had something like that in mind.)

He told me about the case of one teacher which he said fit the purpose of his ballot measure, and he asked me to look into it. I promised him I would, that I would share it with Governor Reagan and that we would talk again after the trip. The case he mentioned turned out to be rather different from what he had described and, if anything, increased concerns that the measure could be misused if passed.

Tactically, Briggs had erred in not putting his case to Reagan and his advisers well before the campaign began. Representatives of the proposition's opposition had asked for an appointment in August with Governor Reagan. They made a quiet, well-reasoned case and answered all of his questions. They also supplied us with detailed background material.

Very late in the campaign, Briggs asked for a meeting with Reagan. He sent a delegation of three persons, one of whom opened the meeting by hinting broadly that if Reagan did not change his position a large number of voters (presumably religious fundamentalists) would turn against Reagan if he ran for the presidency. This was exactly the wrong approach to take with Ronald Reagan. He was furious and minced no words in telling this young man what he thought of his implied political blackmail.

In late October, Reagan put both the Proposition 5 and 6 arguments in perspective in one of his newspaper columns:

> If blue jeans and drive-in churches weren't enough to convince you that California sets trends, Proposition 13 should have left no doubt. Californians aren't stopping with the tax revolt, however. The Golden State's November ballot contains two controversial measures which, pass or fail, have the potential for setting more trends.
>
> One, Proposition 5, would be the nation's toughest anti-smoking law. The other, Proposition 6, would provide for firing teachers who "advocate" homosexuality. The measures are similar in that they would mean more government—Proposition 5 because it would be difficult to enforce except at great cost, and Proposition 6 because it could be overenforced.
>
> Proposition 5 sets out to protect nonsmokers from the fumes of those hooked on the weed. It would prohibit smoking in nearly all public places, but the hitch is that it defines private places of employment as "public." Shades of Newspeak in Orwell's *1984*. Restaurants would be required to have smoking and nonsmoking sections. And, as with offices and factories, the owners would have to foot the cost for the No Smoking signs. . . .
>
> Short of recruiting an army of smoking police, the measure seems unenforceable. Smoking is already prohibited in many public buildings, but this measure goes well beyond, to restrict both personal liberties and private property rights. That reasonable smokers and nonsmokers can use a little common courtesy to work out their differences seems not to have occurred to the proponents of Proposition 5. If it passes, it won't be the first time a false assumption found its way into law and made government grow.
>
> Proposition 6 rests on several assumptions. The most frequently mentioned are that teachers can influence the sexual orientation of children

because they are "role models" and that homosexual teachers will molest their pupils. State Sen. John Briggs, the measure's sponsor, told an interviewer the other day that "Everybody knows that homosexuals are child molesters. Not all of them, but most of them. I mean, that's why they are in the teaching profession."

Although statistics are not kept nationally, informed observers usually put the percentage of child-molesting cases by homosexuals at well under ten percent. The overwhelming majority of such cases are committed by heterosexual male adults against young females.

As to the "role model" argument, a woman writing to the editor of a Southern California newspaper said it all: "If teachers had such power over children, I would have been a nun years ago."

Whatever else it is, homosexuality is not a contagious disease like the measles. Prevailing scientific opinion is that an individual's sexuality is determined at a very early age and that a child's teachers do not really influence this.

Had Proposition 6 been confined to prohibiting the advocacy in the classroom of a homosexual lifestyle (and sex before marriage, "swinging," and adultery, for that matter), it would no doubt enjoy much wider support than it does. Instead, the measure calls for firing teachers who engaged in homosexual activity (something already covered by California law) or homosexual "conduct," which it defines as "advocating, soliciting, imposing, encouraging or promoting private or public homosexual activity." It is that passage—and especially the undefined word "advocacy"—that has generated heavy bipartisan opposition to the measure.

Since the measure does not restrict itself to the classroom, every aspect of a teacher's personal life could presumably come under suspicion. What constitutes "advocacy" of homosexuality? Would public opposition to Proposition 6 by a teacher—should it pass—be considered advocacy?

The measure would require formal school board hearings if a teacher is accused. Under the present law an informal investigation can be conducted to determine the merits of charges against a teacher. Though the formal hearings on Proposition 6 would be private (unless the accused wanted them public), how do you keep such charges private in a small community? And, how do you prevent an overwrought child with bad grades from seeking revenge by accusing a teacher of a homosexual advance or "advocacy?" Under Proposition 6, you don't.

Will California rewrite that old line to read, "As California goes, so goes the nation?" Here is one heterosexual nonsmoker who, where Propositions 5 and 6 are concerned, hopes the answer is no.

On election day, the answer was no, convincingly, to both measures. It was also no to Attorney General Evelle Younger's bid to unseat Governor Jerry Brown, despite a joint television campaign by Reagan and Gerald Ford for him. In late September, in response to an idea advanced by several mutual friends of Reagan and Ford, the Republican state committee arranged for a television taping at the former President's compound at Rancho Mirage, near Palm Springs. Reagan and I flew down from Los Angeles in the morning. Ford and he lunched privately in the Ford home. I had lunch with Ford's chief-of-staff Bob Barrett and his assistant, Dick Wennekamp, in their office. After lunch, Ford and Reagan did several television spots in a spontaneous conversation format, urging votes for Younger and his ticket. Younger arrived and did several more spots with the two men. Following this there was a joint press conference, but nearly all the questions were directed to Younger, whose campaign was faltering.

On the way back to Los Angeles, Reagan said that he and Ford had had a relaxed and cordial visit; that Ford wasn't sure what he would do about 1980. Reagan's impression was that Ford liked what he was doing and, at that moment at least, was inclined to stay out of the race.

Nationally, the Republican party fared not badly at all, with improvements in congressional representation and strong gains in statehouses (including Mike Curb's election as lieutenant governor of California).

Reagan had campaigned since Labor Day for candidates in California, Idaho, Texas, Louisiana, Iowa, Missouri, Ohio, Illinois, Indiana, South Carolina, Virginia, Delaware, Michigan, Minnesota, Kansas, Colorado, Mississippi, and Florida (in several, more than once).

While Reagan was crisscrossing the country in the fall, Dick Allen and I were at work on plans for the Reagans' European trip in late November. I worked on the London portion while Allen coordinated the French and German segments (this would be Reagan's first visit to Germany).

The Reagans, my wife, and I left Los Angeles on Saturday, November 25 for London. Dick Bergholz, *Los Angeles Times* political writer and a long-time chronicler of Reagan's career, accompanied us. The Allens met us in London.

After the long overnight flight we did not schedule anything for Sunday in London. The Reagans met old friends for dinner, so the Allens, Bergholz, and we met Ed and Barbara Hickey (he had been Reagan's security chief in Sacramento) for dinner. During it we were interrupted by a telephone call from California with the news that the mayor of San Francisco, George Moscone, and a county supervisor had been shot and killed in their offices by a fellow supervisor.

The next morning's schedule began with an informal breakfast with several London newspaper writers and editors. Next, we called on the Labor government's foreign secretary, Dr. David Owen. While he was cheerful and polite, Dr. Owen gave the impression that this was a "duty" visit and an act of broad-mindedness on his part. He and Governor Reagan discussed the Middle East and China at length. Allen and I exchanged amused glances when Owen referred to China's Teng Tsiao-ping as "Ping," a misunderstanding of Chinese name usage that would have surprised a freshman political science student.

Following the meeting at the Foreign Office, we went to Margaret Thatcher's office in Parliament. She had larger quarters than when we last visited in 1975. The British elections were not far off and it was widely believed she would become prime minister. She and Reagan greeted one another as old friends. The atmosphere in her study was cheerful, even cozy, with a fire in the fireplace on this chilly fall day. They talked of defense and economics. Mrs. Thatcher urged Reagan to keep working for his goals. She told him that while it might be too late to turn things around in her country, she hoped not and, in any case, would do everything she could to make a success of it. As for America, however, it was definitely not too late to get control of the economy in her view. After a time Winston Churchill, grandson of the late prime minister and Mrs. Thatcher's "shadow" defense minister, came by for a brief visit.

We went on to a meeting with Sir Keith Joseph, the Conservative "shadow" minister for industry; then to a luncheon with several Conservative members of Parliament, led by Humphrey Atkin, the party's floor leader in the House of Commons. The Conservatives were in a buoyant mood, sensing victory for their party around the corner.

Early the next morning we flew to Paris for a full day's schedule which began at the Quai d'Orsay with a meeting with Olivier Stiern, under secretary of foreign affairs. Following that, Baron Nichole Thierry was host at a luncheon at his home on Avenue Foch, attended by about fifteen leading businessmen, editors, and scholars. There was a lively exchange of views about the rise of conservatism in the United States and about hopeful signs in Europe. One guest in particular, Patrick Wajsman, a scholar and regular contributor to Le Figaro, was struck by the encounter with Reagan. He later became a major French interpreter of Reagan's ideas.

In midafternoon we called on François Ceyrac, president of the prestigious Patronat (similar to the Chamber of Commerce of the United States) for an hour's visit. Then we went to a hospital where Jacques Chirac, mayor of Paris, had been taken following an auto accident the night before. He was sleeping, so we paid our respects to Mme. Chirac and returned to our hotel.

That evening, along with Dick Allen's friend Pierre Emanuelli (who had been helpful in arranging the Paris schedule), we watched French National Television to witness a remarkable performance by Richard Nixon. He had come to Paris to do a three-hour live interview. He and his interviewer were in an elegant salon at Nixon's hotel. From time to time the camera would switch from that scene to the television studio where, behind a young man and woman seated before microphones, the viewer saw two lines of telephone switchboards where operators took calls from all over France. Messengers came forth with viewers' questions on small pieces of paper. The young announcers read the questions, then the camera would switch to Nixon for the answers.

At one point the young man described the volume of questions for Nixon as *"une avalanche!"* Nixon was relaxed and calm. He fielded questions about Watergate (he regretted it, he said), on Vietnam, the Soviet Union, SALT II, China, the Western alliance and many other subjects. At the end of three hours he seemed ready to go on for another three. The French people clearly liked him at a time when he was being treated as a sort of nonperson at home. The French considered Watergate a minor incident hardly worth all the fuss.

We had been asked by several news people before we left if Reagan's and Nixon's paths would cross in Europe; however, the timing was coincidental and they did not meet.

The next afternoon we flew to Cologne and motored to Bonn where a full day had been scheduled for Thursday, the thirtieth.

Reagan breakfasted with Manfred Woerner, defense affairs spokesman for the opposition coalition of the Christian Democratic Union and the Christian Social Union. Following that, he called on Helmut Kohl, parliamentary leader of the CDU/CSU caucus. Lunch was with scholars from the Konrad Adenauer Foundation, followed by an hour-and-a-half meeting with Chancellor Helmut Schmidt at his offices. Schmidt gave a bravura performance. His well-known dislike for U.S. policies under Carter came through quickly, though he observed protocol (as did Reagan) by not making the criticisms personal. He talked of his dilemma, facing the armed might of the Russians while being a bulwark of the West. Then, as now, he was doing a balancing act in his own party, the SPD, between its neutralist left wing and its defense-oriented right wing.

From Schmidt's office we called on Economics Minister Otto Graf Lambsdorff of the Free Democratic Party, the smaller party in the ruling coalition. After that, Ambassador Walter Stoessel called on the Reagans at the hotel, and we then went to meet Berlin's governing mayor, Dietrich Stobbe, who was in Bonn for the session of the *Bundesrat* (upper house of parliament), of which he was president. Stobbe was delighted the Reagans were going to Berlin. As we were to learn, West Berliners are warmly appreciative when public figures from other Western nations pay them a visit.

We left for Berlin that evening. On Friday, city officials had arranged a bus tour for us. This ended at the U.S. Army's main base in the city. There, the Reagans had lunch in the mess hall with the GIs. They shook hands, visited, learned of the concerns of the soldiers and Governor Reagan gave brief remarks to all in the hall, followed by a lively question-and-answer session. Then, after a briefing, we were off in army sedans for East Berlin. The U.S. consulate officials with us told us to keep the windows up and to show our passports to the guards at Checkpoint Charlie through the glass (technically, U.S. vehicles and their personnel do not do business with East German border guards, only with Russians). Once across the border, we drove by the Hitler bunker and the ruined Chancellory and on into the commercial center of the city. The weather was damp and overcast and it did nothing to lighten our mood. It was good to get back to West Berlin.

That evening we flew to Munich. Fred Ikle, former head of the Arms Control and Disarmament Agency, was in town and so was Robert Strausz-Hupé. The Reagans asked them both to join us for dinner at our hotel, the Bayerischer Hof. The next morning, Governor Reagan, Dick Allen, and I went to the official residence of the minister president of Bavaria, Franz-Josef Strauss, for breakfast. As chief of the CSU in the opposition coalition, he was a likely candidate of the coalition for chancellor in the next election. A big, hearty man, Strauss swapped anecdotes with Allen from the early days of their friendship, then launched into a lively conversation with Reagan that lasted nearly two hours. The two saw eye-to-eye on many things. It was as if they had been friends for years. Strauss in private belied the fierce image his opponents had created for him publicly.

The Reagans' plane was due to leave for London late that afternoon, but first there was time, on that bright, cold winter morning, to stroll the squares and streets, to enjoy the Christmas market—*Weihnachtsmarkt*—with its greens and holiday ornaments and crafts of all kinds.

As he had with his April trip to Asia and Iran, Ronald Reagan approached his European trip as one in which he would primarily look and listen. Yet, when he did discuss his views, he showed both his basic common sense and an understanding of the European points of view. When he returned, Reagan shared his impressions with his radio listeners and column readers—and these impressions foreshadowed the tone of *President* Reagan's policy views toward Europe.

For his December 8 column, he wrote:

If the words "Berlin Wall" conjure up an image of a hastily constructed concrete block affair with strands of barbed wire on top, you should see what has happened to it in the seventeen years since that August in 1961 when the Soviets decided to seal in the population of East Berlin.

Just before the wall went up, the flow of refugees from the Soviet's eastern sector to the Allied sectors in the western half of the city reached a rate of 2,000 a day. The rush to freedom by East Berliners was crippling the economy of East Berlin and, with it, East Germany. Today, the number of escapees is down to a trickle—a few dozen a year (though, ironically, quite a few of them are East German guards).

Today's Berlin Wall still splits neighborhoods, bisects buildings and snakes its way from north to south the length of this 5-mile-long city, but it does more: It also goes completely around *West* Berlin, cutting off all contact between the free sectors of the city and the East German countryside.

The wall of 1978 is a cast concrete affair; a sophisticated piece of work with a large concrete roll along the top, making it very difficult to climb over. Before a person reaches the wall itself he must go over small ones on the east side; cross a run guarded by attack dogs; come under the glare of searchlights, brave automatically fired machine guns, barbed wire and other obstacles and—in many cases—swim in the River Spree. No wonder so few make it. But, what a testimony to human spirit that any do so under the circumstances.

West Berlin today is full of life, full of prosperity and full of new buildings. Traffic is thick (scarcely a car seems older than last year's model) and people are well-dressed.

We went over into East Berlin to compare impressions. Even allowing for the dark wet skies (the same ones hovering over the colorful streets of West Berlin), the Soviet-controlled sector of the city seems a cheerless place. There are plenty of people on the streets and in the stores, but unlike West Berliners, they are not laughing, talking, jostling. You don't have to take many steps to find evidence of the control over their lives. In a big department store, filled with people and cheap-looking (but not inexpensive) goods, an American newsman with our party was sternly told he could not take photos. Just outside, in Alexanderplatz, within 50 yards of one another, two sets of Vopos (the nickname for the ever-present "people's police") stopped two young men, apparently at random, demanding to see their internal passports.

Beyond that, the buildings are drab. Some are poor copies of Western high-rise buildings of the late '50s; others are heavy and monumental from the Stalin era.

We found ambivalent views in West Berlin about the East-West situation. One American official told us that the U.S. (and Allied) presence in West Berlin makes it possible to preserve the city as a symbol of freedom not only to the two million West Berliners, but "to millions of others in Middle and Eastern Europe who live on hope." He said we must never leave so long as Germany is divided. Yet, later in the conversation when a visitor asked if there were ever any efforts by West Berliners to sabotage the wall so more could escape from the east, he said, "No, we don't encourage escape." In other words, don't rock the boat. Others added that "somehow, time is on our side." Maybe, but I doubt the Russians will be passive while we wait.

The contradictory statements of that American official reflect two distinct views I found in discussions with West German leaders from various areas of the political spectrum. Some want accommodation with the Russians above all, hoping that increased trade will somehow make the Soviets dependent and thus peaceful. Others, more realistic, understand that what the Russians want is not war in Western Europe but control over its industrial capacity and that they will get it by intimidation (their SS-20 rockets can devastate an arc from Peking to London) if they can. The SALT negotiations have not dealt with the particulars of Western European security, and the German realists worry that if the U.S. approves a SALT II treaty that checkmates U.S. strategic weapons, the Soviet hand will be strengthened for future negotiations over Western Europe.

The bottom line is still human freedom. At one section of the Berlin Wall (dubbed "the artists' corner") where President Carter visited (and where the communists lowered workmen over the side the night before to paint out graffiti) there is one huge spray-painted graffito that reads: "Those beyond this wall live in a concentration camp."

On December 12, Reagan's column noted that

Europeans are used to seeing things in a global perspective—certainly more than U.S. politicians seem to. Possibly because of their consciousness of the size of the U.S. economy, plus the fact that they live in the shadow of Soviet military might, the Western Europeans tend more and more to stick together and also to reach out far and wide for new markets and political arrangements that will improve their security.

In the U.S. you might think the governor of a large inland state would be concerned mostly with local and regional matters. I have no doubt that Franz-Joseph Strauss, minister president of Bavaria (equivalent to a state governor) is concerned about such things, but in my meeting with him the only topic purely Bavarian was the delicious breakfast. The discussions moved from one continent to another, back and forth, as complex international relations were explored. Strauss had just returned from a NATO meeting in Lisbon, but his calendar had also included meetings with Leonid Brezhnev and China's Teng Hsiao-ping. And scarcely a political "hot spot" on the globe has failed to get his intense and studious attention. This warm and vigorous leader of the Christian Social Union . . . is very much his own man, but he does share in common with other German leaders I met—Chancellor Helmut Schmidt, opposition leader Helmut Kohl, and Economics Minister Otto Graf Lambsdorff, for example—the faculty of seeing his country's policies and economy in a much larger context.

As for SALT II, those I met with in Britain and on the continent seem agreed only that it is important. Some consider its passage vital; others think it will cripple the U.S. and Western Europe from getting some kind of practical control of the Soviet Union's vastly superior tactical forces and the "gray area" weapons (such as the SS-20 rocket). Europeans are quick to point out that SALT II is a bilateral agreement between the Russians and ourselves and they are anxious to have increased participation in the process, lest their own security interests be neglected. It is odd that U.S. officialdom, echoed constantly by media commentators, seems to think that effective arms control rests with restrictions on intercontinental nuclear weapons. Actually, an increased ability to checkmate Russian strength in Europe may offer us a comparable deterrent.

On December 14, Governor Reagan addressed the Los Angeles World Affairs Council at a sell-out luncheon. He summarized the views he gained from his trip and he projected his concerns regarding U.S. international relations in the new year to come.

Both business and political appointments slowed down as the holidays approached. Soon there would be important decisions to make.

8

1979: The Shape of
Things to Come

As 1978 SLIPPED INTO HISTORY, there was little doubt that an "exploratory" committee would soon be formed by Ronald Reagan's supporters.

Exact timing of a committee's formation would be the subject of much discussion among Reagan's advisers, as would the composition of its management. Remembering the relatively late start of the Reagan committee in 1975 (for the 1976 nomination), most involved in the current discussions wanted to get started much earlier. This time there was no incumbent Republican to challenge; this time, according to the public-opinion polls, Ronald Reagan would be the man to beat. Other potential candidates and their supporters were, not surprisingly, doing their best behind the scenes to weaken Reagan's hold on the lead. At this stage, their vehicle was the age issue.

Among Republicans the matter of Ronald Reagan's age seemed to be covering the country with the speed of a jungle telegraph. "Yes, he's a good man, but isn't he too old?" people would say. (He would be sixty-eight on February 6, 1979.) Many party leaders at the state and county levels would express this view, too. It became almost routine for editorial-page editors and political writers to drop a line in their Reagan stories to the effect that, if elected, he would be the oldest sitting president in our history, seventy years of age shortly after inauguration day. Sometimes they would remind their readers that the historical champion for old age among presidents, William Henry Harrison, caught cold at his inauguration and died within a month.

John Sears had the best explanation for this fascination with the age issue. It seemed hard for most of us around Ronald Reagan to believe it should be an issue, since he looked and acted like someone fifteen to twenty years his junior. "The age issue is a cover," Sears told several of us in the advisory group one day. "A party official who isn't sure who's going to be ahead six or nine months from now and who wants to back a winner, is going to say, 'He's a fine fellow, but I wonder if he isn't too old?' That way," Sears added, "if Reagan is faltering in the polls several months from now, that fellow can say, 'See, I told you he was too old to run.' On the other hand, if Reagan is still ahead, he can say, 'I've been watching him, and I don't think Reagan's age is an issue.' "

As for journalists drumming on the age issue, we tended to dismiss this as predictable. There is a strong herd instinct in the fourth estate. As one of our people put it one day, "After a few 'bell cow' writers write it, everyone else falls into step. As soon as the bell cows change their minds, so will everyone else."

Reagan, when asked during the question-and-answer periods of his speaking engagements about the issue, would give his boyish grin and say modestly, "I feel just fine." He would often follow up with an anecdote he had picked up on his visit to Japan the previous spring. He said that one venerable leader, well up in his eighties, on meeting Reagan said, "I hear many people say that you might be a candidate for president in your country. In my country, you would have a problem with your age. You're too young."

As all this was going on, Mike Deaver and I were having several conversations about our roles in a future Reagan campaign. Mike had been associated with Governor Reagan since 1966; I, since 1974. We shared his philosophy and felt that it—and he—belonged in the White House. Both of us were committed to helping him get there.

This time, however, things were not as simple as they had been for us in 1975. Then, our small public-relations and public-affairs consulting firm had only a handful of clients, including Governor Reagan. Both Deaver and I were able to leave Los Angeles for weeks at a time to be on the campaign trail with him. Back home, our one vice-president, our secretary, and some clerical assistants were enough to tend to our other clients' needs between our return visits.

Now, the picture was different. After the 1976 campaign had ended in Kansas City, we had both worked hard to make our business grow, and it had. We now had several more executives and clients, and we had opened an office in Washington, D.C., in February 1977. We had too many obligations to too many other clients for both of us to be out on the 1980 campaign trail together. We still were not large enough or old enough as a firm to have a team of backup managers to take our places. Every time we talked it over, we came to the same conclusion: one of us could go into a Reagan campaign, but one of us would have to stay behind. At the end of this series of conversations, we concluded that it would be Mike who would go into the campaign and I who would stay with the firm. When the Reagan committee was formed, our plan went into effect as we envisioned it; but before 1979 was over, our plan was to be altered sharply, although we had no inkling of it.

Meanwhile, Governor Reagan's immediate attention early in the year was turned toward international issues. CFTR had created an educational foundation a few months earlier and wanted to kick it off with an all-day seminar, "World Challenges, 1979."

The event was scheduled for January 12 at Pepperdine University's modern campus overlooking the Pacific Ocean at Malibu. Reagan would be the featured luncheon speaker, with a report from his recent trip to Europe and his view of U.S. international relations.

This was preceded by several panels during the morning. I had been asked to put them together and invited economists, and foreign-affairs and defense experts to take part in them from several western colleges and universities.

Several hundred people showed up for the seminar on the kind of California January day that belies the word *winter.* The sky was clear, and the sun warm.

Ronald Reagan's address, as was so often the case, presaged policy themes that he would later sound as president. For example, on trade protectionism he said:

> It is vital for the maintenance of good relations with our allies—particularly those in Europe and Japan—that the free flow of goods not be impeded by the beggar-thy-neighbor policies of protectionism. . . . Our friends are concerned that we may take the first steps to erect damaging barriers to trade and commerce, and they are preoccupied with the long-range consequences of such actions.
>
> While we have always prided ourselves on being resourceful and imaginative "Yankee traders," we are being outcompeted and outsold throughout the world, and even sometimes here at home. . . . In Europe recently, and earlier in Japan, I encountered repeated criticism of U.S. business for not trying hard enough to sell its products in new markets, and for not adapting its products to the special needs of other countries. This may be true in certain instances, but I have also spoken with American businessmen who *have* tried hard and who have been met with arbitrary obstructions, restrictive government practices, and complicated barriers to their products.
>
> But an equally important reason why the Yankee trader has a hard time functioning is because his own government is one of the few in the world that has a basically adversary relationship with its nation's business community. Our government penalizes Americans working abroad by unfair income tax policies. Regulation upon regulation drives up the price of our products, making them less competitive. In most parts of the world, the Yankee trader has been overtaken by the French, German, and Japanese trader because the Yankee trader carries a burden of unnecessary government regulations and punitive taxes.

He went on to review his visits with European leaders and what he had found:

> Much of the dismay, criticism, and dissatisfaction which we encounter seems to add up to an uneasy feeling that the American people have lost their national will. I think that this is not quite accurate. I travel about these United States a great deal, and I sense, instead, a strong grass-roots desire to reaffirm American leadership. Certainly at the polls the voters told us last November that they are sick and tired of government's excesses. In this context, I can tell you that I was frankly amazed at the fascination the British and Europeans alike have with Proposition 13 and the wave of tax revolt that is sweeping the United States. While I had gone to Europe to ask questions of others, I found that business and government leaders were eager to learn of the implications of this movement for them and for their future. As you can imagine, I wasn't bashful about discussing it.

He then turned to the military security of the West, a subject that frequently occupied his thoughts:

> Our national security and the performance of our economy are inseparably linked, and meeting with leaders in Europe and Asia has convinced me that the world wants desperately a *stable, confident, predictable* America.
>
> We may feel from time to time that our friends abroad are altogether too critical of us, and we may resent that criticism. But, what they do know and appreciate is that the United States serves as the guarantor of the peace; that we provide the umbrella of security for them and for ourselves; and that our capabilities and our resolve are absolutely fundamental to their future.

Next, he analyzed Soviet military trends:

> Some sixteen years ago, during the Cuban missile crisis, the United States enjoyed an enormous strategic advantage over the Soviet Union—about eight to one. That clear-cut superiority, coupled with our determination to remove Soviet intermediate-range missiles from our doorstep, enabled us to achieve a satisfactory outcome.
>
> Since that time, the Soviet Union, vowing never again to be caught in a position of such inferiority, embarked upon a no-holds-barred effort to catch up with us. By systematically outspending us in absolute terms and by the steady development and deployment of an awesome array of weapons systems aimed at us, at Europe, and at Asia, the Soviets have largely achieved their objectives.
>
> While there remains a dispute as to where they will go from here, there is no dispute about two fundamental points: (1) what the Soviets are doing in terms of weapons development exceeds by far any legitimate needs they may have for self-defense, and (2) if present trends continue,

the U.S. will be assigned a role of permanent military inferiority vis-à-vis the USSR.

Looking back from 1981, as a "neutralist" movement grows in Western Europe, Reagan's characterization of the range of European opinion in late 1978 and early 1979 is still apt:

> One unmistakable current of opinion holds that recognition of the Soviet juggernaut is but a fact of life and that the best one can do is to accommodate to such a reality, hoping that the Soviets will—once they have achieved what they consider to be strategic equality with the West—begin to devote more of their resources to domestic needs, thus reducing the chance of eventual conflict.
>
> Another bloc of opinion recognizes Soviet might, fears that it will reach new levels and urges arms-control agreements and increased trade as a means to moderate and constrain Soviet ambitions.
>
> A third school of thought believes that the Russians are pursuing a program to achieve clear-cut military superiority over the West. Once this is accomplished they will intimidate, "Finlandize," and ultimately neutralize Western Europe. Those holding this view believe the most effective response by the West is a reinvigoration of NATO and an explicit military deployment program designed to counter the Soviet threat. They do not exclude the possibility of reaching meaningful arms-control agreements, but argue that such agreements must be balanced and must contain mutual advantages; they argue that a one-sided arms-control agreement would be worthless. This range of opinion, running from what I would characterize as "accommodationist" to realist, dominates European discussion about East-West relations.

He returned to the theme of deterrent strength:

> Most Americans have no difficulty in perceiving that in order to achieve a sound national security, we must be strong. To deter war, we and our allies must remain united and we must display a willingness to recognize the challenges which confront us.

Underlying this theme of course was his long-held belief that the Russians best understood and appreciated strength—and exploited weakness. Although he had no intention of endorsing or condemning a SALT II agreement that was then in process of negotiation, he had been frequently critical of the Carter administration's "preemptive" concessions during the negotiations. On several occasions, the administration had announced in advance that it would forgo this or that weapon system in the expectation that the Russians would see these as conciliatory gestures and respond in turn. Reagan had learned long before, in his years as president of his union, the Screen Actors Guild, that you do not waste your bargaining chips, but hold them as long as you can.

Following the CFTR Education Fund's seminar the next day was a meeting of the steering committee of CFTR itself. Nofziger and his staff reported that the PAC's first full-scale election, in November 1978, had been a good one for CFTR. In a little under two years since Reagan had founded it, it had become one of the largest and most active issue-oriented political action committees in the country.

Governor Reagan had devoted a lot of time in 1978 to appearing on behalf of CFTR-supported candidates. Meanwhile, the demand from business, professional, and civic organizations to have him as a conference or convention speaker was greater than ever. With CFTR's needs receding in a nonelection year, he could now accept more of the business engagements. At the same time, he was broadening his contacts both within the Republican party and among issue-oriented people, regardless of their politics.

Little by little the intellectual initiative in the United States had been shifting from the liberals to the conservatives. The emergence of a group of Democratic thinkers who were labeled "neoconservative" (ultimately the label stuck) was especially important. Because of their disenchantment both with our declining world position vis-à-vis the Soviet Union and with the radical excesses in the 1960s, which, for them, were climaxed by the Democrats' nomination of George McGovern in 1972, they were no longer comfortable in the Democratic party. They were not ready to become Republicans, but they were writing about their discontent, which was spreading.

Knowing the demands on Governor Reagan's time, we knew it would not be possible for him to plow through a bundle of opinion journals every week or two. Dick Allen and I hit upon the idea of watching for articles we thought would be especially important, in terms of the new trend toward conservatism, and sending them on to the governor marked for his special attention. We suggested that if he found such articles provocative, he drop the authors a line. In many cases the authors were persons who, a few years ago, would not have thought themselves able to agree with Ronald Reagan on much of anything. We discussed our idea with him. He agreed to it. He would tuck the articles we sent him into his briefcase, read them on his trips and come back with letters to the authors drafted on his familiar yellow pads. He opened many new acquaintanceships this way and ultimately recruited Reagan administration appointees and advisers from among them. A notable example was Jeane Kirkpatrick, now Reagan's ambassador to the United Nations. She first came to his attention with an article on human rights in *Commentary* in late 1979 that Dick Allen had flagged for him.

Another avenue for making common cause across party lines was provided by the Committee on the Present Danger (CPD). This group had been formed about two years before by both Democrats and Republicans, but the driving force came from Senator Jackson's wing of the Democratic party—that is, people who favored a strong U.S. defense network and were deeply concerned by Carter administration trends. Leaders in the organization were Paul Nitze and Professor Eugene Rostow of the Yale law school, both of whom had held important positions in previous Democratic administrations. They were critical of disarmament negotiations under Carter's Arms Control and Disarmament Agency chief, the very dovish Paul Warnke. Nitze had been especially outspoken. Dick Allen arranged with Charles Tyroler, executive director of the CPD, for Governor Reagan to meet Nitze and Rostow over dinner at Nitze's Washington home on January 22. Allen and I attended as well. Not only did the three men see eye to eye on our defense problems and our needs in the years to come, but they got on very cordially on a personal level. (In 1981, both men were to lead the U.S. arms-control effort under President Reagan, and Tyroler was appointed by President Reagan to the Intelligence Oversight Board, a watchdog group for the intelligence community.)

Two days later Governor Reagan addressed the Public Affairs Council, consisting of government-relations officers from several hundred businesses and trade organizations. There was also a round of visits with members of Congress and other political contacts to assess the current mood of the capital.

We returned to the East in late February, in time for the worst blizzard to hit Washington in several years (it moved on to New York when we did). On the twentieth, I went with Nancy Reagan to the offices of *Good Housekeeping* magazine, for a meeting with John Mack Carter, the editor; Bill Adler, her literary agent; and officials of William Morrow & Company, which would publish her autobiography, *Nancy*, the following winter. *Good Housekeeping* was planning to run excerpts in advance of the publication date, and this luncheon was for the purpose of coordinating the schedules and looking over photos Mrs. Reagan had selected from her albums for use in the book. (We had negotiated with Adler for a contract with a major publisher for a book by Governor Reagan, as well. We did not know at the time, of course, that events would postpone his book till after an election and his presidency.)

On March 7, the Reagans were in California, but a large group of the governor's friends and supporters met at the Republican Capitol Hill Club, where Senator Laxalt announced to them and to the news media the formation of the Reagan for President Committee.

The *Washington Post* reported, "In announcing the committee, Sen. Paul Laxalt (R.-Nev.) said Reagan, long the darling of the conservative wing of the Republican party, will not run as a 'fringe' candidate for president in 1980 but as a middle-of-the-roader.

"Reagan hasn't changed, according to Laxalt and other Reagan advisors, but the country has. 'Not since Gen. Eisenhower's first election almost 30 years ago has there been such a perfect fit between the man and the public mood as there is today with Gov. Reagan and the American people,' Laxalt said."

The committee list, more than twenty pages long, contained 365 names from every corner of the country and almost every identifiable segment of the party. It was quite a contrast to 1975, when the 1976 campaign committee was announced with fewer than 10 names on it. This time there were also five senators and twenty-two representatives, far more than Reagan ever received support from in 1976. And, we knew that several more members of Congress planned to announce their support soon. There were also four former cabinet members from the Ford administration.

In Los Angeles, Reagan released this statement: "I am honored and pleased that so many friends in the Republican party have expressed their confidence in me by forming the Reagan for President Committee to explore the possibility of a presidential candidacy. I have been giving this matter serious consideration, and in my travels around the country I do sense a good deal of sentiment for a candidacy by me, but this committee will provide a more objective yardstick as it sets out to determine the full extent of such support and the ability to raise funds for a campaign. I shall await their findings with great interest."

Opinion polling was to be a basic element of the "objective yardstick" to which he referred. In mid-March, Dick Wirthlin presented to the campaign committee's senior staff and a few other advisers the results of the first poll commissioned by the committee. Its results determined, to a great extent, the shape Ronald Reagan's 1980 campaign would take.

Among possible Republican candidates, Reagan had the highest name recognition, above 90 percent, and the highest preference. The components of his public image, however, were more important than the figures themselves. When paired against Carter in terms of assets and liabilities, Reagan was seen as being so strong in terms of his stand on defense that to overemphasize defense issues would run the risk of appearing to be too strong. Carter, on the other hand, was seen as less decisive and effective, but people saw him as "caring about people" more. Up to the eve of the 1980 general election campaign, this "decency" factor remained Carter's major asset with the electorate, since he could not by then point with pride to his record. By election day, he had even lost this last remaining positive factor.

Among the Republicans, Senator Howard Baker showed the most potential strength at that early date, but he had not announced and his name was still not widely recognized. John Connally, on the other hand, ranked second in name identification, but had accumulated by far the highest percentage of negative responses in the poll. Connally's name had been jumping at all of us for several weeks, particularly as we talked with business and financial people. They liked his tough talk, and as I had noticed before with other political issues, in their isolation they were projecting their personal reactions onto the general public.

After we had reviewed the figures, one of the men at the meeting said, "Everyone in this room has worked on at least one presidential campaign. This is March 1979. The first voting will be in Iowa next January, just ten months from now. You know how difficult it is to move public opinion even by a few points. Given the magnitude of the job he has to do and the time he has to do it in, I just can't believe that John Connally can become the nominee." I think each of us left that meeting with a strong sense that Connally was not the looming giant corporate people were saying he was; that George Bush did not have strong enough numbers to win in the long run; that Howard Baker had waited too long; and that the other possible candidates (Dole, Anderson, Crane) would not be major factors. What the poll told us was that Ronald Reagan would win, provided he emphasized his assets and reassured voters he was not strong to the point of recklessness.

At first glance, the Reagan for President headquarters, on the top floor of an office building across the street from the Los Angeles Marriott Hotel and three blocks from Los Angeles International Airport, seemed like a smooth operation. Furniture was in place, secretaries were busy, machines were humming, the first fund-raiser mailing had gone out. But, most of us had our fingers crossed about its management structure.

For months there had been discussions in Governor Reagan's circle about how to organize an exploratory committee and how to man it. We all knew that if Reagan ended up declaring for the presidency later in 1979, this committee would become his campaign organization. So, whoever got it started would be running it then.

Some of the westerners in the group were concerned about the effect of putting Sears in charge, especially since so many grass-roots Reagan supporters felt strongly about him, and Reagan himself the summer before had told the Kingston Group that Sears would play a different role than he had in 1976. Yet, there was a strong feeling that the chief strategist had to be someone whose own base was Washington and who had high credibility with the national political press. Names other than Sears's surfaced and were discussed, but for various reasons none of the other possible managers was available. Finally, after many meetings, a "management team" approach was worked out. Laxalt would again be overall chairman. Sears would be executive vice-chairman, reporting to

Laxalt, and Deaver, as deputy chairman for operations, would be Sears's equal. Also, more or less their equals would be Lyn Nofziger, as deputy chairman for finance, Ed Meese and Jim Lake as "senior consultants" (Meese on issues, Lake for press relations), Martin Anderson as research director, and Charlie Black as national political director.

As Deaver and I had agreed, I did not go into the committee operation itself, since Governor Reagan continued as a client of our firm for management of his personal business. I would work on certain specific assignments on a professional basis. Helping the committee find a possible advertising team became the first of these.

While all the discussions, planning, and announcement activity took place, much of Ronald Reagan's life was business as usual. He still had five radio commentaries each week, two newspaper columns, and many speaking engagements. He also put the finishing touches on a review of Senator S. I. Hayakawa's latest book, *Through the Communication Barrier: On Speaking, Listening and Understanding,* for publication in *Esquire* in April.

By early 1979 Congress was debating the new shape of our relationship with Taiwan. President Carter had suddenly announced on December 15, 1978, that he would recognize the People's Republic of China, on the mainland, and would also withdraw diplomatic recognition from the Republic of China, which controlled all of Taiwan Province and some islands of Fukien Province.

On February 10, Reagan made his customary appearance at the annual dinner of the Conservative Political Action Conference and addressed himself to this issue.

> Bear in mind that the issue here is not *greater* friendship with the people of the mainland of China, and it is not one of attempting to wrest from the office of the Presidency what by law is its prerogative.
>
> The issue *is* our policy toward Taiwan and the methods by which we discharge our responsibilities and keep our word. This is what troubles the American people and troubles our friends abroad. Have we become totally unreliable and capricious? Are we so completely disorganized, so lacking in common decency and morality, so motivated by the dictates of the moment that we can, in an instant and by the stroke of a pen, put 17 million people over the side and escape the consequences?
>
> Along with millions of Americans—Republicans, Democrats, independents; liberals, moderates, conservatives; working men and women, small businessmen and big businessmen; hawks, doves, and neutralists—I again call upon this Administration to face up to the responsibilities which are America's to shoulder. I call for a detailed program of specific guarantees to our friends and allies on Taiwan; a long-range program with clear and unmistakable language; one which will earn and retain the support of the American people and which will help to restore the trust and

confidence of the world in an America which once again conducts itself in accordance with its own high ideals.

He then outlined several steps, most of which were ultimately covered by the Taiwan Relations Act, passed by Congress in the spring. (As it turned out, the Carter administration never activated several of the act's provisions during the remainder of its term.)

Reagan concluded by saying:

> As for the 900 million people of the Chinese mainland—said to make up a quarter of the population of this globe—we can say to them we seek friendship, commerce, and other mutually acceptable goals with you. We hope that the bonds of common interest will grow, and we will continue to hope that your system of government will evolve to provide you with the means of making political choices which will result in your determining your own destiny.
>
> We wish to live in peace with you, and we shall not interfere in your affairs if you do not intervene in ours. We can help you to modernize and update your economy, and we will do so, consistent with our national security objectives. But, when it comes to those 17 million people on Taiwan, we emphatically state that so long as they wish to retain their independence in the world; so long as they declare their unwillingness to be either "liberated" by you or unilaterally "reunited" with you—then, so long will they also have the specific and clear support of the United States of America.

While the matter of Reagan visiting the mainland of China had long since been shelved and was now made entirely moot by Carter's switch in diplomatic recognition, discussions about other overseas travel went forward. There was heavy competition, however, for Governor Reagan's time. His business speaking schedule was back to normal, and if he was to keep open the option of declaring for the presidency, he had to maintain a flow of contacts with Republican political figures. This, too, would take time.

In late February, Dick Allen, Dick Whalen and I met in Washington to reassess the original "wish list" of overseas trips. We quickly agreed that any travels Governor Reagan might make would have to take place within the next six to seven months. If he were to become a candidate, there would be no further opportunity, the demands of campaigning being what they are. We went over the pros and cons of visiting the Soviet Union. Carter had had such difficulty in dealing with the Russians that a trip by a possible presidential contender might obscure those difficulties and seem overtly political. We began to turn from the idea. As for visiting Israel and Arab countries such as Saudi Arabia and Egypt, a good case could be made for this, but it seemed to Governor Reagan and to us that the one area where the Carter administration showed a glimmer of limited success was in its approach to the Middle East. In that case, Reagan did not want to appear to be meddling. As for South America, there were no immediate high visibility issues there for Americans. Reagan had often talked about a new approach to our hemispheric relations, but the realities of scheduling saw this particular trip idea recede, too. Still to be discussed were trips to Canada and Mexico, possibly successive visits within the same week.

Allen and I, on the flight from Paris to Cologne in late 1978 during Governor Reagan's European trip, had hit on the idea of an expanded relationship with Canada and Mexico that involved, initially, more intensive communications, including a possible White House assistant to the president for North American affairs. Whalen, who had had considerable experience in Mexico, added to the discussion process. By late spring, Sears became intrigued with the idea and something called the North American Accord was born. It was to find its way into Governor Reagan's candidacy announcement late in the year and the spirit behind it became fully effective in the Reagan White House, with intensification of contact with leaders of both our neighbors.

Spring moved by quickly. In late March, Martin Anderson and I met with Ken Khachigian, former Nixon speechwriter, about becoming a consultant to Reagan's committee. Khachigian, by fall 1980, was the lead writer on the Reagan campaign plane and then organized the speechwriting office in the Reagan White House before returning to his consulting business in California.

In early April, Helene von Damm, Governor Reagan's executive secretary, in the state capitol in Sacramento and at our firm in Los Angeles, was saying farewell to California. She was going to work in New York for the Reagan for President Committee, to develop its fund-raising program in the northeastern states.

Governor Reagan continued to make some appearances for Republican officeholders. On April 7, for example, we flew to Peoria for a fundraising dinner for Congressman Bob Michel, the Republican whip. Along with such appearances and with his normal radio taping and business speaking schedule, Ronald Reagan met a succession of U.S. and foreign journalists, dignitaries from foreign governments, groups and individuals urging him to run for the presidency, and issues specialists. In late May we were in Washington, and the morning of the twenty-fourth was typical of Governor Reagan's increasingly heavy schedule. Shortly after breakfast, scholars from the Georgetown Center for Strategic and International Studies arrived to brief him—first Roger Fontaine on Latin American and Caribbean issues and then Robert Neumann, former ambassador to Morocco and to Afghanistan, on the Middle East.

Former Secretary of State Henry Kissinger had made one of his periodic requests to see Governor Reagan, and he came by for a half-hour visit, largely to "touch bases," since it was widely known he missed being at the center of power and presumably wanted to be on friendly terms with any Republican who might become president. After Kissinger came a group of conservative journalists with whom Reagan enjoyed visiting whenever it was possible on a Washington trip. Over coffee, *Human Events* editors Tom Winter and Allan Ryskind, author Lee Edwards, and columnist M. Stanton Evans brought the governor up to date on the current thinking of conservative activists.

Late the following month, one could sense the growing momentum for a Reagan candidacy when he appeared in Cleveland at a reception, a dinner and a breakfast the next morning. Although many of the local leaders had not yet made any commitment about 1980, the mood of the crowd seemed very pro-Reagan. The number of people wanting to shake his hand and seek his autograph seemed as great as I had ever seen it, and the events were packed to capacity. We went on to Virginia—Reagan country—for the state Republican convention in Roanoke the next day. There was no question but that Reagan was the man of the hour to delegates and spectators alike.

On the issues front, Dick Allen had been urging a full-scale briefing for Governor Reagan on the SALT II treaty. Negotiations with the Russians had been completed by the Carter administration. General George M. Seignious II (U.S.A., Retired), who had replaced Paul Warnke as head of the Arms Control and Disarmament Agency, telephoned me to ask if Governor Reagan would be interested in receiving an official White House briefing about the treaty. The governor agreed, so long as the briefing would include details about the actual treaty, and we scheduled the briefing for the early afternoon of July 12 in his office within the Deaver & Hannaford suite.

Dick Allen had planned a series of meetings with experts on strategic weapons all morning prior to the White House meeting, and again afterward. He also planned a sort of debriefing breakfast meeting with Governor Reagan and some of his experts the next day, to see if the governor was ready to draw conclusions about the treaty.

Joining Reagan in Los Angeles for the briefings were Sears, Meese, Anderson, Deaver, and me. Allen brought with him from Washington Fred Ikle, head of the arms control agency under President Ford, and Charles Kupperman of the staff of the CPD. Allen, Ikle, and Kupperman led the morning briefings. After lunch, the White House briefer, John Newhouse from the Arms Control and Disarmament Agency, made as strong a case as possible for the administration's position. Then, Dr. Albert Wohlstetter, a well-known nuclear strategy analyst, now at UCLA, came to give his views, as did Dr. William Van Cleave, who had been a member of the Nixon "B" Team, which had critiqued the SALT I negotiations.

Governor Reagan's skepticism about the ultimate value of SALT II deepened. At one point he stopped the briefings and said, "But this treaty doesn't *reduce* arms; it increases them!" Ironically, that is what it would have done.

The next morning at the Reagans' home, Allen, Ikle, and Deaver rejoined Governor Reagan. Having slept on the matter, Reagan had concluded that the measure's weaknesses outweighed any benefits it might have. He said he had decided to oppose Senate ratification of the treaty, but he wanted to make sure his position would be clear so that it would not be reported as simply a quick negative reaction to a Carter initiative. He asked his advisers to round-table the matter and make a recommendation as to how best to announce publicly his position.

Round-tabling was, and is, a method favored by Reagan for getting his advisers to reach consensus. In those days, of course, it was done much more informally than it is in the White House. Since we were scattered around the country, round-table meetings often took the form of conference telephone calls. Or the initiator of an idea would call other advisers one by one. Once he had finished, he would report his findings back to them one by one to see if there was consensus. Then the recommendations would be presented to Governor Reagan.

In this case we were all still in Los Angeles, so we met as a group. Sears pointed out that there was no special urgency for Reagan to make an announcement about SALT II. The news media were not pressing him, it was midsummer, and the issue was expected to simmer for several weeks before the Senate took it up. He proposed that the governor wait until September and then make his position the subject of a speech. We checked the schedule. He would be addressing the California Republican state convention in San Diego on September 15. We recommended that as the forum, and Governor Reagan agreed. Dick Allen was asked to assist him with research on the draft.

At the San Diego convention, Reagan traced the history of our defense posture in relation to that of the Soviet Union:

> Over the past fifteen years we have permitted the Soviet Union to deprive us of our nuclear advantage while at the same time it increased its superiority in conventional forces. Our once unrivaled advantage in naval strength is melting away; our fleet is shrinking almost as fast as theirs is growing.
>
> Of what value can our commitments be if we are inferior both in nuclear and conventional forces? How do we support our friends and defend our vital interests in the Middle East? How do we protect our own free-

dom? And, how in Heaven's name did we get in this perilous situation?

The wrong turn came fifteen years ago when our own military resources were sucked into the war in Vietnam and our strategic defense budgets began to shrink year after year. We were entranced by the notion that if we pounded our swords into plowshares the Soviets would do likewise. They did exactly the opposite. While we made actual reductions in our strategic programs, they made massive investments in theirs.

Oh, they talked about arms control and seemed to hold out the promise of real progress. But somehow progress was always "just around the corner," just another American concession or two away from realization.

A glimmer of improvement had appeared and then faded, he noted:

Toward the end of the last Republican administration the national mood had changed. . . . We began a recovery of our military strength. The B-1 bomber was scheduled for production, the new MX missile was to be accelerated, the decline in our navy was to be reversed, and many other urgent programs were set in motion.

All of these were reassuring to the American people. With the promise of long-range defense programs to provide for our security, we went forward with the SALT II negotiations. But then came a new administration. The B-1 bomber was canceled without any quid pro quo, the MX was slowed down, the cruise missile delayed, the navy's shipbuilding program cut back; and under the heat of a Soviet propaganda attack, Mr. Carter halted development of a weapon [the neutron weapon] that could have neutralized Russia's massive conventional superiority on the NATO front.

He then came to the crux of the problem, Russia's vast increases in arms and the flaw in the treaty, its provisions for arms increases:

The Russians are now spending three times as much as we on strategic arms and are increasing that by 4 to 5 percent a year. We are barely keeping pace with inflation. While Mr. Carter maintains that his defense programs for America are adequate, simple arithmetic tells us that the gap in military strength between us and the Soviets can only grow wider if we continue on our present course. The administration deceives the American people when it tells us the new SALT II agreement will put a brake on the arms race, save money, and be adequately verifiable. SALT II is not strategic-arms limitation; it is strategic-arms *buildup*, with the Soviets adding a minimum of three thousand nuclear warheads to their inventory and the U.S. embarking on a $35 billion catch-up which won't be achieved until 1990, if then.

The SALT treaty now before the Senate should not continue to monopolize our attention nor must it become the cause of a divisive political struggle. This is no time for Americans to quarrel amongst themselves. Our task is to restore the security of the U.S., and we should make it emphatically known to the Soviets and—more importantly—to the nations of the free world that we intend to do just that. At the same time, let us assure the Soviet Union we will join in any arms-limitation agreement that legitimately reduces nuclear armaments to the point that neither country represents a threat to the other.

To suggest, as the administration has, that any shortcomings in this SALT II agreement can be rectified in continuing talks leading to a SALT III agreement is an exercise in futility. It makes no sense at all to ratify a strategic-arms limitation treaty that does not limit arms on either side but vastly increases them while at the same time we are told we'll enter into negotiations for a third such treaty that will make everything alright.

I believe the Senate should declare that this treaty, fatally flawed as it is, should be shelved and the negotiators go back to the table and come up with a treaty which fairly and genuinely reduces the number of strategic nuclear weapons.

That, in effect, is what happened. In time, the Democratic leadership of the Senate advised President Carter that he did not have the votes for ratification. He never did get them and, as it turned out, further arms-limitation negotiations would be left for a Reagan administration to take up with the Russians.

An international matter of another sort was to occupy Reagan a few days after the SALT II briefings in Los Angeles. Sears had become intrigued with the idea of the North American Accord—closer contact between the United States, Canada, and Mexico. While Allen and I saw the issue primarily in terms of Western Hemisphere security and strengthened trade ties, Sears also saw it in a U.S. political context. To propose a new level of partnership between the three countries, to recognize the national pride of our neighbors, would demonstrate Reagan's receptivity to new ideas and an outgoing style of statesmanship. Also, many people on both sides of the U.S.–Mexico border might infer from the proposal a willingness on Reagan's part to solve the illegal-alien program with both compassion and practicality.

When Allen and I had first mentioned the idea, Reagan was interested in the concept, for it fit well with his long-held view that the United States needed to pay closer attention to its relations with its immediate neighbors and the rest of the nations of the Western Hemisphere.

Sears had begun to think of the introduction of the North American Accord as an integral part of a Reagan candidacy announcement. The name had been selected with care to separate it from a "North American Common Market" proposal California's Governor Jerry Brown had been talking up. Brown's idea raised immediate suspicions among the Canadians and Mexicans that such a "common market" would be a disguised grab at Canadian and Mexican natural resources.

Plans were made for Reagan to meet privately with President José López Portillo of Mexico, to sound him out on the concept. We tried to link a one-day visit to Canada into the same trip, but prior commitments on the speaking circuit precluded it. Sears accompanied Reagan to Mexico City on July 17. At the meeting López Portillo seemed interested in the idea of closer communication and more frequent consultation between the two governments. Even the idea of inviting Mexican representatives to sit in on discussions within the U.S. government, and vice versa, affecting the interests of both nations was discussed. On their return, Sears said he was satisfied that if Reagan were to propose publicly the North American Accord, the Mexicans would not react in a surprised fashion and would not denounce it. This was a limited objective, but the quick trip seemed to have achieved it. Dick Wirthlin, who had strong ties to the then-governing Progressive Conservative party in Canada, was going to check out potential reactions north of the border.

With the likelihood increasing that Reagan would announce his candidacy in the fall, time was getting near to begin drafting a standby announcement speech. Sears decided to keep this assignment for himself. For several weeks the status of the announcement draft was a subject of speculation, and Sears said nothing to lessen the mystery.

By midsummer the time had also come to line up a standby team of advertising experts for a possible Reagan campaign. Ruth Jones, who had been under contract to the 1976 campaign to buy media advertising (primarily television), had already agreed to the same role if there was to be a 1980 campaign. So far as the creative and production team was concerned, we had hoped that Phil Dusenberry, who had done such a good job working with Governor Reagan on production of television speeches and spots after the 1976 Kansas City convention, would be able to take leave from BBDO to head the operation. New assignments with his company, however, changed this plan. We then decided that instead of trying to assemble a team from many sources, we would look for an existing advertising agency to do the job. Because I had spent several years in the agency business, I was asked to take on the assignment of screening prospective agencies and recommending some for presentations to the Reagan for President Committee's management team. We decided to do our looking in New York because our media buyer was based there and because the first half of the primary season would largely take place east of the Mississippi.

During July I spent several days visiting agencies. From these I recommended two finalists to make presentations to the management team in Los Angeles on August 27. About a dozen committee senior executives were on hand to hear from the agencies, one of which had several executives who had worked on the 1976 Ford campaign. The other agency had no political experience. Most of its experience was in packaged goods. It was the latter agency that carried the day.

Henry Kornhauser and John Calene of the C. T. Clyne Company (they now head Kornhauser & Calene, Inc.) stood before the group with a cardboard carton in front of them. Kornhauser, a chunky man, began offhandedly to pull samples from the carton. These were packages of client products, ad proofs, charts and diagrams. Kornhauser talked animatedly about ad-campaign case histories, waving the packages about. Then he and Calene turned on a television set for us to see a videotape of their sample spots (so had the people from deGarmo, the other agency). One of the television spots Calene had created for Arm and Hammer Baking Soda promoted two or three uses of the product in the space of thirty seconds, including the idea that if you have a septic tank, you should flush a boxful of the product down the toilet to improve the bacterial action of the septic tank.

After that, Kornhauser unfolded an idea for a Reagan campaign. Both agencies had been told we were not expecting to see speculative samples of creative work for a Reagan campaign. Kornhauser, however, had asked for permission to do so in advance, and it was granted. The two men did more talking than demonstrating. Working without access to any of our polling data, they accurately described the mood of the country; the thirst people had for feeling good about their nation again. They suggested such themes as "Let's make America great again" and "This is a great country, but it's not being run like a great country."

After the delegations from the two agencies had left for New York we round-tabled the presentations. The two agencies were closely matched, but there was something about the intuition of Kornhauser and Calene that had sunk in with many of us. We weighed this against the political experience of the deGarmo group. It was a hard decision to make. Sears suddenly began laughing and said, "Well, I guess anybody who can persuade me to pour baking soda down the toilet ought to be good at almost anything." The room erupted in laughter; then everyone began nodding and the matter was decided. A few days later I notified Kornhauser that the business would be theirs, provided, of course, we had a candidate.

By late summer, strains were beginning to show in the management-team concept of the Reagan for President Committee. Nofziger had taken the job of finance coordinator with some reluctance, since he considered political planning to be his strongest talent. He was also uneasy that Sears seemed bent upon having Reagan depicted not as a conservative, but as a "moderate."

To outsiders, such distinctions may seem both arcane and insignificant, but to those involved, they take on great importance. One conservative close to Reagan once characterized the conservative-moderate tug-of-war this way, in relation to Reagan: "If we're talking about fresh ways to sell Ronald Reagan's conservatism, fine, but if we're talking about ways to change his positions on issues, forget it. He's himself and the fact that he's worked out his positions over a long period of time is one of his strongest attractions."

While it had been agreed almost from the beginning that Sears would be the "most equal" among several equals, many duties among the hierarchy were not clearly defined, and the resulting uncertainty worried several among them that the basic organizing work would not be done in time for a fall campaign announcement. Furthermore, the regime of having several meetings of the entire management team each week, in order to make decisions, was becoming more and more cumbersome.

Sears's talents as a strategist were recognized by the others, but many of his ideas were not translating into operational realities. Deaver had been positioned on the team to be—theoretically, at least—Sears's administrative-operations backup, but Sears was reluctant to share many of his ideas with Deaver, with the result that Deaver was frustrated. So was Nofziger, who, by the last week of August, had decided that in the finance role he could have little effect on the political planning for a 1980 campaign. He resigned to resume his career as a campaign consultant. Thus, Deaver found himself with Nofziger's fund-raising duties on his hands. Sears, by the end of August, had acquired from Governor Reagan the authority to be the last word when it came to executive decisions involving the committee.

Meese and Anderson were to have the development of issues papers under their management; however, in midsummer the committee hired Dr. Gary Jones from the American Enterprise Institute. Sears's plan seemed to be to set up a parallel apparatus in order to gain control of issues development and re-direct Reagan as a "moderate." Jones soon established and staffed a Washington-based research office for the Reagan for President Committee. Sears began working more and more with it. More strains developed in California at the headquarters, and by late fall, Martin Anderson withdrew from active participation in the committee and returned to the Hoover Institution.

An early decision among Reagan's advisers had been that the national headquarters of the committee would be in Los Angeles, at least through the primary season. It was widely felt that Sears had agreed to this only reluctantly and would soon make an effort to move the headquarters to Washington. By fall, he had taken a large space in an office building on L Street in downtown Washington and had begun moving some committee functions into it.

By early October, full preparations were under way for a November 13 announcement by Governor Reagan. This triggered development of the first round of advertising materials by the agency, reviews of scheduling plans for an announcement tour of several cities, and intensification of work on an announcement draft.

I asked Sears if he wanted any help from me on the draft before it went to the governor. He said he would let me know. Later, I was asked to attend a meeting at the committee headquarters in Los Angeles with Sears, Deaver, Anderson, Wirthlin, and Meese to discuss the announcement. Sears said he wanted to propose to the governor that he distance himself from the oil industry because of the heavy attacks in the media on "excess" oil-company profits in recent weeks. He asked me to look over his draft, to make recommendations, and to accompany him to a meeting with Governor Reagan at the Reagans' home on the thirty-first.

Meanwhile, the idea was growing that the announcement speech, which would be on nationwide television, should end with a strong appeal for funds for the campaign. Several fund-raising activities, including a big rally in Boston that Sears had insisted on, had come in below the targeted contribution level, and the committee needed an infusion of money. We decided to ask Michael Landon, the star of television's "Little House on the Prairie," to tape the fund-request message. I called on Landon at MGM on October 30 with a draft for a script. He told me that although he did not know Reagan very well, he liked what he had been saying, and he felt it was time that everyone—including himself—do something to help turn the country around. He approved the copy, and we arranged to videotape his sequence a few days later.

On the thirty-first, Sears and I went to the governor's home late in the day. Reagan was uncomfortable with Sears' copy about the oil companies. Although he held no special brief for the oil companies, he had for years been critical of politicians who tried to make scapegoats of the oil industry. He was concerned that it might seem he was suddenly changing course.

Sears said that Wirthlin's polls showed that the public wanted the government to take remedial action *if* it was found the oil companies were profiting excessively from the recent gasoline distribution shortages and the gas lines of the summer. Reagan took out his pen and worked over the paragraph in question several times. Finally, he had shaped it in a way that satisfied him. He said he would work over the rest of the draft that night and get it back to us the next day.

Meanwhile, Charles Wick and Mike Deaver were in New York working on the big dinner at the New York Hilton that would be the official kickoff of the Reagan campaign. Wick, a man of boundless energy and enthusiasm, was a personal friend of the Reagans who was actively getting into politics for the first time. He and his wife, Mary Jane, and a small band of volunteers and staff in New York had taken on the responsibility for selling more than one thousand tickets in a part of the country that was hardly considered Reagan country. New York had been chosen as the site of Reagan's announcement, to symbolize his recognition of the political importance of the Northeast and of urban America and to make it clear to all that he intended to carry his challenge for the presidency to every constituency and to every corner of the country. This event, in what the media normally thought of as Democratic territory, underscored the belief by Reagan and his advisers that the political map of America was already being redrawn.

Reagan was to give his announcement speech live to the dinner audience at the Hilton. Our plan was to videotape it in New York the day before and then broadcast the speech on a specially organized nationwide television network just after the live delivery. We engaged a New York firm, Syndicast, to put together the special network. Leonard Koch of Syndicast and his staff worked nearly around the clock the last few days before the announcement, clearing time around the country. When they were finished, we were in nearly all of the 150 largest television markets in the country, mostly in prime time.

On Monday morning, November 12, we taped the announcement speech on a Manhattan sound stage. Phil Dusenberry had returned for the occasion to direct the production, working closely first with me and then with Governor Reagan. After the taping, we returned to the Hilton, where Kornhauser and Calene gave the Reagans a preview of the first advertising television spots and other materials.

On Tuesday night, the thirteenth, Ronald Reagan, his wife by his side and surrounded by daughters Maureen and Patti, sons Michael and Ron and daughter-in-law Colleen, faced a full house in the Hilton ballroom. The room fell silent as he began:

> Good evening. I am here tonight to announce my intention to seek the Republican nomination for President of the United States.
>
> I'm sure that each of us has seen our country from a number of viewpoints, depending on where we've lived and what we've done. For me it has been as a boy growing up in several small towns in Illinois. As a young man in Iowa trying to get a start in the years of the Great Depression, and later in California for most of my adult life.
>
> I've seen America from the stadium press box as a sportscaster, as an actor, officer of my labor union, soldier, officeholder, and as both Demo-

crat and Republican. I've lived in an America where those who often had too little to eat outnumbered those who had enough. There have been four wars in my lifetime, and I've seen our country face financial ruin in the Depression. I have also seen the great strength of this nation as it pulled itself up from that ruin to become the dominant force in the world.

To me our country is a living, breathing presence, unimpressed by what others say is impossible, proud of its own success, generous, yes, and naive, sometimes wrong, never mean, and always impatient to provide a better life for its people in a framework of a basic fairness and freedom.

Someone once said that the difference between an American and any other kind of person is that an American lives in anticipation of the future because he knows it will be a great place. . . .

He went on to interpret the nation's current problems:

There are those in our land today who would have us believe that the United States . . . has reached the zenith of its power, that we are weak and fearful, reduced to bickering with each other, and no longer possessed of the will to cope with our problems.

Much of this talk has come from leaders who claim that our problems are too difficult to handle. We are supposed to meekly accept their failures as the most which humanly can be done. They tell us we must learn to live with less, and teach our children that their lives will be less full and prosperous than ours have been, that the America of the coming years will be a place where—because of our past excesses—it will be impossible to dream and make those dreams come true.

I don't believe that. And, I don't believe you do either. That is why I am seeking the presidency. I cannot and will not stand by and see this great country destroy itself. Our leaders attempt to blame their failures on circumstances beyond their control, on false estimates by unknown, unidentifiable experts who rewrite modern history in an attempt to convince us our high standard of living—the result of thrift and hard work—is somehow selfish extravagance which we must renounce as we join in sharing scarcity. I don't agree that our nation must resign itself to inevitable decline, yielding its proud position to other hands. I am totally unwilling to see this country fail in its obligation to itself and to the other free peoples of the world.

The crisis we face is not the result of any failure of the American spirit; it is a failure of our leaders to establish rational goals and give our people something to order their lives by. If I am elected, I shall regard my election as proof that the people of the United States have decided to set a new agenda and have recognized that the human spirit thrives best when goals are set and progress can be measured in their achievement.

True to his promise, a year-and-a-half later, Ronald Reagan as the new president was in the midst of working on both a new economic and foreign- and defense-policy agenda for the nation.

He traced the nation's economic problems and said of the federal government, "We must force the entire federal bureaucracy to live in the real world of reduced spending, streamlined functions, and accountability to the people it serves. We must review the functions of the federal government to determine which of those are the proper province of levels of government closer to the people." He thus signaled his intention, as president, to put into effect the transfer plan he had first proposed in September 1975.

About taxes, he said, "By reducing federal tax rates where they discourage individual initiative—especially personal income tax rates—we can restore incentives, invite greater economic growth, and at the same time help give us better government instead of bigger government."

About energy, he said:

> First we must decide that "less" [conservation] is not enough. Next, we must remove government obstacles to energy production. And, we must make use of those technological advantages we still possess. . . .
>
> We need *more* energy and that means diversifying our sources of supply away from the OPEC countries. Yes, it means more efficient automobiles. But it also means more exploration and development of oil and natural gas here in our own country. The only way to free ourselves from the monopoly pricing power of OPEC is to be less dependent on outside sources of fuel.
>
> The answer, obvious to anyone except those in the administration, it seems, is more domestic production of oil and gas. We must also have wider use of nuclear power, within strict safety rules, of course. There must be more spending by the energy industries on research and development of substitutes for fossil fuels.

He now turned to the sticky matter of oil-company profits:

> In recent weeks there has been much talk about "excess" oil-company profits. I don't believe we've been given all the information we need to make a judgment about this. We should have that information. Government exists to protect us from each other. It is not government's function to allocate fuel or impose unnecessary restrictions on the market place. It is government's function to determine whether we are being unfairly exploited and, if so, to take immediate and appropriate action. As president I would do exactly that.

Reagan went on to a restatement of his belief that we needed to rebuild our defenses in order to have the necessary deterrent strength. He then moved on to two ideas he had never voiced before. First was his advocacy of statehood for Puerto Rico; next was the North American Accord. About the latter, he said, "We live on a continent whose three countries possess the assets to make it the strongest, most prosperous, and self-sufficient area on earth. Within the borders of this North American continent are the food, resources, technology, and undeveloped territory which, properly managed, could dramatically improve the quality of life of all its inhabitants.

It is no accident that this unmatched potential for progress and prosperity exists in three countries with such long-standing heritages of free government. A developing closeness among Canada, Mexico, and the United States—a North American Accord—would permit achievement of that potential in each country beyond that which I believe any of them, strong as they are, could accomplish in the absence of any such cooperation. In fact, the key to our own future security may lie in both Mexico and Canada becoming much stronger countries than they are today.

No one can say at this point precisely what form future cooperation among our three countries will take. But, if I am elected president, I would be willing to invite each of our neighbors to send a special representative to our government to sit in on high-level planning sessions with us, as partners, mutually concerned about the future of our continent. First, I would immediately seek the views and ideas of Canadian and Mexican leaders on this issue and work tirelessly with them to develop closer ties among our peoples. It is time we stopped thinking of our nearest neighbors as foreigners.

By developing methods of working closely together, we will lay the foundations for future cooperation on a broader and more significant scale. We will also put to rest any doubts of those cynical enough to believe that the United States would seek to dominate any relationship among our three countries, or foolish enough to think that the governments and peoples of Canada and Mexico would ever permit such domination to occur. I, for one, am confident that we can show the world by example that the nations of North America are ready, within the context of an unswerving commitment to freedom, to seek new forms of accommodation to meet a changing world. A developing closeness between the United States, Canada, and Mexico would serve notice on friend and foe alike that we are prepared for a long haul, looking outward again and confident of our future, that together we are going to create jobs, generate wealth for many, and provide a legacy for the children of each of our countries. Two hundred years ago we taught the world that a new form of government, created out of the genius of man to cope with his circumstances, could succeed in bringing a measure of quality of human life previously thought impossible.

Now let us work toward the goal of using the assets of this continent; its resources, technology and foodstuffs in the most efficient ways possible for the common good of all its people. It may take the next one hundred years, but we can dare to dream that at some future date a map of the world might show the North American continent as one in which the peoples and commerce of its three strong countries flow more freely across their present borders than they do today.*

He paused for a few moments to let this new idea take root with his audience; then he moved toward his conclusion, once again stating his belief in the power of the American people:

> There remains the greatness of our people, our capacity for dreaming up fantastic deeds and bringing them off, to the surprise of an unbelieving world. When Washington's men were freezing at Valley Forge, Tom Paine told his fellow Americans, "We have it in our power to begin the world over again." We still have that power.
>
> We—today's Americans—have in our lifetime fought harder, paid a higher price for freedom, and done more to advance the dignity of man than any people who ever lived on this earth. The citizens of this great nation want leadership—yes—but not a "man on a white horse" demanding obedience to his commands. They want someone who believes they *can* "begin the world over again," a leader who will unleash their great strength and remove the roadblocks government has put in their way. I want to do that more than anything I've ever wanted. And, it's something that I believe, with God's help, I *can* do.
>
> I believe this nation hungers for a spiritual revival, hungers to once again see honor placed above political expediency, to see government once again the protector of our liberties, not the distributor of gifts and privilege. Government should uphold and not undermine those institutions which are custodians of the very values upon which civilization is founded: religion, education, and—above all—family. Government cannot be clergyman, teacher, and parent. It is our servant, beholden to us.

He then recited—as he had in Kansas City in 1976—the story of John Winthrop and his words to the Pilgrims on their small ship off the Massachusetts coast in 1630. Reagan closed with this:

> A troubled and afflicted mankind looks to us, pleading for us to keep our rendezvous with destiny; that we will uphold the principles of self-reliance, self-discipline, morality, and—above all—responsible liberty for every individual; that we will become that shining city on a hill. I believe that you and I, together, can keep this rendezvous with destiny.

The crowd in the packed ballroom came to its feet clapping and kept it up for what seemed several minutes. There were smiles on the faces, tears in some eyes. You could sense that this crowd *knew* that this time, Ronald Reagan would make it.

---

* Reagan's proposal foreshadowed his actions as president. His open and conciliatory approach in personal dealings with Prime Minister Pierre Trudeau of Canada and President José López Portillo closely reflected his prescription for improved communications. In his meetings with them he sought to gain their personal confidence and trust in his sincerity. His similar approach to the delegates at the Cancun North-South conference in October 1981 was an extension of this.

Reagan left the stage to walk from table to table, greeting virtually each person individually.

The evening had been something of a logistical feat. Charles Wick's committee had filled the ballroom with sixteen hundred people (tickets went for $500 each); Wick's son, C. Z., and some friends had turned out an upbeat film about the life and times of Ronald Reagan that brought cheers from the audience; Jimmy Stewart served as master of ceremonies; and the Reagan announcement speech was seen by millions of television viewers across the nation on a made-for-the-occasion network.

The next day the Reagans began an eleven-state, four-day tour of grueling intensity. There were two reasons for this. First, Sears had made the point that there are two times in the career of a presidential candidate when the eyes and ears of virtually the entire nation are focused on him: when he announces his candidacy and when he accepts his party's nomination. The latter usually gets more attention, Sears noted, so the first one should be extended in order to gain media coverage and increase the candidate's momentum (this was in line with Sears's maxim that "politics is motion"). The second reason was the age issue. It had not gone away. In fact, it was intensifying with the news media. Could Reagan go the distance? they asked. Did he have the stamina? Could he compete against a field of candidates most of whom were several years younger? Reagan and those around him were sure of the answers: of course, he could, and would; however, the only way to prove it was to show it, and a four-day fly-around by chartered jet, working fifteen hours a day, seemed to be the best way to counter the skeptics.

Reagan had deliberately left out of his announcement speech any reference to the Iranian seizure of the U.S. embassy and its personnel in Tehran. The matter was too fresh to have been analyzed thoroughly, and any proposal for solving the dilemma might have seemed self-serving and invited attack. Since Reagan was well ahead in the polls,* there was no point in giving his rivals for the nomination an issue to use against him. At most stops during the announcement tour, however, he did make the point that he would work for restoration of respect for the United States in such a way "that never again will a foreign dictator dare to invade an American embassy and take our people hostage."

Sears's strategy—given Reagan's lead in the polls and the fact that a crowded field tends to favor the leader—had been to let the idea build that Reagan's nomination was inevitable. It was true that organizationally we were far ahead of the other candidates. The Reagan field organization, under Charlie Black, the political director, and Andy Carter, the

---

* *Time*, November 26, 1979, said the spread was 35–45 percent for Reagan, 15–18 percent for Connally, 12–20 percent for Baker, and "less than 5 percent for anyone else."

field director, was well staffed in the most critical primary states. Thus, it seemed logical for Reagan to stick to his basic message and, except for the North American Accord,* to offer no new initiatives. The reasoning was that Wirthlin's polls showed that Reagan's positions were basically popular with the voters. The saying began to make the rounds that the nomination was "his to lose."

Still, there were pitfalls. The first was in Florida. The weekend of November 17 and 18, the state Republican party met at Disney World, near Orlando, for a straw-vote "beauty contest."†. It would have no direct effect on delegate selection to the 1980 Republican convention, but it would have an impact on Reagan's momentum. John Connally, in particular, saw this as an opportunity to derail the Reagan Express. Connally's campaign spent several hundred thousand dollars wooing Florida Republican activists in order to win the straw vote. It did not work. Reagan received 36.4 percent of the votes; Connally, 26.6 percent; and George Bush, 21.1 percent.

Time magazine headlined its coverage of Reagan's first week as a candidate A ROYAL PROGRESS? The Reagan camp did not see it that way, but when you are the leader, you do approach campaigning differently from the way a challenger does. The circumstances in November 1979 were far different for Ronald Reagan and his followers from those of November 1975. It would take some getting used to.

The Reagans were back in California for Thanksgiving week. Most national staff members were back at headquarters near the Los Angeles airport, although some had remained in the East for the holiday.

The day after Reagan's announcement, Mike Deaver had gone on leave of absence from our firm to work full-time on the campaign. Because Governor Reagan's personal business activities—radio commentary, newspaper column, and the commercial speaking circuit—automatically ended the day he became a candidate, he also ceased being a client of our company. There would be loose ends to attend to, but already several people who had worked on his account at Deaver & Hannaford had left to join the campaign organization. A few days later his personal office was moved from our suite overlooking Wilshire Boulevard to an office in the national-headquarters building near the airport.

* Although it had been expected that the Accord proposal would become a staple item in Reagan's campaign stump speech (and Wirthlin's polling data indicated it would be well received), other issues began to crowd it out until it disappeared altogether, resurfacing after Reagan became president. In March, in Connecticut, the disappearance of the Accord prompted one television newsman to quip to his colleagues on the campaign bus that "the North American Accord isn't dead, but it is on a life-support system."

† Several other state parties, Democratic and Republican, picked up the idea of the nonbinding vote as a means of getting media attention. Candidates and their staffs tended to see these as an expensive diversion from their strategies.

The contract our company had with the Reagan for President Committee had been written so as to terminate the day he announced his candidacy, so, with one exception, I thought that my own involvement with the campaign was at an end.

The exception was coordination of advertising. I had recommended to Sears that he hire a full-time coordinator for the campaign staff to act as a liaison to the advertising agency and to Ruth Jones and her media-buying staff. By announcement day this had not happened. He asked if I would be willing to handle this on a volunteer basis for a while. I said that I would but that they would need the staff person no later than the first week of January, when the campaign began full time in the field.

Having spent some part of nearly every day for the past several years working for, and with, Ronald Reagan, I found the new regime unsettling. Now, I could devote full time to our other clients, and did, but I felt there was something missing. Old friends in the media and in the conservative movement called to talk about the previous week's announcement, the tour, and the state of the campaign, but it was not the same as before.

It was not many days later that I was shaken from this. Sunday evening, the twenty-fifth, Mike Deaver telephoned to tell me he had left the campaign.

The worries Deaver had since early summer had never really gone away. At first, I thought they were the natural product of a new organization in its shakedown period, but the duties of the various management leaders were not sharply defined and the tensions continued on into the fall. The Californians around Reagan had worked for him a long time. They were personally devoted to him. Sears and Black and some of their people, on the other hand, thought of themselves as professionals. They had worked for other candidates and would doubtless do so again.

Meese and Deaver had Reagan's ear personally, and this bothered Sears. Yet, because of their long relationship with Reagan, they could hardly be expected to stop having contact with him, especially in view of the management-team concept that had been originally adopted for the committee.

Complaints had persisted that Sears was not translating his strategies into operating realities. Sears, on the other hand, thought Deaver and Meese were making decisions without consulting him.

Deaver had no designs on Sears's job. Anyone who knew him understood this, yet Sears continued to be reluctant to turn administrative functions over to him. One day in early fall, after Mike had visited our office and expressed his sense of frustration, I called Sears (Deaver was unaware of it). I told him that during his career Deaver had often been positioned as a key backup man, knew what to do, and could take a lot of worries off Sears's mind. Sears's reply suggested that he was preoccupied with the fact that Deaver often spoke directly with the Reagans. Although the conversation was cordial, I felt it went nowhere, and I began to wonder if Sears might see Deaver as a threat.

Governor Reagan had suggested that Deaver and Sears meet with him at his home on Sunday afternoon, the twenty-fifth, to see if they could work out their differences. When Deaver arrived, at about four o'clock, he was surprised to find Sears, Black, and Lake talking with Reagan in the living room. The governor asked Mike if he would wait a moment before joining them (he visited with Nancy Reagan in another room). Finally, when he was asked into the living room, he was astonished to hear Sears, after a recitation of complaints, tell Reagan that if Deaver stayed, he, Black, and Lake would all quit the campaign. Despite his shock, Deaver spoke first, in a quiet, controlled voice. "Governor, you don't have to make that decision," he said. "I will. I'm leaving the campaign."

It must have been a moment of agony for Ronald Reagan. The Reagans had felt closer to Mike than to any other of us Californians in their staff circle. At the same time, Sears's ultimatum presented an exquisite dilemma for the man whose campaign for the presidency had just begun. He could hardly afford to lose the top political organizers of the campaign, either. In the unexpected showdown, Deaver had proved to be the biggest man among them, Reagan is reported to have told the others after Mike had left.

Within a few days Mike was back at the firm. He plunged into his work with new energy and enthusiasm. Undoubtedly he wanted to keep his mind off the events of the previous Sunday. It was good for him to do so, and as it turned out, it was good for the firm, for his work brought quick results.

Ed Meese was now the last of the Californians with the campaign. One by one, Nofziger, Deaver, and Anderson had left. And, except for my few remaining advertising coordination activities, I had no further assignments as a volunteer adviser.

Meese, nominally in charge of issue development, was still only a part-time consultant to the campaign. He had planned to join it full-time in January. Meanwhile, he had to make arrangements to disengage from his law-school teaching and criminal justice foundation work in San Diego. During this time, Sears turned his criticism on Meese, complaining that various position papers Meese was supposed to have supervised had not materialized.

When I heard about this criticism, I thought it lacked substance. Thinking back to the 1976 campaign, when Martin Anderson and I grew to realize that one did position papers as the need arose, it seemed to me that at this early stage the production of position papers for a candidate who was leading and whose positions were widely known amounted to so much busywork. I could not shake the thought that Sears might be getting ready to deliver an ultimatum over Meese. Meese was, after all, the one remaining member of the day-to-day management group—other than Sears—who had direct access to the candidate.

In early December, I wrote to Sears to remind him that I would not be able to continue beyond December 31 as volunteer advertising coordinator. He had not yet hired anyone, but I gathered that the duty would fall, at least temporarily, to Charlie Black and his staff.

On December 14, after visiting the advertising agency in New York, I called on Black in the campaign's Washington headquarters. Although there were many empty offices and work spaces, one of the secretaries cheerfully led me on a tour, pointing out that this or that person or unit would soon occupy this or that space. It looked as if the campaign's axis was about to tilt three thousand miles eastward.

Black was cordial. We went over some advertising details and then talked about the campaign in general. Although the news media were beginning to write about an "imperial" candidacy and complain that Reagan was not "accessible,"* Black said he thought everything would be all right "if we can just dodge the flying bullets in Iowa."

The Iowa caucuses, the first test of candidate strength, would be held in little over a month. Sears had been planning to have Reagan stay away from an all-candidate debate in Iowa which would be televised nationally. His reasoning, which fit the logic of the campaign strategy, was that Reagan on the stage would be every other candidate's target and would give them all the kind of increased attention they wanted. Without him, the debate would be flaccid and meaningless. The risk— and Sears was well aware of it—was that the other candidates and the news media might make the idea stick that it was unsporting of Reagan to fail to appear.

Just before Christmas the Reagans invited Deaver and me to their home for cocktails on the twenty-seventh to toast the coming year. Their home—and they—were as warm as ever. Their son Ron was home, and we all visited about many things, but the campaign was mentioned only in general terms. Mike was friendly, but seemed reserved. The events that had taken place little more than a month before in this same home had hurt him deeply. It was a measure of the man, however, that he did not let the hurt linger. The wounds were healing and I had a

* This had actually started a few weeks prior to his candidacy announcement. I tallied up his 1979 "accessibility" and, in an October 19 memo, advised Governor Reagan that since January he had had 31 press "availabilities," 27 broadcast interviews, and 43 print media interviews—a total of 101.

feeling, as we left the Reagans' home that evening, that both they and he had started on the road that would bring them back together.

It would be a funny feeling, I thought, to have a new presidential campaign begin and watch it from the sidelines instead of being in the thick of it. Months before, Mike's and my plan had been that he would go into the campaign and I would stay behind to run the business, helping the campaign as a volunteer adviser now and then. Now, we would both be on the outside looking in. Or so we thought.

9

On the Road to Detroit

As 1980 BEGAN, some misgivings about the Iowa caucuses later that month could be detected inside the Reagan camp, but these were not voiced to the outside world. And, by any measurement, Ronald Reagan was still clearly the man to beat for the Republican nomination.

In contrast to the beginning of his 1976 campaign, this time Reagan had a battery of major Republican names among his early supporters. On his national committee were four cabinet members of the Nixon-Ford years: William Simon (Treasury), Caspar Weinberger (Health, Education, and Welfare), Earl Butz (Agriculture), and Stanley Hathaway (Interior).

John Sears and his political coordinators had been instrumental in getting two popular young congressmen, Jack Kemp of Buffalo, New York, and Tom Evans of Delaware, aboard the Reagan campaign early and in visible leadership roles. Evans was named a senior policy adviser and worked successfully to expand Reagan's support in the House of Representatives beyond the circle of conservative members who had long favored Reagan. Kemp, champion of supply-side economics, was given the title of policy development chairman. Kemp's band of supply-siders considered this a major step in solidifying Reagan's support of the theory that large, across-the-board tax cuts would lead to increased investment and economic growth.

Kemp, along with several members of his staff and advisory circle, was present January 3 at the first of two back-to-back day-long issues meetings with Governor Reagan and his advisers at a hotel near the Los Angeles airport.

Dick Allen and Dick Whalen organized the foreign-policy and national-defense discussions; Martin Anderson, the economic; and Jim Lake, the agricultural. There were about twenty of us present at the first day of round-table talks, but a few less the second day. Specialists came and went, presenting their views on a range of issues that Governor Reagan would be dealing with in the campaign days on the road.

How different it is, I thought at the time, from the start of the 1976 campaign. Then, the issues team consisted of Martin Anderson and me, augmented by frequent, hurried phone calls from pay booths to academic and policy experts in various corners of the country who, if we could catch them at their desks, had agreed to share their views.

This time, Ed Meese had two energetic young researchers to back him up in the Los Angeles office: Douglas Bandow and Kevin Hopkins. In Washington, Gary Jones, the research director, had assembled a small team of professionals from think tanks. All were in attendance as the sessions opened on that first Thursday in January.

Meanwhile, the political strategy in Iowa—developed by Sears and carried out by Charlie Black, the national political director, and his field staff—was to get out a hard core of about twenty-five thousand Reagan voters in order to carry the district caucuses, which would be held throughout the state on Monday the twenty-first.

In 1976, Republican voters had paid little attention to the caucuses in Iowa. The action was on the Democratic side, where Jimmy Carter had decided to stake everything to break from obscurity and move into the lead for his party's nomination. With a combination of intensive grass-roots organizing and personal campaigning, he had made the strategy work. Meanwhile that year, fewer than 5 percent of the half-million Republican voters turned out for their caucuses. Nationally, the Republican spotlight was on New Hampshire.

Reagan's strategists figured that the crowded field would divide approximately 50 percent of the Republican vote and that, even if the number of voters in the caucuses more than doubled, Reagan would carry the day if he pulled twenty-five thousand of his supporters to the gatherings on the twenty-first.

It was a risky strategy, and Sears knew it. Risks were nothing new in politics and certainly not to him. He decided to keep Reagan's presence in the state to a minimum. He said this was to avoid making Reagan seem just like one of a handful of candidates, all scrambling around for votes. Longtime Reagan supporters still called me from various parts of the country, and most had a darker view. They thought Sears was keeping Reagan under wraps for fear that his candidate might make a verbal gaffe.

Sears was aware of the criticism from among Reagan supporters, but stuck to his strategy. He did plan to have Reagan do a live, thirty-minute television broadcast in the state the final Saturday night of the campaign, the nineteenth, but this was no substitute for a Reagan appearance at the all-candidate Iowa debate, which was televised nationally. If Reagan took part with the other Republican contenders, Sears reasoned, their importance would be increased in the eyes of the voters and with such a crowded field the awkward one-at-a-time comments allowed by the debate formula would tend to allow the other candidates to take potshots at Reagan, while his rebuttals would be delayed for several minutes.

Without Reagan there, the other candidates all took potshots at him, as well as trying to separate themselves from one another. All decried his absence. The criticism took hold. Iowans felt snubbed. The *Des Moines Register*, in a post-debate poll, showed Reagan's strength plummeting from 50 percent to 26 percent.

Meanwhile, George Bush was working a variant of the Carter 1976 strategy in Iowa. He spent thirty-one days in the state (to Reagan's three). His strategists (including former Reagan operative from 1976, David Keene) blanketed the entire state with brochures to every Republican household.

By the twenty-first, what had seemed primarily a Democratic party phenomenon only four years before had been built up in 1980 by the twin pressures of media attention and candidate competition to the point where it now became a major early test of strength. Sears and his team had underrated Iowa's importance, as it turned out. The risks came true. On caucus night, Republicans poured out, more than 110,000 in all (about three times what the Reagan campaign had expected). Bush came in ahead of Reagan by 2 percentage points. While that may seem numerically insignificant, in the world of presidential campaigns, where perceptions become realities, the momentum had suddenly passed from Reagan to Bush. For Reagan, because he had been positioned as the "inevitable" nominee, the stakes were very high. In the eyes of the news media and political observers he had to win in Iowa to keep his position as first in the field.

Although by this time my wife and I were in Africa on a long-planned trip, we found that the news media there treated the Iowa results not much differently from those back home. The judgment was quick and clear: Reagan's candidacy was all but finished. If he lost New Hampshire, he was through.

The criticisms of Sears's management of the campaign intensified. Although the line being given out by Reagan headquarters was that Iowa was only a minor setback, it was hard to hide the fact that the morale of Reagan's supporters had been badly shaken by a defeat which, for most of them, had been unexpected.

On the twenty-fourth a large number of Reagan's three dozen supporters in the House of Representatives met with Charlie Black on Capitol Hill. As had many grass-roots Reagan leaders, these members of Congress criticized Sears's strategy of keeping his candidate under wraps while putting himself in the television and newspaper spotlight. It was being called derisively "the imperial candidacy." They wanted Governor Reagan to return to his personal style of campaigning. They minced no words. Nor did Senator Paul Laxalt, who had long worried about Sears's strategy, when he talked to Reagan after Iowa.

Tom Evans personally summarized the views of his congressional colleagues to Reagan on a leg of a campaign flight on the twenty-eighth.

Since Reagan had personally agreed to Sears's Iowa strategy, he considered himself equally to blame for the outcome. Now, having had a few days to reflect on both strategy and outcome and having heard from many of his strongest supporters, he took command. He told Sears that there would be three changes for the New Hampshire campaign (primary day was Tuesday, February 26). First, he would return to people-to-people campaigning. That is, he would ride the bus every day, stop at villages and towns, open with brief remarks, and then have a question-and-answer session with the voters. Second, the week's respite that had been scheduled for the Reagans in California in mid-February would be scrubbed. Third, he would not leave New Hampshire a day or two before primary day, as he had in 1976 on the advice of state chairman Hugh Gregg,* backed by Sears. "This time we'll campaign straight through till election day," he said.

Reagan waded enthusiastically into his dawn-to-dusk daily schedule in New Hampshire. Because federal election law puts a ceiling (based on population) on the amount of money a candidate may spend in each state, the Reagan campaign was to be housed in Massachusetts, a state with a relatively high limit and one in which Reagan was not expected to do much actual campaigning. This way, the housing and feeding costs would be charged against the Massachussetts limit rather than New Hampshire's, which was much lower.

Thus, Reagan's motorcade took off each morning from the Sheraton-Rolling Hills Hotel near Andover. If, as the day progressed, he tired of answering the same questions or making the same points about issues, he did not show it. His ready smile and good color made him seem all the more energetic and youthful in the crisp February air.

Meanwhile, Nancy Reagan was scheduled most days into different towns in order to expand the Reagan contact with voters. Not a speech-maker herself, she is highly effective in extended question-and-answer sessions. Rather than get into minute and technical details when asked about her husband's stands on issues, she gave her answers in terms of his

---

* In 1980, Gregg was Bush's New Hampshire chairman.

philosophical positions, at the same time conveying both a strong sense of support and the feelings of a wife and mother.

Governor Reagan was hitting his stride. It was not showing in the polls yet (Dick Wirthlin's poll showed Reagan, with 28 percent, behind Bush, with 37 percent, a little less than two weeks before election day), but he was feeling it and so was his wife.

Meanwhile, the perceptions of the media commentators and political pros were lagging behind the new reality that the candidate was sensing. George Bush, an ebullient man by nature, had what looked like a well-oiled campaign machine, and he had the apparent momentum of a winner. He called it his "Big Mo."

Reagan had told his staff that he intended to participate in a nationally televised debate among all the Republican candidates in Manchester on February 20—a reversal of the Iowa strategy—but this did nothing to stop columnists and editorial writers from routinely predicting the imminent demise of the Reagan campaign.

In mid-January, Reagan's kitchen cabinet (now expanded and renamed the Executive Advisory Committee) had asked William Casey, a tall, sixty-seven-year-old New York lawyer and former chairman of the Securities and Exchange Commission, to conduct a management audit of the national campaign operation. He set about interviewing the various department and section heads in the national headquarters in Los Angeles. He examined the campaign's books. He was alarmed by what he found. There were so few cost controls that if spending continued at the rate he found, the campaign would reach its federal spending limit by the end of March. To make matters worse, there was a problem of slow cash flow and the bills were not being paid. The Iowa loss, as Casey reported to the Executive Advisory Committee, had cut sharply into the campaign's ability to attract money.

Casey saw as the root of the problem Sears's unwillingness to delegate authority and responsibility beyond his immediate lieutenants, Black and Lake. Since the previous August, Sears had managed to cut off or remove people he saw as potential rivals or obstacles to his effort to concentrate authority, among them Nofziger, Deaver, and Anderson. While Sears was successful in centralizing virtually all day-to-day decision-making in his own hands, he had never developed a keen interest in personal follow-through on operational details. This shortcoming tended to nullify his recognized strengths as a strategist.

The committee members agreed that Casey should make a direct report to the candidate once his review was completed. Meanwhile, at a committee meeting in Los Angeles shortly after the Iowa defeat, as the discussion moved along, assignment after assignment was being passed on to Ed Meese for execution. At one point, Mike Deaver, now a member of the committee at Reagan's request, said, "Ed has more than enough to worry about already, and we're giving him even more. What we should be doing is asking him how we can help shoulder some of the burden." He looked around the room. Casey said in a soft voice, "I'll help." From that two-word answer began the idea, discussed in various conversations over the next several days, that Casey, not having been a part of the Sears or California staff groupings, might be the right man to handle day-to-day administration of the campaign.

Sears, meanwhile, had talked to the Reagans when they were at their ranch in California for a few days following the Iowa loss. He recommended that Reagan's onetime executive assistant in the governor's office, William Clark,* be brought in to handle day-to-day administration. Sears apparently made the recommendation with the belief that he could maintain overall control while reducing criticism of campaign management, since Reagan's confidence in Clark was well known. After several conversations and telephone calls, Clark decided it would not be possible.

Earlier, at a Detroit shop, Jim Lake had told Reagan that the infighting among the staff had to stop and that perhaps it was time to bring in an outsider. This may have been a precursor of Sears's suggestion.

On Friday, February 15 the Reagan campaign was halfway across Massachusetts, in Worcester, where Reagan would give a speech on defense policy that evening at the Lincoln Day dinner of the Worcester Republican Club. Casey, his report ready, arrived at the campaign's temporary headquarters, the Worcester Holiday Inn.

Bill Casey is a good-humored man, but he is also blunt when the need arises. On that winter Friday afternoon he arrived shortly after five. He came right to the point with Reagan. Dick Allen was with them, but Sears was unaware Casey was there.

Casey outlined the campaign's perilous financial position. Some $13 million of its entire primary allowance of $17 million had been spent or committed. "What can be said of a campaign that commits three-fourths of its resources before the first primary?" he added. Apparently, Sears had figured, as he had in 1976, on an early knockout, not allowing for the possibility that funds might be needed for a drawn-out primary season.

Casey said that rather than talking about the role of chief of staff, which he had been asked about in California the week before, he was there to talk about the job of chief of operations. He said he would take the job if he had "real control" of operations. He said that the campaign's financial condition required a drastic cut in staff down to about 150, from 350. "It can and must be done," Casey added.

* Clark, an associate justice of the California Supreme Court, in 1981 became deputy secretary of state.

He wanted to avoid a confrontation with Sears. If it could be made to work, Casey said, Sears would be left with political strategy and delegate-hunting while Casey concentrated on campaign "business." Allen said that Sears might view this as a reduction in status and thus decide to leave. On the other hand, the feeling was growing that Sears might be approaching the point of telling the governor that either he or Meese would have to go. Allen said that if Sears prevailed in such an ultimatum, several other key people would probably leave with Meese. Reagan said he was not going to have any ultimatums but that he wanted to think the matter over. Casey and Allen left.

As they stepped out of the elevator, Linda Gosden, Lake's assistant and the daughter of old friends of the Reagans, stepped in. She looked at Casey as if she recognized him, but did not seem sure. Allen introduced them. Minutes later, Lake encountered Allen with Gary Jones, the research director, and asked what Casey was there for. He said Sears wanted to see Casey. It was too late. Casey had already left the hotel.

Just before they went in to a predinner reception, Jones and Allen gave Reagan a last-minute briefing on some defense points. As they moved away, Gosden approached Reagan and asked him about Casey's visit. It was not a good time to bring up the subject of staff tensions, for Reagan was about to greet supporters and give his speech. The conversation upset him, something that was noticed in his speech delivery by longtime Reagan-watchers among the news people covering the event.

At midnight, just as the Reagan motorcade arrived back at the Andover Hotel, Ed Meese was arriving, too. He had met Casey at the Boston airport. Casey, instead of returning to New York, was staying in a hotel near the airport, in case he was needed.

Tentatively, a meeting had been scheduled for the next day, Saturday the sixteenth, to discuss finances. Sears had hinted in midweek that he might resign if the meeting was held. Several key campaign people, including the finance chairman, Dan Terra, had been asked to stand by in case it was held.

Late that night, tensions spilled over. Sears, Black, and Lake confronted Governor Reagan. They blamed many of the campaign's troubles on Meese. They also claimed they needed to bring in an "expert" on foreign policy, an apparent knock at Allen. They threatened, for the third time since August, to resign as a group unless Reagan reaffirmed Sears's full control of the campaign. They told him that if they left, he would lose New Hampshire. At that point, at three in the morning, they withdrew with the suggestion that "we let it simmer for a few days."

Saturday, Reagan decided to make what would be one last effort to settle the matter. He asked Sears to accept Casey as chief of operations, with day-to-day supervision of the business side of the campaign. Sears seemed to assent, or at least was willing to meet with Casey to discuss it. They did meet the next day, the seventeenth, at the hotel.

At the meeting Sears told Casey he could take any title he wanted and that it would not affect his own decision about the future. Casey inferred from this that Sears was thinking of resigning. Or, he wondered, was this an indirect threat based upon a belief that Reagan needed Sears in order to win? Sears did agree to discuss the range of campaign-management problems with Casey and he appeared to agree in principle to Casey's taking on day-to-day business management. While the conversation was friendly and Sears seemed to offer no objection to Casey's joining the team, he did what he often did when he was dealing with a subject he was not yet ready to resolve—he began a long, circuitous discourse about campaign philosophy and the art of politics. By and by, he was called away to attend to another matter. He said they would reschedule the meeting to bring their discussion to a conclusion. The second meeting never took place.

While Governor Reagan went back on the campaign trail on Monday the eighteenth, thinking the campaign-management problem might be on the way toward a solution, the tensions were still there. On Saturday evening, Allen and Wirthlin had discussed the situation, including what effect the departure of Sears might have on the New Hampshire outcome.

During much of the time in Andover, Sears kept to his room, on the telephone, conferring with aides or simply reflecting on the campaign. Occasionally he would come out for a meal in the large atriumlike dining room of the hotel, but he rarely acknowledged the presence of other staff members or the press in the room. He sat, instead, at a side table with Black, Lake, Gosden, and his secretary, Joan Follick. He was as preoccupied with the campaign's problems as the candidate and his other advisers.

Early in February, after returning from the Africa trip, I read the accumulated—and depressing—press accounts of the Reagan campaign's problems and called Ed Meese to ask if I could be of any help. "It would be good if you could come up to Andover to help with our briefing for the governor before the Manchester debate," he said. Since I was heading east in a few days on business, I told him I would come to Andover on the nineteenth. As it turned out, Allen, Jones, and I were on the same plane from Washington to Boston. We drove together from the Boston airport to the hotel. It was late afternoon. The briefing was to take place over dinner.

When we got to the Reagan campaign's wing of the sprawling hotel, something seemed wrong. The place was too quiet. The staff office had several people in it, but there was not the three-ring-circus atmosphere that is normal in a presidential road-tour staff room. Primary day was only a week away. If anything, the activity level should have been even more frantic than usual, I thought. Instead, the atmosphere was hushed and tense.

In one room, advance men were working quietly on the telephone. In the main office, two young women worked silently at their desks. Joanna Bistany, who was in charge of the office, greeted us warmly, a contrast to the oddly subdued air about the place.

We picked up our room keys (actually plastic cards to be inserted in slots by the doors). There was no one in the halls. The governor and his entourage were still out on the day's tour. Sears, Black, and Follick were apparently holed up in Sears's room.

After we had put our bags in our rooms, Allen and I went to Casey's room. Meese was with him. They quickly brought us up to date. In their view, the campaign's management problems were far from resolved. Rather, they were temporarily in limbo. On the campaign trail there was some good news: Governor Reagan had had his first platform appearances the night before with all his rivals and had done well. Casey and Meese agreed that Reagan had gotten the best of the applause at both a Portsmouth event (a city that had gone for Ford in 1976) and at a gun-owners' candidates' night afterward. At the latter event, John Anderson's performance foreshadowed his later shift to an independent candidacy. Since he was already on the opposite side of the gun-control issue from the gun-owner groups, he made a strong stand for his position. Predictably, liberals and the press editorialists praised him afterward, adding to the general feeling beginning to take root in the press that his was a candidacy of "candor."

It was time to go to the dinner meeting. I still had a business telephone call to make so I stayed back. As the others left, we agreed to meet again later in the evening to discuss the management situation.

Except for Governor Reagan, I was the last one to arrive for the dinner. The others were having a drink. The tension was thick. Sears looked tired. Black looked grim. Meese, Allen, Casey, Hopkins, and Jones looked uneasy. The talk was subdued, inconsequential. It was as if two prizefighters and their seconds were sharing a common holding room before stepping into the ring to belt one another.

Governor Reagan arrived shortly, in good spirits. He greeted us cheerfully and gave me a warm welcome (I had not seen him since Deaver and I had been to his home for a New Year's cocktail in late December). He recounted the day's highlights and seemed satisfied that the day had been a good one. It was plain that his post-Iowa campaign style agreed with him.

While Sears had offered Reagan no resistance when he decided to change the strategy in New Hampshire, it is likely that his long-held theory that "politics in motion" made it hard for him to believe that Reagan's repetitious daily stumping could greatly affect the outcome. This may have caused some of Sears's moodiness. Perhaps he was searching for some move that would arrest the attention of the press and the nation in order to restore Reagan's momentum.

As we sat down around the dinner table, Sears began to speak but was interrupted by Lake rushing into the room. "Before you get into this we've got something more important," Lake announced. He looked at Meese and said, "What am I going to tell the wire services at nine o'clock tonight to substantiate the [Reagan] claim about Alaskan oil?" There seemed to be something accusatory in Jim's tone. It crossed my mind that this might be intended to discredit Ed in front of the governor. Still, that seemed unlike Lake, who had always been very earnest. Probably, I thought, he was just anxious because the press had been hounding him all day.

Some of the traveling news people had been playing a familiar game. We had encountered it in 1976, too. It goes this way: if the candidate slips up on a statistic, question him at every opportunity. Badger his staff for sources to see how they defend his information. Hector the candidate at news conferences to see if he gets testy. Since the primary-election season is a testing ground, the men and women of the media quite naturally consider themselves as key testers.

This time they were challenging a claim Reagan had made at more than one stop to the effect that there was probably more oil untapped in Alaska than in all the other states put together, perhaps enough to make us independent of OPEC. Where had he come up with his assertions? He remembered reading about the matter recently, but could not put his finger on it. The day of this dinner, researchers Hopkins, in Andover, and Bandow, in the Los Angeles headquarters, were working frantically to come up with a source.

Meanwhile, members of the press had contacted officials of the Department of Energy for verification. Not surprisingly, these Carter administration officials pooh-poohed Reagan's claims. Regardless of political affiliation, bureaucrats tend to flow with existing authority and also to defend their own statistics. In the absence of credible sources for Reagan's statistics, the news media were about to declare him dead wrong. This was not a good time to be thrown on the defensive.

Bandow and Hopkins located an Alaskan energy trade association that provided some support, and there were references to an unpublished U.S. Forest Service report for Alaska that was supposedly helpful. An Alaska state agency report was also said to have supporting evidence.

For the present there was enough to go on—just barely—for Lake to give the media a reason to hold their fire.

With the crisis averted, the meeting got down to the briefing for the debate. Sears began. He said that he, Charlie, and Jim had a dinner engagement with some reporters, so would not be able to stay, but he had some comments to make.

His remarks were brief. As was often his habit, he looked downward as he made them, or out toward the distance, without focusing on anyone in particular. He reminded Reagan to be himself, to be relaxed, and to use a little self-deprecating humor. He pointed out that this debate went beyond New Hampshire itself and would give the entire nation its first real look of the year at Reagan contesting for the presidency. Reagan had to convey the look and feel, the reassuring qualities of a national leader, he said. Sears urged him not to be defensive about any past statements or about his record and to glide around categorical rebuttals to his opponents. Instead, he should make the thematic points he wanted to make against Carter, using his immediate primary opponents only as means to get to this real target.

No one could argue with Sears's comments. He understood as well as anyone that television is an impressionistic medium, that Reagan is exceptionally good on television when he is relaxed and confident, and that his appearance could turn the corner for his New Hampshire campaign and perhaps for the year.

Sears, Black, and Lake left and the mood of the place seemed to relax noticeably. The issue-by-issue briefing went on through dinner. We broke up at about nine.

As we left the dining room, I took Casey aside and said, "Bill, I hope you'll come aboard, but I doubt that it will work as long as John is here." "You're probably right," he replied.

We went back to Casey's room to discuss the matter further. Meese seemed a little reluctant to bring the issue to a head with Sears. This was understandable. He had been the subject of criticism by Sears and his lieutenants and, not being a vengeful man, did not want to appear to be getting even. Still, Allen and I argued that the matter had to be resolved and soon; Ronald Reagan's candidacy would be permanently crippled if things were left unresolved much longer. Before Meese, Casey, Allen, and I broke up that evening, we agreed that a plan would have to be developed and presented to the governor; it had to involve Sears leaving and Casey taking over as campaign director. The Manchester debate was the following night. We agreed to have a conference telephone call on Thursday morning to discuss details of a plan.

On Wednesday, Allen and I returned to Washington. I saw the debate on television there and thought that Governor Reagan accom-

plished everything he needed to accomplish. He looked fine, he was relaxed, he used humor well, he was in command of his material, and he
seemed reassuring. As it turned out, reassurance of the voter continued
to be—right through the final debate in the fall—the basic objective of
every one of Ronald Reagan's major 1980 television appearances.

The next morning, Thursday, while I was on an airplane bound for
Los Angeles, Casey, Meese, Allen, Wirthlin, and Deaver took part in the
scheduled conference call. They quickly agreed that the staff tensions
could not continue and that the matter of the campaign's management
needed to be resolved in the next several days. Consensus developed that
a change of management from Sears to Casey should be recommended
to Governor Reagan as soon as possible. Questions of when and how to
effect the change took up the rest of the telephone conference. If it were
done on the weekend, the event might make the campaign appear to be
in disarray and thus affect voters negatively. If it were done after the
New Hampshire results were known the next Thursday night, Reagan
might look like either a sore loser or an ungrateful winner, depending on
the outcome.

Finally, the group decided to recommend that the governor meet
with Sears, Black, and Lake the afternoon of election day, several hours
before the election results would be known. It was also agreed that confidentiality was essential. Aside from those taking part in the call and
me, the matter was to be discussed with no one else until election day,
when a number of key Reagan allies and supporters would be called.

The group decided that I should be interim press secretary from
election day through the end of the next week's campaign trip and perhaps a little longer, my schedule permitting, until Ed Gray, Reagan's
onetime gubernatorial press secretary, could be persuaded to take a
leave from his business to join the campaign as full-time press secretary.

When I left New Hampshire for Washington and California, I had
promised Meese and the others that I would return Saturday to participate in the briefing for the debate in Nashua that evening, which was
being sponsored by the *Nashua Telegraph*. Reagan's New Hampshire
chairman, Gerald Carmen, had provoked the debate. Initially, it was to
be a one-on-one with George Bush, but a series of unexpected events
changed the scenario dramatically late in the week. First, the *Telegraph*,
which had agreed to sponsor and run the debate in a high school auditorium, announced that it could not pay the costs of the event after all,
because to do so might constitute a corporate political contribution.

The Reagan campaign then offered to split the costs with the Bush
campaign. Bush's people declined. Reagan's staff then announced they
would go ahead and pay for the event entirely from Reagan funds.

Meanwhile, the other candidates—senators Howard Baker and Bob

Dole, representatives Phil Crane and John Anderson, and John Connally—were complaining that a two-man debate was unfair and that they should be included. Reagan indicated that he was agreeable to having them participate. Sensing that a "fair play" issue could embarrass the Bush campaign at a critical moment, the Reagan people let the controversy swirl.

Reagan's negotiators told the *Telegraph*, which was still going to run the debate, that Governor Reagan was willing to open it up. The *Telegraph*, which was expected to endorse Bush, was not budging, nor was Bush. It was apparent that the Bush strategists thought their man could beat Reagan in a head-on debate, and they did not want to risk it for a free-for-all with the other candidates.

As it turned out, I was not able to get back from Los Angeles in time for the briefing of Governor Reagan that Saturday afternoon in Andover. I arrived in Boston just in time to rent a car and get to Nashua as the debate was scheduled to begin.

I found the Reagans, Sears and other senior staff members, and all the other candidates except Connally and Bush in a classroom behind the auditorium. It was quite a scene. I crowded past the Secret Service men to find members of the candidates' staffs sitting in tablet desks around the room and the candidates and Nancy Reagan, with Jim Lake and Dick Allen, crowded into a tiny glassed-in teacher's cubicle. Negotiators had been going back and forth down the corridor to *Telegraph* officials and to Bush's quarters. The other side remained adamant. Tempers were rising. Baker, Crane, Anderson, and Dole were getting ready to stalk out and denounce the event (although not Reagan). The *Telegraph* sent word it would cancel the event if Reagan was not in his place in the gym in five minutes. Bush, it seems, was already there. Reagan got the message in the cubicle and told the others he would not debate if they were excluded. Sears and other Reagan staff members knew it was important that he debate Bush and put him on the ropes. Some—including some of the other candidates—said he should go on out by himself, but Nancy Reagan stopped the discussion when she said, "No, you should *all* go on out." And that is what they did.

A phalanx of Secret Service men, candidates, wives, and aides streamed out of the room, heading briskly for the gymnasium door.

Reagan strode in, with the other candidates right behind him. A roar went up from the crowd. Loren Smith, the Reagan campaign's legal counsel, and I were standing at the door, just below the stage where the action was taking place.

Bush sat uncomfortably at the end of the stage nearest us, not looking at the others. Reagan stood by his table at the opposite end of the stage, with the other candidates ranged behind him.

The executive of the *Telegraph* who was in charge called for silence. Reagan stepped up to his microphone to say that he thought the others should participate. Then, the *Telegraph* executive, John Breen, said—for everyone to hear—that Reagan was out of order and he called on the sound engineer to cut off his microphone. That did it for Reagan. In tones that were clear, commanding, and filled with controlled anger, he said the now-famous words, "I *paid* for this microphone Mr. Green [sic]." The crowd went wild. He said a few more words, apologizing to the audience for the confusion and telling them he thought the other candidates should have a chance to speak.

A chant began, "Bring them chairs, bring them chairs." Before I knew it, some teenagers rushed up to Loren Smith and me at the door and handed us each two folding chairs. We hurried them in to the base of the stage, but by then the other candidates were coming down the steps, ready to walk out.

Back at the door, I turned around to see Sears, in his overcoat, standing a few feet away, by a cluster of people. We looked at each other. He was smiling like the Cheshire cat.

No sooner had the other candidates stalked out than they vented their anger at Bush in news conferences, interviews, and television panel shows over the course of the weekend. Meanwhile, in the auditorium, Reagan was in full command. Bush, although he handled himself reasonably well in the debate, seemed preoccupied with what he knew must have been a major mistake, and the distraction made his performance appear far less effective than Reagan's.

Unlike the Manchester debate earlier in the week, which was nationally televised, this one had only local coverage. What was devastating, however, was the brief clip on national television news showing Reagan seizing the microphone and uttering that phrase, "I *paid* for this microphone, Mr. Green!" Those seven words symbolized perfectly a Ronald Reagan in full control of his campaign and his candidacy. Ironically, the event marked the beginning of the end for Bush's presidential candidacy, and it sealed Sears's fate as Reagan's campaign manager.

The original plan, to talk with the Reagans late that evening after the debate about the recommendations to change campaign management, was shelved temporarily. We returned too late, and the buoyant mood was too good to be changed. The matter would have to wait until Sunday.

Some in the press, especially Bob Shogan of the *Los Angeles Times*, sensed that something was going on, but none of us said or did anything to give their suspicions real focus. Earlier in the week, Shogan had written a story speculating about the possibility of Casey joining the campaign, but neither Casey nor any of us reacted to it with the traveling press corps and they did not seek to expand on it.

More details of the plan were shaping up. In addition to Casey as campaign director, senior management would consist of Meese as chief of staff and policy chief and Wirthlin as political strategist. Andy Carter would be asked to step in as national political director, in Black's place. I had already agreed to serve as interim press secretary.

Sunday I drafted the press release that would announce the resignation of Sears, Black, and Lake and the new appointments. I used my portable typewriter in the same hotel room that had been Casey's nearly a week before, when the first discussions about a change of management had taken place. I kept the draft press release and the lists of telephone calls to be made to key supporters locked in my briefcase. Later, after Governor Reagan had reviewed and approved the final draft of the release, I made all the photocopies myself to ensure its security.

Sunday evening, Casey and I followed the Reagan motorcade to a clam chowder supper in Portsmouth. The crowd was in a happy mood, and one supporter sang a country-and-western tune he had composed in Reagan's honor. Then, it was on to Durham and the University of New Hampshire campus, where Reagan visited the local chapter of Tau Kappa Epsilon, his college fraternity. After that we returned to Andover. Meese, Casey, and I followed the Reagans into their suite.

Ed, Bill, and I each briefly addressed elements of the problem and the outline of the plan for changing the management of the campaign. Governor Reagan listened intently. When he spoke, it was clear that he had made up his mind some days before and was waiting for his advisers to reach a consensus on a detailed plan of action. He was now concentrating on the implementation of the plan itself.

"Do you think there is any way we can keep Jim and Charlie?" he said. Both had worked hard for him, but they had locked themselves into Sears's three ultimatums to quit. If they stayed, we said, the new management team would not be able to function effectively.

We talked over all the details and the timetable of the plan.

Mrs. Reagan had tried to keep lines of communication open between the staff groups since the campaign had settled in at Andover, and we asked if she would be willing to talk with Lake or Black to ask the three of them to plan to meet in the governor's suite at the Manchester Holiday Inn, the election day campaign headquarters, after lunch on Tuesday. She said she would. The Reagans would arrive there about noon, after several stops near polling places along the way so they could thank voters for their support.

It was decided that Casey would be the only other person in the room when the meeting took place. The governor said he would hand Sears and the others copies of the press release and explain his timing.

Our meeting was interrupted by a telephone call from Dick Wirthlin, who was in California. He told Governor Reagan that he was going to win New Hampshire by a margin of 17 percentage points. He told him that the campaign really began to turn sharply at the conclusion of the Manchester debate the previous Wednesday evening and that his lead had been building steadily since, getting an extra boost from the previous night's debate in Nashua. Wirthlin was conducting nightly tracking polls, and he had a reputation for cautious analysis, so all of us were cheered by his prediction. By that Sunday, all of us had come to believe that Reagan would probably win, but 17 points still seemed almost too good to be true. In the end, it was 27 points.

Monday dawned clear and cold. The Reagans campaigned all day with an extra measure of confidence. Sears, Black, and Lake were busy countering charges by Bush campaign officials that the Nashua debate had been designed to "sandbag" their candidate. Casey, Meese, and I went over details of the plan for the next day. Governor Reagan would call Paul Laxalt just prior to the Sears meeting. After that, the list would be called—key campaign people and some columnists and other journalists who were not expected to be on hand in Manchester that night. We divided the assignments.

That evening, Meese, Casey, and I picked up Dick Wirthlin at his hotel and drove to the Andover Inn, on the campus of the Phillips Andover Academy, for dinner. There, in the soft light of the large old dining room, with chamber music playing in the background, we enjoyed the first truly relaxed meal any of us had had in many days. We talked of the shape of the campaign to come. Later that night, Casey, Meese, Allen, and I went over details of the plan with the Reagans one last time.

Tuesday, I drove to Manchester in midmorning with Casey and Dan Terra. I was the first staff member at the hotel. After locating the photocopy machine, I arranged to run off enough copies of Sears's resignation announcement for distribution to the press later in the day.

The hotel ballroom was being set up as a press-conference room for the evening. A few local media people were on hand, plus technicians from the networks who were stringing electrical cable. The traveling national press would be along in midafternoon by bus (only a press pool was accompanying the Reagans on their trip from Andover).

The Reagans arrived a little ahead of schedule, just before noon. It was brilliantly clear in Manchester. The air was fresh and bracing on this twenty-sixth day of February.

Nancy Reagan told us that she had talked with Lake that morning and that he, Sears, and Black were planning to have lunch with a journalist in the hotel dining room and that they would be up to see the Reagans at 2:30 in the afternoon.

Casey, as planned, joined the Reagans in their suite. I was in a room down the hall, assembling press releases for staff assistants to hand out downstairs after the meeting had concluded.

The meeting lasted a little under thirty minutes. Reagan told Sears and the others that he appreciated their efforts and that all had tried their best, but that he felt that a change of campaign management was needed and that he planned to issue a statement reflecting both their resignations and the appointment of Casey as campaign director. The action took them by surprise. They read the release, but did not remonstrate with Reagan. (Black even offered to help the campaign in the future as a volunteer.) Although, from their point of view, the worst had happened, the months of growing tension had been broken. There were handshakes all around, and Sears, Black, and Lake left.

Mrs. Reagan went across the hall to talk with Linda Gosden, Lake's assistant. Casey conferred with Andy Carter, asking him to take on Black's duties. Within forty-five minutes of the meeting in the Reagans' suite, Sears, Black, Lake, and Gosden had left the hotel and the campaign. The national press was unaware of it. Their bus pulled in about twenty minutes later.

I stayed upstairs where Meese, Casey, and I began making our assigned telephone calls. I left assistants to face the press with only the release in hand. We wanted some time to pass before sending an official spokesman down to face the cameras. Reports coming back from the main floor of the hotel indicated that our security system had worked. The national media people were as surprised as Sears had been. Not since the day he named Senator Richard Schweiker as his proposed 1976 running mate (a move in which Sears had played a major role) had Ronald Reagan so taken the news media by surprise.

Shortly after I had gone to work for Governor Reagan in Sacramento, Mike Deaver said to me, "Remember, in this business [government and politics], there are no secrets." Time and again, I had seen this proved when news people would call to ask about something I had thought was known only to a few people. This time, however, we had taken special care to keep the timing and composition of our meetings quiet. Because all working papers were kept under lock and key in one hotel room (and no-longer-needed papers were not put in wastebaskets); because no secretary was involved in typing or photocopying; and because so many of our conferences were in the form of long-distance telephone calls, we were able to maintain confidentiality and, thus, the element of surprise.

At five o'clock I went down to the ballroom for a brief news conference. The purpose was to give the media people a chance to vent their curiosity and questions. When was the decision reached? Was the campaign in financial trouble? Why announce it today? Basically, I stuck with the elements of the press release. I felt that the press conference went well, although it all seemed over in seconds.

At seven, we took Bill Casey down to introduce him formally to the national news media in the ballroom. He handled himself in a relaxed style, bantering easily.

The results began to come in. It was going to be a Reagan landslide. The feeling I had back in November, when the governor announced his candidacy—the feeling that he could not be stopped—finally returned. We were on our way.

The rest of the evening was a blur of telephoned congratulations and a succession of well-wishers calling on the Reagans. There were several senators and representatives who had been out stumping for the governor in New Hampshire and elsewhere. The telephones rang constantly. Late in the evening, Governor Reagan did back-to-back interviews with the three television networks. Well after midnight, we began the long ride back to Andover and a good night's sleep.

The next morning, Reagan held a news conference by the big indoor pool in the middle of the Rolling Hills Hotel. He was calm, confident, good-humored. As we were about to break up for the beginning of the next campaign swing, one of the reporters shouted good-naturedly, "Free the Andover 25!"—a reference to the fact that this press contingent had been on the New Hampshire campaign trail with the Reagans nonstop for nearly four weeks.

In midmorning we flew to Burlington, Vermont, for a brief airport stop consisting of a press conference for the local media and a rally. The mood there was buoyant. The following Tuesday, Ronald Reagan won the Vermont primary. That same day, March 4, he did as well as, or better than, expected in Massachusetts, where he had done little campaigning. Bush won, and Anderson placed second, but the three were so closely bunched in the voting results that the delegates were divided nearly equally.

After an hour on the snow-covered ground of Vermont, we headed south—to South Carolina, Georgia, and Florida—for the balance of the week. In Columbia, South Carolina, late that day, we learned that Sears, Black, and Lake had called a press conference at the National Press Club in Washington the next morning.

On Thursday, I called a colleague who had attended to get a report. It had been a long press conference, nearly an hour. He said that Sears, as a professional political consultant, naturally wanted to put his side of the story on the table, which he did. While he did not criticize Reagan, there was implied criticism of others in the campaign organization as well as a rationalization of actions under Sears's management. My informant had been in an elevator filled with reporters leaving the press conference. "They see it for what it was," he said. "I don't think it is going to cause the campaign any serious trouble."

Bill Casey, meanwhile, was already in Washington beginning the uncomfortable but necessary process of cutting operating costs by cutting the size of the staff. Executive-level people who remained were asked to take 25–30 percent salary cuts with no firm promise of restoration of the lost funds later on. Within ten days of his taking over management of the campaign, Casey had managed to cut the staff in both the Los Angeles and Washington offices by nearly half.

Thursday we campaigned in Savannah; Friday, February 29, we were back in Columbia for the South Carolina debate that evening. It was to be held in the same amphitheater on the University of South Carolina campus where Reagan had debated the Panama Canal treaties with William Buckley just two years earlier.

John Connally had decided to make his stand in South Carolina. This would be a make-or-break effort to stop Reagan. He was investing heavily in his South Carolina campaign and the local media were covering it heavily, some pro, some con. Congressman Carroll Campbell and Lee Atwater, who were organizing the Reagan forces in the state, told us that they believed Reagan was holding his lead over Connally and the rest of the field. They doubted that Connally could catch him.

That evening, Reagan stepped in the small ring at the base of the amphitheater, along with Bush, Connally, and Senator Howard Baker. Reagan was relaxed and handled the questions and made his comments with ease. The others seemed more intense, especially Connally and Bush. Connally distracted the audience when he spoke by rattling coins in his trouser pocket. Most of his rhetorical fire was directed at Bush. Baker spoke sincerely but gave the impression that he had more-or-less decided that his candidacy was nearly at an end. Bush seemed uncomfortable.

Anyone looking for a dramatic flourish in the debate would have been disappointed. For Reagan, that was not necessary in any case. All he needed to do, as the leader of the field again, was to hold his own, which he more than did.

On March 8, Reagan swept the state with 54 percent of the vote to Connally's 30 percent and Bush's 15 percent. The defeat resulted in Connally bringing his candidacy to an end. He had spent nearly $10 million and gained only one pledged delegate. In withdrawing, he was gracious and upbeat, calling Reagan "the champ."

Three days later, Reagan won Alabama, Florida, and Georgia. Flor-

ida, which had been such an important early battleground in the 1976
Republican primary race, went for Reagan this time nearly two to one
over Bush.

While Reagan seemed to be pulling away—the most of us felt that
Bush probably could not stop him—the shadow of former President
Gerald Ford seemed suddenly to loom over the entire process.

Back in the fall of 1979, backers of Bush and Connally in California
had sought to get the Republican state convention to scrap the traditional winner-take-all primary and award the state's 168 delegates on a
proportional vote basis. The effort was beaten back by Reagan supporters at the September convention in San Diego by a margin of nearly
three to one. Now, there was talk of a legal challenge to the winner-
take-all primary, with a late Ford candidacy being the presumed bene-
ficiary if it succeeded.

As Reagan's lead grew and more party leaders moved toward supporting him, it began to dawn on the remaining anybody-but-Reagan officeholders and party officials that a Ford candidacy was the only way of
stopping the Californian.

For months the former president had toyed with the idea of running.
He had thus far bypassed the primaries, so it appeared that his only real
chance was for an unlikely grass-roots draft or a deadlocked convention.
He said so at various stops along the speaking circuit. Despite his comfortable postpresidential life-style, it was not surprising that Ford entertained the idea of again occupying the Oval Office. He had lost it by only
56 electoral votes in 1976. To defeat Carter would be a sweet victory
indeed.

Since it was widely reported that Ford felt that Reagan's 1976 challenge had damaged his own November election chances, the prospect of
depriving Reagan of the nomination this time was a likely element in his
consideration. At one point he was quoted by the media as saying that
he found "growing sentiment that Governor Reagan cannot win the
election." He likened a Reagan nomination to a "replay of 1964." While
this view did not square with public perceptions as reflected in our private polls or even in the public polls, it was a frequently uttered thought
by those in the party who were reluctant to rethink old stereotypes.

In the Reagan camp none of us seriously believed the convention would become deadlocked or that its delegates would award the
nomination to a candidate who had not run the gauntlet of primaries.
Governor Reagan put it succinctly to reporters when he said Ford
"should pack his long johns and come out here on the campaign trail
with us."

Bush and Connally also dismissed the "Draft Ford" movement,
which was suddenly the focus of media attention. Still, it was far from

imaginary. The former president was discussing it with many old friends and advisers. Even John Sears weighed in. He took it seriously enough to accept an invitation to visit Ford at his Rancho Mirage home near Palm Springs on March 7. After the meeting, he told reporters he thought Ford could be nominated if he ran. Henry Kissinger, in search of his own restoration, also flew to Rancho Mirage to counsel Ford on nomination strategy.

By mid-March, the Ford boomlet had become a crescendo in the press and in terms of our perception of it. The Reagan campaign was taking it very seriously. The legal people were studying filing rules in each of the states still open to see if it would be possible for Ford to mount a major challenge.

Ford flew to Washington in mid-March for a series of meetings and a GOP fund-raising dinner, where he got a standing ovation.

Apparently, the strategy emerging among Ford's advisers was that Ford had to take a high-risk approach, but one that offered the chance to knock Reagan out in the major states yet to be decided. Tom Reed, both a onetime Reagan adviser and Reagan-selected California national committeeman, was heading a Draft Ford committee. Their advice to Ford was that he had to win seven of the so-called Big Eight primaries: California, Michigan, New Jersey, New York, Ohio, Pennsylvania, and Texas. It was already too late to file for the March 18 Illinois primary. There, the Ford forces hoped John Anderson would defeat Reagan. Reed even talked boldly of beating Reagan in his home state.

The Ford strategy was a tall order to fill. Deadlines were pressing. Filing for California's June primary would close on March 21. While he was in Washington, Ford met with many old friends in Congress, in the hope that his growing interest in challenging Reagan would catch fire with them.* It did not, and he returned to California a disappointed man.

Back at Rancho Mirage, Ford met on the fifteenth with a group of his advisers to assess the situation. The necessary core of congressional support was not there. Many members of Congress were already supporting Reagan; others were committed to other candidates still in the race. Few were enthusiastic about a Ford-Reagan contest, which almost certainly would be divisive at a time when most Republicans sensed that 1980 was their year. The consensus at Rancho Mirage: it was too late.

Over the weekend, Ford announced that he had reached "a final and certain decision. I am not a candidate. I will not become a candidate. I will support the nominee of my party with all the energy I have."

---

* Tom Evans of Delaware, a key Reagan supporter in the House, is quoted by Frank Van Der Linden in *The Real Reagan* as saying, "I really think he [Ford] had made a decision to run, contingent upon strong support in Congress, but he didn't get it."

The news came as the Reagan campaign was moving into the Northeast. The seventeenth and eighteenth were scheduled for Connecticut events; the nineteenth, for New York City. To put the Bush challenge to rest, Reagan needed strong performances in the Northeast. To turn back Anderson, he needed Illinois, which would be decided on the eighteenth.

While Anderson had led in the polls in Illinois, the televised Illinois debate a few nights earlier may have done him in. During the debate, Reagan good-naturedly chided Anderson for having said he preferred Teddy Kennedy as president to Reagan. Congressman Phil Crane reinforced the point later by drawing attention to a fund-raising letter Anderson had signed on behalf of several liberal-to-left Democratic senators, such as George McGovern, Frank Church, and Birch Bayh. Anderson, used to being on the attack, was thrown back by this revelation and did not have an answer that would have satisfied Republican loyalists.

Tuesday the eighteenth, Reagan took Illinois. He beat his fellow native son, Anderson, by 48 percent to 37 percent. Bush and Crane trailed far behind, but Crane, also an Illinoisan, knowing his own candidacy was nearly at an end, had indirectly boosted Reagan by revealing the Anderson direct-mail letter on national television.

Reagan on his second Illinois try, with a dedicated organization headed (for the second time) by State Representative Don Totten, had successfully contested for a major industrial state. Traveling in Connecticut, those of us on the Reagan touring campaign felt the message would not be lost in the industrial states of the East, either.

The next day, having spent two days in Connecticut blue-collar towns addressing friendly, good-sized crowds, Ronald Reagan took his campaign into New York City, via the New Haven line during the early morning commute. Regular riders and railroad workers did a double take as we stepped off the train at Grand Central Terminal and they recognized the governor. They crowded around, shouting good-naturedly. The Secret Service detail formed a wedge as we moved into the huge main terminal room so that the Reagan party could make its way to the street. None of us in the Reagan campaign thought of New York as Reagan country, but after several years of traveling with a major political figure, you develop a hard-to-describe sense about crowds. As we moved through the high-ceilinged terminal, something told me that everyone in this crowd knew they were looking at a winner, and most of them liked the idea.

Out on Vanderbilt Avenue, where our motorcade was waiting, the early spring sky was clear and the air fresh. It was going to be a great day in New York. After a speech at the Waldorf-Astoria, Reagan and his party went on to Queens for a rally in front of the borough's Republican headquarters, followed by a news conference inside. Then, it was on to Brooklyn, where George Clark, Reagan's Brooklyn chairman in both 1976 and 1980, had arranged a luncheon with local party leaders, followed by a large noontime rally in Court House Square. The rally was more like a general election event than the partisan ones that had filled most of the primary schedule. There was even some heckling. In fact, the small knot of hecklers was so persistent and obstreperous that when one of them shouted something about Reagan wanting to start a war, he shot back, "No, I don't want to do that, but if I did, I'd start it right here with you guys." There was no more heckling.

Back in Manhattan, the motorcade drove down from midtown to the financial district, where the New York Stock Exchange was to be the campaign's focus for the afternoon. First, William M. Batten, chairman of the exchange, introduced Reagan to exchange leaders at a reception. Then, the governor met privately with about two dozen New York Jewish leaders, many of them Democrats. The meeting went well and struck me as a promising sign of future support or at least neutrality.

Following this, Reagan had a series of meetings with state Republican leaders arranged by Roger Stone, the campaign's coordinator for New York and Connecticut. Roger took me aside and said that most of the state party leaders had decided Reagan would be the nominee and were getting ready to come over. It was quite a contrast to 1976, when Nelson Rockefeller not only held the New York machinery in place for Gerald Ford but also influenced neighboring states. Now, with Rockefeller gone, the New York Republican party was no longer monolithic. Rather, it had split up into a collection of independent duchies. Reagan, with skillful background work by Stone and his staff and by Max Rabb and other key volunteers, had already received the support of a number of them. Now, it looked as if the rest would be his, too.

If Ronald Reagan needed any further testimony that he was taking New York by storm, the last event of the day provided it. At about three o'clock he was escorted down to the trading floor of the exchange. As he entered the big trading room, word of his arrival spread almost instantaneously among the several hundred traders, brokers, and runners. He was hugged and squeezed by young women runners. Hands shot out for shaking or for autographs. Cheers went up. Blizzards of paper were being thrown into the air. It was pandemonium—all of it friendly.

The careful groundwork in New York paid off on March 25, when most delegate selections were decided in the Empire State. Reagan was the winner. Finally, the inevitability of a Reagan nomination (which Sears had wanted to create with imagery back in November and December) was becoming a reality as a result of Reagan's effective personal campaigning and solid grass-roots organizing.

On the same day, Bush, having put his all into the Connecticut primary, carried his native state. It was close, however, for Reagan, with 34 percent, was only 5 percentage points behind him; Anderson received 22 percent. A week later, Reagan took Wisconsin, with 40 percent to Bush's 31 percent and Anderson's 28 percent. Anderson had pinned his last hopes for a Republican nomination on Wisconsin, with its crossover voting and its reputation for doing the unexpected. After seven tries, he had yet to win a GOP primary. Soon, he was to cut his ties with his party and begin his candidacy as an independent.

As Ronald Reagan moved steadily toward the nomination, media attention, as well as that of the candidate and his advisers, turned more to the development of issues that would be relevant in the general election campaign.

Many in the news media had been after Reagan's senior staff for a definitive position paper on the economy. Reagan's views—that the country needed a significant across-the-board tax cut on the order of the Kemp–Roth bill's 30 percent, along with regulatory reform and budget restraints—were well known. Nevertheless, the pressures on working journalists make it easier for them to comment on a neatly packaged position paper than to wade through tapes of news "availabilities" and speech transcripts. There were also requests for papers on foreign and defense policy, energy, and agriculture.

Martin Anderson, back as coordinator of economic and domestic issues, was in no hurry to develop such a paper on the economy. Most of us advising Governor Reagan felt the same way about the other topics, too. Since his views were generally known, repetitions and expansions were best handled on his terms—that is, in speeches, question-and-answer sessions, and media availabilities. As one adviser put it, "Long papers on issues provide stationary targets." True enough, if "politics is motion" (and I believe it is). The candidate, especially if he is leading, risks diverting attention from his objective—and thus his momentum—if his campaign hands out long policy releases.

Still, we could not dismiss the fact that a problem was brewing over economic issues within the Reagan camp. As Reagan's lead grew, his candidacy attracted more and more advisers. He welcomed this, of course, for it helped fulfill his wish that his candidacy provide a broad umbrella for the whole party. A number of well-known Republican economic advisers who had not previously identified with Reagan joined an enlarged economic-policy advisory committee. Some of them mistrusted individual income tax cuts of the sort Reagan had been advocating. Instead, they favored "targeted" tax cuts, aimed at business and industry.

Some wanted a policy in which each dollar of tax cuts was matched by a dollar of spending cuts. This traditional conservatism was difficult to square with Reagan's oft-stated support for supply-side solutions to the nation's economic ills. One adviser was quoted by the April 7 *Business Week* as saying, "the battle for the heart and mind of Ronald Reagan is on."

Underlying this difference of opinion on economic issues were two basically different views of the American people. Reagan had for years expressed a strong belief in the common sense of the American people. His famous transfer-plan speech of September 1975 summed up his views in its title: "Let the People Rule." By contrast, the more conservative economic advisers beginning to join his campaign viewed "the people" abstractly. They trusted businessmen to know what to do with tax cuts; they were not so sure about the people. This may have been partly a result of decades of Keynesian conditioning (even conservative economists could be affected by it). Most Keynesian tax cuts for individuals were small and of short duration, designed to spur short-term consumer spending in order to "fine tune" the economy.

Within his own campaign, Ronald Reagan was finding that it would not be easy to get his more traditional advisers to understand and appreciate that supply-side theory rested more on knowledge of human behavior than on static sets of numbers.

About this time, Ed Meese asked me to work with Governor Reagan on his forthcoming speech to the American Society of Newspaper Editors. It was scheduled for April 8 in Washington. We were all in California for a few days, about two weeks prior to the event.

I called the governor to talk over the speech. Since this audience, by its nature, would give no more than polite applause to any candidate's speech, why not use the occasion to get some thoughts on the record that he wanted to convey, I suggested. He agreed. We discussed two themes: one would be a sort of report card on the campaign so far, seen from his perspective; the other would be a review of his economic proposals. By covering the latter, he would keep media attention on his economic program and also slake some of the thirst for a long, formal position paper.

What he said to the editors on April 8 foreshadowed several major policy themes he was to develop as president a year later.

> There are several things that set the 1980 presidential campaign apart from all others. This year, by the time we're finished, there will have been thirty-seven primaries. By contrast, just twenty years ago, there was only a handful of them and it took the Democrats two to determine their nominee.
>
> Out on the campaign trail, where I've been for all but a few days of

the last thirteen weeks, I'm often asked in interviews by members of your profession how I can appeal across party lines, to Democrats and independents. It was, after all, another Republican candidate who was supposed to have "crossover appeal." In retrospect, it seems that those who were saying this were thinking in terms of traditionally *liberal* Democrats who found no candidate in their own party satisfying. What they had overlooked was that a different sort of crossover was actually beginning to take place, one that may foreshadow a major change in American politics. This is the crossover voting of increasing numbers of blue-collar workers, ethnics, registered Democrats and independents with conservative values. Am I happy to have these votes? Of course, I am, and the Republican party will need millions of them in November.

The day of appeals to group interests alone is fast disappearing. We are seeing a growing determination on the part of voters to be seen not just as members of economic groups or social classes but as human beings with values held dear. On the farm, in labor unions, on the street corners of the cities, and in white-collar offices; in the suburbs (where the values of the old neighborhoods have been preserved) and in the old neighborhoods themselves, there is a new coalition, and I believe it is coming our way. . . .

This is a new coalition of shared values, and I believe its time has come. The values of this, the American middle class should be deeply involved in the decision-making process in Washington, for these values underlie the strength of our nation. . . .

Right now the most important issue we Americans face is this: Can we stop inflation and still enjoy economic growth and a rising standard of living? Or, as our leaders are telling us, must we endure a mixture of high inflation, unemployment, austerity and limited opportunity for an indefinite period?

I believe we have the knowledge to devise policies that will stop inflation, restore vitality to our economy and provide private employment for all willing Americans. We certainly know that today's policies have not worked. The present administration does not seem to know or to believe that the American people have the will to succeed. . . .

He moved on to a review of the hapless state of the economy; then to his proposals:

I don't think anyone objects to paying reasonable taxes. And, we all agree on the need to help the less fortunate. But, rich or poor, young or old, a person's reward for working *more* should always clearly exceed his reward for working *less.*

The government's refusal to adjust (or "index") income tax rates for inflation not only stops all Americans from climbing higher on the economic ladder, it also pushes some people off the bottom rung every year. Two million more Americans are considered permanently unemployed today than only 10 years ago.

Those who do manage to keep their grip on the ladder still face dismal prospects. In half of all households, rich and poor alike, the government takes at least 50 cents of every $1 wage or salary increase, and the average is 46 cents. At these rates, you need to increase your income about twice as fast as inflation just to stay even after taxes. Americans aren't losing their confidence; they're losing their shirts! . . .

We don't need to abolish government or its safety net of programs, but we must change the government's policies to get it working on our side rather than against us.

He outlined six proposals, in addition to his support for income-tax indexing:

I would tell our monetary authorities that they have only one job: to restore and maintain a sound dollar at home and abroad. They would be directed to create as few or as many dollars as it will take to stabilize the value of what a dollar will buy.

In proceeding toward the goal of full employment without inflation, I would ask Congress to act immediately to begin the necessary reform of our tax system, to restore the rewards for working and saving by cutting income-tax rates and adjusting them automatically for inflation. My goal would be to cut the tax rates of all Americans by at least 30 percent over three years. And I would ask Congress to widen the tax brackets yearly thereafter to prevent any further tax 'bracket creep' caused by inflation.

Next, he proposed that Congress adjust corporate-tax rates for inflation: "It is only fair that businesses be allowed to account for the true cost of replacing their plants, equipment and inventories. This is necessary if American business is to stand up to the fierce international competition of the 1980s."

Next, he called for abolition of federal gift and estate taxes. "The federal government," he said, "never imposed such death taxes, except in emergencies, until the Depression. Before that, the property-tax base traditionally belonged to the states. Is it only coincidence that the number of farms in this country has dropped every year for forty-four years straight since the estate-tax rates were first hoisted to their current levels?"

He then said, "I would go after excessive federal spending. A freeze on federal hiring would be one step. Seeking out and eliminating waste and fraud would be another. . . . Inflation adds to the government's cost. It is estimated that every 1 percent of inflation increases spending about $5 billion. Every 1 percentage point added to the unemployment rate costs the government between $25 billion and $29 billion."

Next came a revival of his transfer plan: "As part of the process of streamlining government, we should take a close look at the efficiency of various federal programs to determine which could be handled more effectively by state and local government. Those that can should be transferred—and in an orderly, phased manner—along with the tax sources to pay for them."

He went on to underscore the importance of his tax-cut philosophy:

> Critics of major tax cuts usually cry that these will aggravate inflation by enlarging the federal deficit. They don't take into account the fact that the additional money the people get to keep isn't buried in a tin can in the backyard. It's put into savings and investments, into a new car, a vacation, a new room on the house—all the things people do when they make decisions in the marketplace. That money spreads through the economy. It means more production, so there would be more jobs. . . .
>
> Recent history shows that significant tax cuts, rather than throwing sand in the gears of the federal machinery, actually help it. For the five years just prior to the round of tax cuts proposed by President Kennedy's administration, federal tax receipts increased by 25 percent. But, during the five years they were taking effect, federal receipts increased by more than 50 percent! Inflation wasn't a factor. During the earlier five-year period it averaged only 1.6 percent, and only 2.3 percent during the second period. A more productive economy produced the added revenue. . . .
>
> The program I am talking about is not a 'free lunch,' but a plan for economic growth. We must have growth. Other nations have not waited, militarily or economically, for the United States to squabble over matters that should have been settled long ago. The world is a more dangerous and challenging place today than when our leaders turned inward to debate whether America would continue to be great. We have no choice but to be great. The world has never begged more clearly for us to serve as its "shining city on a hill," a place of refuge, as well as an example and proof of democracy's strength.

He concluded, "Here in America our choice is not between liberal and conservative, young and old, black and white, rich and poor, Sunbelt and Snowbelt, consumer and producer, or Democrat and Republican. No, our choice is between up and down—up to the ultimate in individual freedom consistent with an orderly society or down through statism and government intervention to authoritarianism or even totalitarianism. To me, the signs are everywhere and they are unmistakable—the American people want to go up."

It was about this time that Reagan's economic-policy advisory committee had scheduled a meeting with him at his home in Pacific Palisades. Privately, some of the newer advisers had been talking about "bringing him around" on economic matters, especially his espousal of supply-side tax cuts. After the meeting, the advisers, about twelve in all, joined Governor Reagan for an impromptu news conference outside the house. There, with the candidate beaming his pleasure, they pledged unanimous support for his entire economic program.

Reagan had made it clear not only to his economic advisers but also to the news media that while he welcomed a range of views and diversity of thought, he would draw the ultimate conclusions. Thus, the battle for the heart and mind of Ronald Reagan had been fought—and won by Ronald Reagan.

Although Governor Reagan's lead for the nomination was growing steadily, no one in the Reagan camp was taking victory for granted. Bush was putting up a determined fight, and there was the danger that if he beat Reagan convincingly in, for example, Pennsylvania, Texas, and Michigan, the leader's lead might evaporate.

Because he was the leading candidate, Reagan was being subjected to an intensified barrage of questions from the news media. This was part of the trial-by-fire process the media employ every four years, and it is as basic to the American political system as voting itself. My notes for an April 2 meeting at the Reagan for President Committee headquarters in Los Angeles list, "New themes from the press: Are you worried about right-wing 'boarding parties'? When are you going to beef up your staff? When are you going to make an economics speech and other 'substance' speeches or issue papers? Are you afraid of complacency setting in?"

Some in the media were playing the "facts" game again. In late March in Wichita, Reagan had fumbled a question about farm price parity. He had discussed the subject knowledgeably a number of times over the years, but as can happen to any person faced with dozens of questions a day—as a candidate is—he momentarily went blank on the subject. He recovered at the next stop, but the fumble brought on a fresh round of inquiry from the media about whether he was well informed, well prepared, and perceptive.

The press was also restless about the style of the campaign's leadership. Bill Casey's style, for example, was deceptive. At first glance, he might have seemed casual, almost offhand about the campaign. In actuality, he was anything but that. His offhand demeanor was protective coloration for an analytical mind, constantly probing for more effective ways for the campaign to operate.

Casey, Ed Meese, and Dick Wirthlin operated comfortably as a trio, talking or meeting with one another several times daily. Still, the media liked the idea of a single strong leader and often cited the three-man leadership as evidence that the campaign was in "disarray" (a favorite media word).

In April, the campaign traveling squad gained more depth when Jim Brady, a canny Washington veteran with an irrepressible sense of humor who had been a key adviser to Connally, joined it to augment the issues operations and to help Ed Gray, the press secretary.

As to the right-wing "boarding parties" the press was asking about, there was increasing worry among the media that religious fundamentalists-turned-political-activists would assume an important role in the Reagan campaign. Those of us who had been with Reagan for some time knew this would not be the case. While Reagan considered himself a "born-again" Christian,* he did not wear his religion on his sleeve. Religious conservatives found his views generally congenial, but he did not share their doctrinaire approach on many issues. Many of them were moving to Reagan partly because he was acceptable and partly because they felt betrayed by the famous born-again occupant of the White House. Reagan was not going to turn down their support, but neither was he going to be co-opted by them—or by anyone else.

In mid-May, we headed for a last visit to Michigan, with a stop at Portland, Oregon, on the way. The Portland sky was flat gray, a pall created by the volcanic smoke and ash from Mount St. Helens. This did not dampen the enthusiasm of the big rally crowd.

Saginaw, Flint, and Detroit, Michigan were grim cities. Unemployment in the auto industry was bad and getting worse—12 percent. In Flint, Reagan had lunch with a dozen or so out-of-work members of the United Auto Workers to learn firsthand of their problems. In Detroit, he addressed the Detroit Economic Club on the fifteenth. He surprised his audience by announcing he would talk about *optimism.* "On the way in today," he said, "a fellow stopped me and asked what I was going to talk about. 'Optimism,' I told him. He said, 'You sure picked a heckuva time and place to do it.' "

He continued, "At first glance, he may seem right. Unemployment nationally is above 7 percent and in Michigan it is nearly double that. The very life of the U.S. auto industry seems threatened and its problems affect scores of related industries.

He went on to detail the auto industry's plight and the bias of some in the federal government against the automobile itself: "It is fashionable in some Washington circles to be hostile to the automobile, especially the American automobile. After all, everything in Washington is close by and even those without limousines and Volvos can get around on the taxpayer-financed Metro subway. But, those who must get from one place to another in such locales as Texas, Kansas, or Los Angeles can't afford the luxury of seeing cars taxed and regulated into oblivion. . . .

"Automobiles have been everyone's favorite scapegoat for the failures of energy and economic policy. Yet, the production of automobiles

---

* Reagan explained to questioners that in the church of his childhood, the Christian Church, young people were asked to recommit themselves to their faith as a deliberate act, even though they had been baptized as infants; hence, his view that he had been "born again."

is vital to the health and well-being of the nation. The U.S. auto industry remains the best in the world. It simply needs the freedom to compete, unhindered by whimsical bureaucratic changes in energy, environmental, and safety regulations. It needs a predictable and stable economic environment where people can make the sort of long-term commitment that an auto purchase entails."

As to the optimism he mentioned at the beginning of his address, it was embodied in his description of the growing "coalition of values" he had been discussing for some weeks, and in his proposals for economic reform as outlined in April to the American Society of Newspaper Editors and reiterated in Detroit.

During the question period, he was asked for an example of overregulation in the auto industry. He cited the number of persons General Motors had to employ to deal with regulation compliance; the figure was on the order of twenty thousand. The press jumped on it. Several news people called General Motors, sure that Reagan was exaggerating. It turned out he had understated the figure.

Although his Detroit speech was well received and widely reported, he lost Michigan to Bush. Pennsylvania also went to Bush, while Reagan carried Texas.

Bush declared he would fight down to the wire—the big June 3 primary day that included California, Ohio, and New Jersey, but on Memorial Day, he brought his campaign to an end. Reagan was going to be nominated anyway, so Bush's withdrawal prior to the final primary day provided a gracious final note to a contest that had gone on for nearly seven months.

On the night of June 3, as the results from the final round of primaries came in, several thousand Reagan supporters gathered in and around the Ambassador Hotel on Los Angeles's Wilshire Boulevard, just as they had done four years earlier.

When the Reagans appeared it took several minutes to quiet the cheering crowd. Ronald Reagan stepped to the microphone, beaming, and said: "First, there are two very important words that I have for each of you here, and for everyone who is watching or listening who helped make this night possible. Those words are *Thank you.* Thank you for volunteering to walk through the snow; thank you for organizing rallies, breakfasts, luncheons, and dinners; thank you for spending hours on the telephone; thank you for typing and writing letters; thank you for stuffing envelopes."

He went on to recite some statistics his staff had compiled: "In the nearly seven months since I announced my candidacy . . . we have visited 318 cities and towns (some of them three and four times each) and have traveled, by air alone, 166,450 miles. That's an average of 855 miles a day. Those statistics are important only in terms of contact with people. This campaign has given me a special opportunity to listen to the concerns—and the hopes—of the American people in every corner of the country."

Briefly, he recapitulated the nation's economic troubles and added: "Mr. Carter, when he was campaigning in 1976, concocted something he called a 'misery index.' This was the sum of the rates of inflation and unemployment. Then, it was 12.5 percent. Today, thanks to his policies, it is almost twice that—24.5 percent. The administration's policies are built on a theory that was once widely held but has long since been discredited. The theory is that for one person to prosper, another must suffer."

Reagan recounted his meetings with some of the people thrown out of work: the auto workers in Flint, small contractors in Oshkosh. He spoke of the shared values of those who supported him: "More and more as I traveled from state to state, I've found a growing consensus of shared values. I have seen a growing determination on the part of voters to be seen not just as members of this or that economic group or social class, but as human beings with values they hold dear. At the center of their values are five very important words: *family, neighborhood, work, peace,* and *freedom.* Their values cross party lines; they go beyond politics. In place after place, saying the same thing to different groups, I've seen the artificial barriers fall away, barriers that had kept Americans with shared values but with different economic, social, or geographic backgrounds from each other. These shared values of which I speak are values that transcend economic or social class, and they should be heeded in Washington, for they underlie the strength of our nation."

Moving to conclude his brief remarks to a crowd that was attentive but obviously wanted to get on with its celebrating, Reagan added, "Perhaps the Carter administration's greatest failing is that it seems to see Americans as statistical units, not as a great collection of individuals. I see them as individuals, and although I have no elixir to make our troubles go away, I do believe wholeheartedly in the common sense of the American people. They are our greatest resource. Beginning in January, if we couple a new administration which brings sensible tax, spending, and regulatory policies together with renewed freedom for the power and initiative of the American people themselves, we can make the 1980s a new era of hope, not only for our nation, but for all mankind."

The long road to the nomination was all but behind Ronald Reagan now. It was time to turn attention to the selection of a running mate, to development of political strategy and issues for the fall campaign, and to plan for the Republican convention in Detroit in mid-July.

10

"Hang in There, America"

WITH THE LAST ROUND of primaries behind him, Ronald Reagan had three things to occupy his full attention: strategy and themes for the general election in the fall, selection of a vice-presidential candidate, and his own acceptance speech for the Republican National Convention in Detroit, a little over a month away.

Dick Wirthlin was developing the strategic basis for the fall campaign while discussions were going forward about the other two subjects. A few days after the June 3 primaries, I attended a meeting at the campaign headquarters in Los Angeles. Governor Reagan was there, along with several members of his senior staff. Ed Meese had asked me to coordinate draft contributions from various sources for Governor Reagan's acceptance speech and to work with him on it.

When the subject of the speech came up, Reagan made the point that he wanted to restate his basic themes about the economy and America's role in the world but that he also wanted the speech to be, in effect, the beginning of his general election campaign. He may have been thinking of John Sears's statement of many months earlier, to the effect that a presidential candidate has the full attention of the nation twice—when he announces his candidacy and when he accepts his party's nomination. In retrospect, it seems to me that a candidate gets more attention at the latter event. Certainly, the news media give the acceptance speech more serious, detailed coverage than they do an announcement of candidacy.

The words *thematic* and *inspire* kept coming up in the discussion. Governor Reagan said he did not want a laundry list of specific shortcomings of the Carter administration. Instead, he wanted to tie together the things he had been saying about a "community of shared values," to dramatize the idea that people with seemingly disparate backgrounds had values in common that were being abused by an unresponsive government that had grown too large and pervasive.

We discussed the speech timetable. I said I would ask for all suggestions to be in Friday, June 27, so that a first draft could be in Governor Reagan's hands early the next week. He and Mrs. Reagan were planning a visit to a friend's ranch in northern Mexico over the long Fourth of July weekend. He said he would leave all other work home and concentrate on the acceptance speech while he was there.

Meanwhile, many meetings and discussions were taking place about the vice-presidency. Casey, Meese, Wirthlin, and Deaver talked frequently with one another, with Governor Reagan, and with Senator Paul Laxalt. The Executive Advisory Committee, of which Deaver was a member, had frequent discussions about the subject at this time, too.

From the beginning of the discussions, George Bush's name figured prominently. Those who argued for Bush made these points: he had virtually earned it by running the gauntlet of all the primaries gallantly; most of his supporters were not Reaganites, so his inclusion on the ticket would cement them to the ticket for the fall campaign; Bush's ebullient style suggested that he would be a loyal and effective campaigner.

Among Reagan's grass-roots supporters, however, there was resistance to Bush. Prolife forces were suspicious of his views on abortion. He had declared his opposition to federal funding but stopped short of supporting a constitutional amendment banning abortions altogether.

The New Right beamed its strongest opposition toward Senator Howard Baker, another possibility discussed by party moderates. Many conservatives still smoldered over Baker's support for the Panama Canal treaties. The prolifers and the increasingly activist evangelical Christian groups were upset over Baker's Senate votes for federal funding of abortions. The traditional conservative weekly, *Human Events,* became a powerful voice in opposition to Baker, too. It cataloged what it felt were Baker's shortcomings in detailed articles over several weeks. Jack Kemp was the candidate *Human Events* appeared to favor. This was not surprising, considering its strong support for supply-side economics as the key to a Reagan victory and to a conservative resurgence. *Human Events* had long been staple reading for Ronald Reagan. This fact may not have been lost on Senator Baker. In any case, he responded to the heavy conservative attacks on him by, in effect, taking himself out of contention.

Within the kitchen cabinet there was some sentiment for former Treasury Secretary William Simon. Simon had been an early supporter of Reagan's 1980 bid and was himself a member of the committee. Some of the committee members had come to like his crisp, forthright style and his economic views. Many other names were mentioned in the news media,* but none were really in serious contention save one: that of Gerald Ford.

Bryce Harlow, widely respected throughout the party, was probably the first one to put forth the idea of a Reagan-Ford ticket. He said it was the best guarantee of a defeat of Carter in November. Reagan, two days after the California primary, had gone to Ford's desert home near Palm Springs, not only to ask for his active help in the campaign to come but also to ask him to take the second spot on the ticket. Ford declined, but he emphasized that Reagan should pick a moderate in order to give the ticket the broadest possible appeal. He also told Reagan he could count on his support for November.

As June moved on, there was no firm decision on a vice-presidential nominee. Indeed, contrary to the circumstances of 1976, when Reagan had startled the nation by announcing his choice of Schweiker three weeks before the Republican convention, this time the Reagan camp considered advance selection to be a mistake. Better to keep the options open until the convention, they believed, than risk irritating disappointed aspirants and their supporters. On the other hand, there was never any question about throwing the matter into the laps of the delegates. Reagan believed he had a responsibility to make his personal choice known and would do so in time.

Bill Casey continued to be intrigued by the possibility of a Ford candidacy, despite Ford's initial refusal. He continued to discuss the idea informally within the Reagan circle.

Now that the Reagan forces had triumphed in the primary campaign, many grass-roots leaders pressed for a shake-up in the staff of the Republican National Committee. Several of them harbored long-simmering resentment toward the committee staff. They felt that it was not only non-Reaganite in composition, but actually anti-Reagan. Added to this was the unhealed wound caused by Chairman Bill Brock's refusal, back in late 1977, to provide committee monetary support for the anti–Panama Canal "truth squad."

Reagan's campaign leadership took up the discussion of quickly replacing the committee leadership with trusted Reagan supporters. Brock, alarmed, flew to California to meet with Reagan and Casey to make his case for staying on.

Brock came away from the meeting saying he expected to stay on through the November election. Others in the Reagan high command, led in this case by Laxalt, said that Brock should stay only through the convention and that Drew Lewis, Reagan's Pennsylvania chairman,

* Paul Laxalt was the sentimental favorite of much of the Reagan circle, especially the Californians, but it was generally agreed that a ticket of two Westerners from neighboring states was a political impossibility.

should take over at that time. This view was close to unanimous and was finally recommended to Governor Reagan when Brock mounted a vigorous campaign to keep his position as chairman. Elected Republicans around the country began to call Reagan and his senior advisers, saying, in effect, that the benefits of Reaganite control of the committee would not be worth the cost in terms of party disharmony.

William Timmons, Nixon's congressional liaison and, since then, a highly respected Washington lobbyist, had been asked to join the campaign as national political director, commencing with planning for the convention. Time was short, and Timmons, a friend of Brock, was withholding a decision until the controversy was settled. Ultimately, former President Ford weighed in, in favor of Brock's retention. With the Reagan–Ford relationship having been carefully rebuilt and with Ford's help in the campaign seen as important, his support for Brock became decisive.

In mid-June, Brock again flew to Los Angeles to call on Reagan. A compromise was worked out. Brock would continue to chair the committee; Lewis would become deputy chairman; Brock's deputy, Ben Cotten, would step down to a lesser position; and Mary Crisp, cochairman and an outspoken Reagan critic, would go.*

While all this was going on, Reagan and his campaign were not idle on the issues front. Mindful of the planned introduction of a tax-cut bill by congressional Republicans the next day, Reagan on June 25 released a statement to increase the pressure on the Carter administration, which was facing increased unemployment and record inflation.

> The answer to this depressing situation lies in *immediate* action by the Congress to reinvigorate the economy. The answer lies in a tax cut—a genuine tax cut—to be effective on January 1, 1981.
>
> Consistent with the tax reduction approach I have been outlining for months, it should take the form of an across-the-board 10 percent cut in income-tax rates on individuals, as well as an effective accelerated depreciation schedule to revive the flow of investment into American business so it can become more productive and more competitive. . . .
>
> Given the deteriorating economy, we simply can't afford to wait any longer to take the steps necessary to put such a productivity-oriented tax cut on the books by year's end. . . . I want to emphasize again that such tax cuts must be coupled with substantial reductions in the rate of growth in government spending. . . . Jimmy Carter says we cannot cut taxes until we balance the budget. But, his policy of fighting inflation with higher taxes, mounting unemployment and deepening recession only guarantees there will be no balanced budget at all—next year, or ever. . . .
>
> Moreover, the phased-in tax cut I have proposed is just the first in-

---

* In one interview, Crisp had spoken warmly of John Anderson. Ultimately, she took a position in Anderson's independent campaign.

stallment of an overall program to get the country back on its feet and moving again . . . a program to steadily reduce today's stifling tax burdens on citizens and businesses, large and small.

Besides the three-year, 10-percent-a-year reduction in income-tax rates on individuals, these cuts must be made real and permanent in the fourth year by indexing all federal personal income taxes, so that today's new incentives are not taken away by tomorrow's inflated tax collections. . . . Only a permanent, inflation-proof, continuing tax-reduction program can restore growth, jobs, and prosperity to the nation. A "tax of the month" gimmick . . . will only compound the nation's problems. Any such plan—to lower one tax and raise another, or reduce taxes this year and then inflate wages and salaries into higher brackets next year—will only compound the nation's problems.

Still, a firm handle on federal spending is absolutely essential for long-term control of inflation. My goal as president would be to gradually reduce the amount of federal spending relative to the total economy, or Gross National Product—reminiscent of the Kennedy administration when the nation provided adequately for both national defense and domestic needs and also had stable prices.

Next, Reagan took the first step to implement a strategy using a favorite medium, radio. Wirthlin, following suggestions by Allen and Anderson, had been considering for some time the idea of proposing to Reagan that he do a series of fifteen-minute radio addresses on a national network, to lay down a foundation of basic positions on a variety of issues. Reprints of the speeches would become position papers, the basis to which his staff and campaign workers could always refer. It was agreed that the pilot project would be such an address on the subject of leadership and the presidency, to be broadcast first on July 2 during the morning commute hours and then again on Sunday the sixth on CBS. A major advantage of this media strategy, Wirthlin had concluded, was that the radio addresses cost a fraction of such presentations on television; the time was easier to clear; the production was far simpler; and television could be saved for major and timely campaign presentations. The pilot speech became the single manifestation of the plan; the idea for a series never materialized.

The short address is a concise statement of Reagan's view of the job he was to assume a few months later:

Often during the months of campaigning, I have been asked which president I most admire. Such a question may seem easy to answer. Washington, Jefferson, Lincoln—what American doesn't admire such leaders? But, when you think about it, a question about one's favorite president is really a question about values, not about specific leaders.

I think it is important for the people to know where a candidate stands regarding the nature of leadership as it is for them to know where he stands on specific issues. Issues change. Today's blaring headline is forgotten as tomorrow's takes its place. But, values and principles remain.

It is one of the ironies of recent political history that a commitment to political principles and social values has often been seen as a sign of rigidity and an inability to change, but there is an old saying that the best statesman is one who has the *disposition* to *preserve* and the *ability* to *improve.* I agree. A leader must have the ability to improve, to change, to adapt to new circumstances. But, that ability must be tempered by a deeply rooted understanding of the need for continuity in basic principles and a dedication to fundamental values. Indeed, without such an understanding, a leader will drift to and fro—as we have seen happen so often with the present administration. Seneca said, "He who knows no ports to sail for, finds no winds favorable."

Leadership in the presidency means something more than making decisions as the chief executive. It means understanding that the United States has many sources of leadership, not just one. When a president forgets that fact, when he begins to believe that leadership is limited to what he does or to what is done in Washington, D.C., he in effect cuts himself off from the real strength of the nation. In every city and town, every county, every state, there are elected leaders. They are not somehow less important to America than a president; they are important in different ways. Once a president gets the idea he can do *their* jobs better than they can, the very foundations of our nation are weakened.

Leadership in America is not now and never has been *synonymous* with elected or appointed public office. There are leaders in neighborhoods and communities who have never been elected to any office but who serve as spokesmen for the places where they live, men and women who lead every day without making headlines, and their contribution to America is priceless. . . .

We have one president, but we have many leaders. Too often, in recent years, when we have talked about the need for leadership, it has been only in terms of the need for leadership in Washington. Heaven knows, we need it there, but just as urgently we need to have a federal government whose lust for ever-increasing amounts of power is curbed so that power can once again be exercised by many leaders—in civic, social, business, union, professional, and community groups.

My vision of government is one in which presidential leadership complements, but does not overshadow, other forms of leadership. In those areas where he has the constitutional responsibility, a president must be bold, vigorous, prudent, and willing to use the powers granted him. But, at the same time, he should take care that his powers and those of government in general don't become so strong and widespread as to smother the natural capacity for leadership in our society that has long been America's strength and hope. . . .

Ironically, it is precisely when a president begins to think he needs more power that he finds himself powerless. A president may think he needs bigger federal budgets in order to get his job done. But, bigger budgets—unchecked—lead to inflation. Higher taxes for those budgets lead to reduced savings, less investment, lower rates of productivity, and more people out of work—problems we are saddled with today. So, the president who tries to gain more power finds himself without the very thing he needs most: a strong, confident, resourceful people, able and willing to put their ingenuity to work.

The wisest course for a president—the course seen so clearly by the founders of our country—is to concern himself with those duties strictly limited by the Constitution, and let the American people themselves do the rest.

Daniel Webster said, "Hold on, my friends, to the Constitution of the United States of America and to the republic for which it stands. Miracles do not cluster. What has happened once in six thousand years may never happen again. Hold on to your Constitution, for if the Constitution shall fail, there will be anarchy around the world." . . .

There is a great movement abroad in the land today, and I think it is unstoppable. It is the movement to return power to the people and the states, as called for in the Constitution. It is the refreshing idea . . . that the money you earn is yours and that government had better give you a good reason for asking for it in taxes, the idea that families prosper best when least burdened by government interference. . . .

There are seven attributes I believe a president should bring to the Oval Office to help activate the community of values. They are a view of government based on clearly defined principles and a vision of what this nation should be; the effective communication of those principles and that vision to the American people and to the world; "a bold, just and impartial spirit" in dealing with national problems; the cooperation of talented and dedicated men and women in making certain that the principles and the vision shape every decision made by government; the capacity to identify, analyze, and adapt to changing conditions in the nation and in the world; the courage to make what at first may seem to be unpopular decisions, but ones based on an understanding of national needs; and, finally, the willingness not only to admit error, but also to learn from it.

Shortly after the Brock controversy was settled, Bill Timmons officially joined the campaign team, his first assignment being the supervision of the Republican National Convention. He worked quickly, assembling his leadership cadre mostly through a series of telephone calls. This time, since there would not be a contest for the presidential nomination, there would be a high degree of coordination among all the party dignitaries who would speak and take active roles at the convention. The GOP intended to show the world that it was united.

Timmons called to ask if I would be director of research and writing. I accepted. He assigned my unit a large suite equipped as an office, on the sixty-eighth floor of the Detroit Plaza Hotel. Martin Anderson, concentrating on domestic policy for the platform, and Dick Allen, working on foreign policy, would share the working quarters and hold meetings with their various technical advisers there. My wife and I would be assigned a bedroom next to the office suite. The Andersons and Allens would be nearby. This proved to be a good arrangement, for we were in and out of our office dozens of times, day and night, during the nearly two weeks we were in operation.

Marty Anderson said that his assistant, Barbara Honegger, would organize the typists, staff assistants, and volunteers; Timmons was watching the budget carefully, so all operating units would rely heavily on volunteers. The budget did not cover hotel rooms for two of our junior volunteers, so they flopped down in the office in sleeping bags each night.

I made a series of telephone calls to line up a writing team. Bill Gavin, in Washington, could not come to Detroit but offered to help by telephone (he was already working on an important memo for Governor Reagan's acceptance speech). Dave Gergen, at the American Enterprise Institute, said he would be available, as did Jim Robinson who had once done research at Deaver & Hannaford on some of Reagan's newspaper columns and radio commentaries and was now executive assistant to Congressman Gerald Solomon. Dick Fairbanks, a Washington lawyer and onetime Nixon aide, volunteered and proved to be invaluable. Marty Anderson's capable research associates, Doug Bandow and Kevin Hopkins, would be on hand, and Misty Church and my son Dick volunteered to be "gofers" for the unit.

As June drew to a close, memos and draft ideas for Governor Reagan's acceptance speech began to come in. Gavin, who had offered many good ideas over several years, made a major contribution. Peter Rusthoven, a young Indianapolis attorney whose essays I had seen from time to time in Bob Tyrrell's iconoclastic magazine *The American Spectator,* submitted a full draft that contained many good ideas.* In my transmittal memo to Governor Reagan with the first draft, I noted that "it owes much to . . . conversations, ideas, and phrases from Bill Casey, Ed Meese, Dick Allen, Marty Anderson, Mike Deaver, Lyn Nofziger, Dick Whalen, and Roger Fontaine."

Although I had read the submissions as they came in, I set aside Friday, June 27, to stay at home in order to concentrate full attention on them. This was followed by a weekend of developing a full draft for Governor Reagan to work on. On Monday, the draft was typed in final form. It went with him the next day as he and Mrs. Reagan left for Mexico.

---

* Memos and draft ideas from George Gilder, Bob Smalley, and the Reverend Don Shea of the Republican National Committee arrived after the first draft had been completed.

In my cover memo, I noted that Gavin had analyzed Franklin Delano Roosevelt's 1932 acceptance speech, which is considered by speechwriters to be a model of its kind. I added, "We have worked against a checklist developed from the FDR model, including such things as appreciation to the delegates and to the people who voted for you in the primary campaign; formal acceptance of the nomination; acceptance of the platform; an appeal to those outside the party (the Community of Shared Values); an overview of the major issues (economic, energy, national defense); a look at what you will do to correct problems; a 'new' idea (a 'new compact for America'); criticism of the Democrats, but stated thematically, without a detailed statistical rundown."

Thus, the draft submitted to him responded to his original charge to me and the others. When he returned to Los Angeles the following Monday, he gave his revised copy to Chuck Tyson, the scheduling chief, to telecopy to me, for by then I was in Washington. Although all telecopy paper is soft gray, I knew that back in Los Angeles the draft had the familiar look of all drafts returned by him: the typed pages would be interspersed with lined yellow pages bearing his familiar handwriting, and such marginal notes as "Pete, let's try this instead." As I read his revisions I had a déjà vu sensation. I found myself thinking, as I had often in the past, "Why didn't I think of that?" Ronald Reagan's long years of experience in radio, films, television, and public speaking had given him an ability, unique among American politicians, to think primarily of how a word or a sentence would sound, rather than how it would look. He has always written for the ear, rather than the eye. Although I have done a good deal of radio and television writing over the years, it was nothing compared to his experience, and like many writers who work with major political figures, more of my experience had been in print media than in broadcasting. In addition, Reagan has the advantage of having developed over the years a telling sense of imagery. For example, at one point in the draft I had referred to the nation's economic plight under Carter as an "economic miracle," the quotation marks denoting a sarcasm that he would have to convey by tone of voice. When we talked about it, Reagan said, "Nobody will understand the quotation marks. Let's try this: 'Mr. Carter has created an economic stew that has turned the national stomach.' " And that is the line he used.

We discussed inclusion of an FDR quotation. Reagan had been a New Deal Democrat in the 1930s, admired FDR, and felt, as did many Democrats in recent years, that the party had moved away from Roosevelt's precepts. I proposed a quotation in the draft. Reagan chose another one. His turned out to be more apt, for the quote, regarding Democratic party intentions in 1932, let Reagan make the point that it would be the Republicans who would now redeem the Roosevelt promises of forty-eight years before.

Dick Wirthlin and I went over the governor's changes and agreed to have a telephone conference with him on Saturday the twelfth (I would be in Detroit, Reagan and Wirthlin in California) and then asked him to "sign off" for the last time shortly after his arrival in Detroit on Monday, July 14.

Although I arrived in Detroit the evening of the eighth, a week before the actual convention was to begin, there were already hundreds of people crowding the walkways, hanging gardens, lobby, elevators, restaurants, and bars of the vast Detroit Plaza Hotel (since renamed the Westin Hotel). The Committee on Resolutions (known by everyone as the Platform Committee) had held its first session on Sunday the sixth. This meant that not only all its members would be there but so would many convention staff personnel and countless numbers of cause-pleaders seeking a hearing before the committee.

The Detroit Plaza Hotel stands at the hub of the Renaissance Center, a huge complex on the shore of the Detroit River. The hotel is a seventy-story cylinder, dwarfing the four fifty-story office buildings that surround it. In addition, there are several floors of shops and restaurants. The lobby ceiling seems to be a hundred feet or more high. Despite the complex's great size, when it is filled with people, it seems warm and cheerful. The Republicans were all of that. An air of revelry, optimism, and joviality was apparent as you passed through the groups of people chatting, hailing, or just watching one another.

Later that evening I met with Timmons to report to him on the organization of the research and writing unit. He told me that party leaders would be fanning out the next weekend to brief all the state delegations on the platform and the Reagan program. Our unit would be asked to prepare remarks and briefing sheets for them. In addition, once the platform was adopted, there would have to be short presentation speeches for all its major segments. And some twenty or so party leaders would address the full convention sessions. Many of them would want drafts from our unit, Timmons said. Others would provide their own, but he was asking all of them to send their final drafts back to us to review in order to avoid duplication. There would be nominating and seconding speeches and, no doubt, some speeches we did not yet know about. Timmons said that there would be a meeting early each morning over coffee and rolls of the convention leadership cadre.

Timmons and his convention-planning team had worked swiftly and well to organize the logistics for this several-thousand-person drama. He handed me a green folio bulging with a hundred pages or more that amounted to a comprehensive guide to the convention. There were phone numbers, room assignments, code names, daily agendas, lists of receptions and parties, convention officers, floor plans of the hotel, and instructions for using phones and paying hotel bills. There was even material on sightseeing in Detroit, something I doubt anyone on the staff ever got to do.

The convention organization chart was headed by a box labeled "Candidate." Under it were boxes for the national chairman, Paul Laxalt; the campaign director, William Casey; and the convention director, Timmons. Off to one side were boxes for the chief of staff, Ed Meese; the senior advisers, Dick Wirthlin and Mike Deaver; the press secretary, Ed Gray; and the scheduler, Chuck Tyson. Then, there was a row of special operating units and those in charge of them: the director of arrangements, Keith Bulen; the director of communications, Lyn Nofziger; the director of promotion and advertising, Peter Dailey; the director of political operations, Clif White; the director of operations, Chuck Tyson; and the director of research and writing, myself. Not shown on the chart but soon to play an important role at the convention (and through the general election) as a political adviser was Stu Spencer who had comanaged Reagan's first gubernatorial campaign in 1966 and had worked for Ford in 1976.

All week long the crowds kept streaming into the hotel. Most of us on the staff never left the complex. There was no need to, for the place was so large and there were so many restaurants and stores that one could attend to one's needs simply by riding down an elevator.

On Sunday the thirteenth, the *New York Times* reported, "Riding a tide of optimism, planeloads of delegates converged on Detroit today for the 32nd Republican National Convention since the party's founding in 1856, with Ronald Reagan's choice of running mate the only real item of suspense." The newspaper went on to note that Reagan had that day issued a four-point economic recovery program geared to the U.S. auto industry. In the program, Reagan referred to the industry's unemployment rate of 30 percent as "a tragedy of the first magnitude." Plans were afoot for him to meet with Detroit Mayor Coleman Young and United Auto Workers President Douglas Fraser. Meanwhile, the Reagan program called for new tax breaks for the auto industry to speed retooling for small cars, repeal of federal gasoline allocation, and a moratorium on future auto-industry regulations. At the same time, he repeated his opposition to import quotas. As it had been for a long time, Reagan's view was that a revived, newly competitive U.S. auto industry was the best answer to the import tide.

Saturday evening I dropped by Bill Casey's suite on the sixty-ninth floor. The lights of Windsor, Ontario, winked far below us and across the river. Beyond that, the flat Canadian countryside was nearly black.

I asked Casey if he thought the Ford vice-presidential option was still alive. Yes, he said. If the governor really wants Ford, I said, there is a way to do it that will inject real drama and excitement into a convention that the news media expect to be dull. I noted that the Reagans' schedule showed them calling on the Fords on their seventieth floor suite shortly after their arrival Monday. After that they would go to Cobo Convention Center nearby for a forty-minute appearance at a huge reception for all the convention's delegates and alternates, some seven thousand persons in all. If Reagan intended to reintroduce the subject of the vice-presidency with Ford, that first meeting might be the best time to do it, I said. He could emphasize how important Ford's presence on the ticket would be and then tell him he wanted to mention their conversation to the delegates in the reception hall. By doing so, he would be asking the delegates to call on Ford to accept a genuine draft.

Casey mulled this over and then said, "It might work. Let's round-table it, then talk it over with the governor." Meanwhile, he asked me to draft the sort of brief remarks the governor might use to break such news to the delegates. I said I would have them back to him within the hour.

When the idea was proposed to the governor, he said he thought that would put the former President in too tight a spot. He thought the best time to discuss the subject would be at the meeting the two of them had scheduled in the Reagan suite for 3:45 Tuesday afternoon. It would be one on one, and if Ford still felt the same as he had when Reagan called on him in Rancho Mirage, well, he would understand.

The Reagans arrived to a tumultuous welcome at the Detroit Plaza late Monday afternoon, the fourteenth. People seemed to be hanging over every inch of every balcony. The Reagans stepped out onto one of the round concrete platforms that seem to float in space here and there in the huge lobby. Briefly they addressed the throng.

When they arrived in their suite, Casey and Meese briefed them, and we all began discussing one problem that had arisen from the Platform Committee deliberations: equal rights for women.

James Flansburg, writing in the *Des Moines Register* the day before, had summed it up well: "The platform writers decided against repeating the party's 1976 endorsement of the Equal Rights Amendment. That left the anti-ERA types laughing and proclaiming victory and the pro-ERA types gnashing their teeth as if the party had advocated returning to the days when women were regarded as chattels.

"In fact, the plank, as proposed for adoption by the convention last week, is a first-rate compromise. The views of both sides were blended, and their reactions to the outcome had more to do with state of mind than with objective assessment."

The state of mind·of one group of Republican women leaders was the subject at hand. Dissatisfied with the plank and worried about the party's commitment to women's rights, they had gone public. The media, with not much else to report, were giving them plenty of attention. What this group wanted, it seemed, was a personal reaffirmation by the head of the ticket himself in the matter of equal rights for women. To them, the constitutional amendment on the subject had become a litmus test of conviction.

It could be argued (and our briefing sheet prepared for the caucus briefers did so) that the compromise plank represented the first time the party had actually been united on the issue. In the past, support for the amendment was the only measurement of support for the broader subject of women's rights. This time the plank read, "We acknowledge the legitimate efforts of those who support or oppose ratification of the Equal Rights Amendment. We support equal rights and equal opportunities for women, without taking away traditional rights of women such as exemption from the military draft. We support the enforcement of all equal-opportunity laws and urge the elimination of discrimination against women. We oppose any move that would give the federal government more power over families.

"Ratification of the Equal Rights Amendment is now in the hands of state legislatures, and the issues of time extension and recision are in the courts. The states have a constitutional right to accept or reject a constitutional amendment without federal interference or pressure. At the direction of the White House, federal departments launched pressure against states which refused to ratify the ERA. Regardless of one's position on the ERA, we demand that this practice cease."*

How should Reagan deal with the matter? Tuesday morning his schedule called for meeting with Republican women officeholders. This could be expanded to include the group dissatisfied about the women's rights plank. At that meeting, Reagan would, he said, reaffirm his personal commitment. He also said he wanted to insert a statement about it in his acceptance speech, and very early in the speech, "so there's no mistaking my intentions," as he put it. At that point, he sat down with a yellow pad and wrote out, "I know we have had a quarrel or two, but only as to the method of attaining a goal. There was no argument about the goal. As president, I will establish a liaison with the fifty governors to encourage them to eliminate, wherever it exists, discrimination against women. I will monitor federal laws to insure their implementation and to add statutes if they are needed." It was to become the third paragraph in his speech.

* The Carters had campaigned heavily for ratification in several states, providing the leadership for a barrage of telephone calls from Washington to legislators.

That was the only aspect of the acceptance speech we were able to cover before it was time for the Reagans to leave for the Fords' suite to convey good wishes on the former President's sixty-seventh birthday. Wirthlin and I would have to take up the review of the full draft with Governor Reagan some time the next day.

Tuesday did not offer many spare moments for the candidate, as it turned out. The day started with a briefing over breakfast, followed by a visit from Henry Kissinger, followed by the meeting with Republican women leaders, who seemed greatly relieved to learn of Reagan's strong sense of commitment to women's rights. The late morning was occupied by a series of meetings with various party leaders, a lunch with policy advisers, and a reprise meeting with the group of unemployed auto workers from Flint with whom he had had lunch in the city in May. Most were still unemployed.

At 3:45 in the afternoon, Reagan and Ford met, as scheduled. They were alone for a little over an hour. There was a new sense of comradeship between the two, a feeling of having a mission to share. Reagan's renewed request to Ford to consider taking the vice-presidential nomination apparently came as a surprise to the former President. Reagan made it clear that this was not a spur-of-the-moment whim on his part. Ford said nothing to encourage him. After all, he had held both jobs before and now was leading a life he greatly enjoyed, a mixture of business and pleasure. Still, his strong sense of duty kept him from giving a flat no, and so, as they parted, he agreed to call Reagan the next morning. This was the door left open.

That was enough to put the Reagan group into action. In the early evening, Casey called Henry Kissinger to ask him to stop by before he left for a dinner engagement. Kissinger agreed. In Casey's suite, he, Meese, and Deaver told Kissinger that Reagan was serious about having Ford on the ticket, that time was short, and that they hoped he would help persuade Ford to accept. Would he visit the former President right away? Kissinger told them a better time would be after dinner when he would join Ford and his party on publisher John McGoff's yacht, anchored in the Detroit River.

Meanwhile, Reagan had invited Chairman Bill Brock to his suite that evening to watch the convention proceedings on television. He told Brock of his conversation with Ford. Brock was delighted with the idea and apparently surprised. Later that evening he called the convention chairman, Congressman John Rhodes, to ask him to breakfast the next morning to talk about the "dream" ticket. He invited senators Howard Baker and Bob Dole and several other leaders. Brock intended to join the persuade-Ford effort and to enlist others.

After the Ford party returned from the yacht to the former President's suite about midnight, discussions about the ticket lasted nearly two hours. Betty Ford sat in, as did Ford's chief of staff, Robert Barrett, and his old friend and former White House aide John Marsh. At one point, Ford and Kissinger retired to another room to discuss the matter alone. Ford knew it was unlikely that Reagan, if elected, would name Kissinger as his secretary of state, although he would have been Ford's choice. Kissinger is reported to have urged Ford to accept on the basis of patriotism and to disregard such considerations as Kissinger's personal future or that of any other adviser.

Although I had dropped by Governor Reagan's suite once or twice that evening, I had spent most of the time after dinner working on the redrafting of his acceptance speech. We had only had time to go over the speech in very short breaks between his various meetings that day and evening.

The evening hours were relatively quiet in the research-and-writing unit's office. I had found it nearly impossible to concentrate for any length of time during the day on doing some of the fine tuning on the draft Governor Reagan had asked me to do. Now, with evening wearing on, I saw a deadline of Wednesday morning facing us.

The days in our big office—with its panoramic view of Windsor and the green Canadian countryside and the river traffic below us—were filled with the comings and goings of our staff and volunteers. There were reports from members of the team on various projects, approvals of drafts for this or that speech or statement, and endless telephone calls. I thought the noise level was high, but Theodore White, author of the *Making of the President* books, wandered by Tuesday afternoon, looked in, chatted for a few moments, and then proclaimed this the most serene place he had found in the entire hotel and asked if he could borrow a desk to write up his notes. I did not know how he would be able to concentrate in this bedlam, but we all welcomed him and I turned back to the latest crisis.

At 12:30 A.M., by now Wednesday the sixteenth, I put a large paper clip on what I hoped would be the final draft of the governor's speech and bounded up the steps to the next floor. I hoped he would have a few minutes to look it over before retiring. That would reduce the time our final review meeting the next day would require. Nancy Reagan had also asked me to look over her notes for her remarks at Wednesday's Federated Republican Women's luncheon. I had these with me, too.

Reagan, Deaver, Meese, and Ed Gray were in the parlor of the suite when I got there. Mrs. Reagan was in the bedroom talking on the phone with Mrs. Ford.

Governor Reagan said that most of the governors, members of Congress, and friends (such as kitchen-cabinet members) who had called on him that afternoon all spoke up for Bush. Someone else said, "That's because they all want to win very badly, and they don't see any alternative." Someone else added that on balance, Bush would still be a positive factor on the ticket. (Ford had told Reagan in their afternoon meeting that he thought highly of Bush, felt he had done well in all his government jobs, and would be a loyal teammate on the ticket.) According to my notes, "Someone says that a Bush choice would send out the right signals to the voters. All seem to agree that RR's conservative supporters would accept him. We discuss whether Bush's primary-campaign criticism of what he called 'voodoo economics' would hurt, but conclude that it would not present a problem."

Mrs. Reagan reported that Mrs. Ford was very cordial but not enthusiastic about her husband going back into politics and government. According to my notes: "All disappointed. M—— says, 'Tomorrow we send in the next team [William Simon, George Schultz, Caspar Weinberger, Alan Greenspan] to see if they can help persuade Ford.' No one believes it will work."

When it came time for the morning network television shows, Ford (who had been scheduled for some time) was on NBC's "Today." His remarks—although not mentioning the still-secret discussions—were interpreted in the Reagan camp as still keeping the door ajar. Brock's breakfast with John Rhodes and several other party leaders centered around a discussion of "remaking" the vice-presidency under Ford. Some of the participants were later reported to have been uneasy about the idea of tinkering with the powers of the presidency. Some suspected that the dream ticket, if it got elected, would founder on the inevitable competition between the two men's staffs. Still, the election appeal of the ticket intrigued others. Pollster Bob Teeter presented his latest poll data, indicating that Ford would pull 11 percent more support than anyone else as Reagan's running mate.

Brock and some of his breakfast group called on Ford at ten to renew their urgings. He was still skeptical but agreed to listen to any proposal they might develop with Reagan's people regarding how a Ford vice-presidency might work in relation to a Reagan presidency.

Meanwhile, one floor down, Dick Wirthlin, Ronald Reagan, and I were seated in the Reagans' bedroom, going over his speech draft for the last time. The day before, he had asked me to "boil five minutes out of it," to make sure he would not go over twenty-five minutes, including interruption allowances for applause. I hated to see some of those paragraphs go; so did he, but Ronald Reagan knew better than anyone else that if the price of a speech that would hold his audience's full attention was the elimination of a few paragraphs, he would be willing to pay it.

Reagan had also met that morning with several New Right leaders, none of whom wanted Bush, Baker, or Ford. Reagan did not mention the Ford discussions, although he did tell them that Baker's name was not under consideration. All in the Reagan circle had decided to maintain the Ford discussions as confidential until a decision had been reached. It was our impression that Ford and his advisers would do likewise. With no commitment from Reagan, the New Right group left unsatisfied.

These morning meetings took place against the backdrop of a thun-der-and-lightning storm ferocious enough to please the ghost of Richard Wagner. The sky had grown nearly black in a matter of minutes early that morning. High winds angrily hissed rain against the all-glass walls of the suite. Lightning danced across the ink-black sky for nearly an hour. The seventy-story building creaked as it swayed in the wind.

It was nearly eleven in the morning when Reagan made his last no-tation on the speech draft and said, "Okay, let's go with it." I gathered up the papers spread across the bed and shuffled them back into page order. There was much to be done with the speech before he would give it the next night. Meanwhile, a meeting on the Ford matter was about to begin in the parlor. Casey, Meese, Deaver, Timmons, Spencer, and Tyson were assembled there when we came out of the bedroom.

Since Ford had not yet telephoned, we talked about contingency plans. These centered around George Bush. Earlier, in the bedroom meeting, Wirthlin had remarked, "The more time Ford takes, the more likely he will say yes." Still, we could not count on it, and we had to be prepared for a no. It was decided to try to get the process moving to-ward a conclusion one way or the other. The meeting broke up, and Casey telephoned the Ford suite to suggest a meeting of representatives of the two men to see if they could develop a plan acceptable to both principals. Ford agreed. Shortly thereafter, Casey, Meese, and Wirthlin met with what was to become the Ford negotiating team: Kissinger, Greenspan, Barrett, and Marsh. The ground had already shifted. Kis-singer and Greenspan, who had been enlisted by the Reagan staff to plead the Reagan case to their former chief, were now negotiating on his behalf.

In the first meeting they reviewed the various White House staff functions. The idea of a "deputy president" role for the vice-president began to take shape. After a time, Casey offered "to get something" on paper to take up with the other side after lunch. All agreed.

Back in the dining room of the Reagan suite, Casey, Meese and Wirthlin showed several of us their first draft during the noon hour. From start to finish, they described this only as a "talking paper." (By evening, the news media were referring to this paper variously as a "codicil," a "co-presidency agreement" and "The Treaty of Detroit.") It was careful to convey the intention of including the vice-president in the information "loop" at the White House, by channeling the paper flow from the Office of Management and Budget, the National Security Council, and the Council of Economic Advisers *through* the vice president, but it did not mention any change in the authority or powers of the president.

At 2:30 P.M. the Reagan and Ford teams met again. Casey presented the talking paper. The atmosphere was cordial and cooperative. In addition to channeling the White House paper flow through Ford—thus making him a key adviser to the President on virtually all matters—the paper suggested merging the presidential and vice-presidential staffs to avoid the friction that would be inevitable between parallel staffs. The Ford negotiators thought the plan was reasonable, but they began to raise a number of questions about how it would work in detail. They wanted to know, for example, what role the vice-president would have in the selection of cabinet officers.

Ford's negotiators said they would take the plan to him despite the unanswered questions. Ford, after reading the talking paper, commented that it was in line with the assurance of broadscale participation that Reagan had discussed with him the day before. His mood, however, seemed to be changing. The pressure had been growing all day—from friends, party leaders, the Reagan people, the news media. If he were going to abandon his good life for public service again, it would have to be worthwhile.

He telephoned Reagan and suggested a brief meeting to clarify the powers that would be given him under the proposed arrangement (back in the suite, Reagan's advisers were recommending against any firm commitments—let alone more documents—that went beyond the original talking paper). Reagan asked Ford to come down. Ford did and got right to the point; indicating he would want a say in the selection of the cabinet, and he was particularly interested in having Kissinger and Greenspan seriously considered for secretary of state and treasury, respectively. Reagan made no commitments.

In retrospect, that meeting seems to have been the turning point. It was downhill from then on. At seven, Ford astonished Reagan and those of us with him in the suite by going public with the matter in a CBS interview with Walter Cronkite in the network's booth above the convention floor. Ford had accepted the Cronkite invitation well beforehand and felt duty-bound to honor it. By then, however, the restless media were beginning to report on the various meetings between the Ford and Reagan camps, although their information was sketchy and the rumors they were reporting frequently drew smiles, even laughs, among those watching in Reagan's suite.

In the CBS booth, Ford heard Dan Rather give a report about the meetings. He was later reported as feeling that he had no choice at that point but to be straightforward with Cronkite about the matter.

At the start of the interview Ford seemed skeptical about the vice-presidency but warmed to the subject as it progressed. "I would not go to Washington and be a figurehead vice-president," he told Cronkite."I have to have responsible assurances," he said, that his role would be "meaningful . . . across the board in the basic and crucial decisions that have to be made." Cronkite asked him if this meant something like a "co-presidency." Although he did not reply directly, Ford said, "The point you raised is a very legitimate one."

Back in the Reagan suite, the governor watched the Ford interview in silence, his lips drawn thin, a sign that he was highly displeased. Everyone in the room felt the same thing, and some voiced it: a confidence had been broken.

Soon, the television networks were proclaiming that the Reagan-Ford ticket was a reality and that the two would be appearing in the arena that night.*

The negotiating teams continued to talk, but the tone had changed. Increasingly, Kissinger, the seasoned shuttle diplomat, had taken the lead and was trying to shape the discussions. He pressed for concessions.

About eight, Bill Simon came to the suite to see Reagan. He was worried that if the negotiations went as far as had been demanded by the other side, Reagan would be in danger of losing the ability to implement his programs once he was president. (It reminded me of something one of Reagan's California cabinet secretaries, Frank Walton, had once said in a cabinet meeting: "But Governor, that's not what we came here to do!") Simon said what many of us were beginning to think. Reagan listened attentively.

Meanwhile, the convention was in a frenzy. The delegates, intoxicated by the "news" from the media that there would "definitely" be a Reagan-Ford ticket, were demonstrating wildly. This was to be a big night for Ronald Reagan, the night of his official nomination as his party's candidate. But, there had been no expected excitement in the scheduled proceedings, and a convention thirsting for action was responding to the media reports like tinder to a match.

At nine, Reagan telephoned a weary Ford (he had had little sleep the night before) and told him that he would have to have a decision that night. This ran counter to a proposition Kissinger and the other Ford

---

* Hours earlier, this had been discussed as a dramatic way to announce such a ticket, and I had drafted some brief remarks for the governor to look over for such an event.

negotiators were about to put to Casey and his team—namely, that the convention adjourn without an announcement that night and that everyone sleep on it and conclude the negotiations the next morning, Thursday. Ford's answer to Reagan was noncommittal. Despite his lingering skepticism about the whole thing, if his negotiators could get the right assurances soon, it might be worth doing after all.

Reagan went back to watching the convention on television with his wife, daughters Maureen and Patti, and sons Michael and Ron. As he had in 1976, Paul Laxalt placed his friend's name in nomination. The convention crowd, already "high" on the Reagan-Ford rumors, went wild demonstrating for Reagan, even though the vote result was a foregone conclusion.

At a little after ten, as Casey was calling back a report from the negotiating room on the floor above, the television commentators were reporting that the Reagan motorcade, with Ford in it, was now forming at the hotel for the short ride to the convention arena.

The proposal of the Ford negotiators to put off the decision until the following morning struck one of my colleagues as a clever ploy by Kissinger. "He knows that if we wait till morning," he said, "we'll have no choice but to go with Ford, whatever the terms. In that way, they expect we will ultimately accept the deal on their terms. If we do, our colleagues will have given away Ronald Reagan's presidency." He added, "You've known the governor for a long time. Don't you suppose he thinks this has gone on long enough? If you ask him, I bet he'll agree. Why not talk to him now and bring this to a conclusion?"

I mulled that over, but not for long. "You're right," I said, and walked into the next room. The governor was sitting on the edge of a sofa, only half-watching the television, obviously deep in thought. There were several other people in the room, but I did not notice them. I walked over to him and briefly repeated the argument for not letting the matter string out until morning. "Why don't some of us go up there and bring it to a conclusion right now? If Ford says no, and he probably will, you still have time to call George Bush, then go down to the arena." He looked at me with a half-smile and said, "Yes."

It suddenly struck me: he had known for hours—probably since the detailed negotiations had begun late in the morning—that it was not going to work but that the simplicity of yesterday's one-on-one visit with Ford, now having given way to a complex drama with many players, just had to run its course. He had been waiting for the rest of us to catch up with his realization of it. It was about over.

I turned back to the other room and found Deaver and Nofziger. I repeated the whole thing. "Let's go," Nofziger said, and the three of us bounded out the door toward the stairs. A Secret Service agent stopped us. Nofziger and I were in our shirt sleeves; our jackets and their "pass" buttons were in our rooms. Deaver, who was wearing his jacket and button, vouched for us, and we took the stairs two at a time. We burst into the room where the negotiations had been going on, only to find the two teams standing silently at opposite ends of the room. Barrett, Greenspan, and Kissinger were near the door, and Casey, Meese, and Wirthlin, several feet away. Deaver had led us in. He walked up to the Ford advisers and said, "Look, that convention is about to go up in smoke, out of control, any minute if we don't give them a decision. If we wait till morning their expectations will be crushed if it isn't Ford, and if it is, it will be an anticlimax."

After a very brief silence, Barrett said, "I'll go talk to him [Ford]." He left the room for a few minutes. When he came back, he said, "He's going downstairs and I think the answer is no." He turned and went back into the Ford suite. Deaver, Nofziger, and I bounded downstairs to the Reagan suite. Ford appeared a minute or two later, a serious look on his face. He and Reagan went alone into the dining room and closed the door. Ford told Reagan that, after all was said and done, "it just won't work." He left to return to his own suite. Reagan came out and broke the news. He asked Chuck Tyson to get Bush on the phone.

Bush had, by then, retired for the night, having figured there was no hope after the convincing rumors coming from the news media all evening. Reagan's call took him by surprise. In asking him to be his running mate, Reagan also asked Bush if he could wholeheartedly support the party's platform. Bush unhesitatingly said he could. Allen and Anderson then rushed over to Bush's hotel to meet with him and his staff.

Arrangements were quickly made with Timmons, in the command post in the arena, for Reagan to appear at the convention. We all scrambled downstairs to the basement and the waiting motorcade within minutes. The Secret Service agents led the Reagans and their senior staff through a maze of stairs, halls, and small rooms until finally Reagan stood at the podium of the arena, looking out at thousands of cheering delegates, alternate delegates, and visitors. It was midnight. The crowd fell silent. He acknowledged that he was breaking precedent by appearing before them prior to his acceptance of their nomination, but he said he felt he owed it to them to "clear up the rumors." He explained that he and Ford had "gone over this and over this" and that they had "come to the conclusion, and he believes deeply, that he can be of more value as the former President campaigning his heart out, as he has pledged to do, and not as a member of the ticket. I respect him very much for the decision."

Reagan beamed at the crowd and gave them his surprise: he had selected "a man who has great experience in government and a man who told me that he can enthusiastically support the platform across the board . . . George Bush."

If anyone in that auditorium was unhappy with Reagan's decision, they would have had a hard time registering it. The crowd thundered its approval. The tension had been broken. There was a joyous outburst of applause and cheers.

The next morning, George and Barbara Bush, along with Jim Baker, the Bush campaign director; Pete Teeley, Bush's press secretary; and adviser Dean Burch, arrived after breakfast at the Reagan suite for a meeting with Casey, Timmons, and the Reagan and convention senior staffs. Coordination of schedules and arrangements went smoothly and quickly. Vic Gold was already at work on Bush's acceptance speech. The various staff members continued working on details, while the Bushes excused themselves to meet privately with the Reagans at the other end of the suite.

Every day that week, *Newsweek*'s senior editors had been meeting at lunch with one or two senior Reagan staff members for background views of the upcoming general election. Today, they had asked Martin Anderson and me. Not surprisingly, they focused their attention on economic issues, and Marty, as Reagan's chief domestic-issues adviser and an economist, fielded their questions. I was content to eat in peace. Just before dessert and coffee, however, Marty's paging beeper went off, and he excused himself. After a brief silence, a few questions were asked of me about that evening's speech by the governor. Then, one of the editors asked me if we expected anything unusual in the campaign against Carter.

In the Reagan circle, we had been discussing recently the possibility that Carter might spring some surprise, such as the release of the American captives in Iran, in the later stages of the campaign, in order to upstage Reagan completely. Considering the widespread public perception that Carter's policies were a failure, most of us believed that a dramatic surprise would be a likely Carter stratagem. We had begun to call it, among ourselves, "the October surprise." If Carter pulled it off successfully, it would show him as both decisive and effective.

The question by the *Newsweek* editor was a perfect opportunity for me to float this trial balloon. I discussed our reasoning for such a stratagem and said we expected "a surprise along about October." What might it be, I was asked? I didn't know, I replied. Sudden release of the hostages was an obvious possibility, but it might be something closer to home. More or less facetiously, I said, "Perhaps an invasion of Jamaica to protect our bauxite supplies, should Manley call off the election."

From across the large table, another editor asked,"What steps can you take? How can you anticipate such a thing?" Before I could answer, one of his colleagues said, "He just did."*

The Reagans had left the hotel late in the morning to drive to the suburbs, where they would have a quiet lunch together at a friend's home. Most of the afternoon had been set aside there for the governor to study his speech.

That evening, my wife and I sat among some of the Reagan's friends at one end of the arena. Just below us, on the convention floor, was the Texas delegation. My eye was drawn to a woman standing by an aisle seat of the delegation. She had a look of confidence on her face. She was about sixty and wore a bright floral-print blouse, dark blue slacks, and a ten-gallon hat. She held a sign that read, "Hang in there, America, the Republicans are coming!" How right she was, I thought. Ronald Reagan's final drive to take his party to the White House begins here, in this hall, tonight.

The arena fell dark. A single spotlight shone on the podium. Ronald Reagan stepped into the light. The crowd clapped and cheered. When it died down, he began, his voice quickly hitting a cadence that made it seem the words were just now coming to him, even though he had spent hours going over them.

> More than anything else, I want my candidacy to unify our country, to renew the American spirit and sense of purpose. I want to carry our message to every American, regardless of party affiliation, who is a member of this community of shared values.
>
> Never before in our history have Americans been called upon to face three grave threats to our very existence, any one of which could destroy us. We face a disintegrating economy, a weakened defense, and an energy policy based on the sharing of scarcity. . . .
>
> We need a rebirth of the American tradition of leadership at *every* level of government and in private life as well. The United States of America is unique in world history because it has a genius for leaders— many leaders—on many levels. But, back in 1976, Mr. Carter said, "Trust *me.*" . . .
>
> "Trust me" government asks that we concentrate our hopes and dreams on one man, that we trust him to do what's best for us. My view of government places trust not in one person or one party, but in those values that transcend persons and parties. The trust is where it belongs— in the people. The responsibility to live up to that trust is where *it* belongs, in their elected leaders. That kind of relationship, between the

---

* Despite Carter's eleventh-hour flurry of activity to release the hostages before election day, there never was an October surprise. By then, Reagan and his staff had mentioned the possibility so often, and the media had reported it so often, that any such "surprise," short of the hostage release, would have been robbed in advance of spontaneity.

people and their elected leaders, is a special kind of compact, an agreement among themselves to build a community and abide by its laws.

He put the concept of a compact of the people in historical perspective:

> Three hundred and sixty years ago, in 1620, a group of families dared to cross a mighty ocean to build a future for themselves in a new world. When they arrived at Plymouth, Massachusetts, they formed what they called a "compact," an agreement among themselves to build a community and abide by its laws. The single act—the voluntary binding together of free people to live under the law—set the pattern for what was to come.
>
> A century and a half later, the descendants of those people pledged their lives, their fortunes and their sacred honor to found this nation. Some forfeited their fortunes and their lives; none sacrificed honor.
>
> Four score and seven years later, Abraham Lincoln called upon the people of all America to renew their dedication and their commitment to a government of, for, and by the people.
>
> Isn't it once again time to renew our compact of freedom, to pledge to each other that all that is best in our lives, all that gives meaning to them—for the sake of this, our beloved blessed land?
>
> Together, let us make this a new beginning. Let us make a commitment to care for the needy, to teach our children the values and the virtues handed down to us by our families, to have the courage to defend those values and the willingness to sacrifice for them.
>
> Let us pledge to restore, in our time, the American spirit of voluntary service, of cooperation, of private and community initiative, a spirit that flows like a deep and mighty river through the history of our nation.
>
> As your nominee, I pledge to restore to the federal government the capacity to do the people's work without dominating their lives. I pledge to you a government that will not only work well, but wisely, its ability to act tempered by prudence, and its willingness to do good balanced by the knowledge that government is never more dangerous than when our desire to have it help us blinds us to its great power to harm us.

He went on to summarize the nation's economic problems, but not in statistical terms. He said:

> Ours are not problems of abstract economic theory. These are problems of flesh and blood, problems that cause pain and destroy the moral fiber of real people, people who should not suffer the further indignity of being told by the White House that it is all somehow their fault. . . .
>
> Can anyone look at the record of this administration and say, "Well done"? Can anyone compare the state of our economy when the Carter administration took office with where we are today and say, "Keep up the good work"? Can anyone look at our reduced standing in the world today and say, "Let's have four more years of this"?

He moved on to speak about priorities:

We must have the clarity of vision to see the difference between what is essential and what is merely desirable, and then the courage to use this insight to bring our government back under control and make it acceptable to the people.

We Republicans believe it is essential that we maintain both the forward momentum of economic growth and the strength of the safety net beneath those in society who need help. . . .

Beyond these essentials, I believe it is clear our federal government is overgrown and overweight. Indeed, it is time for our government to go on a diet. Therefore, my first act as chief executive will be to impose an immediate and thorough freeze on federal hiring. Then, we are going to enlist the very best minds from business and labor and whatever quarter to conduct a detailed review of every department, bureau, and agency that lives by federal appropriation. We are also going to enlist the help and ideas of many dedicated and hard-working government employees at all levels who want a more efficient government as the rest of us do. . . .

Our instructions to the groups we enlist will be simple and direct. We will remind them that government programs exist at the sufferance of the American taxpayer and are paid for with money earned by working men and women. Any program that represents a waste of their money—a theft from their pocketbooks—must have that waste eliminated or the program must go, by executive order where possible, by congressional action where necessary. Everything that can be run more effectively by state and local government, we shall turn over to state and local government, along with the funding sources to pay for it. We are going to put an end to the money merry-go-round where our money becomes Washington's money, to be spent by the states and cities only if they spend it exactly the way the federal bureaucrats tell them to.

He moved on to the center of his economic plan, tax reductions:

We are going to initiate action to get substantial relief for our taxpaying citizens and action to put people back to work. None of this will be based on any new form of monetary tinkering or fiscal sleight of hand. We will simply apply to government the common sense we all use in our daily lives.

Work and family are at the center of our lives, the foundation of our dignity as a free people. When we deprive people of what they have earned or take away their jobs, we destroy their dignity and undermine their families. We cannot support our families unless there are jobs; and we cannot have jobs unless people have both money to invest and the faith to invest it.

He spoke of his long advocacy of a 30 percent reduction in income-tax rates over a three-year period. "When I talk of tax cuts," he said, "I am reminded that every major tax cut in this century has strengthened the economy, generated renewed productivity, and ended up yielding new revenues for the government by creating new investment, new jobs, and more commerce among our people."

Business tax reform to stimulate investment in plants and equipment came next and then: "We will also work to reduce the cost of government as a percentage of our Gross National Product."

Next, he turned to the problems of minorities:

> When those in leadership give us tax increases and tell us we must also do with less, have they thought about those who have always had less—especially the minorities? This is like telling them that just as they step on the first rung of the ladder of opportunity, the ladder is being pulled up. That may be the Democratic leadership's message to the minorities, but it won't be ours. Our message will be: we have to move ahead, but we're not going to leave *anyone* behind. . . .
>
> It is time to put America back to work, to make our cities and towns resound with the confident voices of men and women of all races, nationalities and faiths bringing home to their families a decent paycheck they can cash for honest money.
>
> For those without skills, we'll find a way to help them get skills. For those without job opportunities, we'll stimulate new opportunities, particularly in the inner cities where they live. For those who have abandoned hope, we'll restore hope and we'll welcome them into a great national crusade to make America great again!

Reagan then moved on to problems abroad and the incumbent's response to them. About the broader subject of peace, he said:

> We are not a warlike people. Quite the opposite. We always seek to live in peace. We resort to force infrequently and with great reluctance—and only after we have determined that it is absolutely necessary. We are awed—and rightly so—by the forces of destruction at loose in the world in this nuclear era. But neither can we be naive or foolish. Four times in my lifetime America has gone to war, bleeding the lives of its young men into the sands of beachheads, the fields of Europe, and the jungles and rice paddies of Asia. We know only too well that war comes not when the forces of freedom are strong, but when they are weak. It is then that tyrants are tempted. We simply cannot learn these lessons the hard way again without risking our destruction.
>
> Of all the objectives we seek, first and foremost is the establishment of lasting world peace. We must always stand ready to negotiate in good faith, ready to pursue any reasonable avenue that holds forth the promise of lessening tensions and furthering the prospects of peace. But let our friends and those who may wish us ill take note: the United States has an obligation to its citizens and to the people of the world never to let those who would destroy freedom dictate the future course of human life on this planet. I would regard my election as proof that we have renewed our resolve to preserve world peace and freedom. This nation will once again be strong enough to do that.

He moved on to recounting briefly the odyssey he and his wife had taken for so many months, through the primary campaigns, to arrive at this place, this night.

I ask you to trust that American spirit which knows no ethnic, religious, social, political, regional, or economic boundaries, the spirit that burned with zeal in the hearts of millions of immigrants from every corner of the earth who came here in search of freedom.

Some say that spirit no longer exists. But I have seen it—I have felt it—all across the land, in the big cities, the small towns, and in rural America. The American spirit is still there, ready to blaze into life if you and I are willing to do what has to be done, the practical, down-to-earth things that will stimulate our economy, increase productivity and put America back to work.

He summarized his main themes, starting each one with "The time is now." He then moved on to a quotation from Franklin Delano Roosevelt's address to the Democratic National Convention in 1932 that ended, "I propose to you, my friends, and through you that government of all kinds, big and little, be made solvent and that the example be set by the President of the United States and his cabinet."

Reagan ended thus: "The time is *now,* my fellow Americans, to recapture our destiny, to take it into our own hands. But, to do this will take many of us, working together. I ask you tonight to volunteer to help in this cause so we can carry our message throughout the land. Yes, isn't *now* the time that we, the people, carried out these unkept promises? Let us pledge to each other and to all America on this July day forty-eight years later, we intend to do *just that."*

The crowd was hushed. There was not a sound. The single figure in the spotlight was surrounded by darkness. He began again: "I have thought of something that is not a part of my speech and I'm worried over whether I should do it.

"Can we doubt that only a divine providence placed this land, this island of freedom, here as a refuge for all those people in the world who yearn to breathe freely—Jews and Christians enduring persecution behind the Iron Curtain; the boat people of Southeast Asia, of Cuba, and of Haiti; the victims of drought and famine in Africa, the freedom fighters of Afghanistan; and our own countrymen held in savage captivity.

"I'll confess that I've been a little afraid to suggest what I'm going to suggest. I'm more afraid not to. Can we begin our crusade joined together in a moment of silent prayer?"

The utter stillness continued for half a minute or more.

Ronald Reagan then said, his voice subdued, "God Bless America."

The silence continued for just a moment as he stood in the spotlight. I felt tears stream down my face. A release from all the tension of the last two weeks, no doubt, but also a sense of pure joy that this good—and great—man might, at last, be president of the United States. It was no longer just a distant hope.

Up went the lights. The band began to play, the crowd erupted in applause and cheers, everyone stood. Nancy came out to stand by his side, then the Bushes, and then the Fords. It was a buoyant climax for the thousands of people there, and I thought, if Ronald Reagan's right, it is the beginning of a new beginning for America.

Celebrations went on all over Detroit until late that night. The next morning, the Republicans began to pack and head toward home. Detroit had been a wonderful host. One of my colleagues said, "It's as if everyone here had gone to charm school before the convention. I haven't met a single Detroiter who didn't smile and make me feel welcome."

The Reagan campaign was off to a running start, judging from all the reviews of the candidate's official kickoff the night before. The stock market responded with a net gain of 32.6 points in the Dow-Jones average for the week. The newspapers called it "the Reagan Rally."

11

"There You Go Again"

THE SUSPENSE and intensity of the Reagan-Ford drama at Detroit quickly faded into the past. On reflection, most in the Reagan circle felt that things had worked out for the best. An Associated Press–NBC News poll, released the Tuesday following convention week, seemed to bear them out. Of those surveyed, 54 percent said the selection of Ford as Reagan's running mate would have made no difference in their November vote. The rest were nearly evenly divided between being more or less inclined to vote for Reagan if Ford were on the ticket. Even more important to the Reagan camp was the 10-point lead their candidate was showing over Jimmy Carter in most polls.

Friday morning, the eighteenth, the day most delegates packed and left Detroit, Reagan was meeting with his state chairmen to discuss the job ahead of him and them.

Earlier in the year, Carter's people had been underestimating Reagan in the same way so many others had in previous years. They would tell journalists that they hoped Reagan would be the Republican nominee because he would be the easiest to beat. It was clear that they would portray him as an amiable dunce, incapable of making the important decisions presidents are called on to make.

Now, in July, that approach had changed, in the opinion of Reagan and his strategists. Reagan told his state chairmen they could expect a "mean, ruthless, vicious, vindictive" campaign from the Carter camp.

Behind Reagan's prediction was this analysis of the Carter strategy: Carter's performance as president had fallen so badly in the public eye that a typical incumbent's "point with pride" campaign, reciting his accomplishments, was no longer possible. It would have no credibility with voters. Thus, Carter would have to "view with alarm" the prospect of his opponent occupying the White House. He would have to tear down Reagan, make him into a heartless, warlike bogeyman. If he succeeded in frightening enough voters with this Reagan imagery, he might win. The danger in such a strategy, however, is that Carter's one remaining public-opinion asset, the view that he was a decent, honest man, might be lost in the process. Reagan and his strategists were sure that it would be, since a slashing, negative campaign against Reagan would be a sharp contradiction of Carter's "decent, honest man" image. Once the perception began to change and show up in the polls, Carter would become more desperate and shrill. Hence, Reagan's prediction that it would be a mean campaign.

Ed Meese spoke to the group about Carter's shrewdness as a campaigner. He reflected the prevailing view of the Reagan circle when he said that Carter might not be a very good president, but he would be hard to beat in a campaign. As the incumbent, he could manipulate events to his advantage. And if anyone had any doubts about his skills as a political strategist and campaigner, they need only review the events of 1976, when Carter seemingly came from nowhere to capture the Democratic nomination, then go on to unseat an incumbent president.

Most of the rest of July was devoted to moving the Reagan campaign headquarters from Los Angeles to a leased office building in Arlington, Virginia, across the Potomac River from Washington. The Reagans themselves leased a country home near Middleburg, Virginia, and would move in in late August for the duration of the campaign, after a working vacation at Rancho del Cielo. At Wexford, their Middleburg home, in Virginia's rolling horse country, there would be plenty of room (but little time) for Ronald Reagan to go horseback riding.

The campaign high command had been beefed up. Bill Timmons became national political director, joining Bill Casey, Ed Meese, and Dick Wirthlin in the Arlington headquarters.

With the convention behind us, Mike Deaver and I planned to reactivate our original plan whereby he would go into the campaign and I would stay behind to run our business. The plan had been derailed back in November 1979, when Deaver suddenly left the campaign. Since then, I had spent far less time with our business than I had expected to. It was time now for me to give it nearly full attention. While I would be available for volunteer assignments now and then, the convention was to be my last period of intense involvement with the campaign. Mike, on the other hand, would go on full leave of absence from our company to work full-time as the campaign's tour director, accompanying Governor Reagan on *Leadership 80*, the chartered campaign plane.

Joining Deaver on the campaign tour would be political strategist Stu Spencer; Martin Anderson, the chief domestic-issues adviser; Ken Khachigian, a fine writer who had been on the Nixon White House speechwriting staff; Jim Brady, as issues coordinator; Lyn Nofziger, press secretary; and, from time to time, Dick Allen, the chief foreign- and defense-issues adviser.

From early to mid-August the spotlight shifted to the Democrats, who would hold their convention in New York City, in Madison Square Garden. The Carter forces kept tight control, beating off the efforts of Kennedy's people and assorted other anti-Carter elements seeking an "open" convention. Carter's declining popularity within his own party's leadership would have made such a convention risky.

Kennedy electrified the delegates with a speech that tugged at their hearts, but it was Carter, with his icy eyes, who was in control. In his acceptance speech on the fourteenth, he lived up to Reagan's predic- tion: he launched an all-out assault on his opponent.

Carter told his audience that he offered "a stark choice between two futures." The Democratic choice, he said, would bring "confidence, hope, and a good life." The Republican choice, according to Carter, would mean "surrender to the merchants of oil" and an economic plan that involved "a bizarre program of massive tax cuts for the rich, service cuts for the poor, and massive inflation for everyone."

The Reagan camp made no effort to draw attention from the Demo- crats and their quarrels in New York. Instead, there would be a series of major Reagan speeches and events immediately after the Democratic convention, the intention being to show an upbeat contrast to the downbeat Democratic gathering.

Dick Allen called me one day early in August to say that he had been working with Governor Reagan on a speech entitled "Peace: Restoring the Margin of Safety." This would expand on the peace theme Reagan had sounded in his acceptance speech. It would, Allen said, be a rhe- torical foundation to which the governor could return again and again when talking about national defense. Thus, he would be able to put the lie to Carter's efforts to depict him as warlike. Allen said Reagan would give the speech at the Veterans of Foreign Wars (VFW) convention in Chicago on August 18.

As a companion speech, he said, they wanted to develop one under the title "Friends," basing it on the need for the United States to strengthen and restore its alliances around the world. I suggested mak- ing it a preamble to a speech on Latin America. I knew that Reagan wanted to focus more attention on our neighbors in the Western Hemi- sphere and had a good speech on draft, waiting for an occasion to use it. We talked over timing. The next major speaking forum after the VFW would be a gathering of evangelical ministers in Dallas. We agreed that now that Reagan was the nominee, no speech had to be topical to the audience addressed. Rather, its content and timing had to be considered in terms of national media coverage. Allen asked me to draft the "Friends" preamble and discuss the idea with Reagan. I did, but he was skeptical. He asked me to send it over, but he was concerned that the topic was so far from what was on the ministers' minds that if he gave it, "they would scratch their heads, wondering why." The growing political activism of evangelical Christian groups was making some other voters nervous, but Reagan said he felt he could avoid the pitfalls of some of the potentially divisive issues associated with evangelical political groups. He said his inclination was to speak extemporaneously and thematically, and that is what he ended up doing.

Reagan's "Peace" speech to the VFW was a measured exposition of his views on the state of U.S. security, our need to rebuild our defenses and to seek genuine arms reduction with the Soviet Union. It had almost no applause lines in it, and not wanting to disappoint the audience before him, he ad-libbed his conclusion, calling the Vietnam War "a noble cause."

So far as coverage by the news media was concerned, the carefully crafted speech might as well never have been delivered. The only thing that came through in the headlines and that evening's network television news was the "noble cause" line.

For the second time, Reagan had inadvertently given his opponent an opportunity to throw him on the defensive. Just two days before, at a send-off news conference in Los Angeles for George Bush, who was on the way to Peking, Reagan said that he wanted to restore "official" ties with the Republic of China on Taiwan. While Reagan's support for our longtime ally, Nationalist China, and his opposition to the method and timing of Carter's "normalization" of diplomatic ties with the Communist Chinese on the mainland were well known, to suggest restoring "official" ties with the rival Chinese government in Taipei was to jeopardize the Bush trip. The trip had been intended to show Reagan's intention to be friends.

Peking had for months been chiding Reagan for his support of the Nationalists, but this was nothing compared to the firestorm of criticism unleashed now. Watching the network coverage, it struck me that the combined Carter administration and Peking blasts at Reagan were too smoothly timed to be accidental. It was almost as if they were coordinating their efforts.

Bush was treated coolly and lectured by the Peking leadership. A second news conference in Los Angeles on the twenty-fifth was designed to contain the damage. Bush and Reagan released what would be their definitive statement on the issue. Reagan said he had made a misstatement at the earlier news conference. He said he would follow the terms of the Taiwan Relations Act (some of which the Carter administration had ignored) and would improve U.S. relations with Taipei entirely within the framework of the act, which set forth the basic elements of unofficial relations with the Republic of China.

On Labor Day, September 1, Reagan committed another of what the news media were calling "gaffes" when he remarked that Carter was opening his campaign "down in the city that gave birth to, and is the parent body of, the Ku Klux Klan." He was wrong. Carter was speaking in Tuscumbia, Alabama. The Klan had been founded in a small town in Tennessee. Furthermore, Carter had been attacking the Klan, not embracing it. As Reagan had done, Carter refused the Klan's endorsement.

Reagan, who had been counting on penetrating Carter's Deep South, suddenly found himself the object of outraged cries from southern politicians (most of them Carter supporters) who claimed Reagan had impugned their region's honor. Again, he was thrown on the defensive.

Worried congressional Republicans conferred with the Reagan high command. He had to resist off-the-cuff remarks, they insisted. He had to eliminate the risks inherent in spontaneous comments, or he would be thrown on the defensive time and again, they argued.

At the White House, gleeful Carter aides were telling journalists that Reagan was turning out to be just the sort of candidate they always expected him to be: inept and bellicose. The gloom of August had given way to cheer in September. The Carter people were nearly euphoric. Already, they could taste victory.

Reagan, however, had gotten the message from his key supporters and his strategists. He proved it on the third with a strong pro-Israel speech to the national convention of the B'nai B'rith in Washington. The Jewish leaders, who had soured on Carter, applauded Reagan nearly three dozen times during the course of the speech as he criticized Carter's assorted "zigzags" and "flipflops" in Middle East policy.

Carter's appearance before the group the next day drew little applause and some booing, but he proved an incumbent can control events by announcing that the deadlocked Israeli-Egyptian negotiations would resume the following week.

On balance, the media consensus of the campaign's first "official" week was that it was Carter's. As John Sears had said, however, politics is motion, and Reagan, with his flawless and well-received speech to the B'nai B'rith, had taken the offensive.

Now, Reagan began quoting the Kennedys, especially the late President and Ted, who had delivered some slashing lines in his primary campaign against Carter. Reagan served them up again with a smile.

At one stop, in response to Carter's claim that the battered economy was suffering only a "mild recession," Reagan said, "If it's a definition he wants, I'll give him one: a recession is when your neighbor loses his job;

a depression is when you lose yours. Recovery is when Jimmy Carter loses his." The crowd rocked with laughter.

On the ninth, Nancy Reagan telephoned me from Philadelphia. They were getting great response from blue-collar and ethnic voters at their stops, she said. Already, her husband's message of economic recovery and restoration of American leadership in the world was cementing his "community of shared values"—which included many traditional Democrats.

It was typical of Nancy Reagan at the end of a campaign day to call friends and acquaintances in various parts of the country to check her own impressions against other perspectives. The synthesis of her impressions would be shared with her husband.

Throughout the 1980 campaign (as she had in previous campaigns), Mrs. Reagan was either at her husband's side each day or appeared on his behalf in one set of towns while he was in another. Almost always, they began and ended the day together. Both at parting in the morning and greeting in the evening, they had a brief moment between them that, no matter how many others were in the room, was intensely private. They had eyes only for one another.

My mother once said to me that if a couple still held hands after years of marriage, you could be sure they were very much in love. After nearly three decades of marriage, the Reagans still hold hands.

While Nancy Reagan is very much a part of her husband's story— and his success—she has not figured prominently in this narrative because she has chosen for herself a supporting role. In their years together she has rarely been in the limelight by herself.

Nancy Davis abandoned a budding film career in the early 1950s to become Mrs. Ronald Reagan. The career she wanted was to be a wife and mother. Since then, she has always seen herself primarily as Mrs. Ronald Reagan. Although this traditionalism may be out of fashion at the moment, Nancy Reagan never hesitates to say that, for her, it is a natural role. It is one with which she is clearly comfortable.

Over the years, she has often been asked by interviewers to compare her outlook and life-style with those of other women in public life. She declines to make comparisons. She freely acknowledges that while her way is best for her, others choose other ways and she does not judge them.

Along the way, Nancy Reagan has become widely known for her poise, her handsomely styled, understated clothes, and a smile that is sometimes big and open, sometimes wry (even enigmatic), and sometimes just on the edge of laughter (her hazel-colored eyes are the key).

Some who know her say she is shy; others say she is reserved, reticent. Whatever the truth, she is protective of the little privacy she and her husband and family have as public figures. She knows and accepts the fact that governors and their wives, presidential candidates and their wives, and presidents and their wives surrender most of their privacy when they become these things. It goes with the job, so to speak. To her, that is all the more reason for guarding whatever privacy is left to them.

The Reagans have experienced many of the tugs and pulls any American family might experience. There have been the changing relationships with their daughter and son as they passed through the growing-pain years and into adulthood. For Mrs. Reagan there have been the extended family relationships with her husband's daughter and son by his previous marriage. As she has often noted, each of the four is a distinct individual and each has developed his or her talents in a different way. She says this warmly, with a touch of pride. The details of how the Reagans work out family relationships and problems, however, remain a part of their private lives, as is the case with most families.

All of this has led, over the years, to frustration among some of the media people who have covered Nancy Reagan. In many interviews she is not what a reporter would call "good copy" because she does not bare the details of her or her family's private life. And she does not criticize other public figures. Since it is controversy that makes a good story, a reporter will occasionally be so frustrated that she (it has always been a woman reporter) will vent that frustration by writing a sharp, satirical article about Mrs. Reagan. Some of these appeared during the 1980 campaign.

While the wives of some public figures are outspoken, Nancy Reagan is comfortable as a sort of silent partner. She and her husband share most of their experiences, talking them over at the end of the day. She is a sounding board for him; however, she emphasizes that it is he who makes the decisions. She does not involve herself in technical discussions on issues. As to the so-called social issues, when she makes a public appearance or gives an interview, she will express her philosophy. On such things as drug abuse, abortion, and women's rights, her views closely parallel her husband's, but she states them in her own terms, from a woman's perspective. If she is on a platform by herself and asked about such things as foreign policy or economic matters, she will usually summarize her husband's position, figuring that the audience primarily wants to know what *he* thinks about it.

Is it unusual for the wife of a public figure to agree with his positions on most issues? After nearly three decades of marriage—itself a working partnership—it would be unusual if she did otherwise. While all husbands and wives may occasionally disagree in private, it would be unusual for a couple in love after many years of marriage to present anything but a shared view to the world.

For as many years as I have known Nancy Reagan, she has declined to give formal speeches. I think this is partly due to shyness and partly to her desire not to be in the limelight apart from her husband. During campaigns, however, she is often scheduled apart from her husband in order to extend the Reagan exposure. Fall of 1980 was no exception. During these times she had been given a heavy schedule of appearances. For these she prefers a question-and-answer format instead of a campaign speech. She opens with very brief remarks and then invites questions. Her soft voice and smile are enough invitation to get the questions flowing. The resulting dialogue is a natural medium of exchange for her. She answers all the questions extemporaneously (although she admits that when she has given an answer she is not satisfied with, the better answer often comes to her later in the bathtub). Her question-and-answer sessions are as close to living-room conversation as is possible in a campaign in which thousands of people must be reached every day. Indeed, they were reaching, between them, thousands in person and millions each night on the television news programs.

Beyond the new buoyancy that the Reagans themselves were experiencing on the campaign trail, the Carter administration had just handed the Republicans a fresh opportunity to prove that politics is motion. Reagan charged the administration with leaking data about the secret "Stealth" aircraft technology, technology that could render a new U.S. military aircraft impervious to Soviet radar. Former chief of Naval Operations, Admiral Elmo Zumwalt, backed up the Reagan charge. Zumwalt said that Carter had permitted the leaks in order to reduce criticism of his decision to kill the B-1 bomber. The leakage, he claimed, permitted the Soviets a five-year head start in developing countermeasures.

Now it was Carter's turn to be on the defensive. Allen and the Reagan national-security advisers coordinated a barrage of criticism of the administration from assorted defense experts.

Next, Reagan and Bush appeared on the U.S. Capitol steps on September 15 with the Republican congressional delegates en masse—a pointed contrast to Carter's bumpy relationship with congressional Democrats.

Reagan's campaign to pull voters from the old-time Democratic coalition was working with every group except blacks. He was moving well in the polls.

On the sixteenth, Carter went to Atlanta and exclaimed from the pulpit of the Reverend Martin Luther King, Sr., that Reagan had injected "racism" and "hatred" into the campaign. The shock and outrage was widespread. A *Washington Post* editorial critical of Carter's remarks was headed "Running Mean."

While criticism was being heaped on Carter from left and right, Reagan's strategists knew the real cause of Carter's attack from the pulpit: he was afraid of losing. Carter was playing out the strategy Reagan and his advisers had predicted back in July. A few more mean, vicious attacks from him, and his reputation as a "decent, honest man" would be gone.

Reagan had by now moved ahead in the polls in most of the large states. The League of Women Voters' nationally televised debate was coming up on the twenty-first. Conventional wisdom has it that the incumbent should avoid such an event because it gives his opponent "peer-level" exposure. That had been Sears's advice about the Iowa debate in January, when Reagan was way ahead of his Republican rivals in the polls. Reagan had taken the advice and lost the Iowa caucuses. Such an "incumbent" strategy is not risk-free, of course, and Carter was willing to take the risk of skipping the debate. Without him there, Carter figured that Reagan, whom he regarded as a lightweight, would bumble away the debate through slips of the tongue.

Carter's avoidance of the debate in Baltimore turned out to be a serious mistake. The League of Women Voters (and many editorial writers) was critical of Carter for failing to appear before the American public. At one point, the League seriously considered putting an empty chair, representing the missing Carter, on the stage with Reagan and John Anderson.

Anderson, despite a deep third-place position in the polls, was as articulate as ever during the debate. His biting criticism of the Carter administration showed he could become a genuine threat to the incumbent by chipping away suburban liberals.

In preparation, Reagan's strategists had pressed Congressman David Stockman into service as a surrogate Anderson (he had once worked for Anderson). They set up the garage at Wexford as a mock-debate set. Stockman played Anderson well and Reagan went into the debate ready to handle any frontal attack from his fellow Illinoisan. As it turned out, in order to advance his cause, all Reagan needed to do was convey the impression that he was a reasonable, peaceful man, concerned about people's needs. This he did. Anderson did well, too. The only loser was the absent man: Carter.

Back in August, Reagan had told a group of several thousand evangelical Christian ministers at the Dallas gathering, that as president he would make sure the "awesome power of government respects the rights of parents and the integrity of the family." He would, he added, "Keep Big Government out of the school and the neighborhood and, above all, the home."

This was the libertarian side of Ronald Reagan speaking. Although they probably shared his views for other than libertarian reasons, the ministers gave him a rousing ovation. Many actively began working among their parishioners for the Reagan-Bush ticket after this meeting. The Reverend Jerry Falwell and his Moral Majority drew the most press attention of the evangelical groups. The White House took note, too. On the twenty-third, Patricia Harris, the secretary of Health and Human Services, who had echoed Carter's charge of "hatred" and "racism" against Reagan, took up cudgels against the evangelicals at a speech on the Princeton University campus in New Jersey.

Falwell came out swinging. At a press conference outside Harris's office on September 29 he accused her of making "vicious . . . attacks on the literally millions of Jews, Catholics, Mormons, and Protestants whose only crime has been to register to vote."

If Carter, the self-proclaimed born-again Christian, was expecting to get the evangelical and fundamentalist vote this time, his expectations appeared to be misplaced. Unlike those in 1976, the leaders of these movements in 1980 seemed to be making real progress in getting their traditionally apolitical flocks to register, and Reagan seemed to be their favorite.

Carter's strategists were reading Patrick Caddell's polls and the news was not good. Carter's "decent, honest man" image was eroding and the attacks on Reagan were not taking hold. It was time to tone down the supercharged rhetoric, but Carter could not bring himself to do it. On October 6, in Chicago, he let go another verbal fusillade. "You will determine," he said, "whether or not this America will be unified or, if I lose the election, whether Americans might be separated, black from white, Jew from Christian, North from South, rural from urban."

The day before, I had telephoned Governor Reagan at Wexford. He was in fine spirits and sounded confident. Later I talked with Mike Deaver, who said all seemed to be going well and that Wirthlin's latest polls "show us ahead by 17 percent in California."

Still, Carter was ahead with women voters, who were apparently still worried about Reagan over the peace issue. On October 14, at a Los Angeles news conference, Reagan said he would commit American troops to combat only as a last resort. In the same news conference, he pledged to appoint a woman to the Supreme Court. While the latter point got mixed political and media reviews, he was to make good on that pledge less than a year later.

On the nineteenth, Reagan underscored the theme of his original August peace speech, in a nationally televised speech entitled "Strategy of Peace in the '80s."

He appealed to traditional Democrats: "The Carter administration, dominated as it is by the McGovernite wing of the party, has broken sharply with the views of Harry Truman, John Kennedy, and many contemporary Democrats."

He played back another Ted Kennedy quotation critical of Carter. Then, he went straight to the heart of voter worries when he said, "As president, I will make immediate preparations for negotiations on a SALT III treaty. My goal is to begin arms *reductions."* (The failed SALT II treaty called for limited increases.) First, he said, he would restore "the margin of safety" in our defenses as an inducement to the Soviet Union to negotiate.

Carter replied the next morning as he left the White House for a campaign swing. Reagan "doesn't understand," he complained, that to go beyond SALT II to a renewed commitment to strong defenses (Carter called it "nuclear superiority") would have "serious consequences."

Behind the scenes there were two important developments. Jim Baker was negotiating with the Carter people for a one-on-one Reagan-Carter televised debate. And, the Reagan camp's intelligence detected that the Carter White House was negotiating for the release of the American captives in Iran. It was the October surprise!

Reagan responded to Carter's latest blast by turning it around. He admitted, he said, "I don't understand why we have had inflation at the highest peacetime rates in history. . . . I don't understand why his answer to inflation was to put 2 million people out of work. . . . I don't understand why our defenses have weakened. . . . Lastly, I don't understand why fifty-two Americans have been held hostage for almost a year now." He blamed a weak Carter foreign policy for permitting the conditions that led to their captivity.

On the twentieth, Carter seemed to verify the existence of secret negotiations over the captives when he announced that if they were freed, he would "unfreeze" Iranian assets in U.S. banks, drop his trade embargo, and begin to resume normal trade with Iran. "It is to our advantage," he said, "to see a strong Iran, a united Iran." (Iran was by now at war with its neighbor Iraq and was losing.)

The next day, Gerald Ford told a St. Louis audience, "Carter is so anxious to get elected, he might do anything." Ford warned that U.S. military involvement in the Iran-Iraq war could prove "worse than the war in Vietnam."

Reagan, not wanting to appear to be opposed to release of the captives, had indicated general acceptance of Iran's terms and pledged a bipartisan effort. This was not universally popular among his senior advisers, but it seemed to be the only choice under the circumstances. Still, the Reagan high command worried. If Carter actually did pull off a cynical October Surprise, he would dominate the news for four or five days in a huge media spectacular that would eclipse Reagan in the climactic days of the campaign.

The suspense was hard to bear in the Reagan camp as it prepared for the television debate with Carter on October 28 in Cleveland. Word went around that Carter expected to swamp Reagan with his superior knowledge of the details of government operations. If it was encyclopedic information they wanted to put across, that would be fine with the Reaganites. It would only prove that Carter did not understand television. From long experience, Ronald Reagan knew that television is the most personal of the media. He knew that when he looked into the camera, he was really looking at one person, or one family, seated before a set in the living room. What he would have with them was a quiet conversation, just as if he was in the living room with them. In his television appearances, Carter had so far not shown that he understood how personalized television is. As so many politicians did, he treated it as if he was talking to a huge audience. He was to prove again in Cleveland that he had not mastered the medium.

Reagan's objective that night was to be relaxed and calm, to appear to have a good working knowledge of the issues, and to be reassuring about his position on peace. The Reagan strategists expected Carter to renew his attack on the Reagan bogeyman he had been trying to create for weeks.

Carter had two things to buoy his confidence going into the debate: the fact he had bested Gerald Ford in debate four years before, and a new poll from Gallup that showed him moving into a tiny (three-point) lead over Reagan.

As the debate began, Carter quickly moved to take charge. He repeatedly described Reagan as "dangerous" and his views "disturbing." He said Reagan was "heartless" and his tax-cut plans "ridiculous." Reagan rebutted, but quietly.

Carter's fatal mistake was to attack Ronald Reagan on the same platform, to his face. Carter said Reagan was "dangerous" and would start a war, but one look at this kindly, affable man, and you or I watching the debate on television could not believe that.

Still, the Carter tirade continued. At one point, he said his young daughter, Amy, had told him that the nuclear arms race was the major issue. Carter's insensitivity, juxtaposed with the incongruity of the statement, caused the live audience to laugh.

Carter opened a fresh attack on Reagan. He said Reagan "began his political career campaigning around the nation against Medicare" and now opposed compulsory national health insurance and, by implication, disease prevention and hospital cost control.

That was too much for Reagan. Like an uncle watching a rambunctious teenage nephew, he shook his head and with a tolerant smile said, "There you go again." That said it all for the millions watching. Carter may have won on encyclopedic details, but Reagan got the sympathy of those watching. Reagan was likable and believable, and many were making up their minds to vote for him the following Tuesday.

ABC invited people to call in to have their opinions tallied as to who had won the debate. The vote, although it was no scientific sample, gave the Reagan forces a lift. Callers chose him two to one over Carter. The Carter campaign cried foul. Besides, based on some early reports by media commentators and their own feelings (misunderstanding the uses of television as they had), the Carter high command thought Carter had bested Reagan.

Carter redoubled his attacks the next day. Time and again, he linked Reagan's name to such words as "dangerous," "radical," "nuclear war." Reagan struck back the same day. He said, "I can hardly have a warm feeling in my heart for someone who's been attacking me on a personal basis for many months now in the campaign."

Aside from responding to the attacks, Reagan had reason to feel good about the way things were going. Dick Wirthlin's nightly tracking polls were showing him moving away from Carter. He was ahead in Carter's home region, the Deep South, way ahead throughout the West and Southwest, and ahead in most of the big industrial states. There was even a possibility he would take New York.

Reagan's confidence came through as he moved along the campaign trail after the debate. At one stop he said, "Sorry I'm late, but I was busy starting a war." At another he said, "I recall when my kids were young, we used to sit around the living room after dinner talking about nuclear proliferation."

On Thursday, the thirtieth, I stopped by the Arlington headquarters with a speech draft I had promised Meese and found I was in time to sit in on the morning senior staff meeting. I had not sat in on one of these since the convention. I was impressed by how smoothly and quickly the business was attended to. These people were professionals, carefully meshing their respective responsibilities with one another.

Wirthlin said, as the meeting broke, "Come over to my office and sit in on the morning polling report meeting." There, Richard Beal and another Wirthlin researcher were poring over the data from the previous night's calls. The trends were getting stronger. It looked as if Reagan was going to do more than squeak through (the public pollsters and the media had routinely been predicting for some time a cliff-hanger finale). The one wild card, according to Wirthlin, was the October surprise—the sudden return of the captives from Iran. We talked about this for some time. Even if Carter got them out the next day, he looked to be too far gone to make the ensuing media spectacular truly effective for him. Even though the data and common sense told us it was probably too late for Carter, this did little to ease the suspense everyone in the Reagan camp felt.

The Iranian parliament was to debate the subject of the captives' release. Parliamentary maneuvering was delaying it. It finally took place on Sunday, November 1. It was almost the first anniversary of the Americans' capture when the Iranian parliament set conditions for their release.

Carter got the news early Sunday morning in Chicago, where he had been campaigning. He canceled the day's campaign schedule and flew back to Washington. My friend Jim Fuller, who had organized Reagan's business-issues advisory panel earlier in the year, put the next move in a nutshell after watching television and calling me from New York. "When he left Chicago, Carter was wearing a Chessy-cat grin, like a guy who expected to play an ace. But something happened on the way to Washington. He arrived with that tight-lipped expression he sometimes wears. Mondale put his arm around him (like someone who was consoling a man who had just lost his mother), but Carter thrust him away and took a piece of paper from Brzezinski. Obviously, Carter's ace had turned out to be a deuce."

Whatever Carter had learned about the impossibility of getting the captives out of Iran, he was going to milk the situation if he could. A little after six o'clock, Washington time, he went to the White House press room to briefly address the nation on television. He described the Iranian parliament's action as a "positive basis" for finally freeing the American captives. "I wish I could predict when the hostages will return, but I cannot," he said. That was his hand. The ace was a deuce after all, although he was playing it with all the trappings of a world leader from his command post.

The performance was enough to keep the Reagan campaign tour strategists on edge that night, worried that somehow the unpredictable old Ayatollah Khomeini and his hot-blooded mullahs would let Carter snatch victory out of the jaws of defeat.

Monday dawned brighter for the Reagan campaign, however, as Wirthlin's researchers assembled the previous night's polling data. Carter was not receiving a burst of renewed strength with the voters as a result of the renewed activity to free the captives. Indeed, voters were suspicious of Carter's motives at this late date.

Ronald Reagan flew home to California buoyed by this news and concluded his tour at a noisy rally in San Diego where he told a heckler, "Aw, shut up." He said to the audience that his mother had always told him he should not use that phrase, but he figured it would be okay just this once. The crowd loved it.

The Reagan campaign finale was a nationally televised speech in which he reprised, as he had at the conclusion of the Cleveland debate the week before, some of the haunting questions he had been putting to the voters since he began his campaign with his acceptance speech in Detroit. This time he asked, "Is our nation stronger and more capable of leading the world toward peace and freedom, or is it weaker?"

He called on his fellow Americans: "Together, tonight, let us say what so many long to hear: that America is still united, still strong, still compassionate, still clinging fast to the dream of peace and freedom, still willing to stand by those who are persecuted or alone."

Carter meanwhile continued crossing the country in a last desperate search for votes. He flew to the Pacific Northwest on Monday to see if he could pry Washington and Oregon from Reagan's grip. The weary President headed home for Plains, Georgia, on Air Force One when his press secretary, Jody Powell, broke the news to him that Pat Caddell's polls showed him facing certain defeat the next day.

The next morning, Carter addressed a gathering in Plains that was widely broadcast. He made an emotion-choked plea for his party to stick with him. His voice sounded tired, reflecting the wearing pace of the last days of the campaign.

On election day in California the Reagans voted in the morning in Pacific Palisades near their home. It was late in the afternoon, California time, when the call came from Jimmy Carter in the White House. He was calling to congratulate the President-elect. Carter pledged his full help in the transition to a Reagan administration.

As the Reagans drove down their driveway to go to a dinner party with friends they found all their neighbors lining the street, waving and cheering. It was a bright send-off to a night of victory.

By the time they arrived at the Century Plaza Hotel, the news was tumbling in about the Republicans taking control of the Senate. At 6:50 P.M., Los Angeles time, Carter conceded publicly. The size of the Reagan victory was stunning. He carried forty-four states, leaving only six and the District of Columbia to Carter. The popular vote was 51 percent for Reagan, 41 percent for Carter, 7 percent for Anderson, and 1 percent for minor candidates. The electoral vote landslide was 489 for Reagan, 49 for Carter. Reagan had 45.8 million popular votes; Carter, 35.4 million; and Anderson, 5.7 million.

According to the "exit" polls of the networks, Reagan had won 52 percent of the independents; 35 percent of the Jewish votes; two-thirds of the evangelical vote; 44 percent of the labor vote; 27 percent of all Democratic votes; 70 percent of the voters earning more than $20,000 a year; and 51 percent of those earnings between $5,000 and $10,000. He had also carried the women's vote. As columnist John Lofton was to write a few days later about these and other statistics, "Reagan got a solid majority among farmers and small-town residents, a strong edge among white-collar workers and a narrow plurality among blue-collar workers. Some coalition."

Right after we congratulated the Reagans in their suite, they were off for the ballroom, where the President-elect spoke to several hundred campaign workers. "When I accepted your nomination for president, I hesitatingly asked for your prayers at that moment," he said. "I won't ask for them at this particular moment, but I will just say that I will be very happy to have them in the days ahead."

To a great extent the news media had been stunned by the size of the Reagan and Republican party victory. Much of this resulted from the fact that the public polls had stopped collecting data several days before the election, thus missing the sharp upswing in the Reagan trendline.

Richard Wirthlin told *Advertising Age* magazine that as early as October 16, the Reagan research showed him winning by 6 points and 320 electoral votes.

Wirthlin's colleague Vincent J. Breglio told the magazine, "The situation we saw on October 16 just kept getting better." By the thirtieth, the Reagan research data yielded a prediction of a 7-point victory; on the thirty-first, 9 points; on November 1, 10 points; on the second and third, 10 to 11 points. (Reagan's actual victory margin was nearly 11 points.)

Breglio added, "We ran our final simulation [vote projection] at 11 P.M. Monday night, the third, and it said we'd have at least 395 electoral votes and a maximum of 480. We never released those findings to Governor Reagan; we were too conservative."

Ronald Reagan had awakened that morning as a former radio announcer, former film actor, former governor, and a candidate for president. When he went to bed that night, it was as all of those things, minus the last. Now he would be the fortieth president of the United States.

Epilogue

IT WAS TUESDAY, just two days before Christmas, 1980, when I headed West on Wilshire Boulevard to go to the Reagans' Pacific Palisades home for what would be the last time. It was five in the afternoon, and the western sky had that suffused orange-peach flame look to it that is typical of a late fall afternoon in Southern California, as the haze refracts the light. Night was falling quickly.

I thought back over the events of the last year, the determination and spirit of the Reagans as they worked their way to the final goal, and the help and support of so many people. The night before the election, I had heard John Sears, now an occasional commentator on National Public Radio, say on a broadcast that he thought the election was too close to call. I thought now about something one of my campaign colleagues had said soon after Ronald Reagan was elected: "Sears made it possible for Ronald Reagan to win. What he gave him was the ability to take control of his own destiny. By late 1979, after Nofziger, Anderson, and Deaver had all left the campaign, Reagan began to seriously question, in his own mind, if he was in control of the situation. At some point thereafter, I think he decided that the only way he could be true to himself and win was to just *be* himself, not something or someone others wanted. All this was crystallizing over a period of several months. It culminated in Sears's firing."

What a mixture of influences a campaign is; the constantly changing interplays of personalities, ideals, sometimes conflicting motivations.

The transition to a Reagan administration was now well underway. How would Ronald Reagan deal with the Presidency? One thing seemed certain, I thought. He would not be overwhelmed by it.

Over the years I have had many discussions with liberals and conservatives over the matter of politicians who are "pragmatic" or "practical," versus ones who are "ideological," as if all of them fit neatly into such compartments. I have yet to meet one who does. In Ronald Reagan's case, over a period of years he worked out a clear set of principles about the role of government and, on holding public office, never altered his principles, though he was quite willing to compromise in terms of accomplishing specific program elements. As Governor of California, he proved he was consistent, but also practical. He knew that a successful chief executive and politician could not fight every battle as if it were Armageddon. His political acumen was and is probably based on many factors in his background: his mother's steadfast belief in God and good works in the temporal world; his father's good humor; his tolerance for idiosyncrasies and unconventionality, probably developed during his film career when he had to get along with a wide variety of temperaments; his instinct for negotiating, forged during his six terms as president of the Screen Actors Guild; his belief that government was growing out of control, developed strongly in his years with General Electric and his many contacts with business people and plant workers.

There was no reason to believe he would not apply the same approach to the federal government. Would he be served well by those around him, or would he suffer from the inevitable "turf" disputes that plague the early months of most administrations (Mike Deaver's words of early 1974 came back to me. I had commented, after only a few days in the governor's office, how smoothly things worked and how well everyone got along together. "Remember, we've had seven years practice," he said. "You should have been around here the first year.")

Ronald Reagan's years of public life have been marked by the intense loyalty he has received from those around him. He manages, in his low-key way, to inspire his people. I knew the "Reaganauts" who would be going into the administration with him would help him make his programs work. Many new people would join them. Well, if history was a guide, most of them would become "Reaganauts."

I parked below the driveway, identified myself to the Secret Service men and walked up to the Reagans' home. The governor looked tanned, fit and relaxed in slacks and a sport shirt. Nancy wore a trim hostess gown. They greeted me warmly. He was still working on key appointments to his new administration and interrupted our conversation at one point to take a call from Ed Meese about one of them.

We visited for awhile, then exchanged Christmas gifts as we had for several years. On Christmas Day, I found that one of them, from the governor, was a bottle of Taittinger champagne. My mind flashed back to that night in Washington, the eve of his first presidential campaign announcement in late 1975 when Mike Deaver and I had toasted the Reagans' success in champagne.

On New Year's Eve, my family and I opened the Taittinger and toasted the beginning of The Reagan Era.

Index